For You in Full Blossom

10

story and art by
HISAYA NAKAJO

HANA-KIMI
For You in Full Blossom
VOLUME 10

STORY & ART BY HISAYA NAKAJO

Translation/David Ury
Touch-Up Art & Lettering/Gabe Crate
Design/Izumi Evers
Editor/Jason Thompson

Editor in Chief, Books/Alvin Lu
Editor in Chief, Magazines/Marc Weidenbaum
VP of Publishing Licensing/Rika Inouye
VP of Sales/Gonzalo Ferreyra
Sr. VP of Marketing/Liza Coppola
Publisher/Hyoe Narita

Hanazakari no Kimitachi he by Hisaya Nakajo © Hisaya Nakajo 1999
All rights reserved. First published in Japan in 1999 by HAKUSENSHA, Inc.,
Tokyo. English language translation rights in America and Canada arranged with
HAKUSENSHA, Inc., Tokyo. New and adapted artwork and text © 2006 VIZ
Media, LLC. The HANA-KIMI logo is a trademark of VIZ Media, LLC. The stories,
characters and incidents mentioned in this publication are entirely fictional. Some
art has been modified from the original Japanese edition.

Published by VIZ Media, LLC, P.O. Box 77010, San Francisco, CA 94107

Shōjo Edition
10 9 8 7 6 5 4 3 2

First printing, January 2006
Second printing, March 2007

www.viz.com
store.viz.com

PARENTAL ADVISORY
HANA-KIMI is rated T+ for Older Teen and is recom-
mended for ages 16 and up. Contains strong language, sexual themes and alcohol and tobacco usage.

CONTENTS

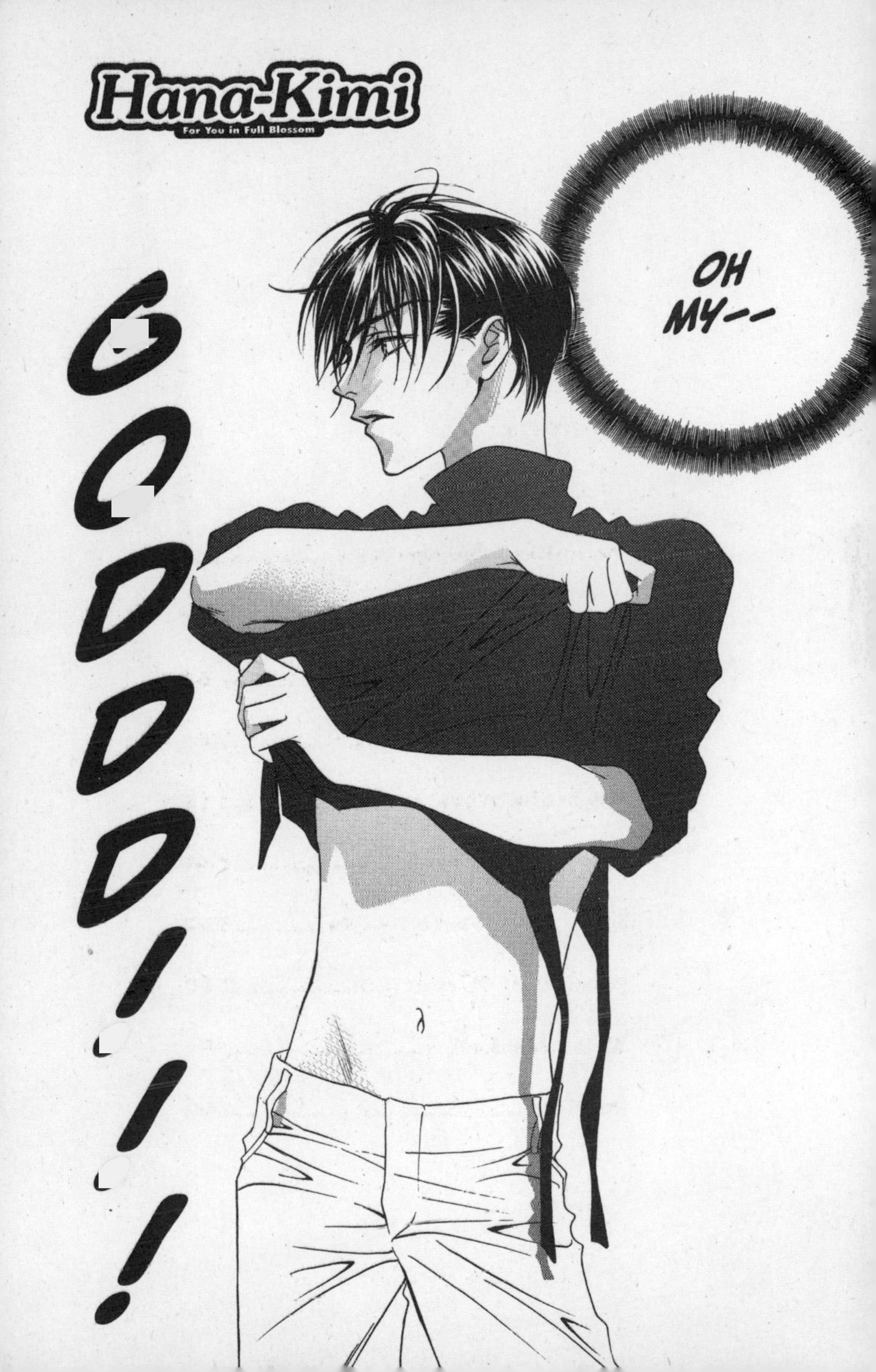
Hana-Kimi
For You in Full Blossom
OH MY--
GODDD!!!

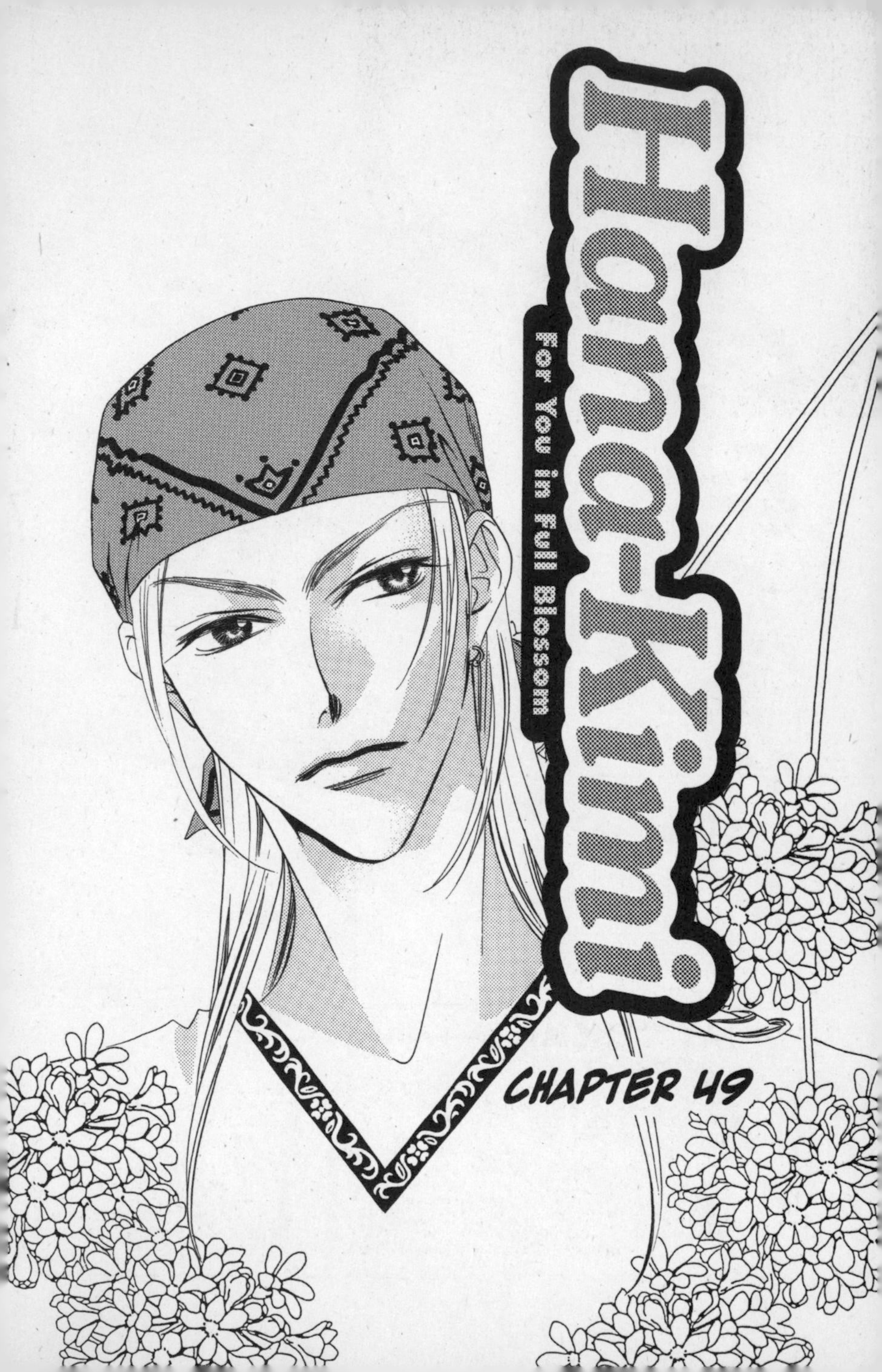
Hana-Kimi
For You in Full Blossom
CHAPTER 49

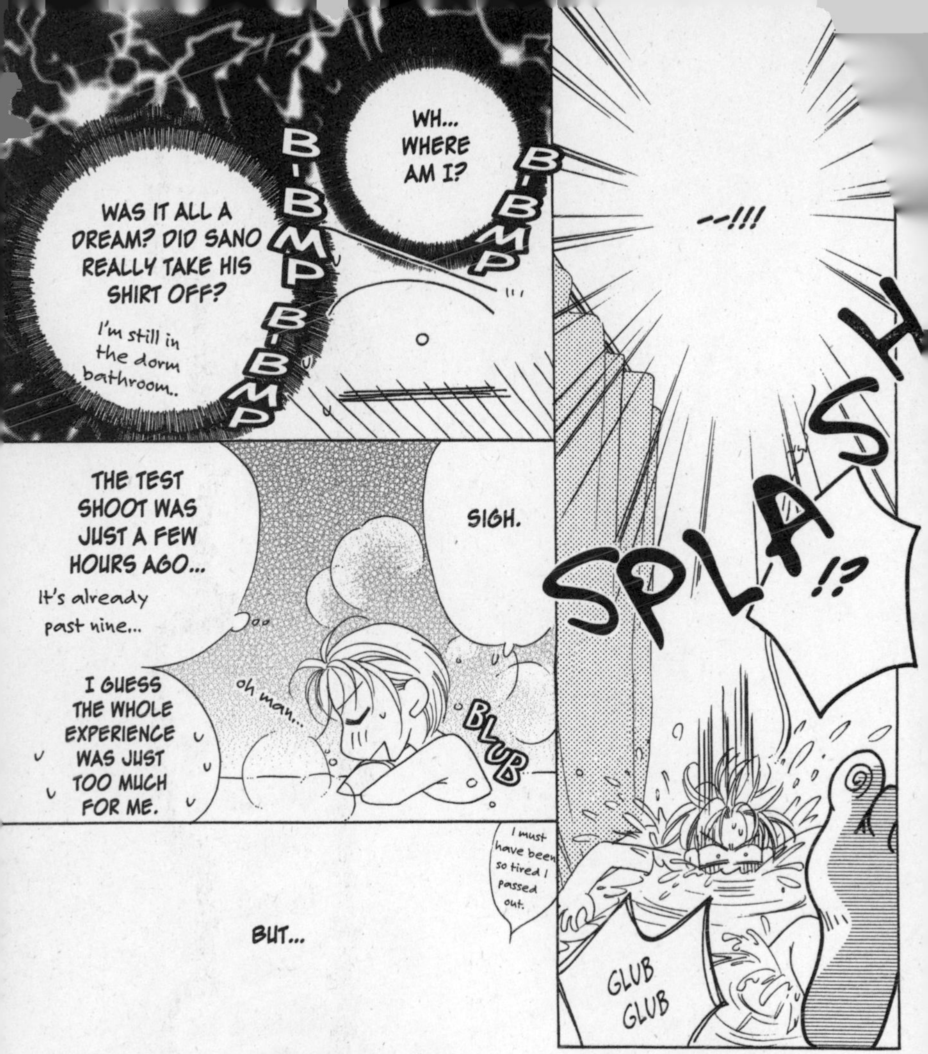
WH... WHERE AM I?
B-BUMP
WAS IT ALL A DREAM? DID SANO REALLY TAKE HIS SHIRT OFF?
I'm still in the dorm bathroom..
B-BUMP B-BUMP
SIGH.
THE TEST SHOOT WAS JUST A FEW HOURS AGO...
It's already past nine...
oh man...
BLUB
I GUESS THE WHOLE EXPERIENCE WAS JUST TOO MUCH FOR ME.
I must have been so tired I passed out.
BUT...
--!!!
SPLASH
!?
GLUB GLUB

MY CINEMA

My Favorite Obscure Films, Part One:

FLOWERS IN THE ATTIC

AFTER THE DEATH OF HER HUSBAND, A MOTHER OF FOUR CHILDREN HAS NO CHOICE BUT TO MOVE BACK WITH HER WEALTHY PARENTS, WHO DISINHERITED HER BECAUSE THEY DISAPPROVED OF HER CHOICE OF MARRIAGE. SHE TRIES TO RECONCILE WITH HER FAMILY, BUT IN THE PROCESS, HER FOUR CHILDREN ARE TAKEN FROM HER AND LOCKED IN THE ATTIC. THE CHILDREN ARE CONVINCED TO WAIT "UNTIL YOUR MOTHER PATCHES THINGS UP WITH YOUR GRANDFATHER," BUT GRADUALLY THEIR MOTHER SHOWS UP LESS AND LESS. SOON, THE HAPLESS DOLLENGANGER CHILDREN ARE LEFT ENTIRELY IN THE CARE OF THEIR WICKED GRANDMOTHER, WHO MISTREATS AND NEARLY STARVES THEM. ONE DAY THE CHILDREN DISCOVER THE SECRET OF THEIR BIRTH, AND FINALLY ATTEMPT TO ESCAPE FROM THE ATTIC...AND THE SHOCKING TRUTH IS REVEALED! I THOUGHT IT WAS A VERY WELL-MADE FILM, ALTHOUGH IT WASN'T ANYTHING FANCY.

THE LEAD IS KRISTY SWANSON FROM "SUPERGIRL."

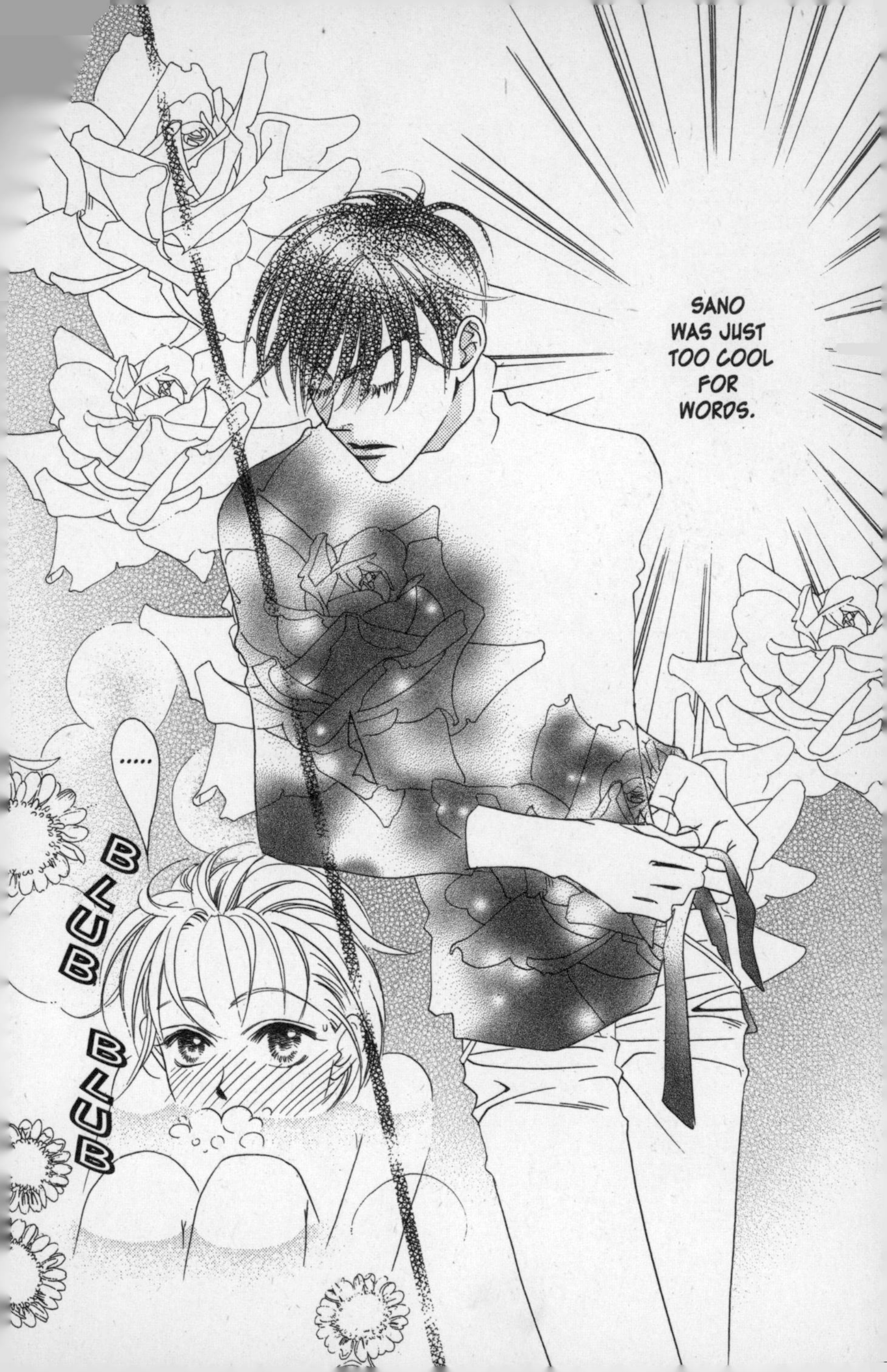
SANO WAS JUST TOO COOL FOR WORDS.
.....
BLUB BLUB

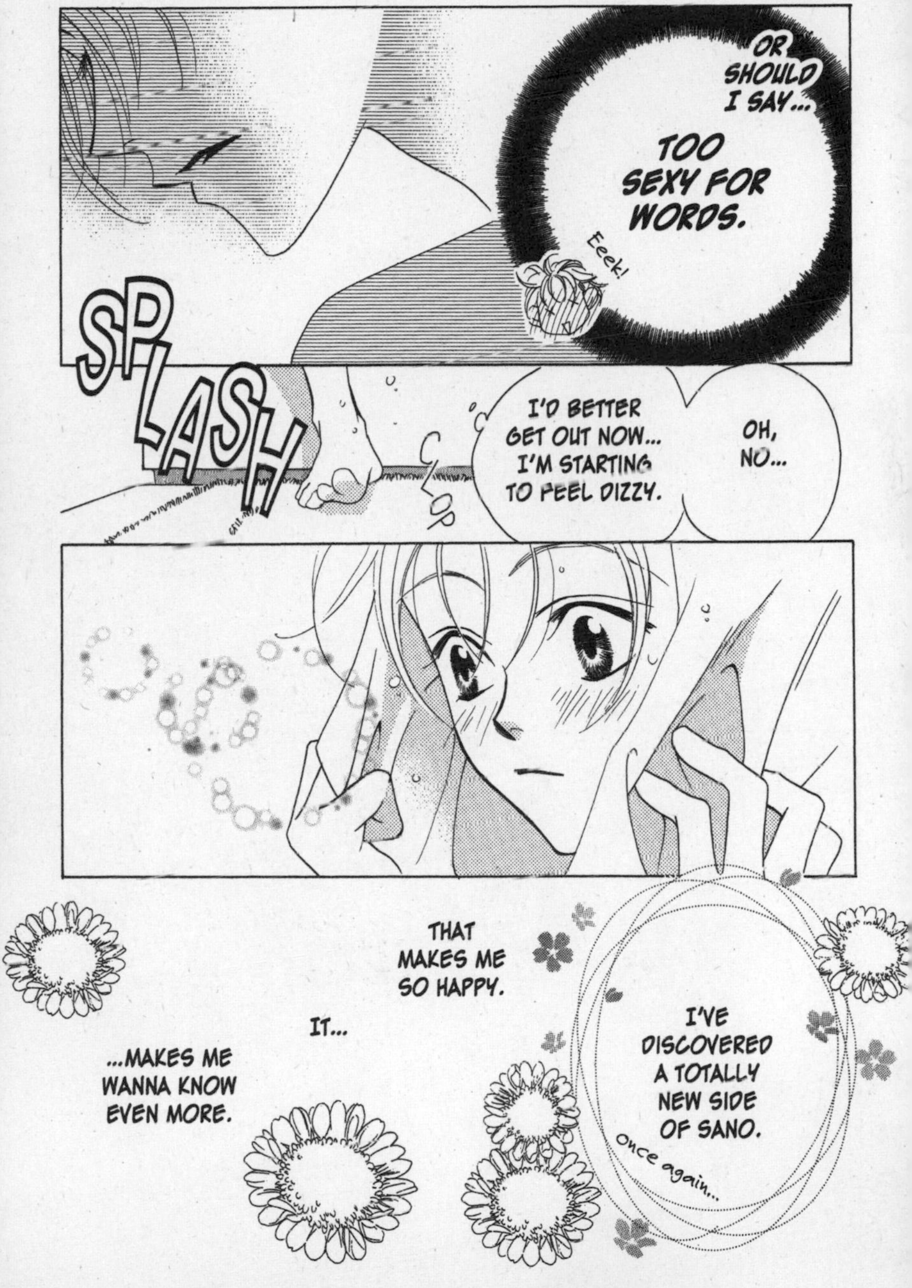
OR SHOULD I SAY...
TOO SEXY FOR WORDS.
Eeek!
OH, NO...
I'D BETTER GET OUT NOW... I'M STARTING TO FEEL DIZZY.
CLOP
SPLASH
I'VE DISCOVERED A TOTALLY NEW SIDE OF SANO.
Once again...
THAT MAKES ME SO HAPPY.
IT...
...MAKES ME WANNA KNOW EVEN MORE.

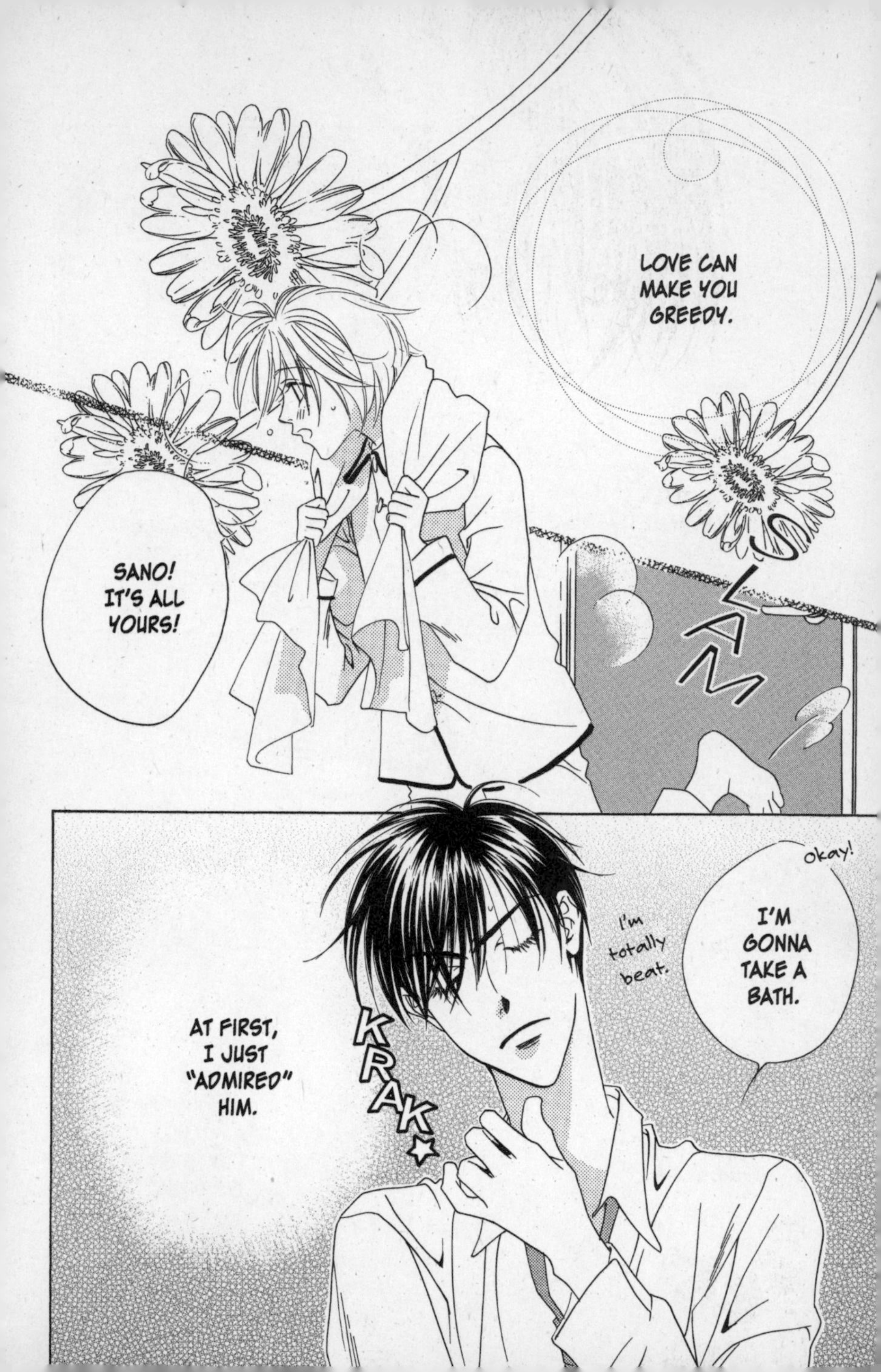
LOVE CAN MAKE YOU GREEDY.
SLAM
SANO! IT'S ALL YOURS!
Okay!
I'M GONNA TAKE A BATH.
I'm totally beat.
KRAK
AT FIRST, I JUST "ADMIRED" HIM.

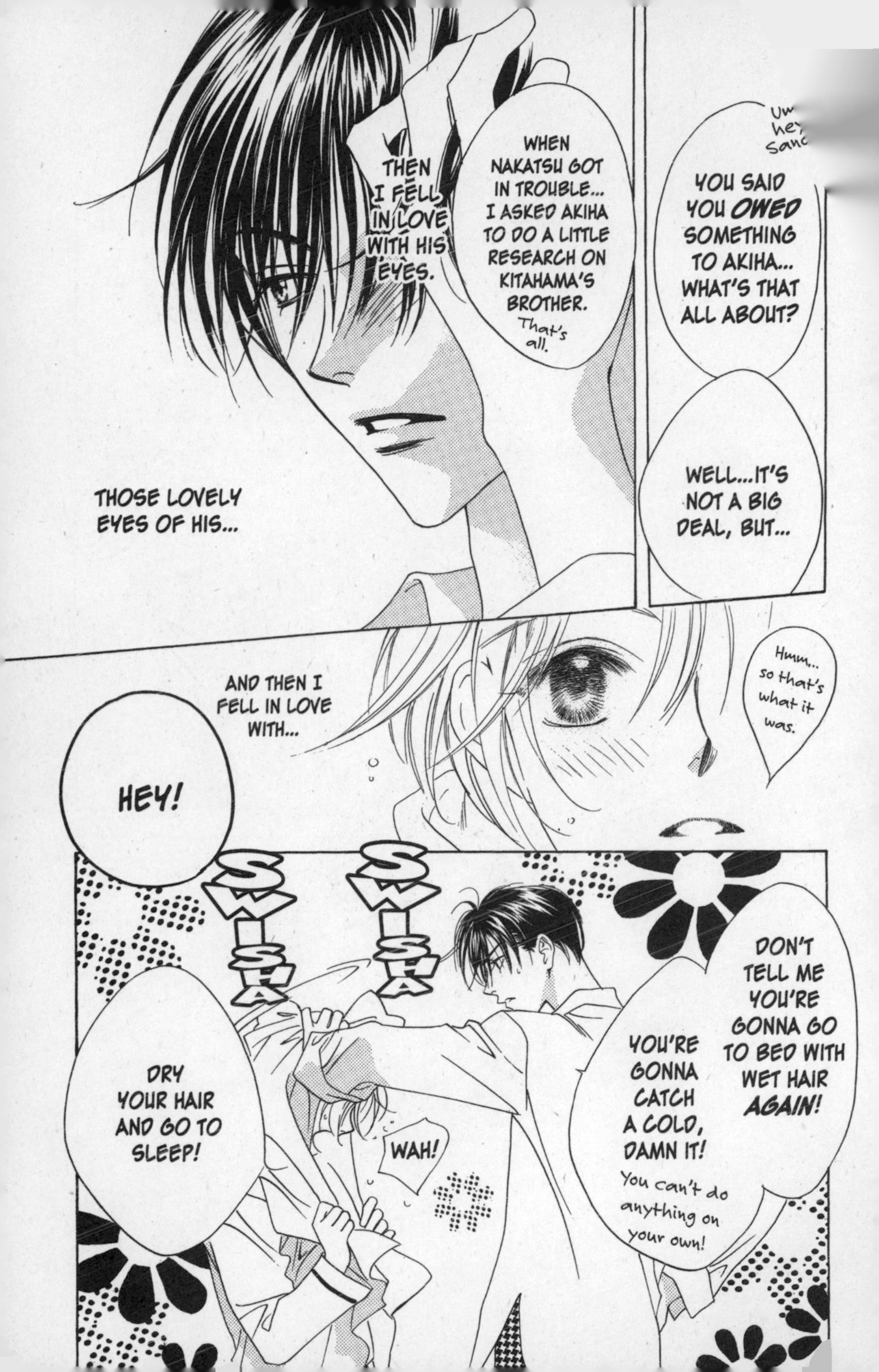
YOU SAID YOU OWED SOMETHING TO AKIHA... WHAT'S THAT ALL ABOUT?
WELL...IT'S NOT A BIG DEAL, BUT...
WHEN NAKATSU GOT IN TROUBLE... I ASKED AKIHA TO DO A LITTLE RESEARCH ON KITAHAMA'S BROTHER.
That's all.
THEN I FELL IN LOVE WITH HIS EYES.
THOSE LOVELY EYES OF HIS...
Hmm... so that's what it was.
AND THEN I FELL IN LOVE WITH...
HEY!
DON'T TELL ME YOU'RE GONNA GO TO BED WITH WET HAIR AGAIN!
YOU'RE GONNA CATCH A COLD, DAMN IT!
You can't do anything on your own!
SWISHA
SWISHA
WAH!
DRY YOUR HAIR AND GO TO SLEEP!

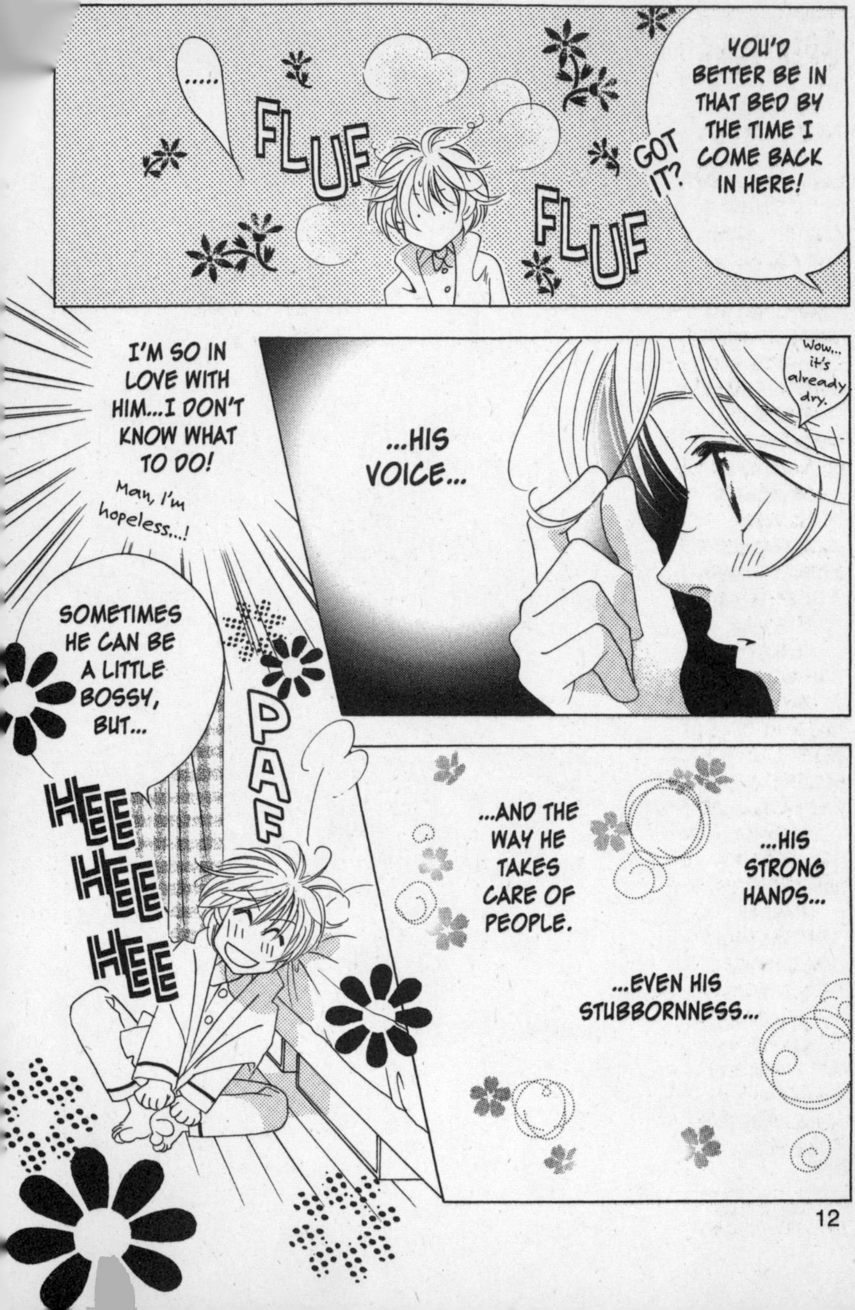
YOU'D BETTER BE IN THAT BED BY THE TIME I COME BACK IN HERE!
GOT IT?
FLUF
FLUF
.....
Wow... it's already dry.
...HIS VOICE...
I'M SO IN LOVE WITH HIM...I DON'T KNOW WHAT TO DO!
Man, I'm hopeless...!
...HIS STRONG HANDS...
...AND THE WAY HE TAKES CARE OF PEOPLE.
...EVEN HIS STUBBORNNESS...
SOMETIMES HE CAN BE A LITTLE BOSSY, BUT...
PAF
HEE HEE HEE

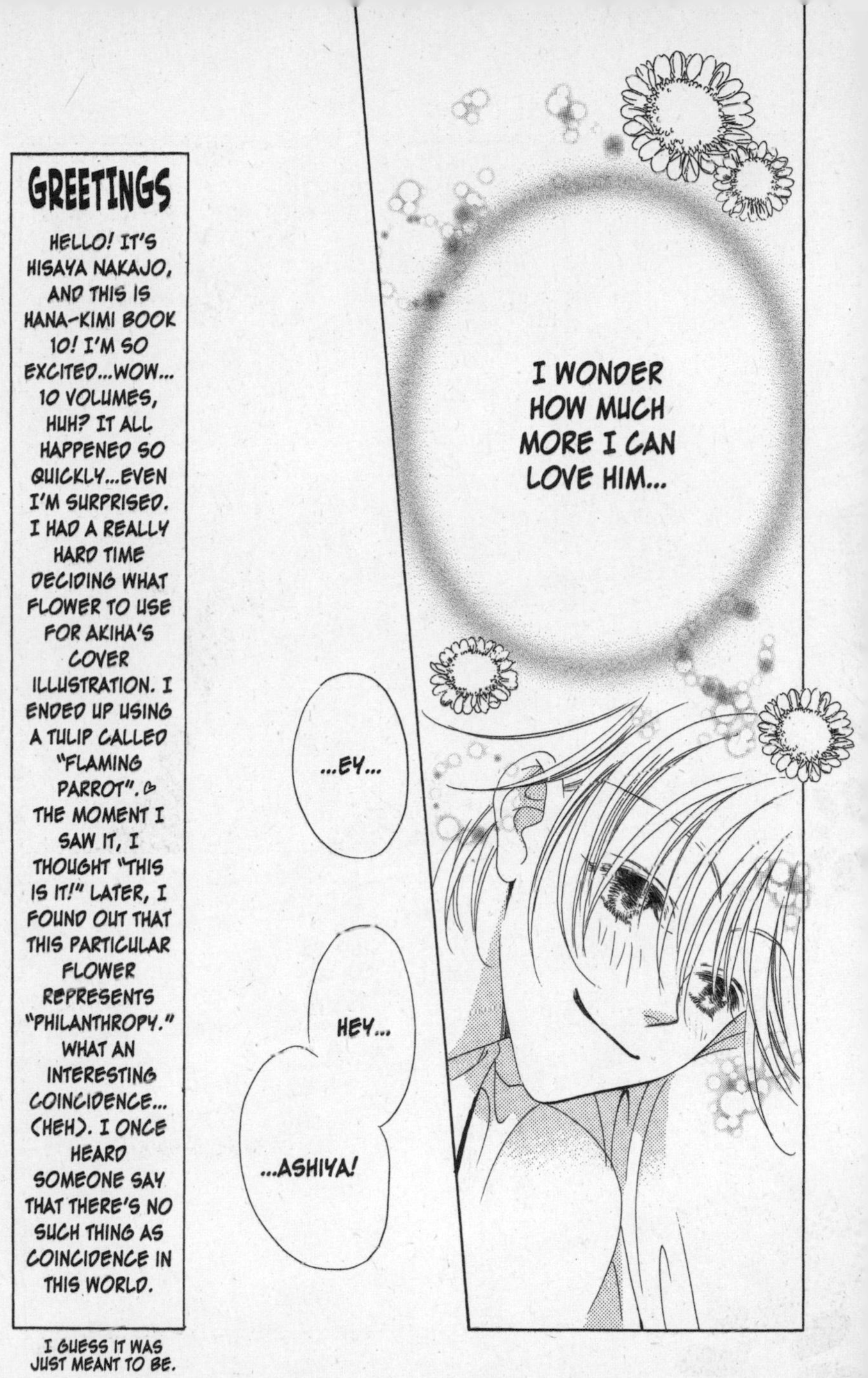
I WONDER HOW MUCH MORE I CAN LOVE HIM...
...EY...
HEY...
...ASHIYA!

GREETINGS

HELLO! IT'S HISAYA NAKAJO, AND THIS IS HANA-KIMI BOOK 10! I'M SO EXCITED...WOW... 10 VOLUMES, HUH? IT ALL HAPPENED SO QUICKLY...EVEN I'M SURPRISED. I HAD A REALLY HARD TIME DECIDING WHAT FLOWER TO USE FOR AKIHA'S COVER ILLUSTRATION. I ENDED UP USING A TULIP CALLED "FLAMING PARROT".♡ THE MOMENT I SAW IT, I THOUGHT "THIS IS IT!" LATER, I FOUND OUT THAT THIS PARTICULAR FLOWER REPRESENTS "PHILANTHROPY." WHAT AN INTERESTING COINCIDENCE... (HEH). I ONCE HEARD SOMEONE SAY THAT THERE'S NO SUCH THING AS COINCIDENCE IN THIS WORLD.

I GUESS IT WAS JUST MEANT TO BE.

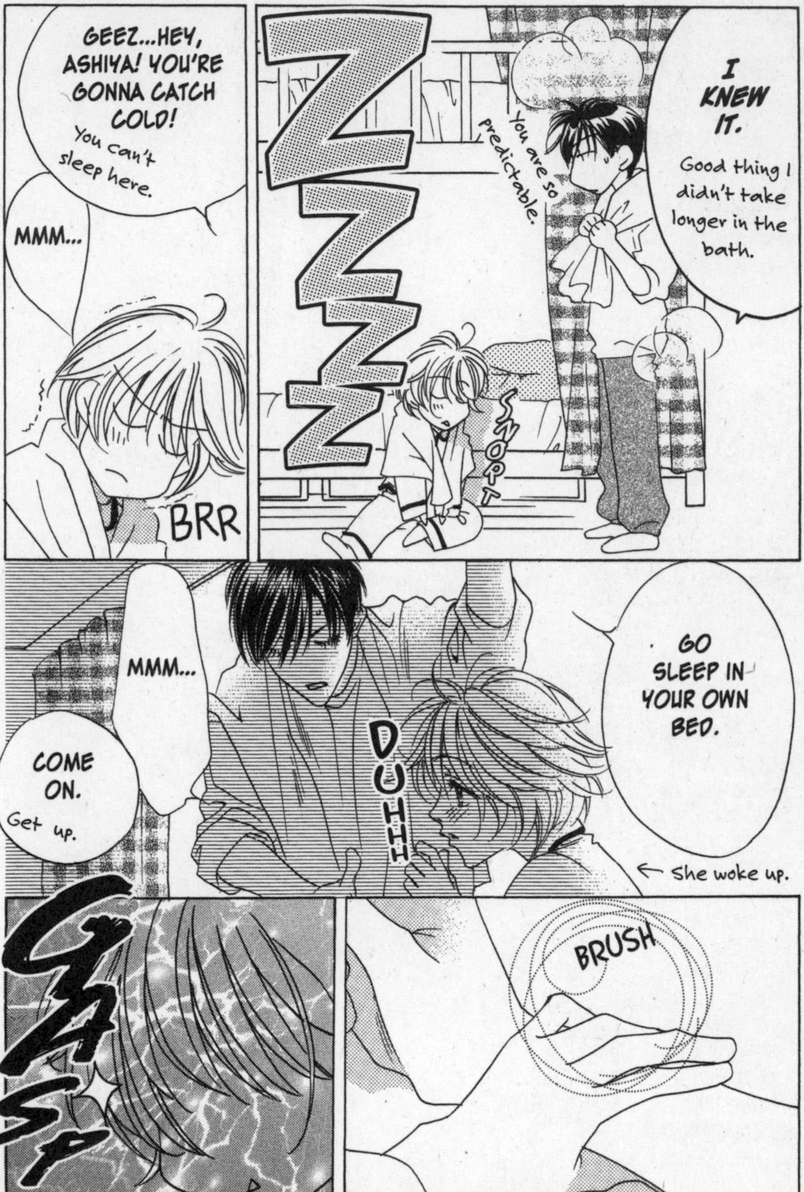
I KNEW IT.
Good thing I didn't take longer in the bath.
You are so predictable.
ZZZZ
SNORT
GEEZ...HEY, ASHIYA! YOU'RE GONNA CATCH COLD!
You can't sleep here.
MMM...
BRR
GO SLEEP IN YOUR OWN BED.
← She woke up.
DUHHH
MMM...
COME ON.
Get up.
BRUSH
GASP

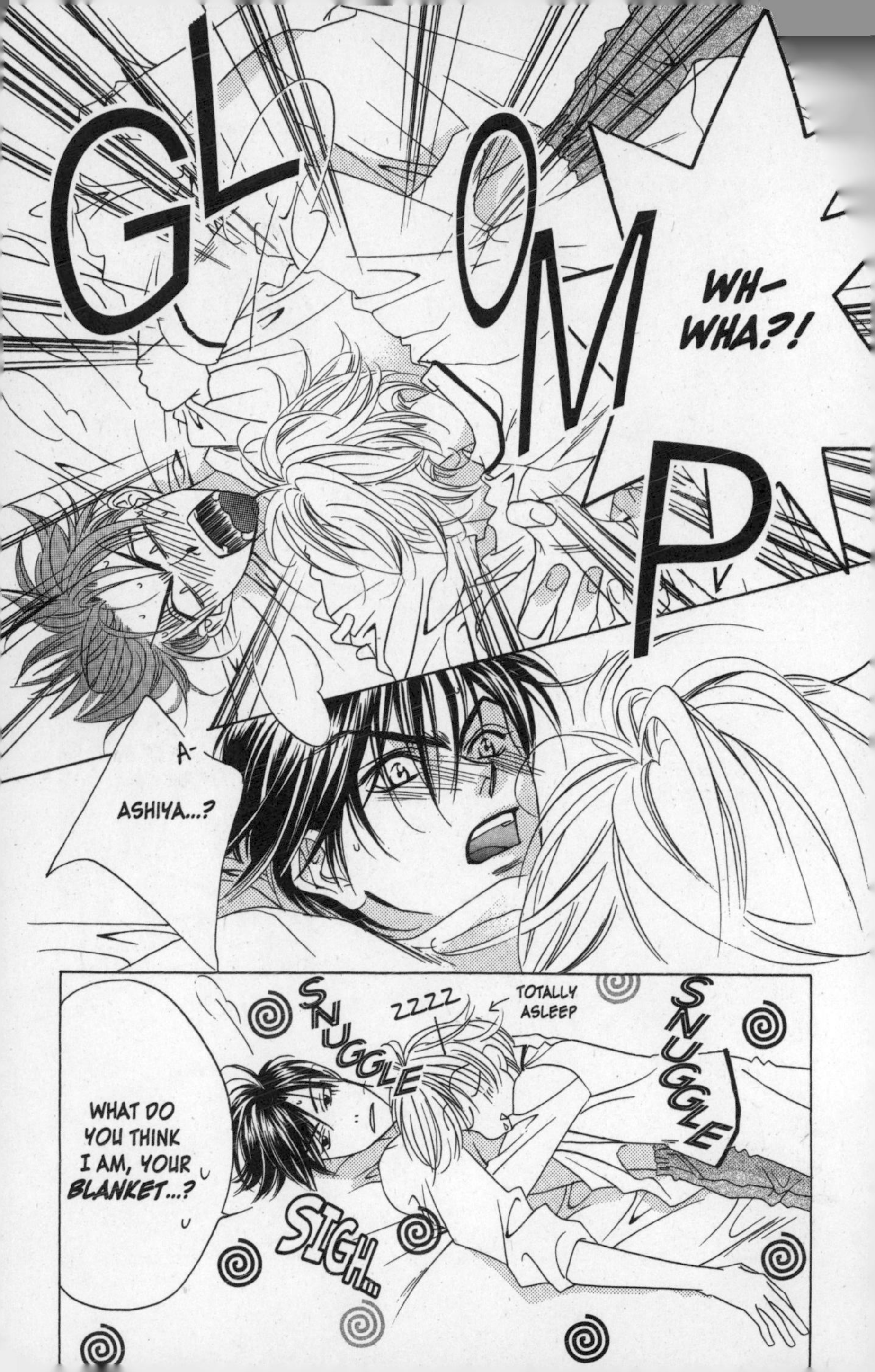
GLOMP
WH-
WHA?!
A-
ASHIYA...?
SNUGGLE
TOTALLY ASLEEP
ZZZZ
SNUGGLE
WHAT DO YOU THINK I AM, YOUR BLANKET...?
SIGH...

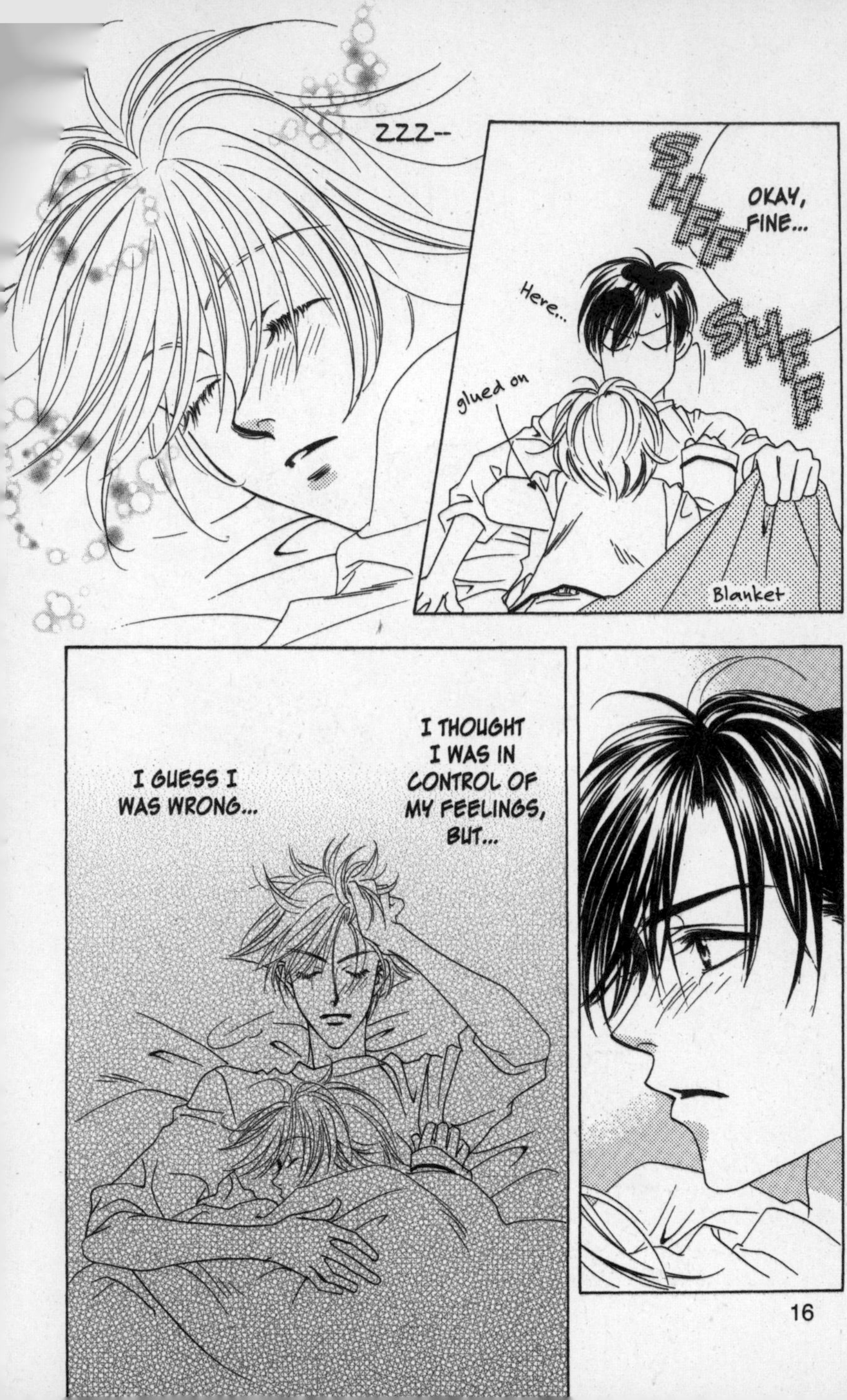
OKAY, FINE...
SHFF
SHFF
Here...
glued on
Blanket
ZZZ--
I THOUGHT I WAS IN CONTROL OF MY FEELINGS, BUT...
I GUESS I WAS WRONG...

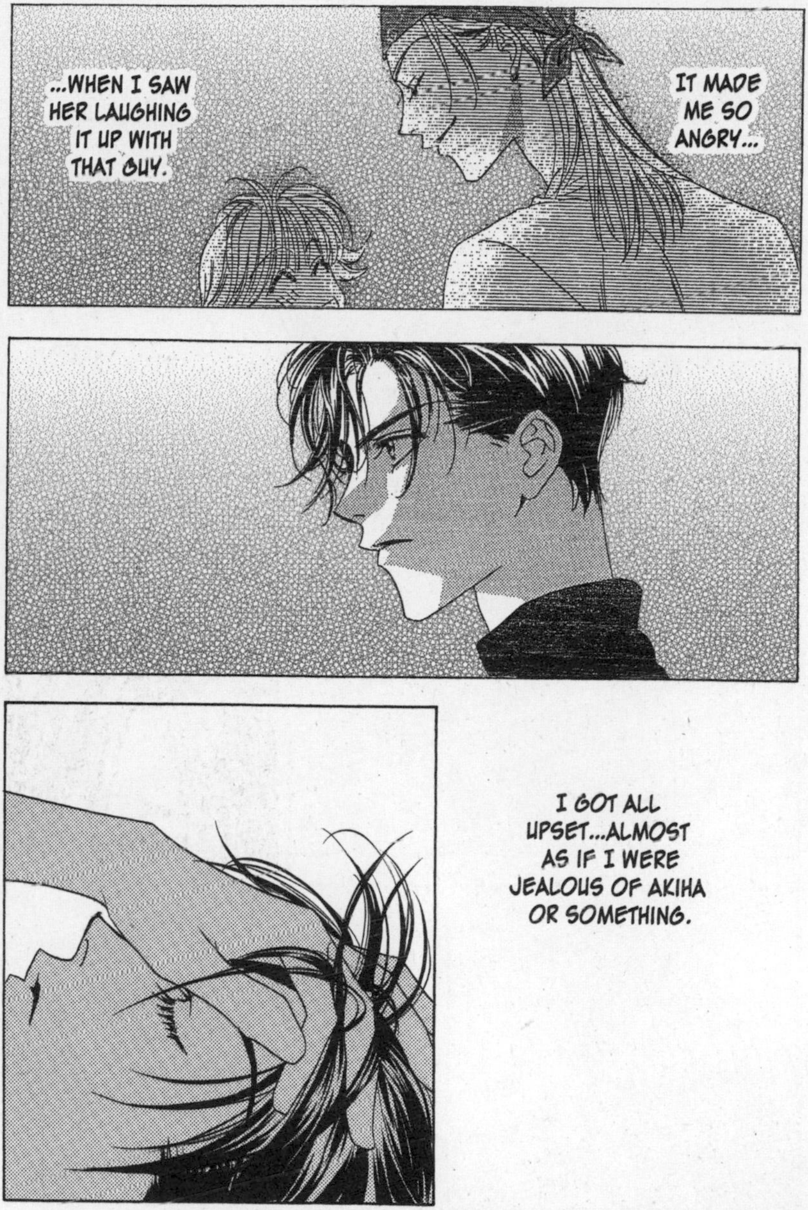
IT MADE ME SO ANGRY...
...WHEN I SAW HER LAUGHING IT UP WITH THAT GUY.
I GOT ALL UPSET...ALMOST AS IF I WERE JEALOUS OF AKIHA OR SOMETHING.

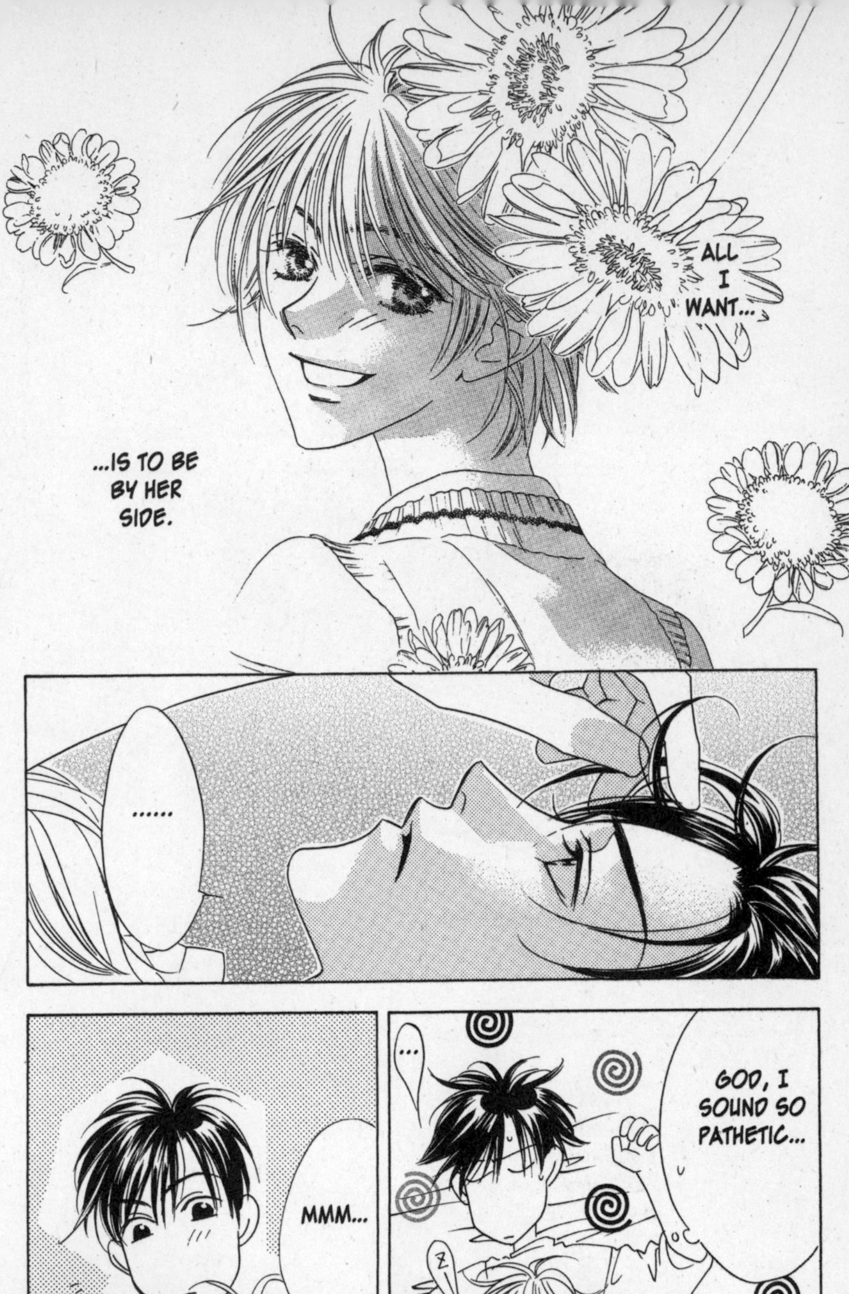
ALL I WANT...
...IS TO BE BY HER SIDE.
......
GOD, I SOUND SO PATHETIC...
...
MMM...

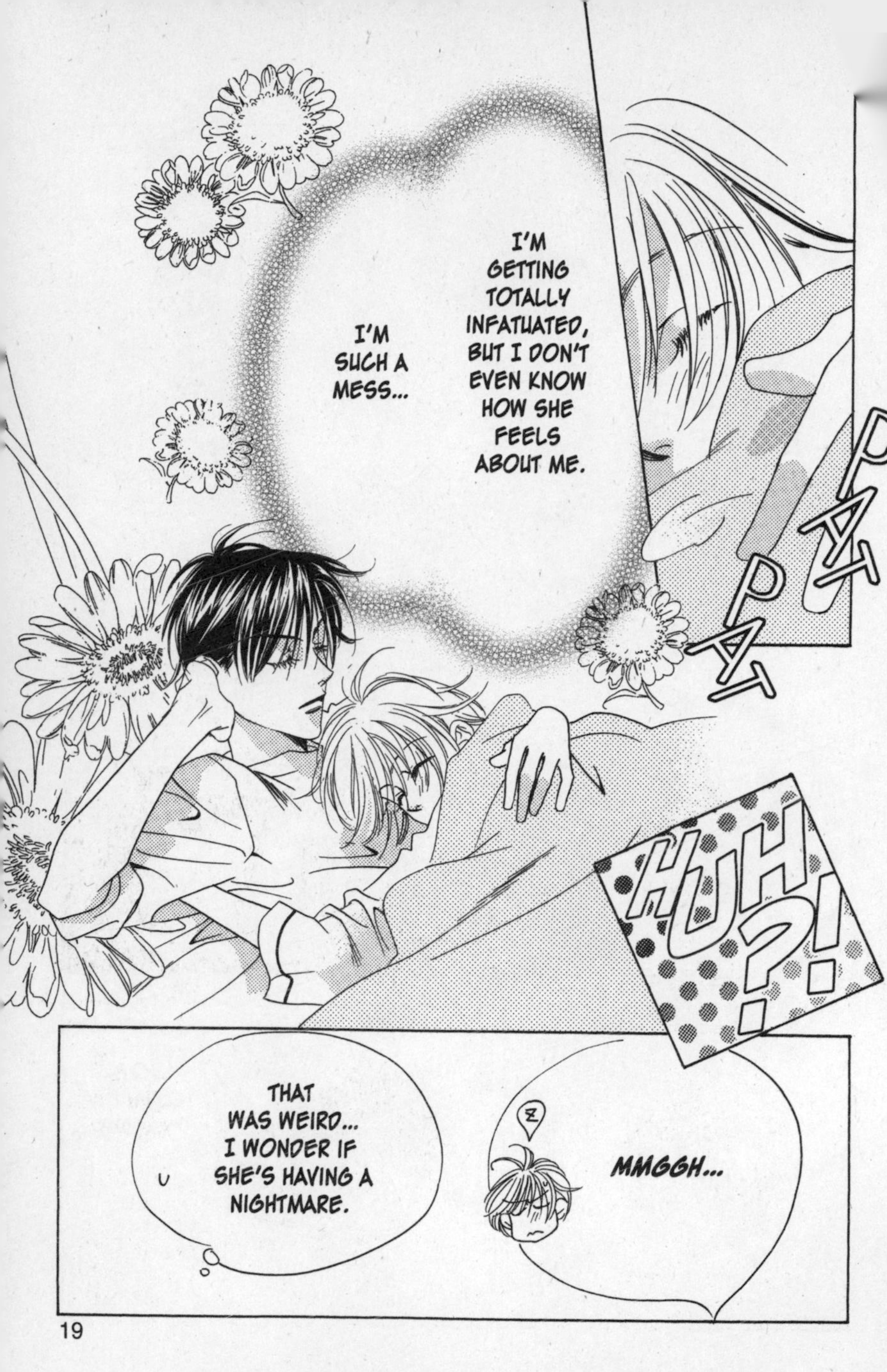
PAT PAT
I'M GETTING TOTALLY INFATUATED, BUT I DON'T EVEN KNOW HOW SHE FEELS ABOUT ME.
I'M SUCH A MESS...
HUH?!
MMGGH...
Z
THAT WAS WEIRD... I WONDER IF SHE'S HAVING A NIGHTMARE.

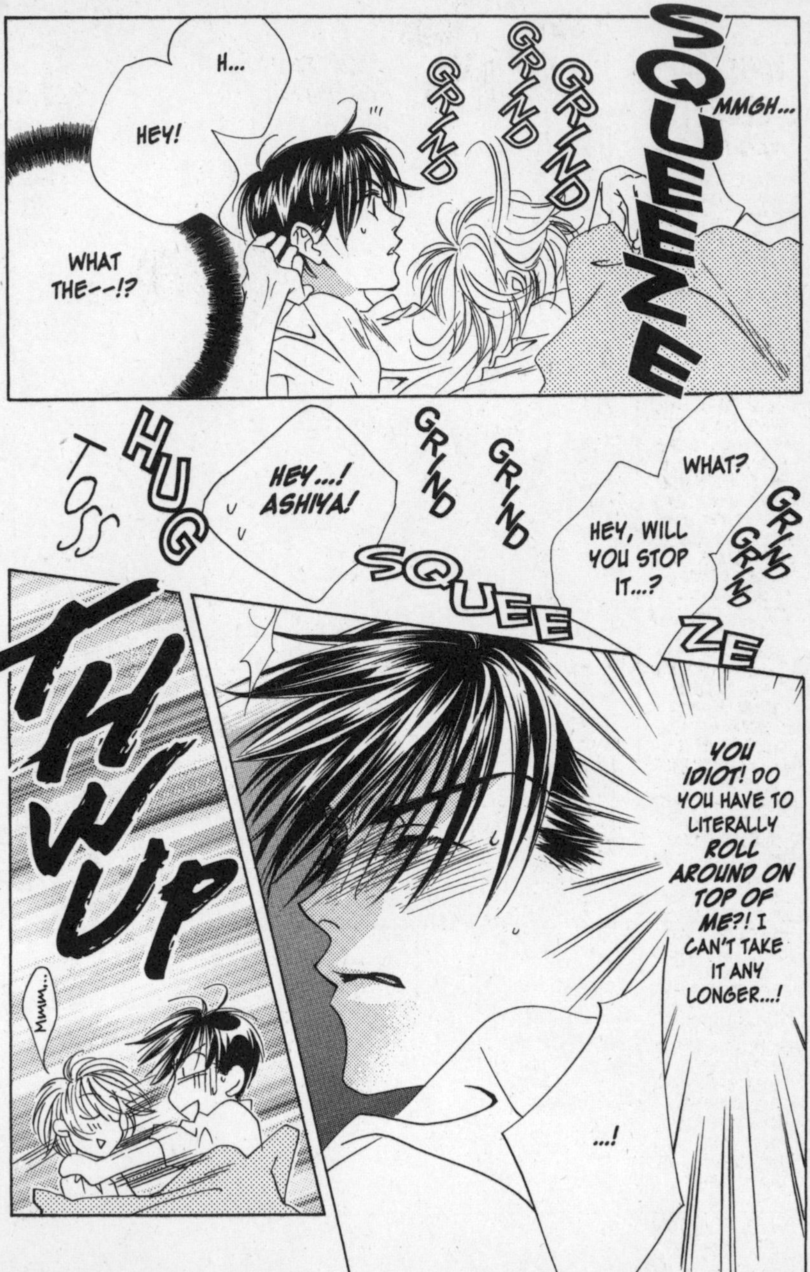
SQUEEZE
MMGH...
GRIND
GRIND
GRIND
H...
HEY!
WHAT THE--!?
WHAT?
HEY, WILL YOU STOP IT...?
GRIND
GRIND
SQUEEZE
GRIND
GRIND
HEY...! ASHIYA!
HUG
TOSS
YOU IDIOT! DO YOU HAVE TO LITERALLY ROLL AROUND ON TOP OF ME?! I CAN'T TAKE IT ANY LONGER...!
...!
THWUP
Mmm...

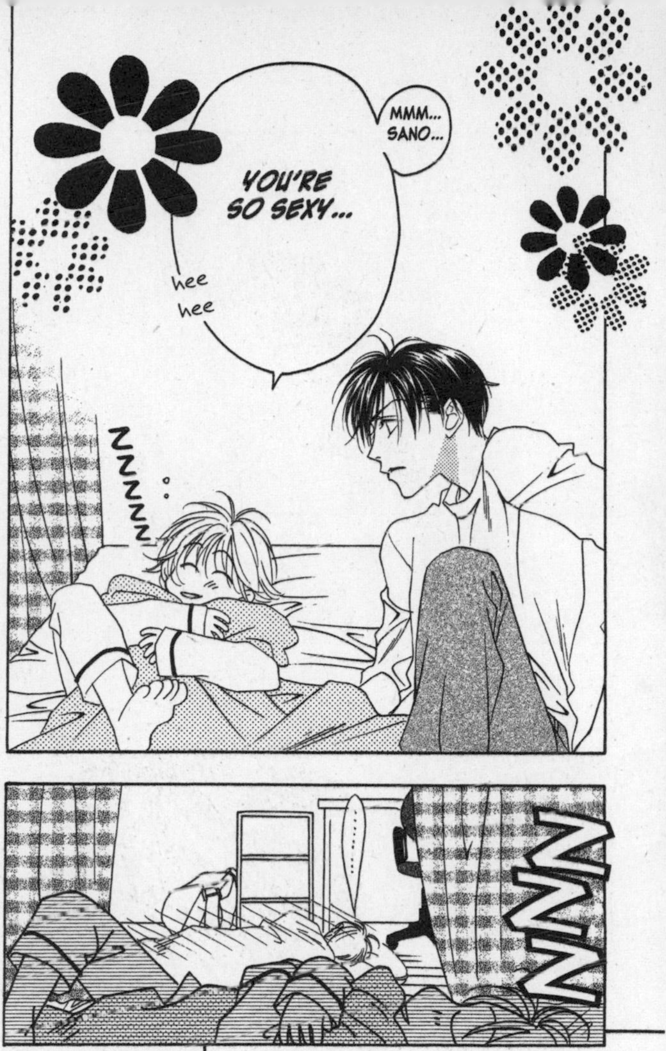
MMM... SANO...
YOU'RE SO SEXY...
hee hee
ZZZZZ
...

WHISPERED SECRETS

NOSTALGIA

EVER SINCE I SET UP MY NEW OFFICE IN TOKYO, I'VE BEEN COMMUTING TWICE A MONTH FROM OSAKA. WHENEVER I GO BACK HOME AFTER WORK, I ALWAYS CRAVE OKONOMIYAKI!* FOR ANYBODY FROM THE KANSAI DISTRICT, OKONOMIYAKI IS THE ULTIMATE FOOD THAT TAKES YOU BACK HOME. IT'S THE FOOD THAT BRINGS PEACE TO OUR SOULS. (I'M EXAGGERATING, BUT JUST A LITTLE.) JUST LIKE KIMCHEE IN KOREA, EVERY FAMILY HAS THEIR OWN SPECIAL RECIPE, AND EVERYBODY HAS THEIR FAVORITE WAY OF PREPARING IT. SINCE MY GRANDMA USED TO OWN AN OKONOMIYAKI RESTAURANT, I'M PRETTY PICKY ABOUT HOW MY OKONOMIYAKI IS PREPARED. BUT SINCE THE WORD "OKONOMI" MEANS "WHATEVER YOU LIKE", I THINK EVERYBODY SHOULD HAVE THE FREEDOM TO ENJOY THEIR OKONOMIYAKI HOWEVER THEY LIKE IT BEST. ALL THAT MATTERS IS THAT IT TASTES GOOD.

*A PANCAKE-LIKE FRIED FOOD WITH VARIOUS FILLINGS, OFTEN CALLED "JAPANESE PIZZA"

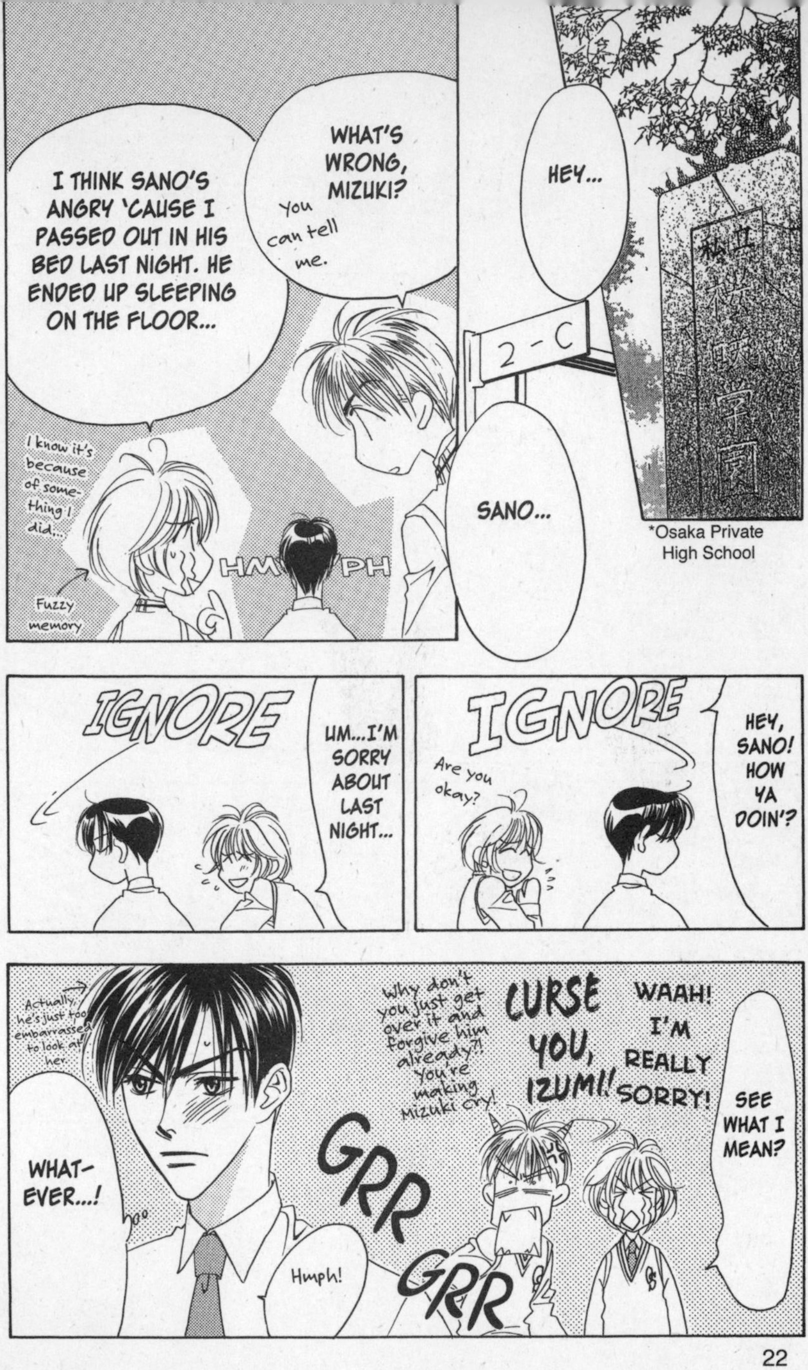
HEY...
SANO...
*Osaka Private High School
2-C
WHAT'S WRONG, MIZUKI?
You can tell me.
I THINK SANO'S ANGRY 'CAUSE I PASSED OUT IN HIS BED LAST NIGHT. HE ENDED UP SLEEPING ON THE FLOOR...
I know it's because of something I did...
Fuzzy memory
HMPH
HEY, SANO! HOW YA DOIN'?
IGNORE
Are you okay?
UM...I'M SORRY ABOUT LAST NIGHT...
IGNORE
SEE WHAT I MEAN?
WAAH! I'M REALLY SORRY!
CURSE YOU, IZUMI!
Why don't you just get over it and forgive him already?! You're making Mizuki cry!
GRR
GRR
Hmph!
WHAT-EVER...!
Actually, he's just too embarrassed to look at her.

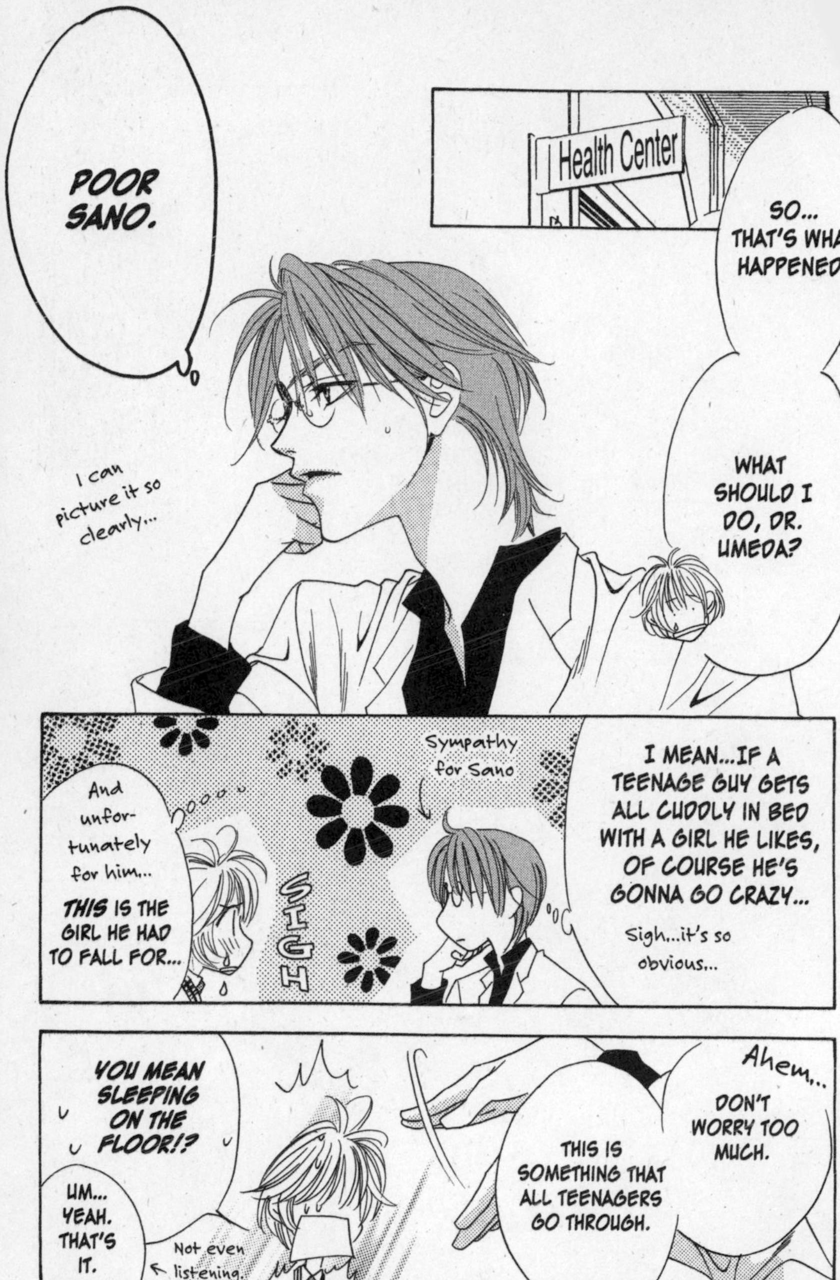
Health Center
SO... THAT'S WHAT HAPPENED.
WHAT SHOULD I DO, DR. UMEDA?
POOR SANO.
I can picture it so clearly...
I MEAN...IF A TEENAGE GUY GETS ALL CUDDLY IN BED WITH A GIRL HE LIKES, OF COURSE HE'S GONNA GO CRAZY...
Sigh...it's so obvious...
Sympathy for Sano
SIGH
And unfortunately for him...
THIS IS THE GIRL HE HAD TO FALL FOR...
Ahem...
DON'T WORRY TOO MUCH.
THIS IS SOMETHING THAT ALL TEENAGERS GO THROUGH.
YOU MEAN SLEEPING ON THE FLOOR!?
UM... YEAH. THAT'S IT.
Not even listening.

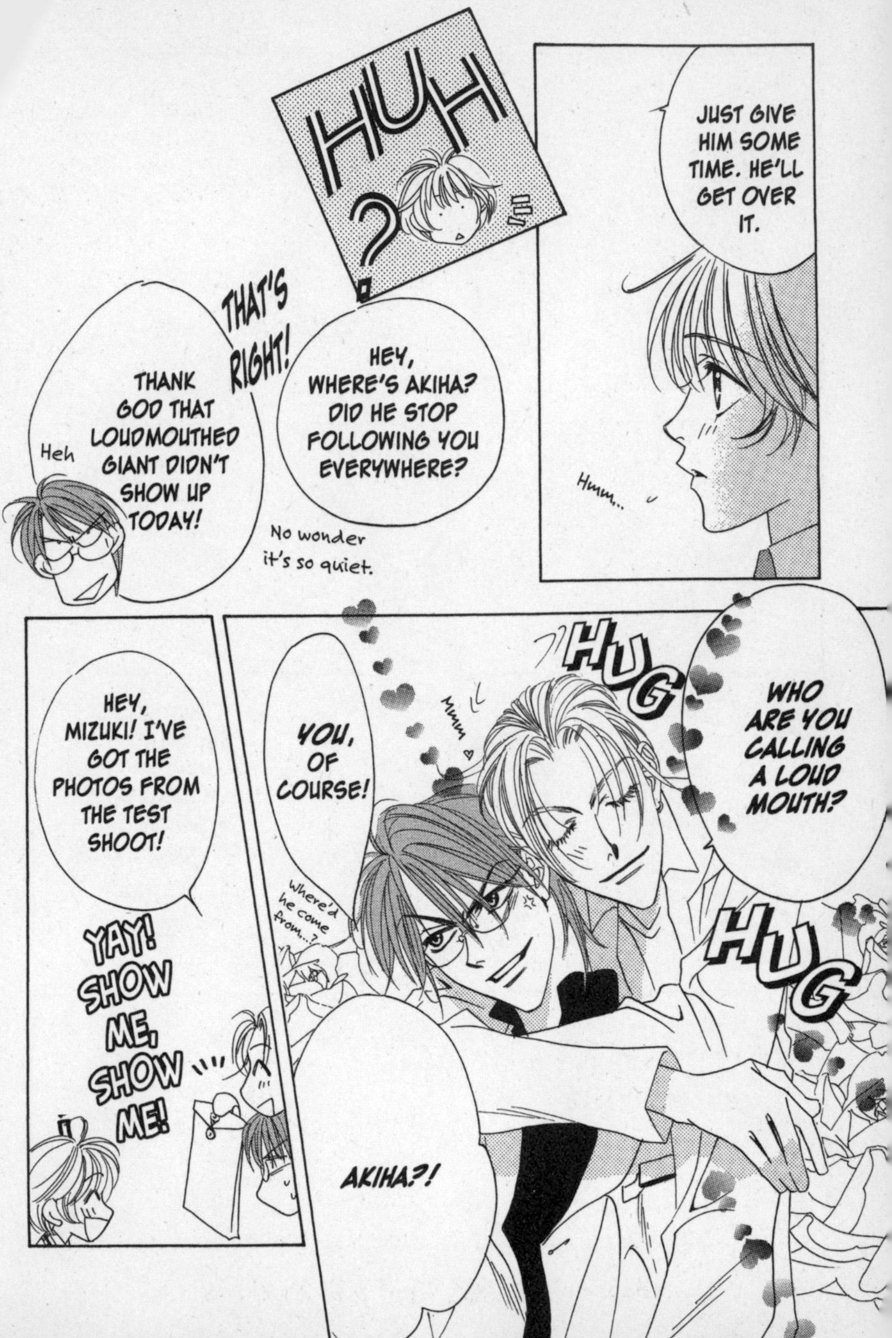
JUST GIVE HIM SOME TIME. HE'LL GET OVER IT.
Hmm...
HUH?
HEY, WHERE'S AKIHA? DID HE STOP FOLLOWING YOU EVERYWHERE?
THAT'S RIGHT!
THANK GOD THAT LOUDMOUTHED GIANT DIDN'T SHOW UP TODAY!
Heh
No wonder it's so quiet.
HUG
WHO ARE YOU CALLING A LOUD MOUTH?
Mmm
YOU, OF COURSE!
HUG
Where'd he come from...?
AKIHA?!
HEY, MIZUKI! I'VE GOT THE PHOTOS FROM THE TEST SHOOT!
YAY! SHOW ME, SHOW ME!

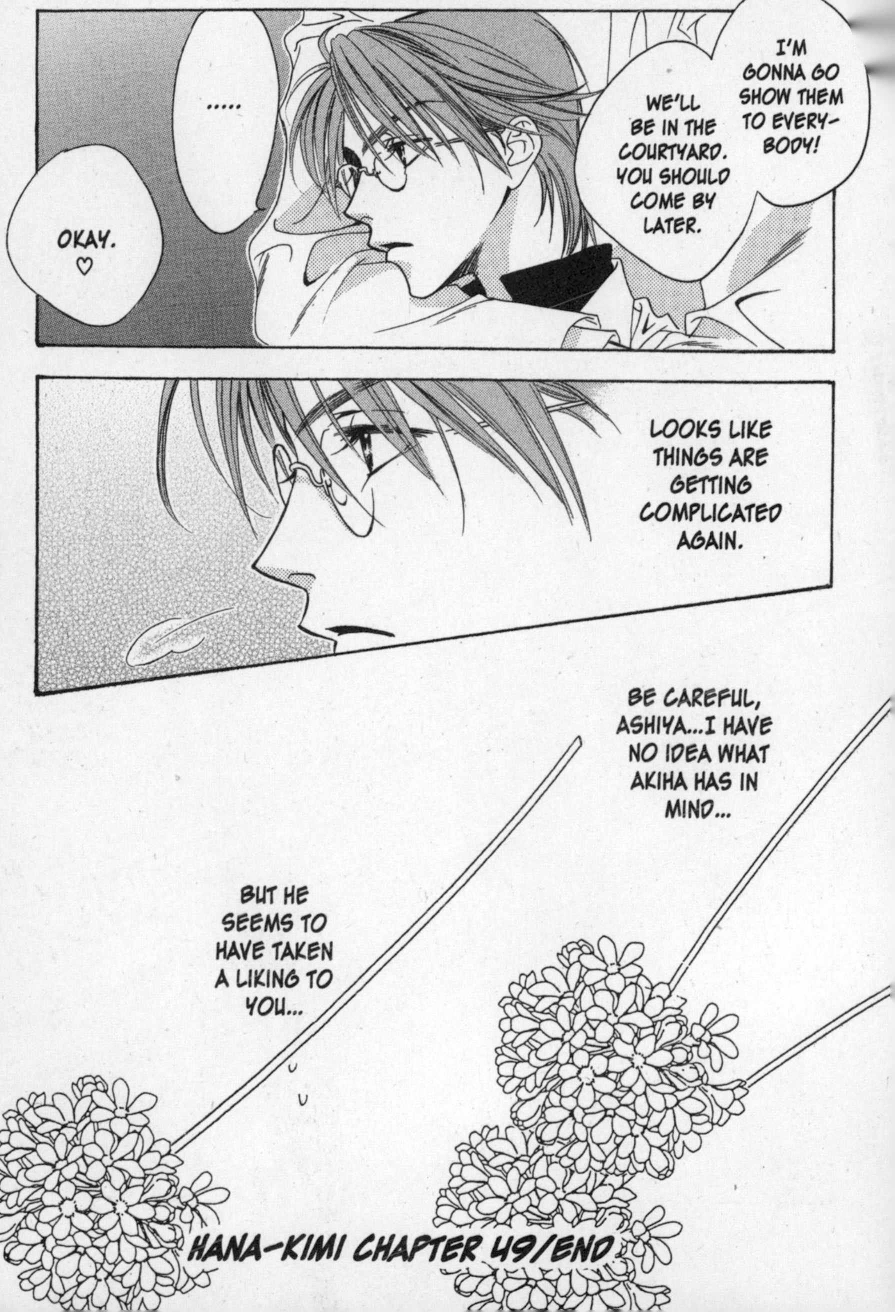
I'M GONNA GO SHOW THEM TO EVERY-BODY!
WE'LL BE IN THE COURTYARD. YOU SHOULD COME BY LATER.
.....
OKAY. ♡
LOOKS LIKE THINGS ARE GETTING COMPLICATED AGAIN.
BE CAREFUL, ASHIYA...I HAVE NO IDEA WHAT AKIHA HAS IN MIND...
BUT HE SEEMS TO HAVE TAKEN A LIKING TO YOU...
HANA-KIMI CHAPTER 49/END

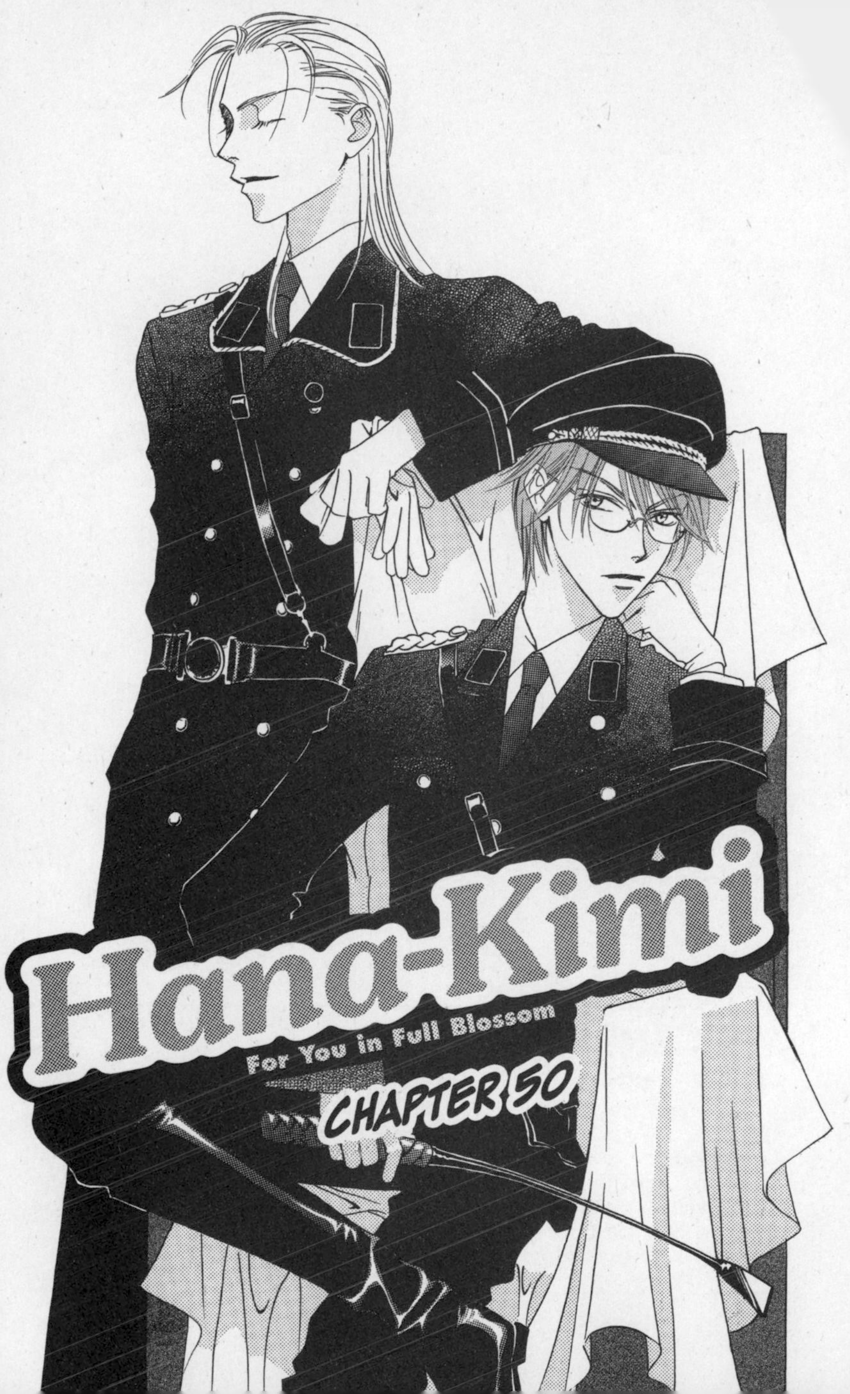
Hana-Kimi
For You in Full Blossom
CHAPTER 50

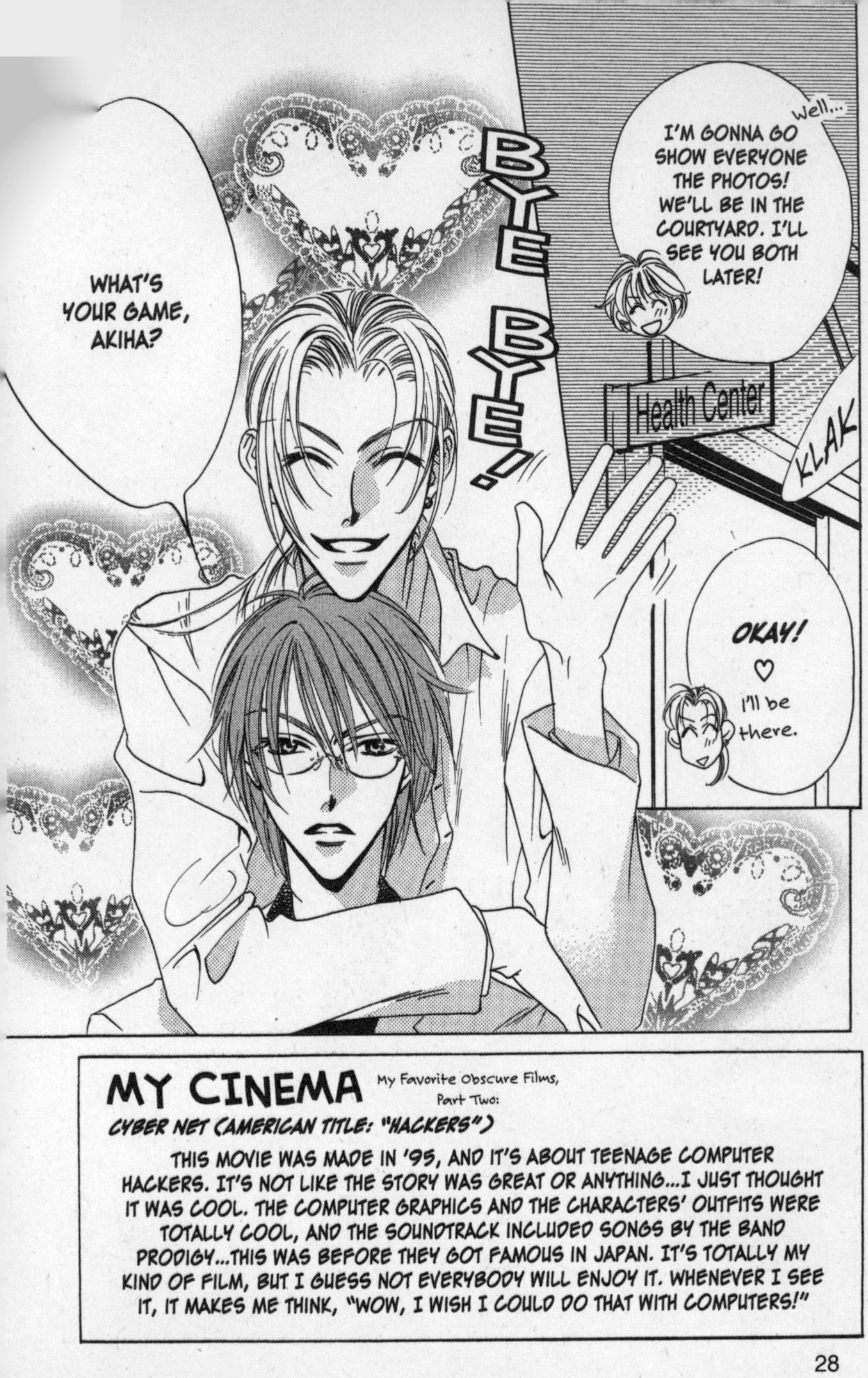
Well...
I'M GONNA GO SHOW EVERYONE THE PHOTOS! WE'LL BE IN THE COURTYARD. I'LL SEE YOU BOTH LATER!
Health Center
KLAK
OKAY! ♡ I'll be there.
BYE BYE!
WHAT'S YOUR GAME, AKIHA?

MY CINEMA

My Favorite Obscure Films, Part Two:

CYBER NET (AMERICAN TITLE: "HACKERS")

THIS MOVIE WAS MADE IN '95, AND IT'S ABOUT TEENAGE COMPUTER HACKERS. IT'S NOT LIKE THE STORY WAS GREAT OR ANYTHING...I JUST THOUGHT IT WAS COOL. THE COMPUTER GRAPHICS AND THE CHARACTERS' OUTFITS WERE TOTALLY COOL, AND THE SOUNDTRACK INCLUDED SONGS BY THE BAND PRODIGY...THIS WAS BEFORE THEY GOT FAMOUS IN JAPAN. IT'S TOTALLY MY KIND OF FILM, BUT I GUESS NOT EVERYBODY WILL ENJOY IT. WHENEVER I SEE IT, IT MAKES ME THINK, "WOW, I WISH I COULD DO THAT WITH COMPUTERS!"

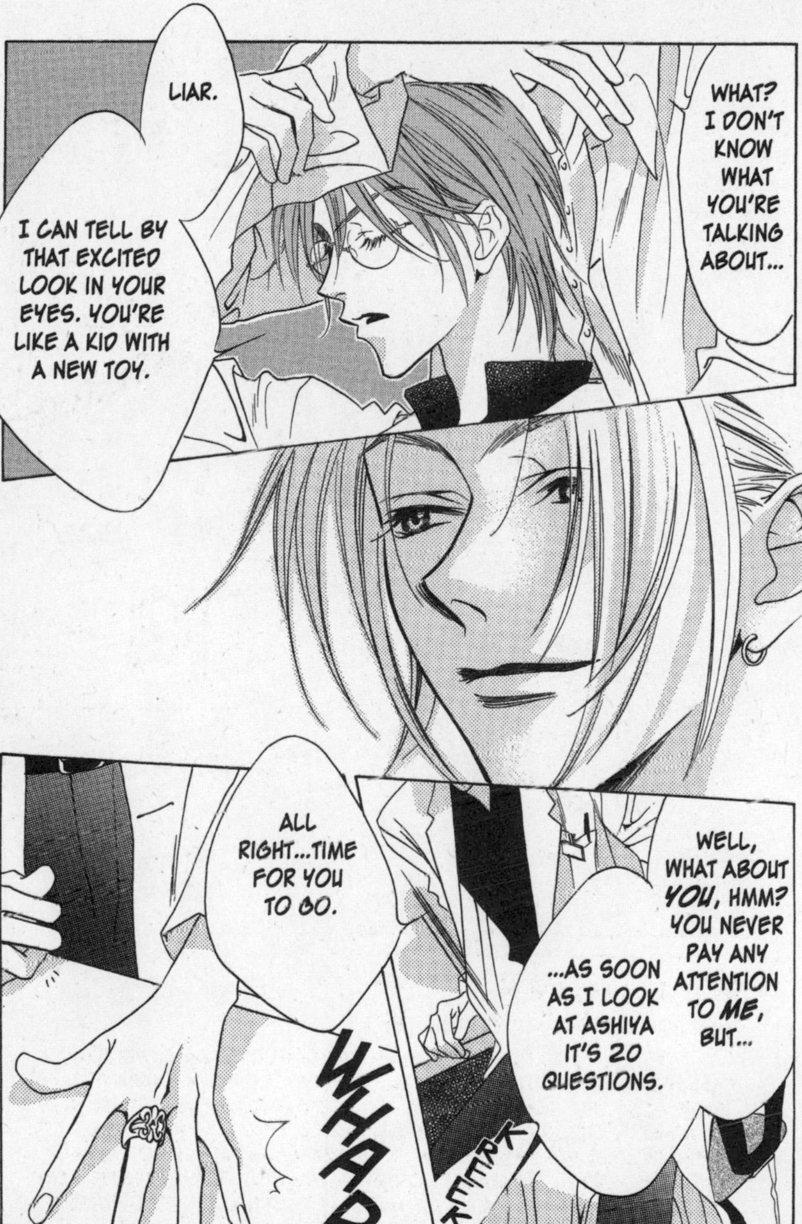
WHAT? I DON'T KNOW WHAT YOU'RE TALKING ABOUT...
LIAR.
I CAN TELL BY THAT EXCITED LOOK IN YOUR EYES. YOU'RE LIKE A KID WITH A NEW TOY.
WELL, WHAT ABOUT *YOU*, HMM? YOU NEVER PAY ANY ATTENTION TO *ME*, BUT...
...AS SOON AS I LOOK AT ASHIYA IT'S 20 QUESTIONS.
KEERK
ALL RIGHT...TIME FOR YOU TO GO.
WHAP

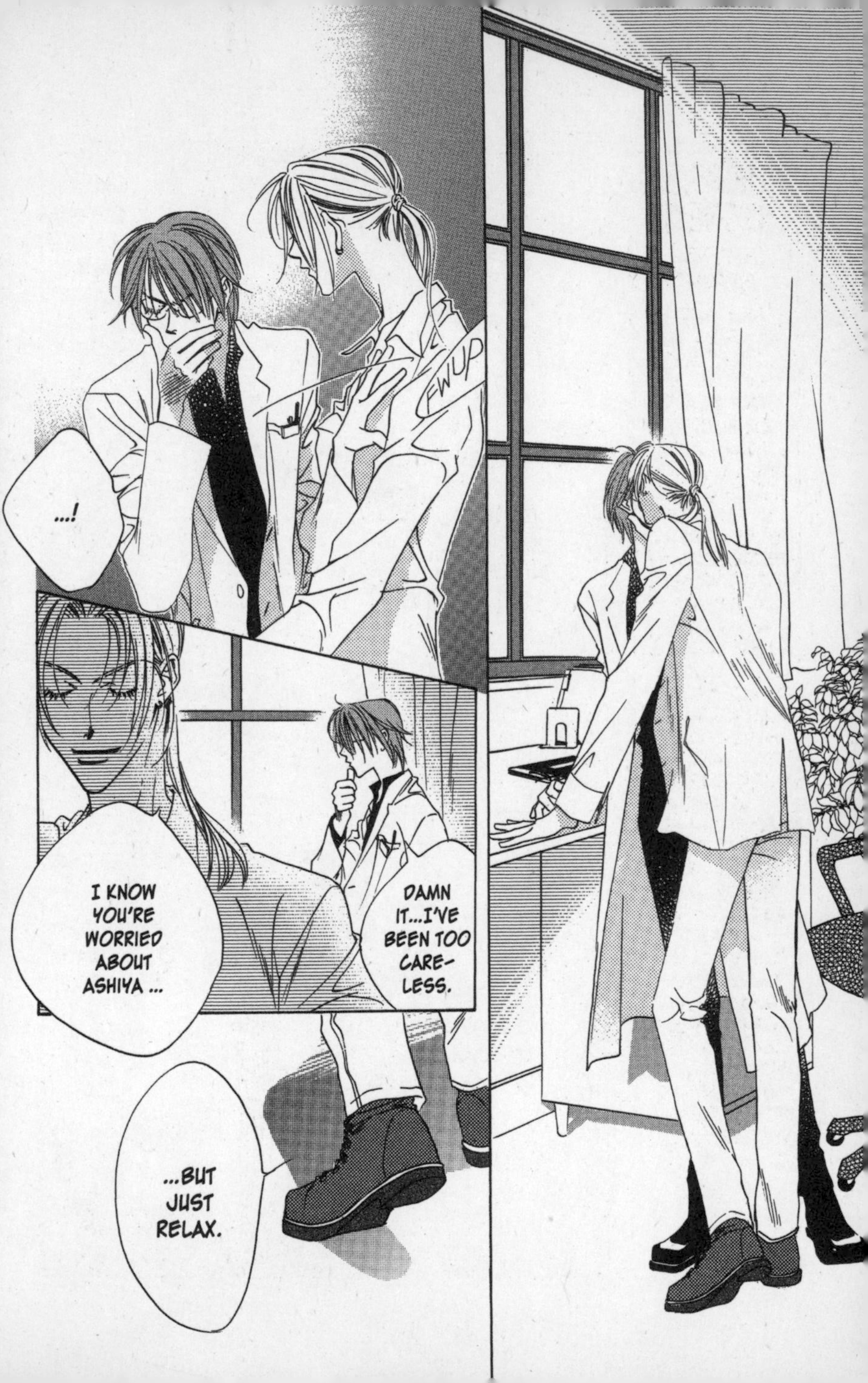
FWUP
...!
DAMN IT...I'VE BEEN TOO CARE-LESS.
I KNOW YOU'RE WORRIED ABOUT ASHIYA ...
...BUT JUST RELAX.

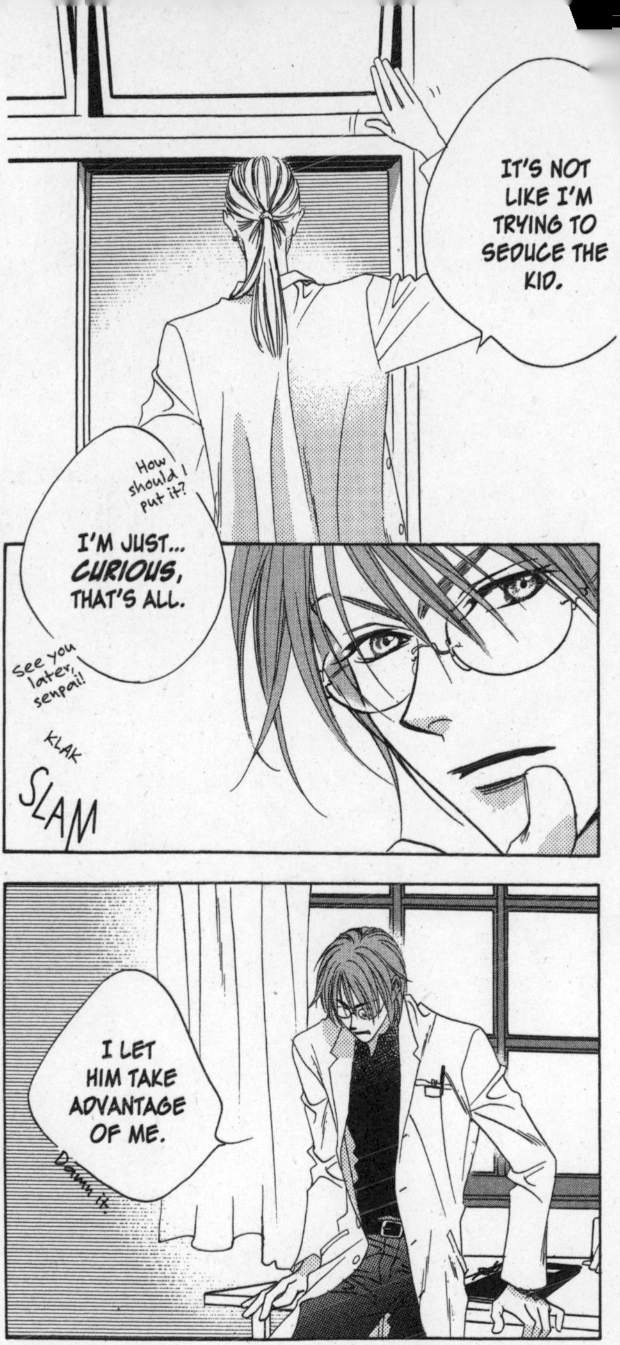
IT'S NOT LIKE I'M TRYING TO SEDUCE THE KID.
How should I put it?
I'M JUST... CURIOUS, THAT'S ALL.
See you later, senpai!
KLAK
SLAM
I LET HIM TAKE ADVANTAGE OF ME.
Damn it.

WHISPERED SECRETS

UNIFORM FETISH

I LOVE MILITARY UNIFORMS! HEH, HEH. I WAS SUPPOSED TO DRAW THEM IN COLOR, BUT I THOUGHT THEY MIGHT BE SEXIER IN BLACK & WHITE. MY FRIEND "M" LET ME BORROW A REFERENCE BOOK.♥ BUT I DIDN'T FEEL LIKE DRAWING A REPLICA, SO I MADE MY OWN ORIGINAL VERSION. MANY OF MY FANS SEND ME LETTERS SAYING "PLEASE DRAW UMEDA IN A MILITARY UNIFORM!" SO WHAT DO YOU THINK? (SEE PAGE 27.) I ALSO LIKE TO DRAW HIM IN HIS LAB COAT, AND IN STREET CLOTHES. OH, AND I LOVE DRAWING SOMMELIER AND MAID OUTFITS TOO! I JUST LOVE THEM! TWO-TONE, BLACK & WHITE UNIFORMS ARE SO GORGEOUS. TRES BIEN! ✧

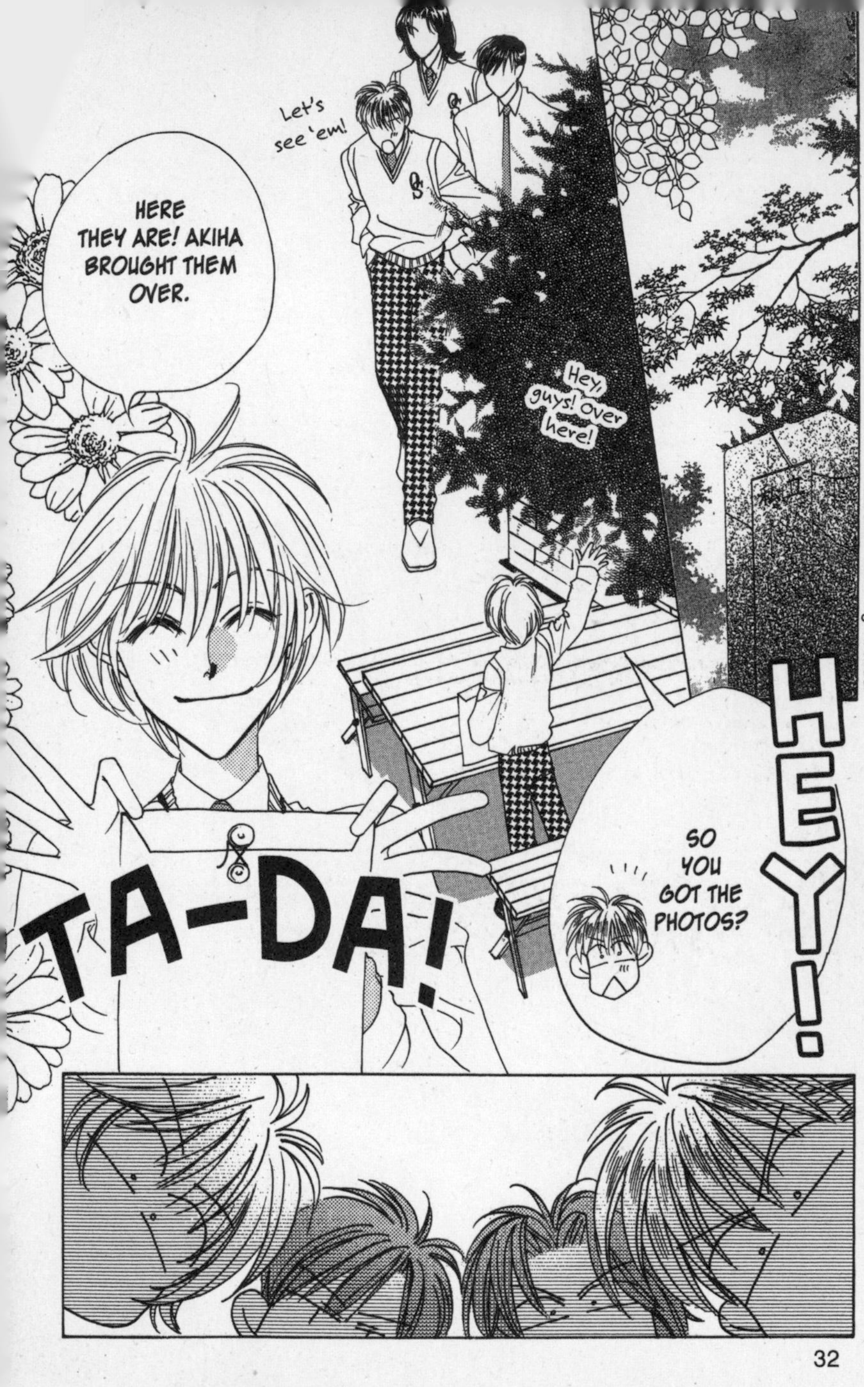
Osaka Private High School
HEY!
SO YOU GOT THE PHOTOS?
Hey, guys! over here!
Let's see 'em!
HERE THEY ARE! AKIHA BROUGHT THEM OVER.
TA-DA!

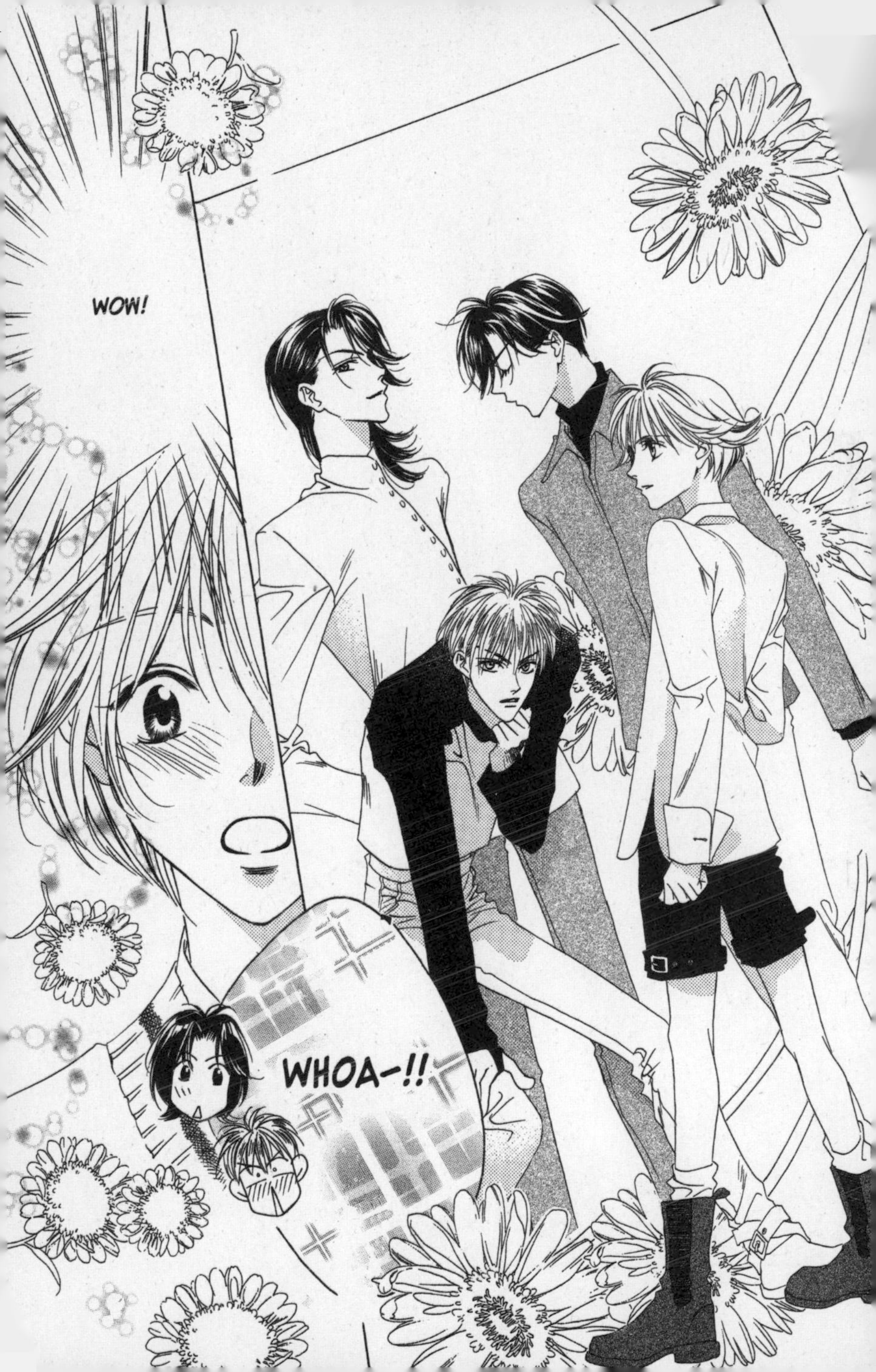
WOW!
WHOA-!!

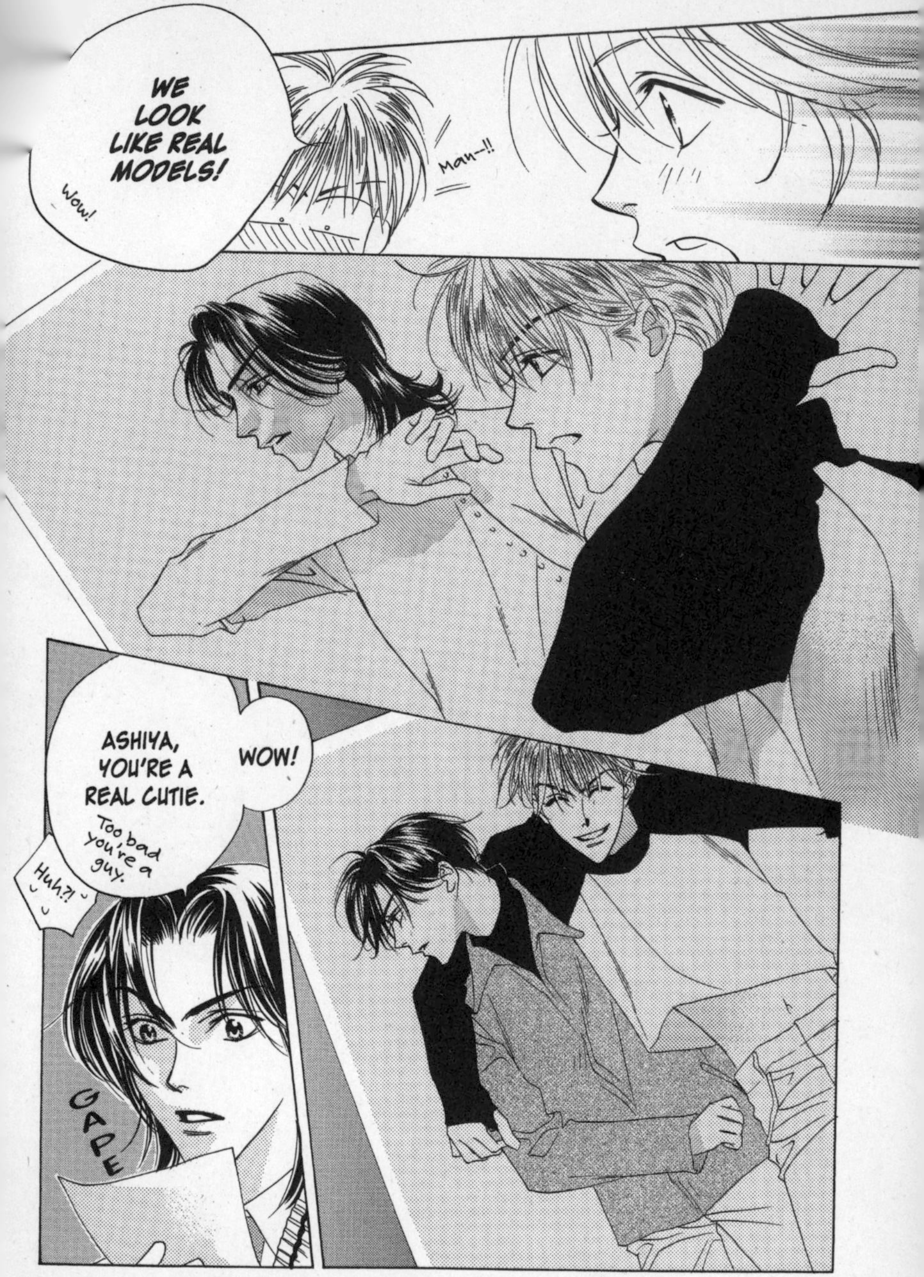
Man—!!
WE LOOK LIKE REAL MODELS!
Wow!
WOW!
ASHIYA, YOU'RE A REAL CUTIE.
Too bad you're a guy.
Huh?!
GAPE

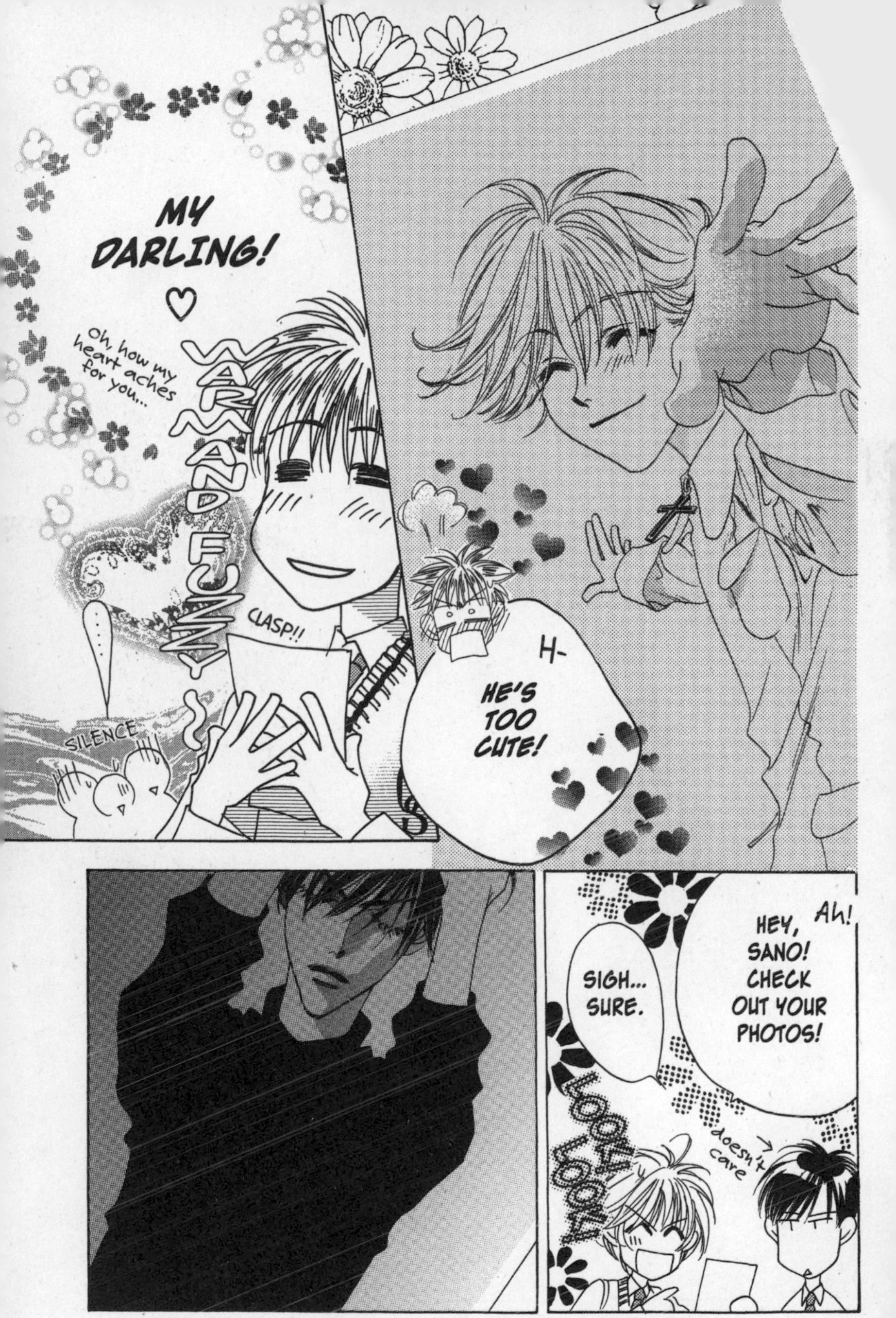
H- HE'S TOO CUTE!
MY DARLING! ♡
Oh, how my heart aches for you...
WARM AND FUZZY
CLASP!!
SILENCE
AH!
HEY, SANO! CHECK OUT YOUR PHOTOS!
SIGH... SURE.
LOOK LOOK
doesn't care

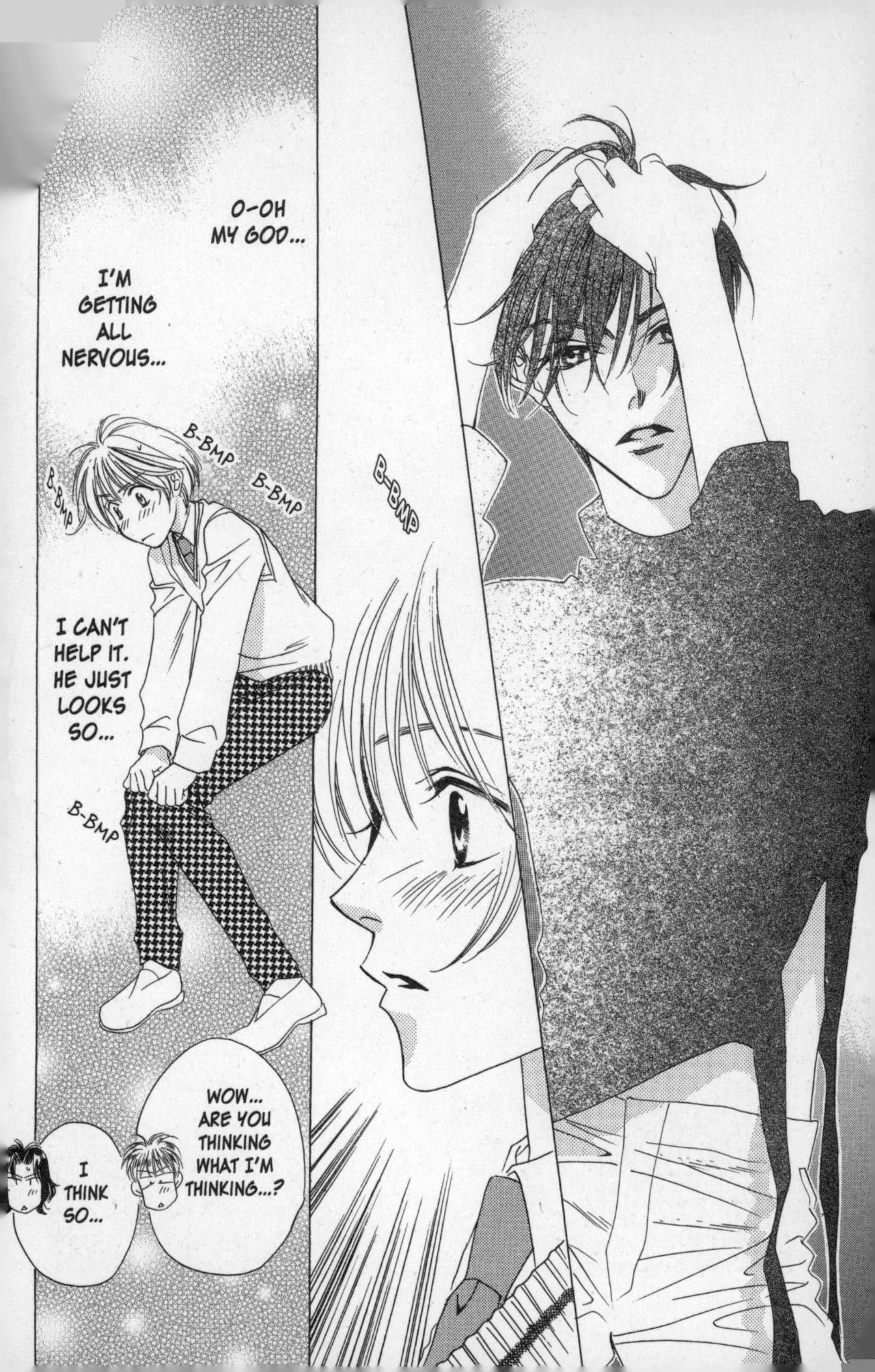
B-BMP
O-OH MY GOD...
I'M GETTING ALL NERVOUS...
B-BMP
B-BMP
B-BMP
I CAN'T HELP IT. HE JUST LOOKS SO...
B-BMP
WOW... ARE YOU THINKING WHAT I'M THINKING...?
I THINK SO...

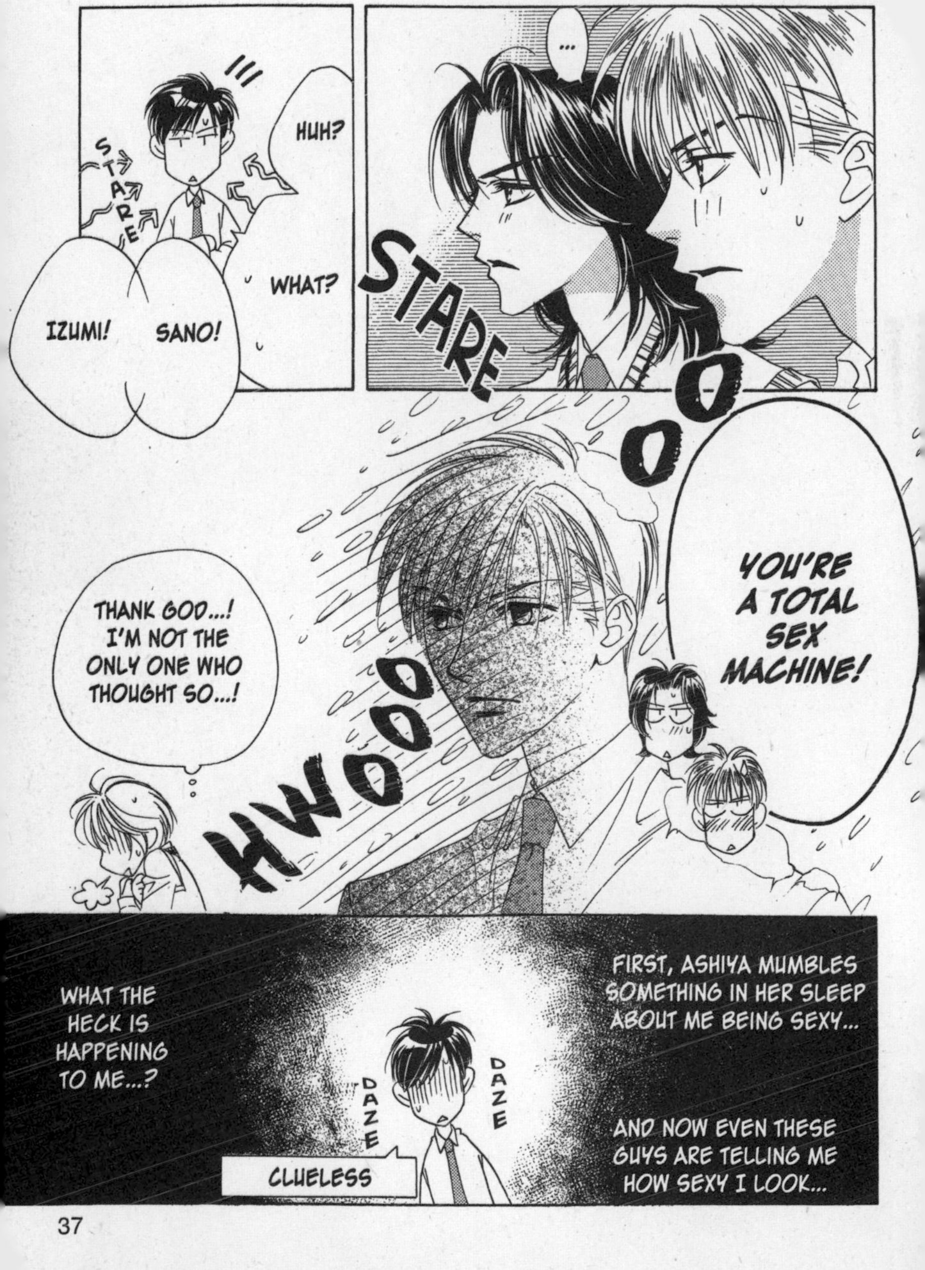
…
STARE
HUH?
WHAT?
STARE
SANO!
IZUMI!
YOU'RE A TOTAL SEX MACHINE!
HWOOOOOO
THANK GOD...! I'M NOT THE ONLY ONE WHO THOUGHT SO...!
FIRST, ASHIYA MUMBLES SOMETHING IN HER SLEEP ABOUT ME BEING SEXY...
AND NOW EVEN THESE GUYS ARE TELLING ME HOW SEXY I LOOK...
DAZE
DAZE
CLUELESS
WHAT THE HECK IS HAPPENING TO ME...?

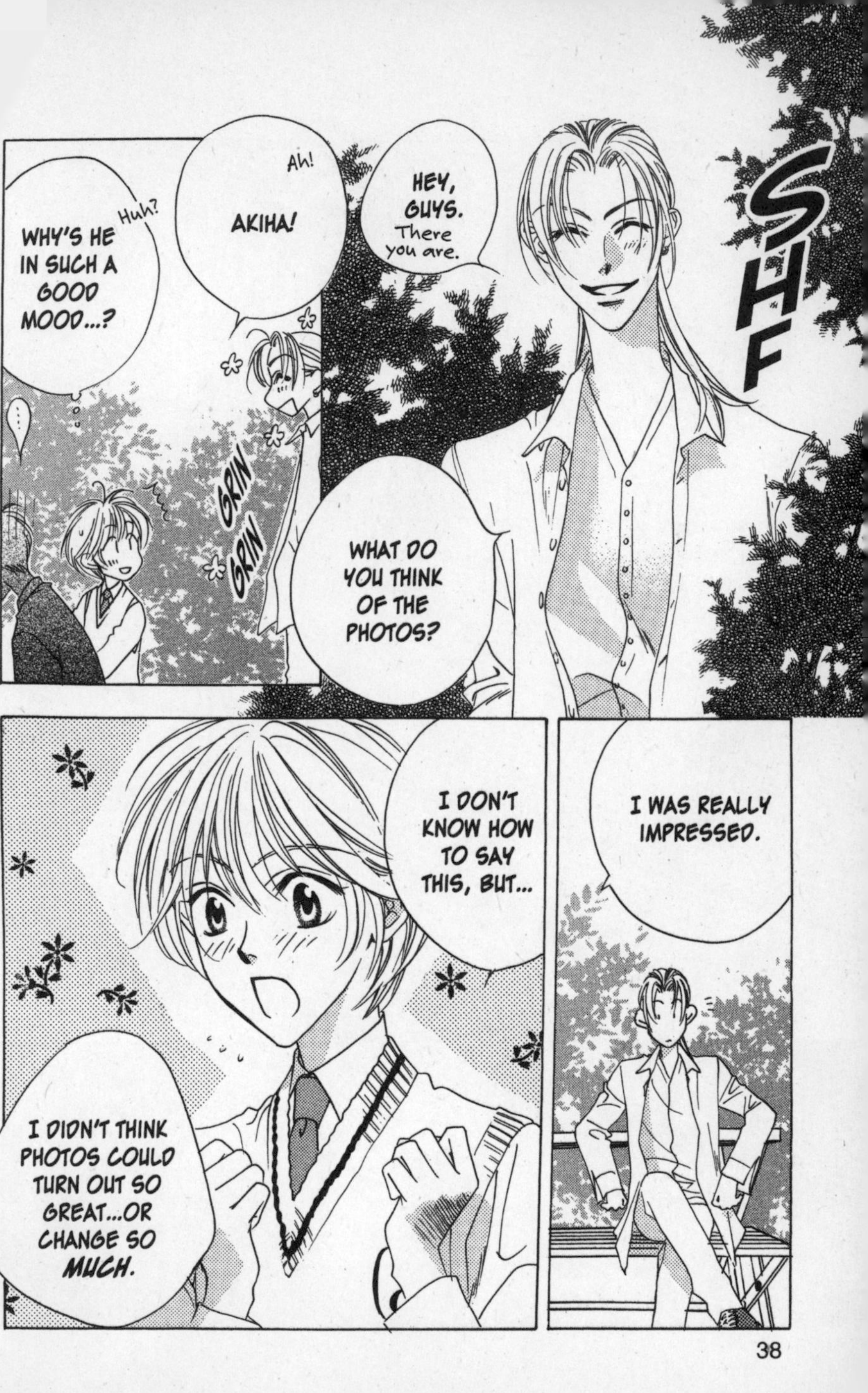
SHF
HEY, GUYS. There you are.
Ah!
AKIHA!
Huh?
WHY'S HE IN SUCH A GOOD MOOD...?
...
GRIN GRIN
WHAT DO YOU THINK OF THE PHOTOS?
I WAS REALLY IMPRESSED.
I DON'T KNOW HOW TO SAY THIS, BUT...
I DIDN'T THINK PHOTOS COULD TURN OUT SO GREAT...OR CHANGE SO *MUCH*.

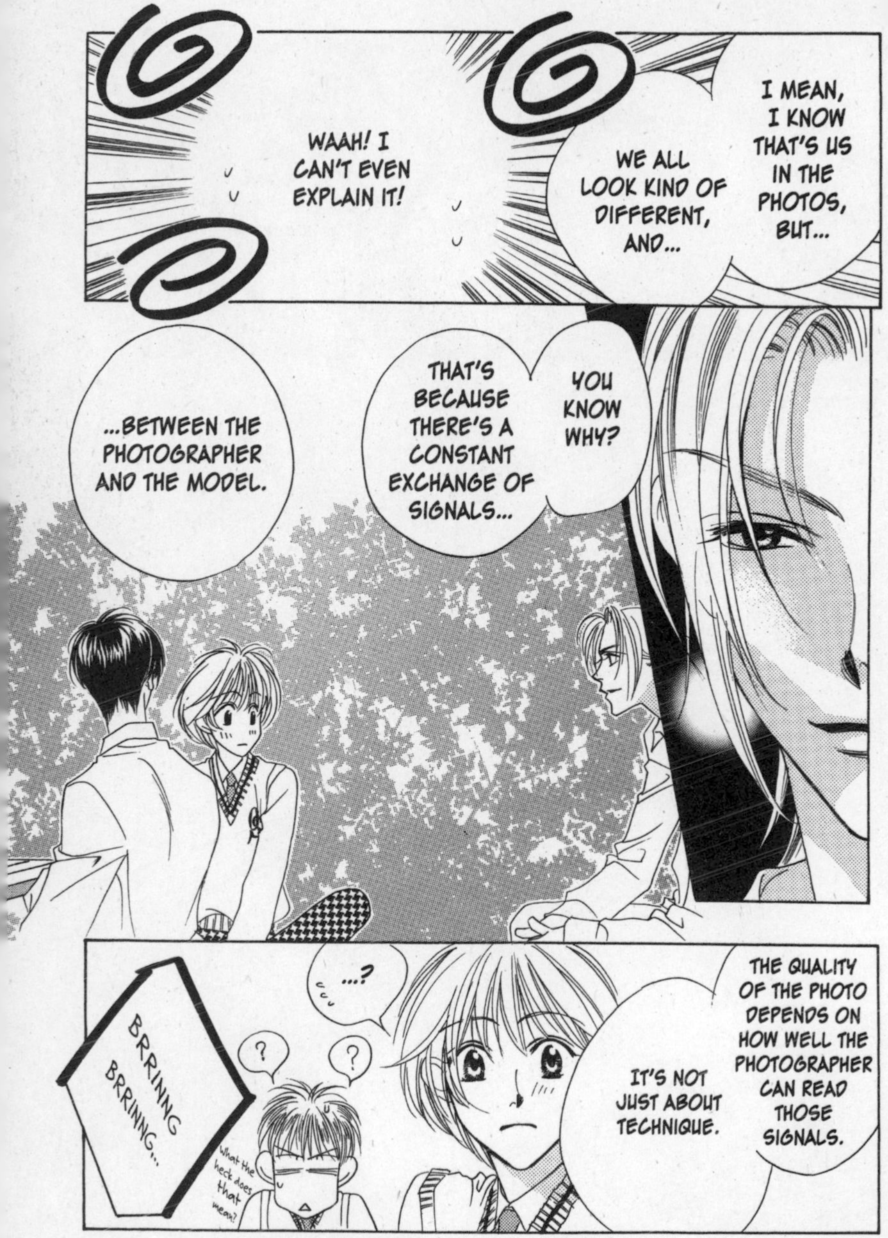
I MEAN, I KNOW THAT'S US IN THE PHOTOS, BUT...
WE ALL LOOK KIND OF DIFFERENT, AND...
WAAH! I CAN'T EVEN EXPLAIN IT!
YOU KNOW WHY?
THAT'S BECAUSE THERE'S A CONSTANT EXCHANGE OF SIGNALS...
...BETWEEN THE PHOTOGRAPHER AND THE MODEL.
THE QUALITY OF THE PHOTO DEPENDS ON HOW WELL THE PHOTOGRAPHER CAN READ THOSE SIGNALS.
IT'S NOT JUST ABOUT TECHNIQUE.
...?
?
?
What the heck does that mean?
BRRINNG BRRINNG...

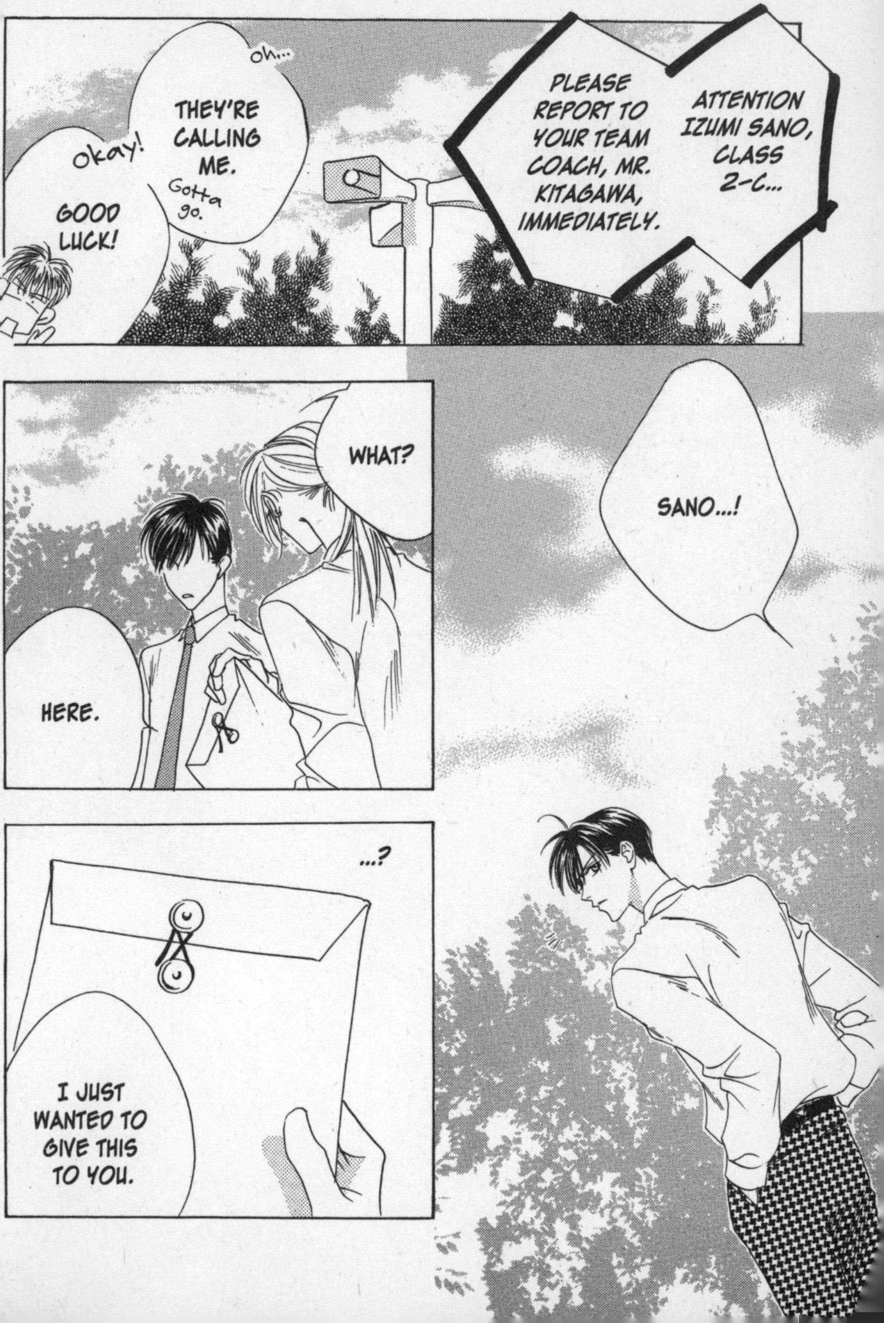
ATTENTION IZUMI SANO, CLASS 2-C...
PLEASE REPORT TO YOUR TEAM COACH, MR. KITAGAWA, IMMEDIATELY.
oh...
THEY'RE CALLING ME.
Gotta go.
Okay!
GOOD LUCK!
SANO...!
WHAT?
HERE.
...?
I JUST WANTED TO GIVE THIS TO YOU.

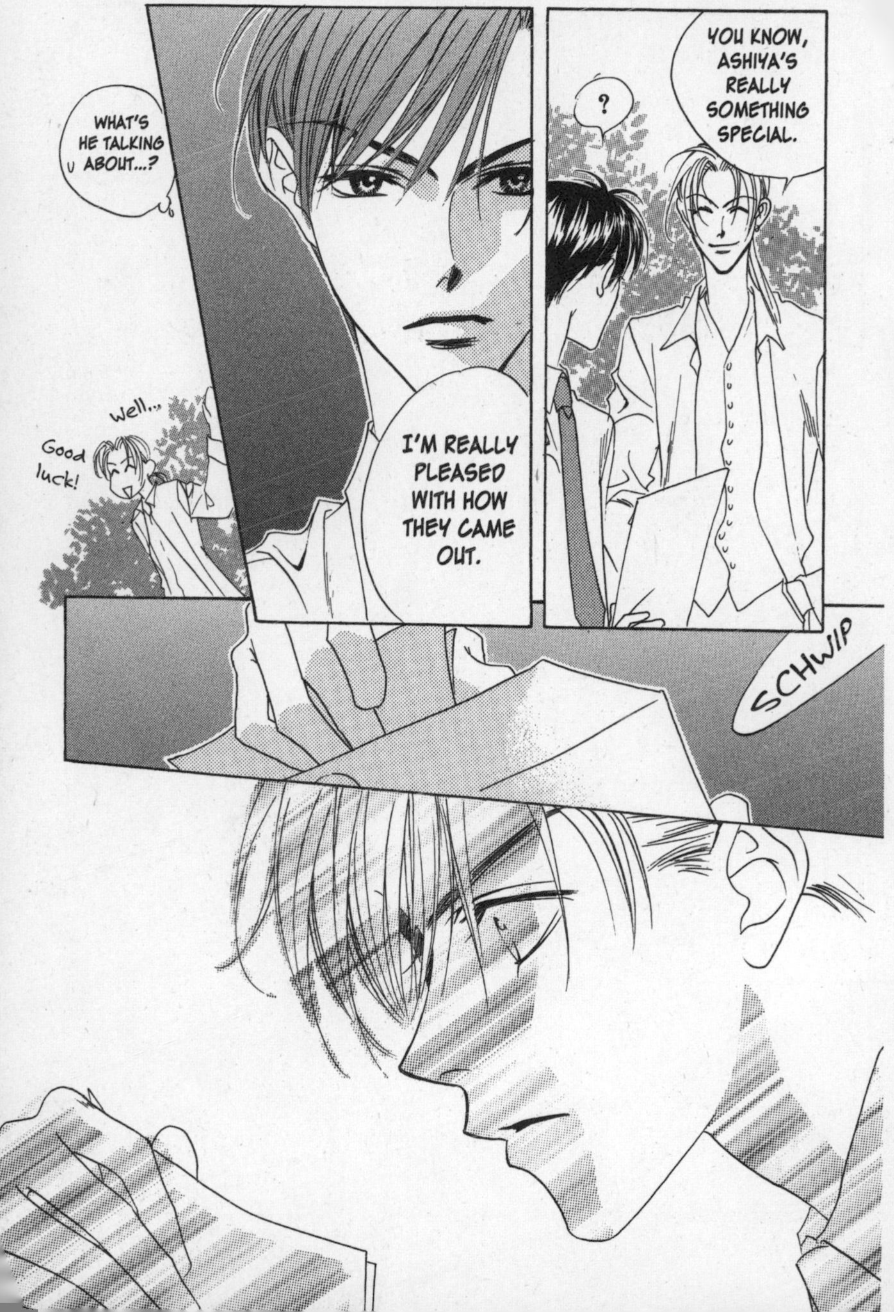
YOU KNOW, ASHIYA'S REALLY SOMETHING SPECIAL.
?
I'M REALLY PLEASED WITH HOW THEY CAME OUT.
WHAT'S HE TALKING ABOUT...?
well..
Good luck!
SCHWIP

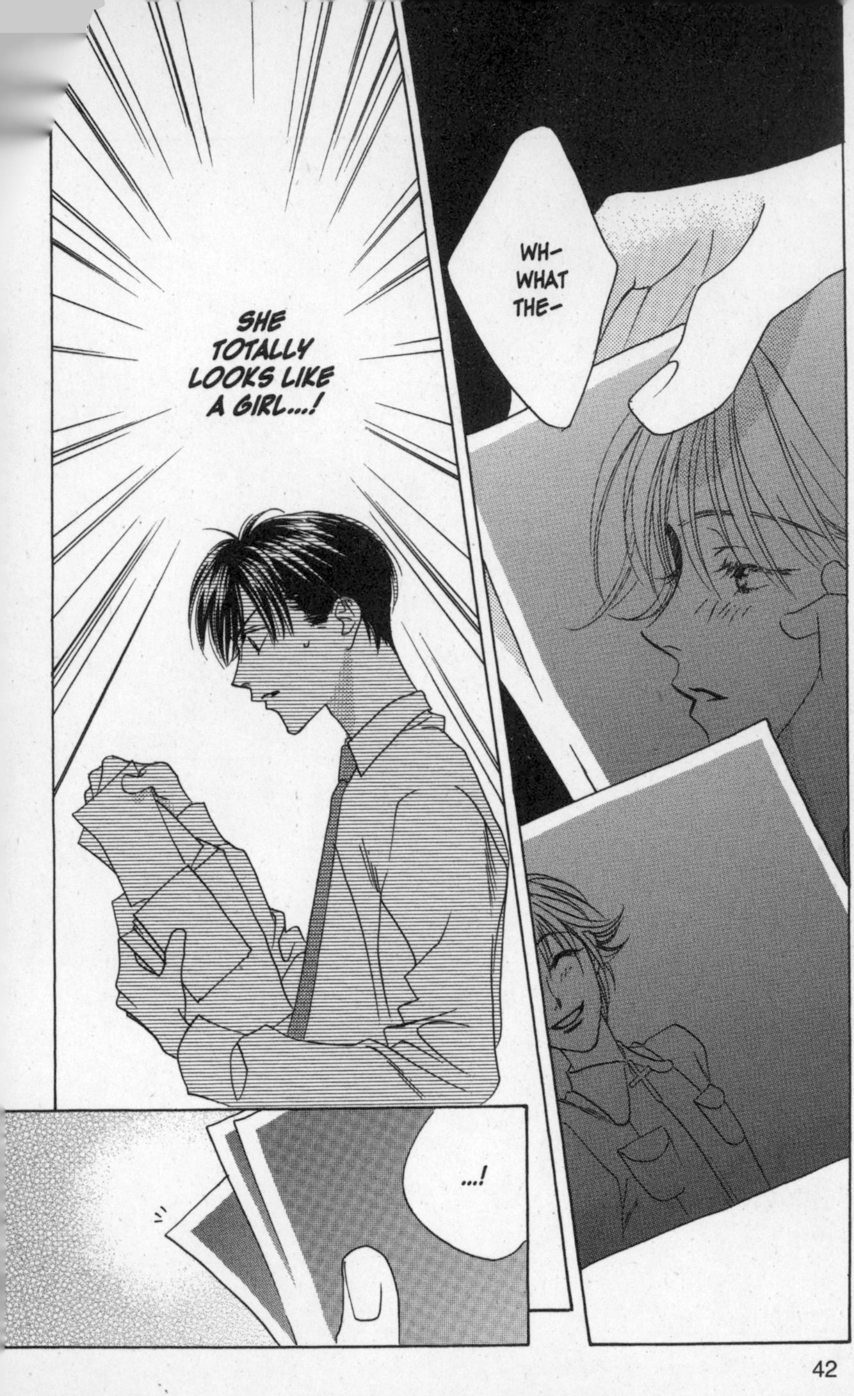
WH- WHAT THE-
SHE TOTALLY LOOKS LIKE A GIRL...!
...!

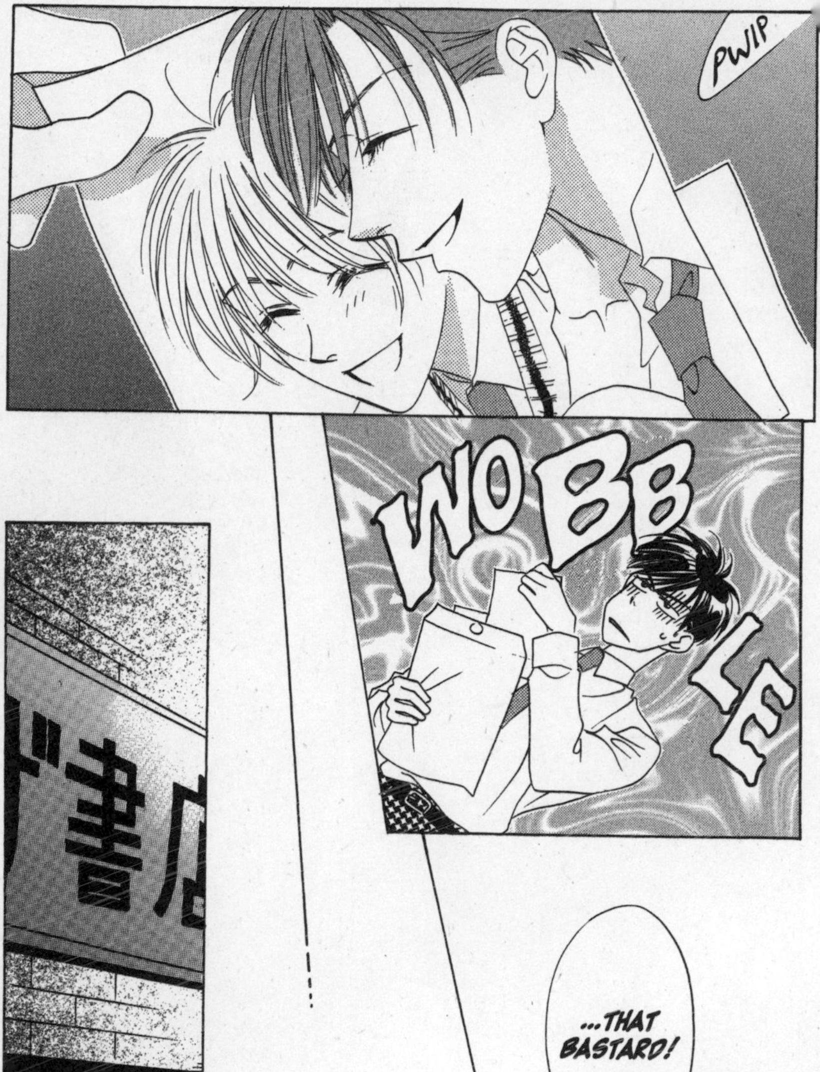
PWIP
WOBBLE
...THAT BASTARD!
when did he...?
書店
世紀末の謎

* Big Sign = Bookstore
* Small Sign = Mysteries of the Millennium

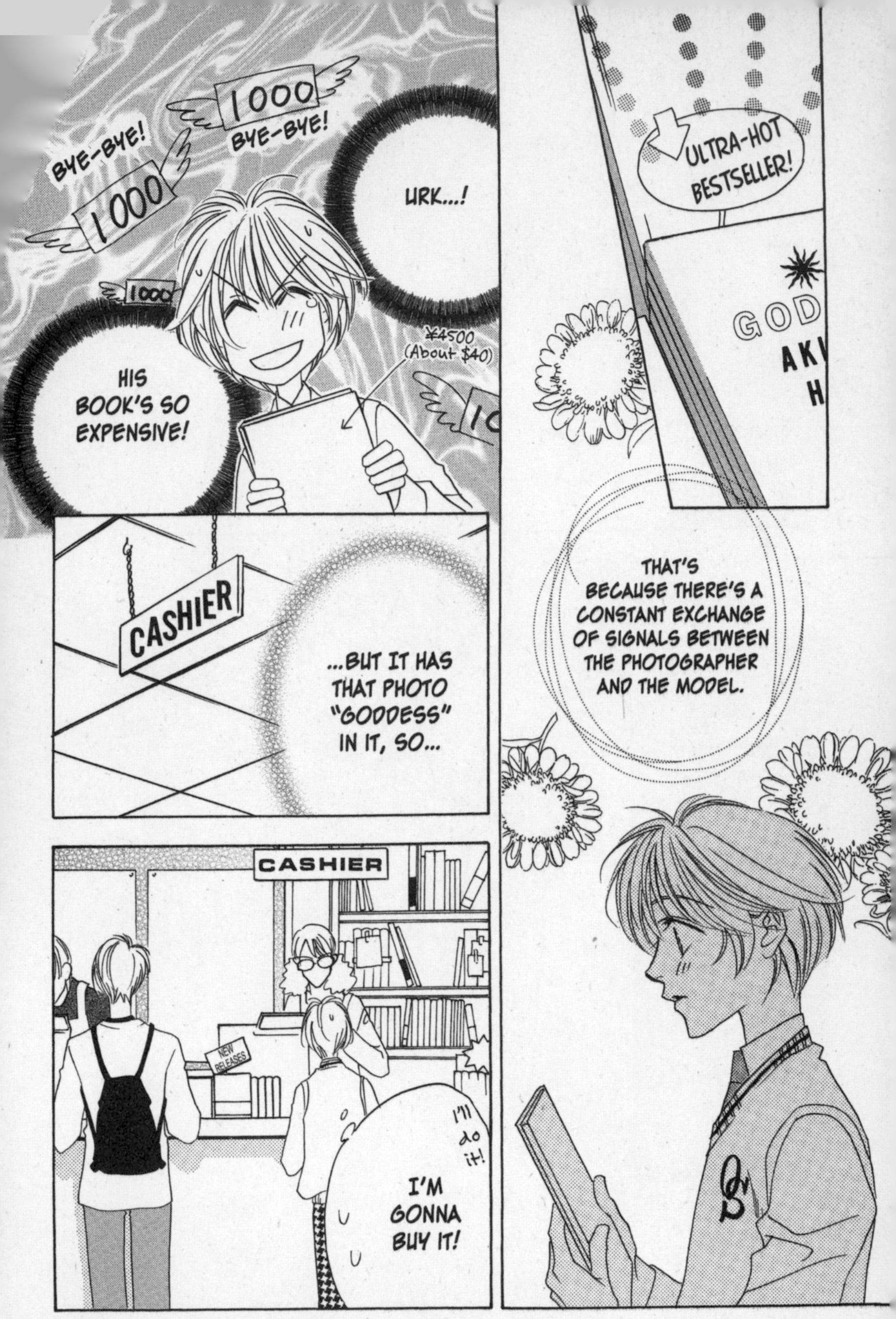
ULTRA-HOT BESTSELLER!
THAT'S BECAUSE THERE'S A CONSTANT EXCHANGE OF SIGNALS BETWEEN THE PHOTOGRAPHER AND THE MODEL.
URK...!
1000
BYE-BYE!
BYE-BYE!
1000
HIS BOOK'S SO EXPENSIVE!
¥4500 (About $40)
CASHIER
...BUT IT HAS THAT PHOTO "GODDESS" IN IT, SO...
CASHIER
NEW RELEASES
I'll do it!
I'M GONNA BUY IT!

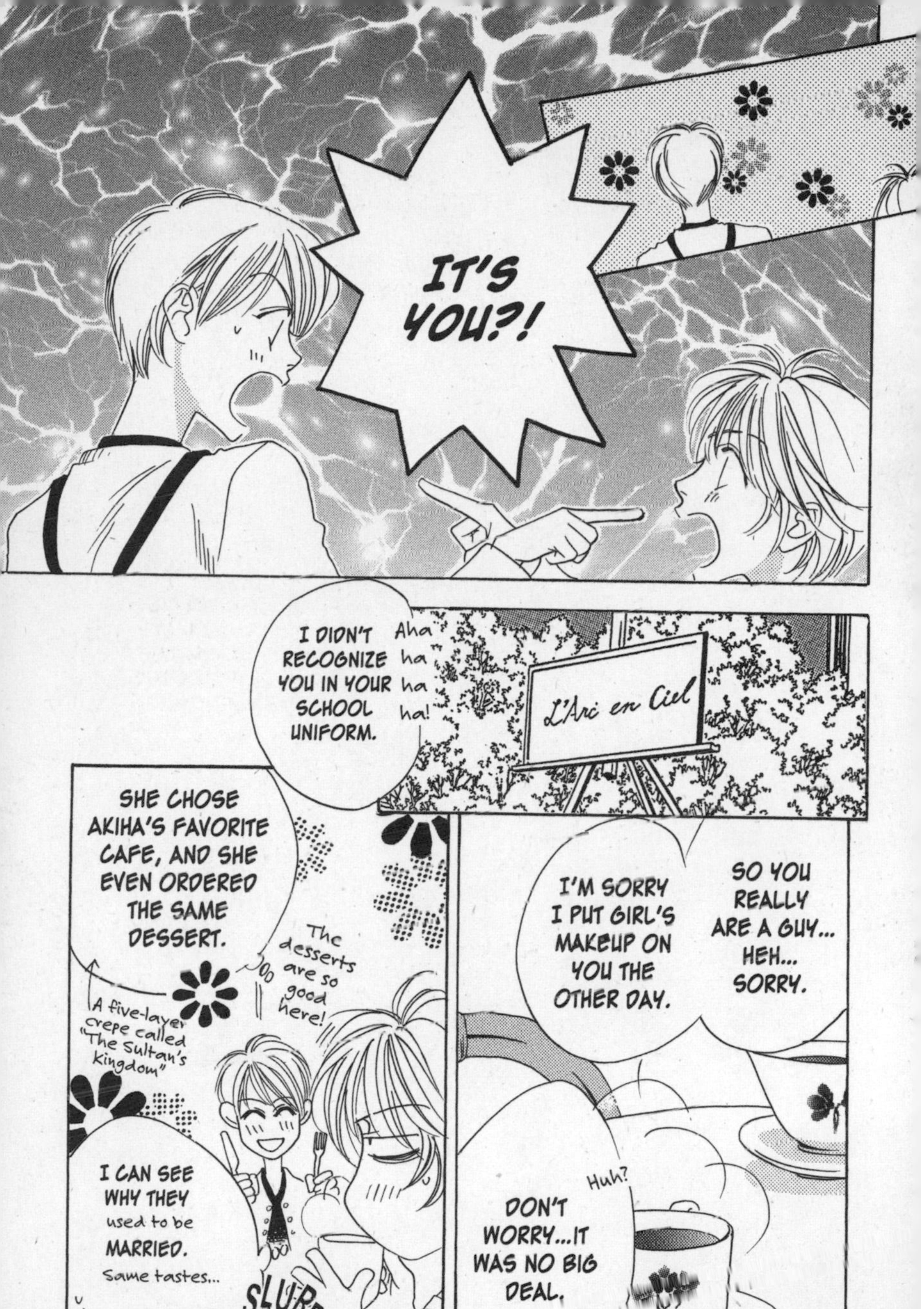
IT'S YOU?!
I DIDN'T RECOGNIZE YOU IN YOUR SCHOOL UNIFORM.
Aha ha ha ha!
L'Arc en Ciel
SO YOU REALLY ARE A GUY... HEH... SORRY.
I'M SORRY I PUT GIRL'S MAKEUP ON YOU THE OTHER DAY.
Huh?
DON'T WORRY...IT WAS NO BIG DEAL.
SHE CHOSE AKIHA'S FAVORITE CAFE, AND SHE EVEN ORDERED THE SAME DESSERT.
The desserts are so good here!
A five-layer crepe called "The Sultan's Kingdom"
I CAN SEE WHY THEY used to be MARRIED. Same tastes...
SLURP

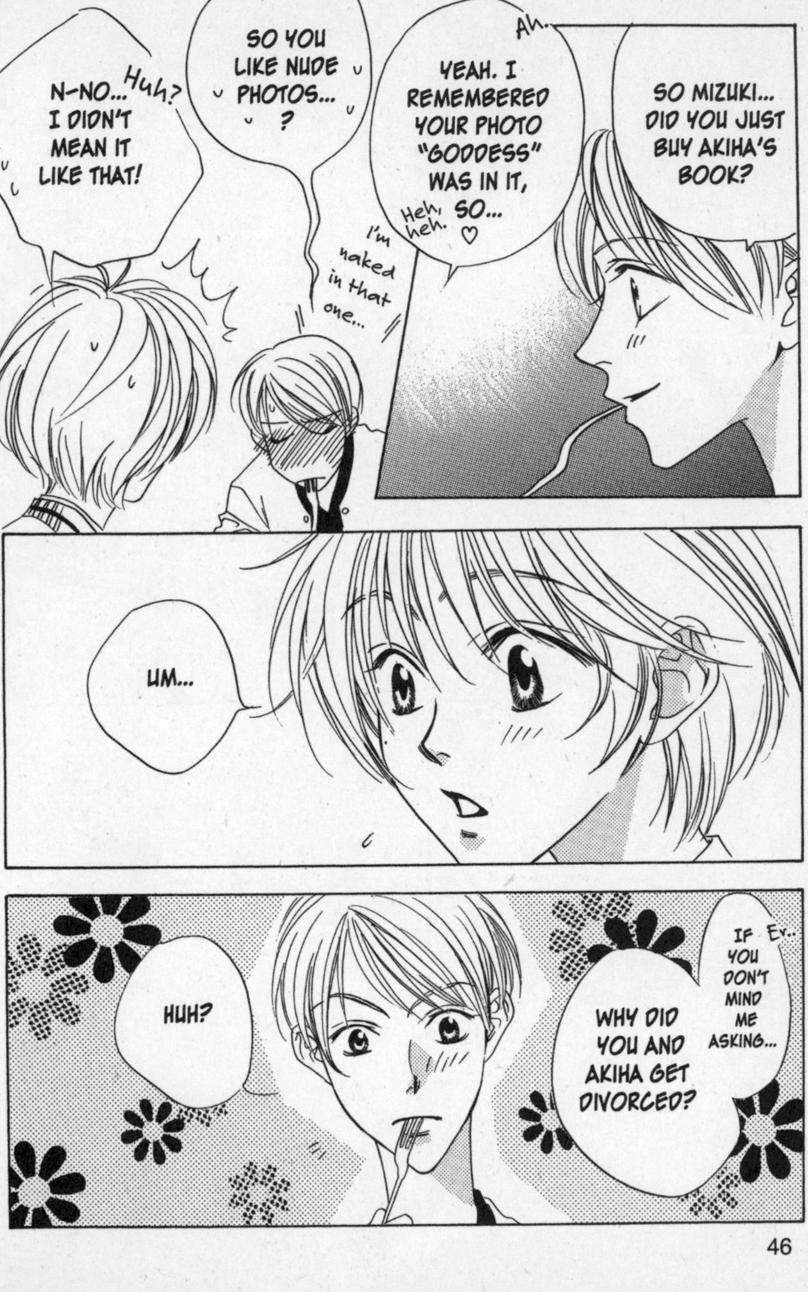
SO MIZUKI... DID YOU JUST BUY AKIHA'S BOOK?
Ah.
YEAH. I REMEMBERED YOUR PHOTO "GODDESS" WAS IN IT, SO... ♡
Heh, heh.
SO YOU LIKE NUDE PHOTOS...?
I'm naked in that one...
Huh?
N-NO... I DIDN'T MEAN IT LIKE THAT!
UM...
Er..
IF YOU DON'T MIND ME ASKING...
WHY DID YOU AND AKIHA GET DIVORCED?
HUH?

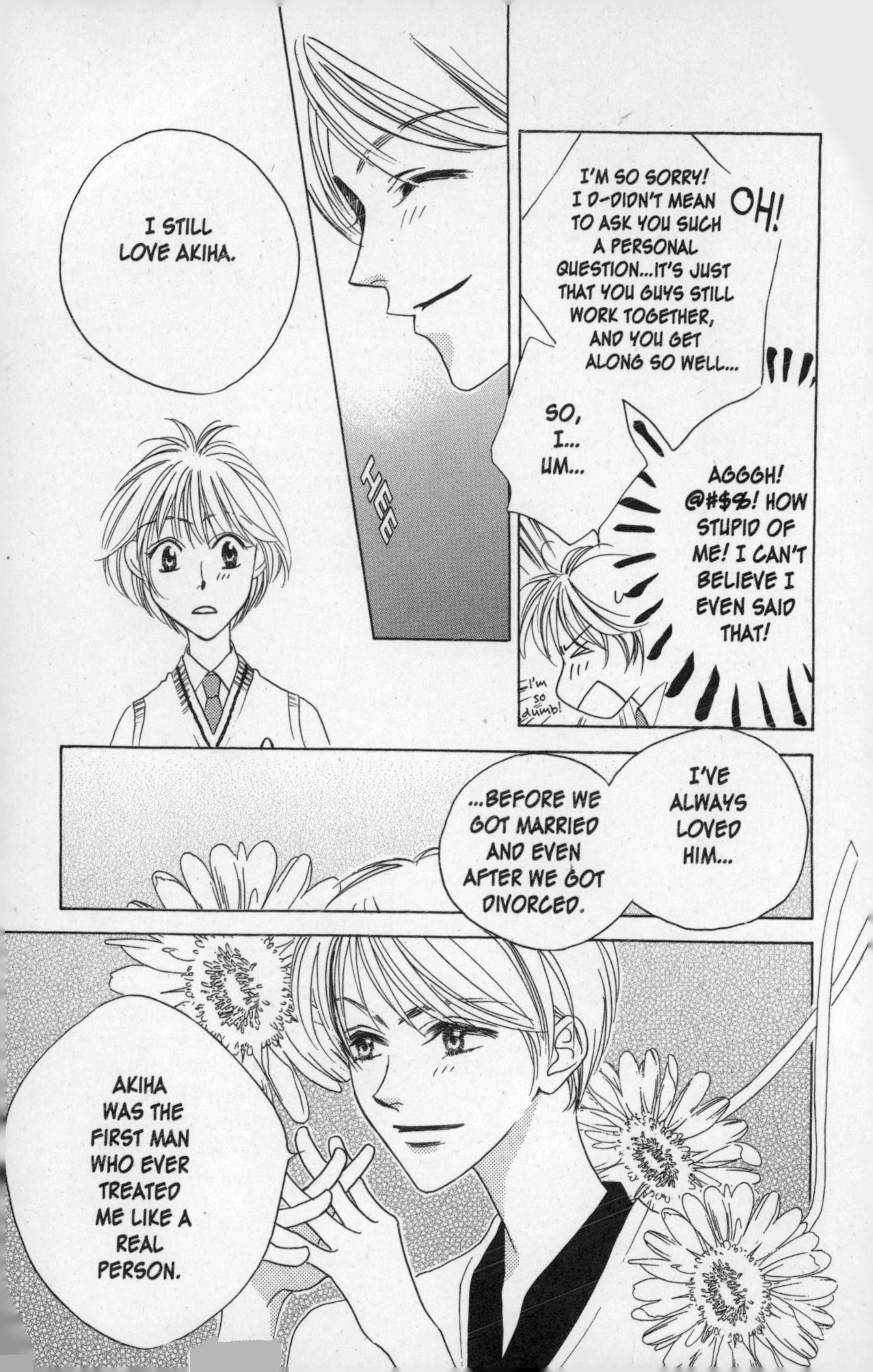
OH!
I'M SO SORRY! I D-DIDN'T MEAN TO ASK YOU SUCH A PERSONAL QUESTION...IT'S JUST THAT YOU GUYS STILL WORK TOGETHER, AND YOU GET ALONG SO WELL...
SO, I... UM...
AGGGH! @#$%! HOW STUPID OF ME! I CAN'T BELIEVE I EVEN SAID THAT!
I'm so dumb!
HEE
I STILL LOVE AKIHA.
I'VE ALWAYS LOVED HIM...
...BEFORE WE GOT MARRIED AND EVEN AFTER WE GOT DIVORCED.
AKIHA WAS THE FIRST MAN WHO EVER TREATED ME LIKE A REAL PERSON.

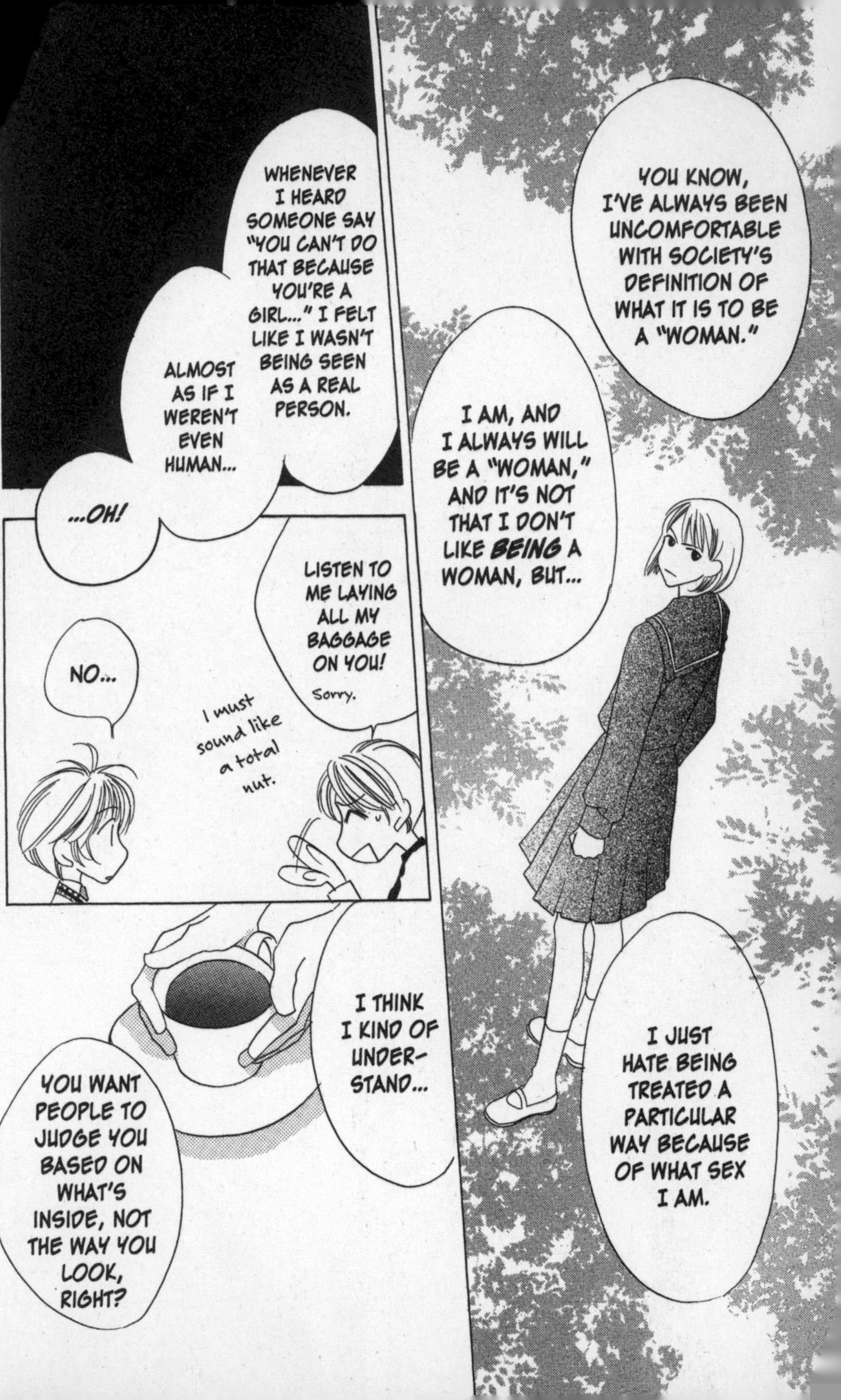
YOU KNOW, I'VE ALWAYS BEEN UNCOMFORTABLE WITH SOCIETY'S DEFINITION OF WHAT IT IS TO BE A "WOMAN."
I AM, AND I ALWAYS WILL BE A "WOMAN," AND IT'S NOT THAT I DON'T LIKE *BEING* A WOMAN, BUT...
I JUST HATE BEING TREATED A PARTICULAR WAY BECAUSE OF WHAT SEX I AM.
WHENEVER I HEARD SOMEONE SAY "YOU CAN'T DO THAT BECAUSE YOU'RE A GIRL..." I FELT LIKE I WASN'T BEING SEEN AS A REAL PERSON.
ALMOST AS IF I WEREN'T EVEN HUMAN...
...OH!
LISTEN TO ME LAYING ALL MY BAGGAGE ON YOU!
Sorry.
I must sound like a total nut.
NO...
I THINK I KIND OF UNDER-STAND...
YOU WANT PEOPLE TO JUDGE YOU BASED ON WHAT'S INSIDE, NOT THE WAY YOU LOOK, RIGHT?

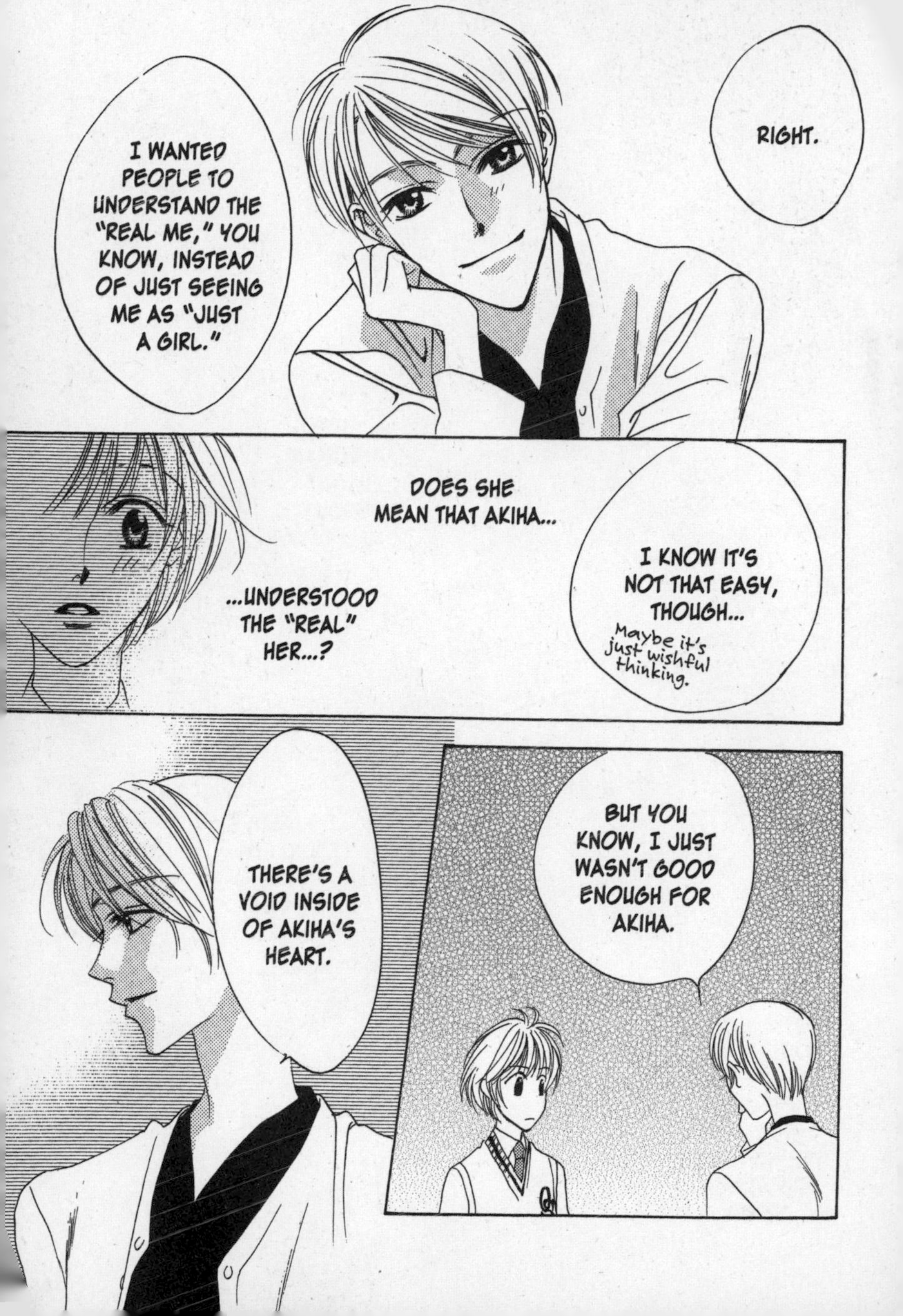
RIGHT.
I WANTED PEOPLE TO UNDERSTAND THE "REAL ME," YOU KNOW, INSTEAD OF JUST SEEING ME AS "JUST A GIRL."
I KNOW IT'S NOT THAT EASY, THOUGH...
Maybe it's just wishful thinking.
DOES SHE MEAN THAT AKIHA...
...UNDERSTOOD THE "REAL" HER...?
BUT YOU KNOW, I JUST WASN'T GOOD ENOUGH FOR AKIHA.
THERE'S A VOID INSIDE OF AKIHA'S HEART.

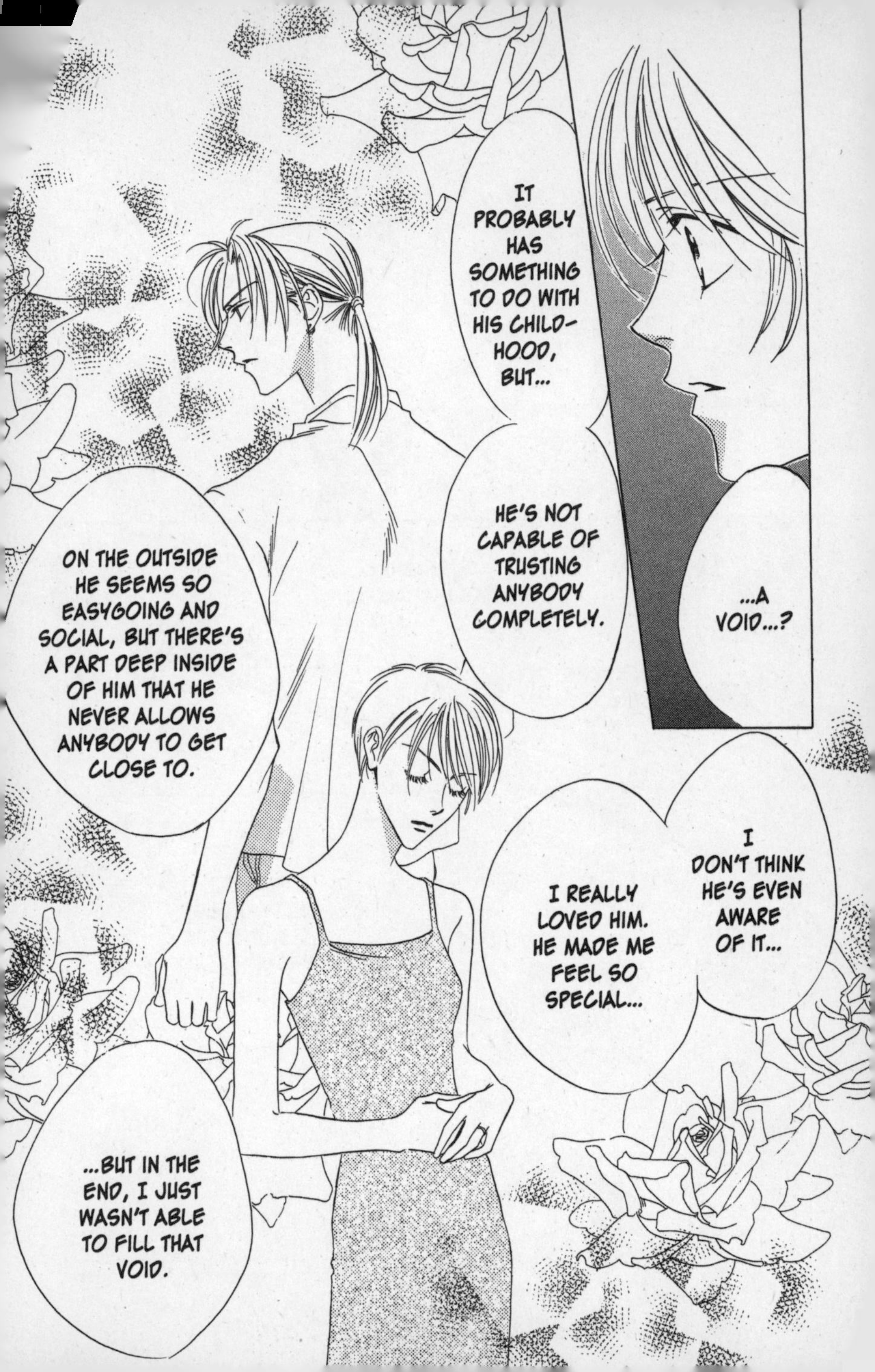
...A VOID...?
IT PROBABLY HAS SOMETHING TO DO WITH HIS CHILD-HOOD, BUT...
HE'S NOT CAPABLE OF TRUSTING ANYBODY COMPLETELY.
ON THE OUTSIDE HE SEEMS SO EASYGOING AND SOCIAL, BUT THERE'S A PART DEEP INSIDE OF HIM THAT HE NEVER ALLOWS ANYBODY TO GET CLOSE TO.
I DON'T THINK HE'S EVEN AWARE OF IT...
I REALLY LOVED HIM. HE MADE ME FEEL SO SPECIAL...
...BUT IN THE END, I JUST WASN'T ABLE TO FILL THAT VOID.

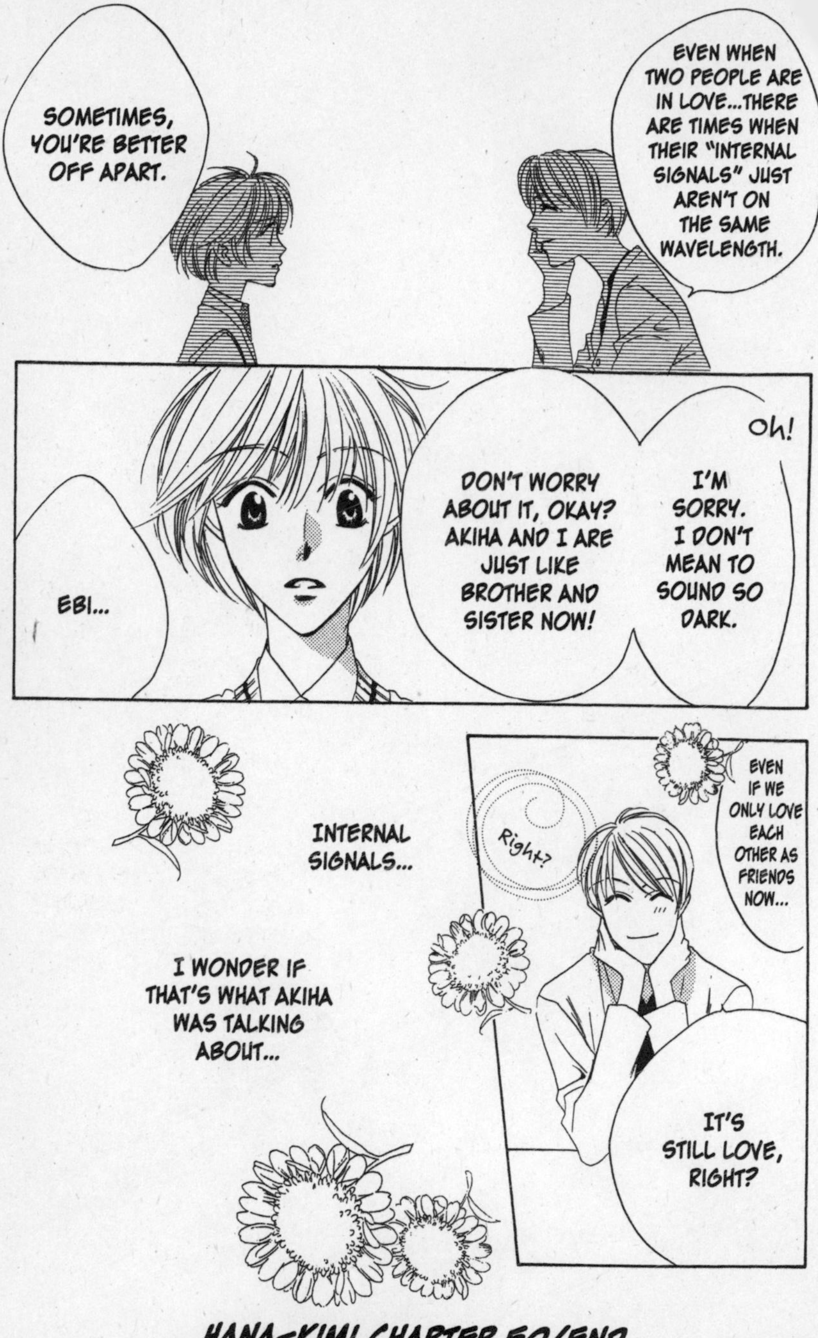
EVEN WHEN TWO PEOPLE ARE IN LOVE...THERE ARE TIMES WHEN THEIR "INTERNAL SIGNALS" JUST AREN'T ON THE SAME WAVELENGTH.
SOMETIMES, YOU'RE BETTER OFF APART.
Oh!
I'M SORRY. I DON'T MEAN TO SOUND SO DARK.
DON'T WORRY ABOUT IT, OKAY? AKIHA AND I ARE JUST LIKE BROTHER AND SISTER NOW!
EBI...
EVEN IF WE ONLY LOVE EACH OTHER AS FRIENDS NOW...
Right?
IT'S STILL LOVE, RIGHT?
INTERNAL SIGNALS...
I WONDER IF THAT'S WHAT AKIHA WAS TALKING ABOUT...

HANA-KIMI CHAPTER 50/END

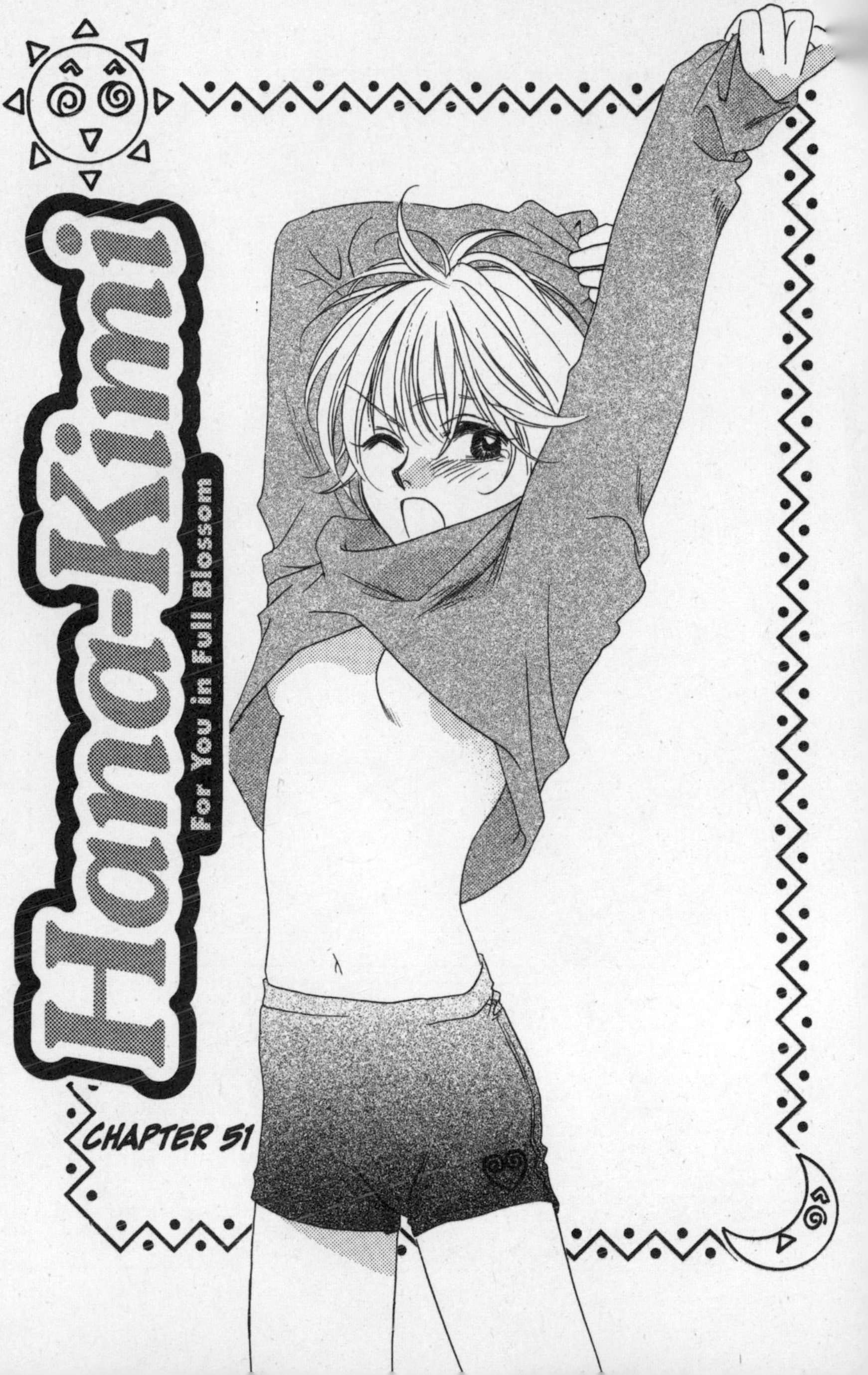
Hana-Kimi
For You in Full Blossom
CHAPTER 51

Osaka High School Dormitory

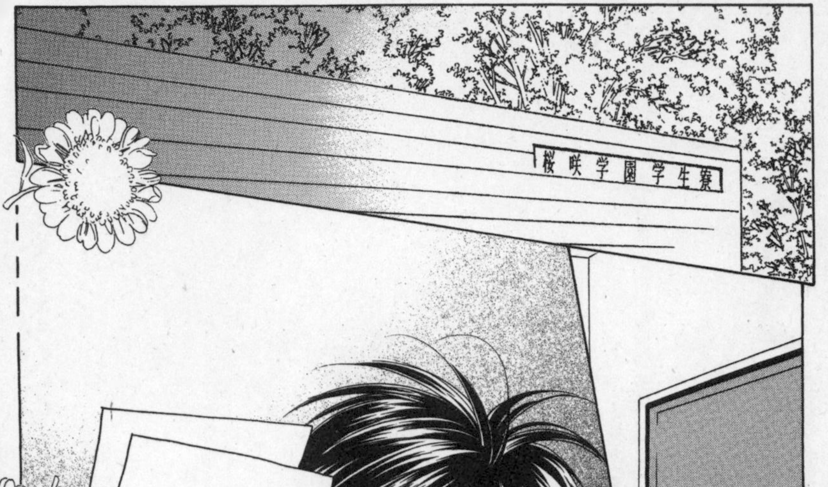

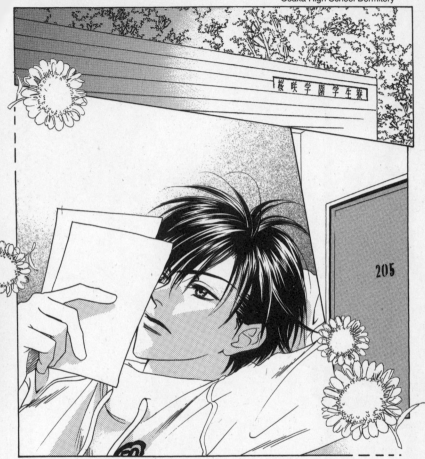

桜咲学園学生寮
205

MY CINEMA

My Favorite Obscure Films, Part Three:

MORTAL KOMBAT

THE STORY WASN'T REALLY THAT GOOD, BUT IF YOU LIKE THESE KINDS OF MOVIES, YOU'LL BE INTO IT. (WHOA...I JUST TELL IT LIKE IT IS!) THERE'S A SEALED GATE THAT DIVIDES THE HUMAN WORLD AND THE OUTWORLD. WHENEVER THE GATE IS ABOUT TO BE OPENED, HUMANS MUST BATTLE AGAINST THE EVIL CREATURES FROM THE OUTWORLD IN ORDER TO GAIN CONTROL OF THE GATE. THAT'S PRETTY MUCH WHAT THE STORY'S ALL ABOUT. (THE WINNER OF THE BATTLE IS REWARDED WITH THE RIGHTS TO THE GATE, WHICH THEY ARE ALLOWED TO HOLD ON TO UNTIL THE END OF THEIR GENERATION. THE BATTLE HAS BEEN REPEATED FOR GENERATION AFTER GENERATION.) THE BEST PARTS OF THE FILM WERE THE ALL-GIRL BATTLE SCENES! THEY WERE SO COOL! IT WAS AS IF THE VIDEOGAMES "TEKKEN" AND "VIRTUA FIGHTER" HAD COME TO LIFE! THEY REMINDED ME OF NINA, SARA, PAI AND MICHELLE! THE LEAD LOOKED LIKE A MORE MACHO VERSION OF KOICHI DOMOTO... [LAUGH]

I LOVE FIGHTING GAMES.

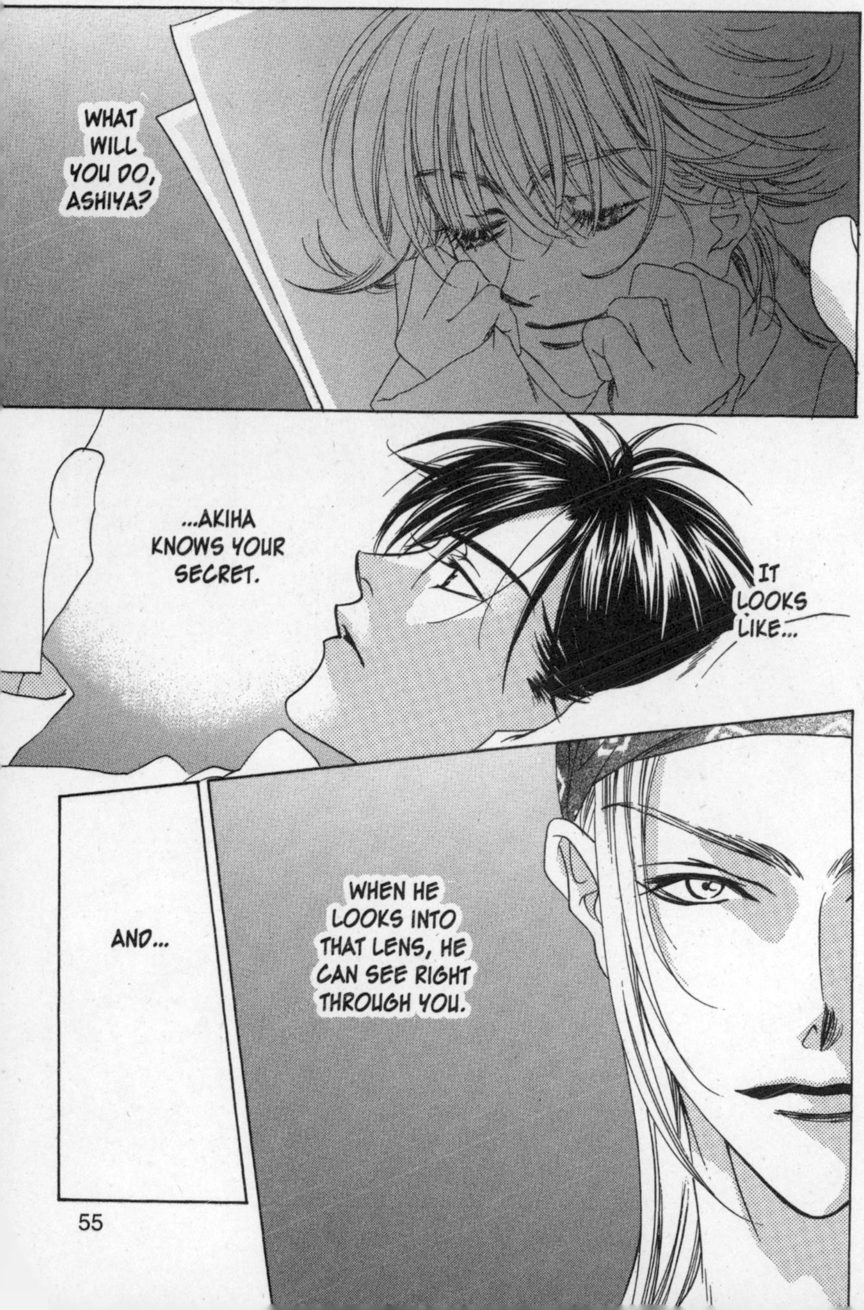
WHAT WILL YOU DO, ASHIYA?
IT LOOKS LIKE...
...AKIHA KNOWS YOUR SECRET.
WHEN HE LOOKS INTO THAT LENS, HE CAN SEE RIGHT THROUGH YOU.
AND...

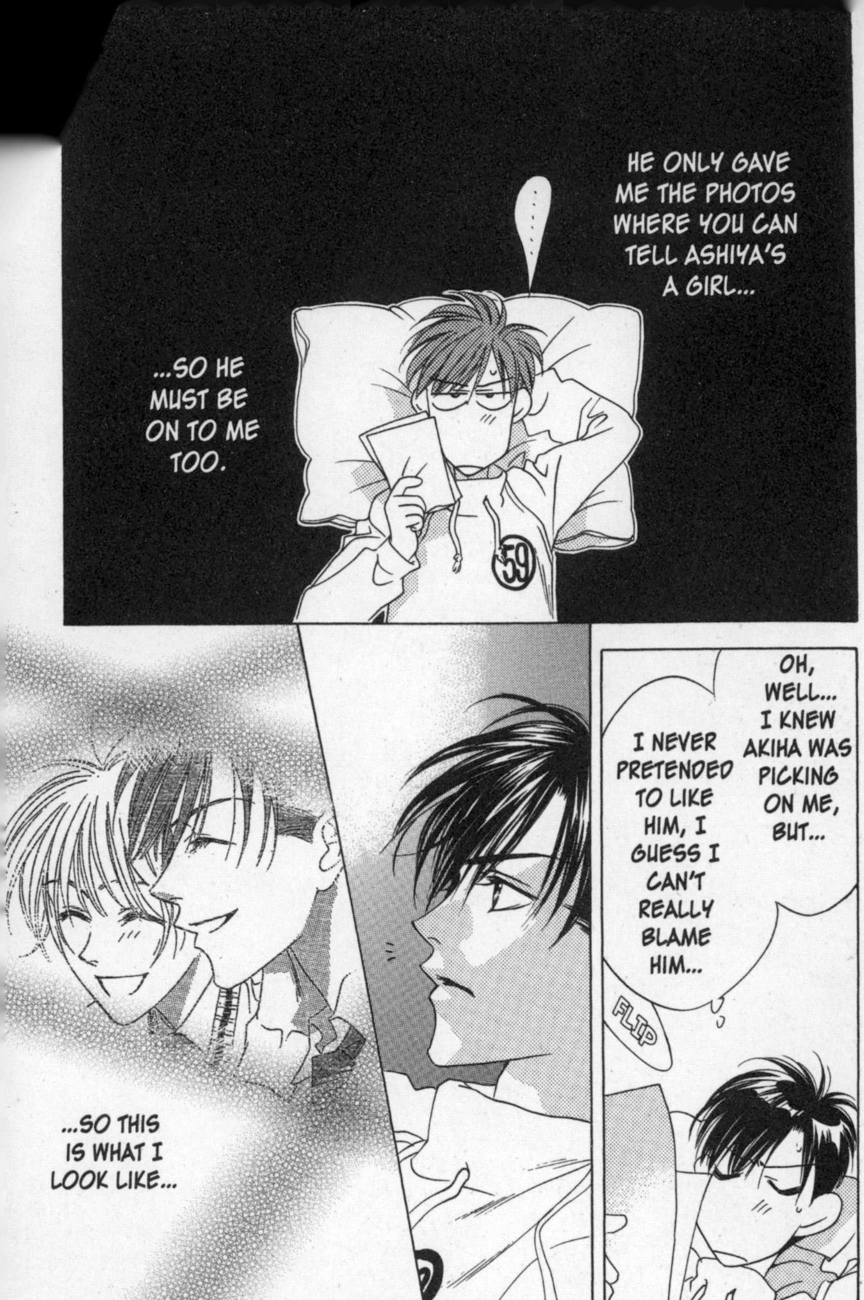
HE ONLY GAVE ME THE PHOTOS WHERE YOU CAN TELL ASHIYA'S A GIRL...
...SO HE MUST BE ON TO ME TOO.
OH, WELL... I KNEW AKIHA WAS PICKING ON ME, BUT...
I NEVER PRETENDED TO LIKE HIM, I GUESS I CAN'T REALLY BLAME HIM...
FLIP
...SO THIS IS WHAT I LOOK LIKE...

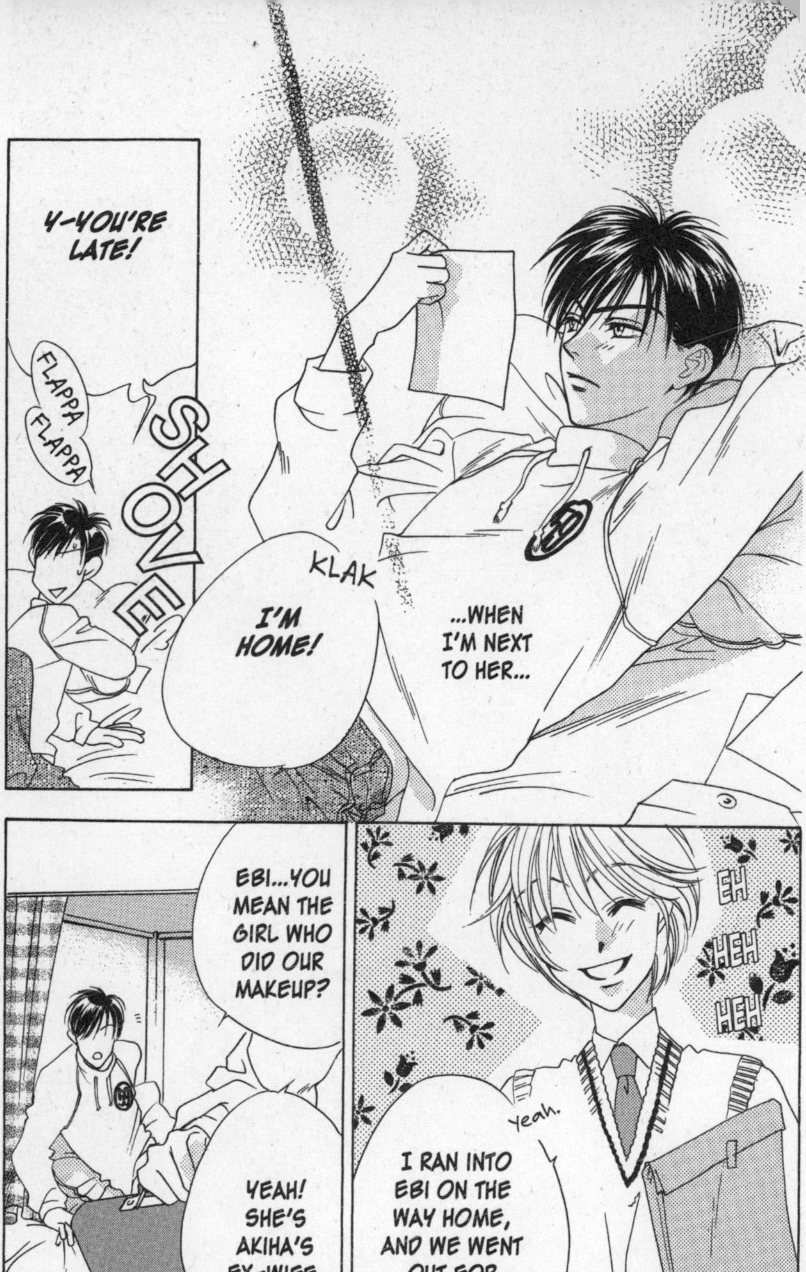
...WHEN I'M NEXT TO HER...
KLAK
I'M HOME!
Y-YOU'RE LATE!
FLAPPA FLAPPA
SHOVE
EH HEH HEH
Yeah.
I RAN INTO EBI ON THE WAY HOME, AND WE WENT OUT FOR COFFEE.
EBI...YOU MEAN THE GIRL WHO DID OUR MAKEUP?
YEAH! SHE'S AKIHA'S EX-WIFE.

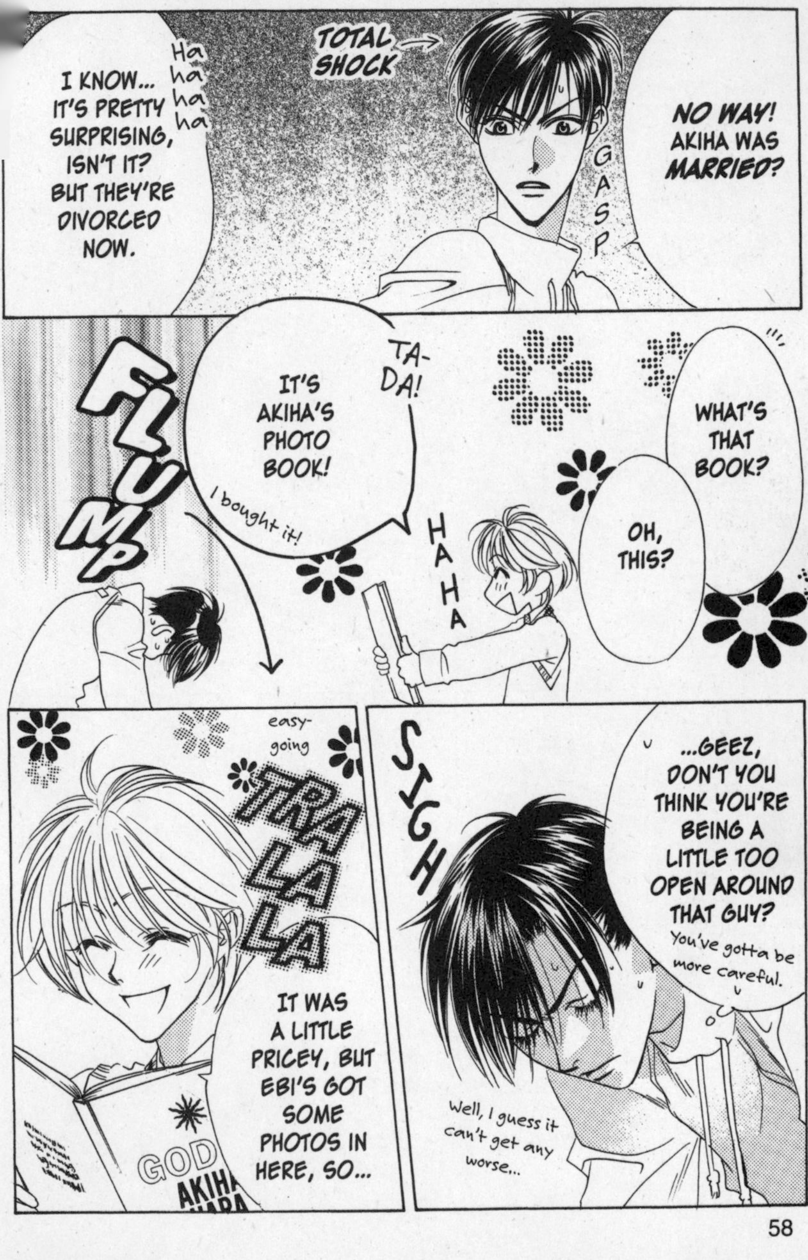
NO WAY! AKIHA WAS MARRIED?
GASP
TOTAL SHOCK
I KNOW... IT'S PRETTY SURPRISING, ISN'T IT? BUT THEY'RE DIVORCED NOW.
Ha ha ha ha
WHAT'S THAT BOOK?
OH, THIS?
HAHAHA
TA-DA!
IT'S AKIHA'S PHOTO BOOK!
I bought it!
FLUMP
SIGH
...GEEZ, DON'T YOU THINK YOU'RE BEING A LITTLE TOO OPEN AROUND THAT GUY?
You've gotta be more careful.
Well, I guess it can't get any worse...
easy-going
TRA LA LA
IT WAS A LITTLE PRICEY, BUT EBI'S GOT SOME PHOTOS IN HERE, SO...
GOD
AKIHA

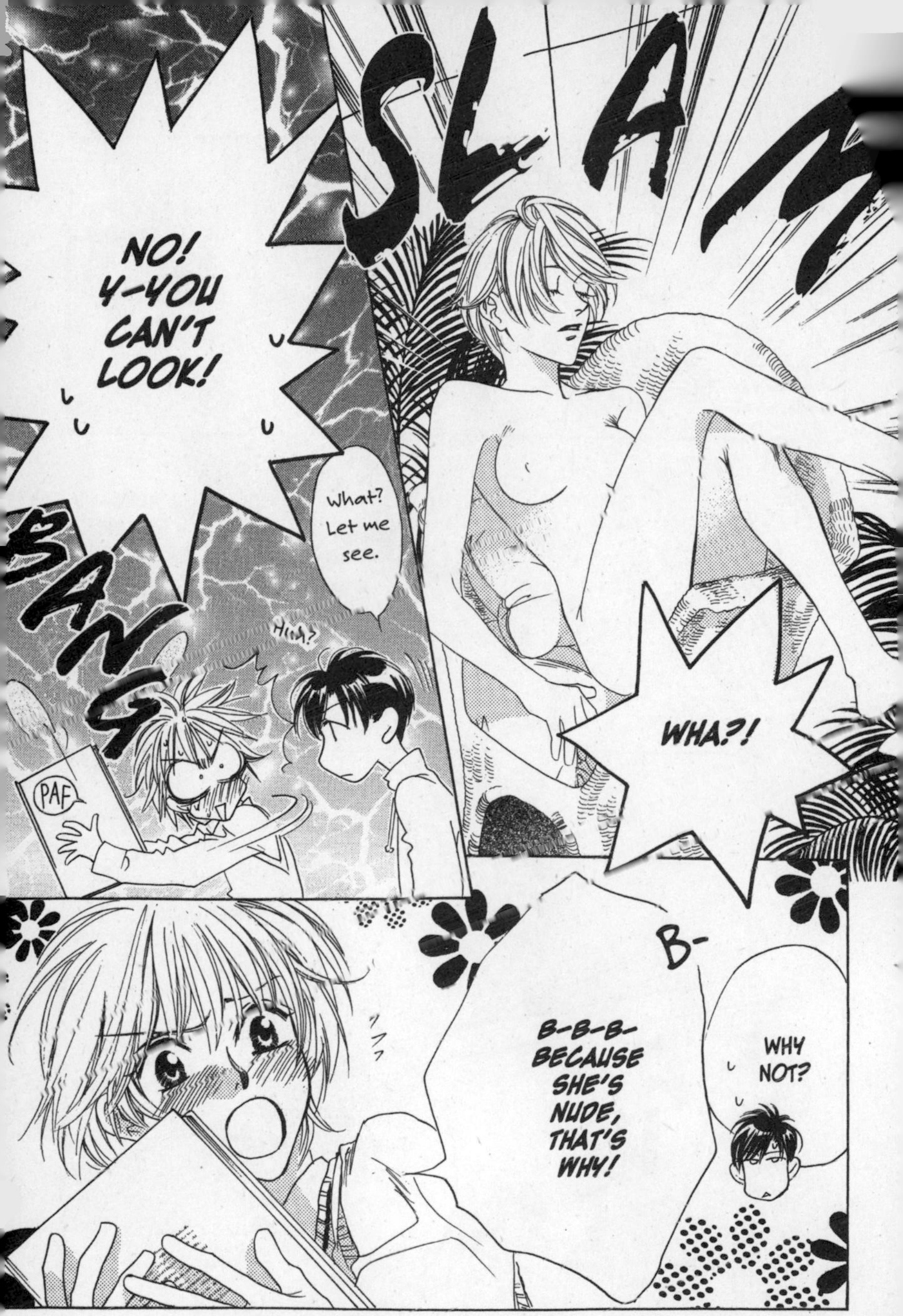
SLAM
WHA?!
What? Let me see.
Huh?
NO! Y-YOU CAN'T LOOK!
BANG
PAF
B-
WHY NOT?
B-B-B-BECAUSE SHE'S NUDE, THAT'S WHY!

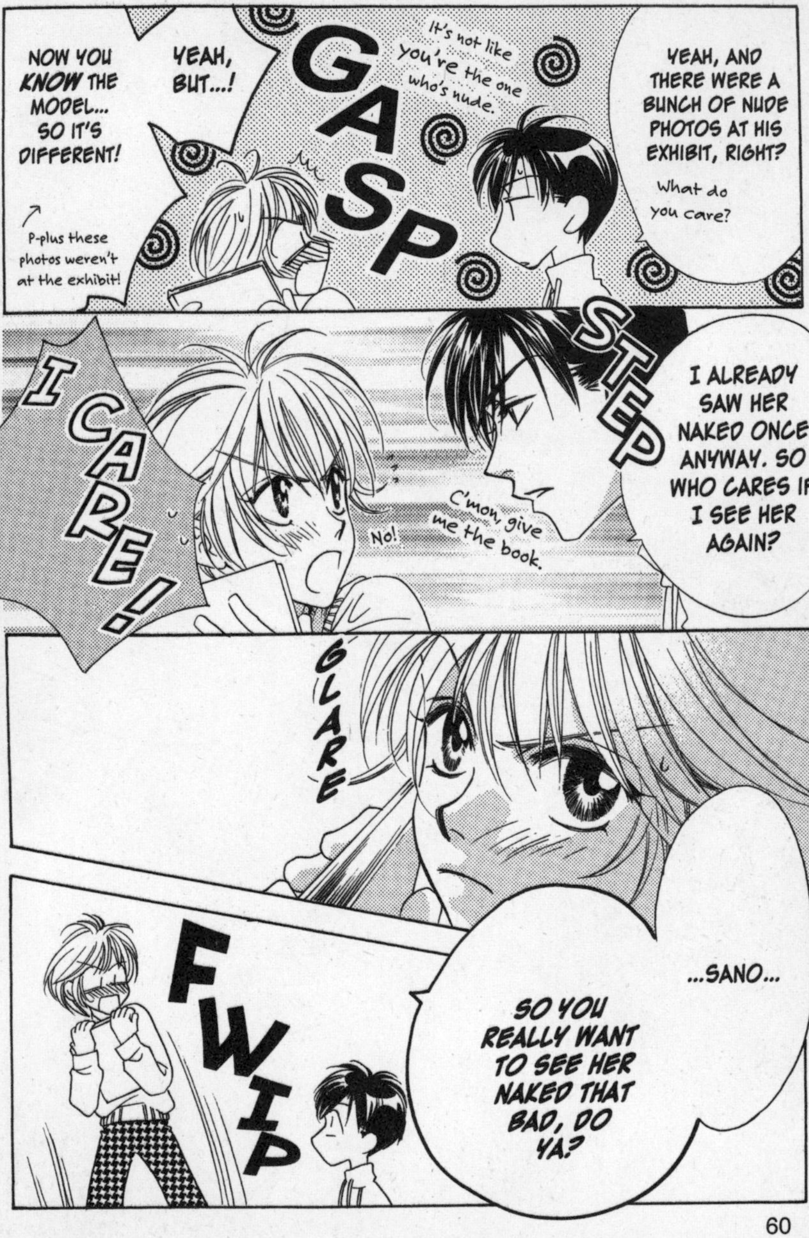

YEAH, AND THERE WERE A BUNCH OF NUDE PHOTOS AT HIS EXHIBIT, RIGHT?
What do you care?
GASP
It's not like you're the one who's nude.
YEAH, BUT...!
NOW YOU KNOW THE MODEL... SO IT'S DIFFERENT!
P-plus these photos weren't at the exhibit!
I ALREADY SAW HER NAKED ONCE ANYWAY. SO WHO CARES IF I SEE HER AGAIN?
STEP
C'mon, give me the book.
No!
I CARE!!
GLARE
...SANO...
SO YOU REALLY WANT TO SEE HER NAKED THAT BAD, DO YA?
FWIP

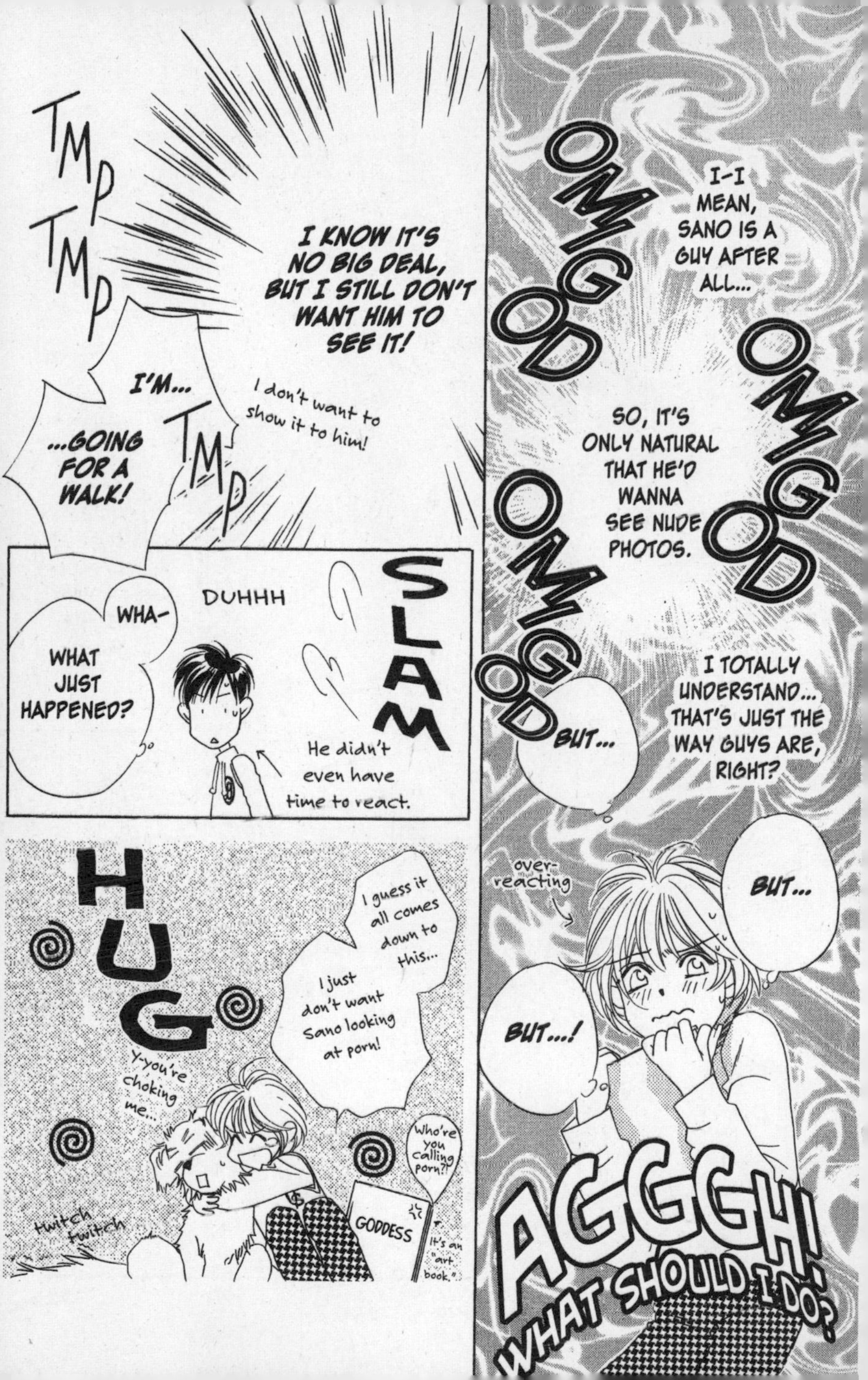
OMGOD
OMGOD
OMGOD
I-I MEAN, SANO IS A GUY AFTER ALL...
SO, IT'S ONLY NATURAL THAT HE'D WANNA SEE NUDE PHOTOS.
I TOTALLY UNDERSTAND... THAT'S JUST THE WAY GUYS ARE, RIGHT?
BUT...
BUT...
over-reacting
BUT...!
AGGGH!
WHAT SHOULD I DO?
TMP TMP TMP
I KNOW IT'S NO BIG DEAL, BUT I STILL DON'T WANT HIM TO SEE IT!
I don't want to show it to him!
I'M...
...GOING FOR A WALK!
TMP
SLAM
He didn't even have time to react.
DUHHH
WHA-
WHAT JUST HAPPENED?
HUG
I guess it all comes down to this...
I just don't want Sano looking at porn!
Who're you calling porn?!
It's an "art book."
GODDESS
Y-you're choking me...
twitch twitch

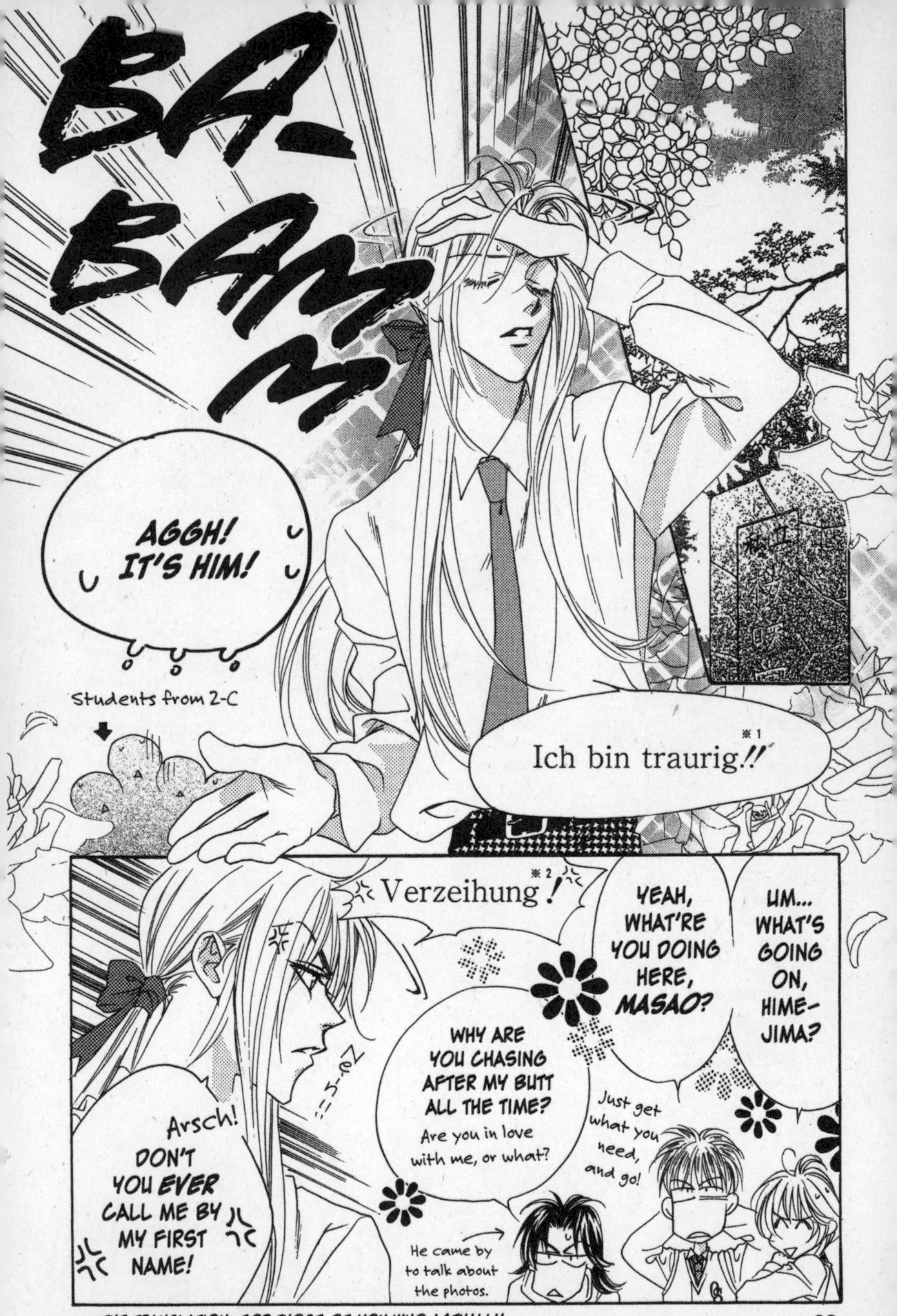
BA-BAMM
Ich bin traurig!![*1]
AGGH! IT'S HIM!
Students from 2-C
UM... WHAT'S GOING ON, HIME-JIMA?
YEAH, WHAT'RE YOU DOING HERE, MASAO?
Verzeihung![*2]
Just get what you need, and go!
WHY ARE YOU CHASING AFTER MY BUTT ALL THE TIME?
Are you in love with me, or what?
He came by to talk about the photos.
Arsch!
DON'T YOU EVER CALL ME BY MY FIRST NAME!

THE TRANSLATION, FOR THOSE OF YOU WHO ACTUALLY CARE WHAT HIMEJIMA'S SAYING... *1: HOW SAD! *2: HOW RUDE!

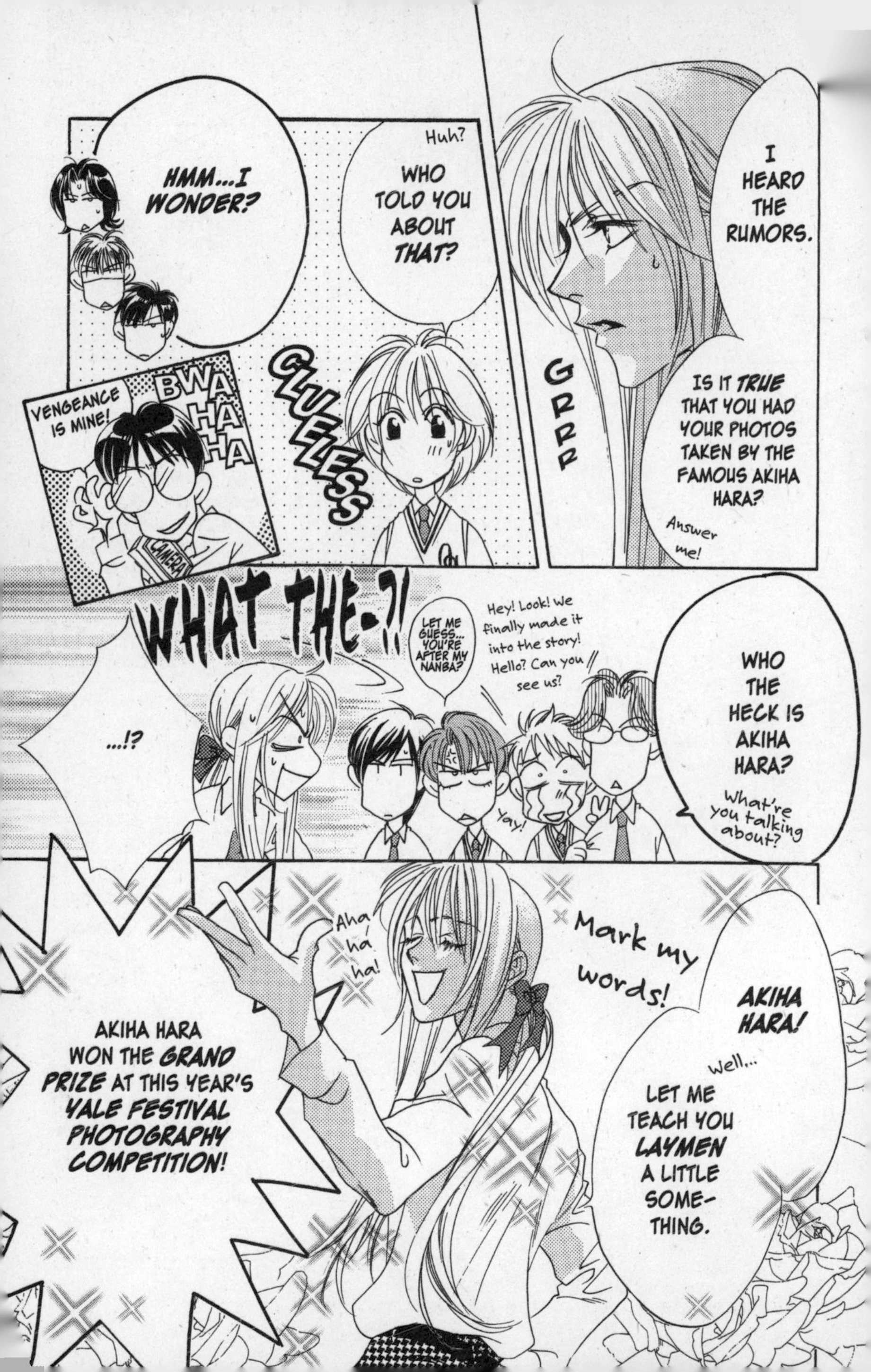
I HEARD THE RUMORS.
GRRR
IS IT TRUE THAT YOU HAD YOUR PHOTOS TAKEN BY THE FAMOUS AKIHA HARA?
Answer me!
Huh?
WHO TOLD YOU ABOUT THAT?
CLUELESS
HMM...I WONDER?
VENGEANCE IS MINE!
BWA HA HA HA
CAMERA
WHO THE HECK IS AKIHA HARA?
What're you talking about?
Hey! Look! We finally made it into the story! Hello? Can you see us?
LET ME GUESS... YOU'RE AFTER MY NANBA?
Yay!
WHAT THE-?!
...!?
Mark my words!
AKIHA HARA!
Well...
LET ME TEACH YOU LAYMEN A LITTLE SOME-THING.
Aha ha ha!
AKIHA HARA WON THE GRAND PRIZE AT THIS YEAR'S YALE FESTIVAL PHOTOGRAPHY COMPETITION!

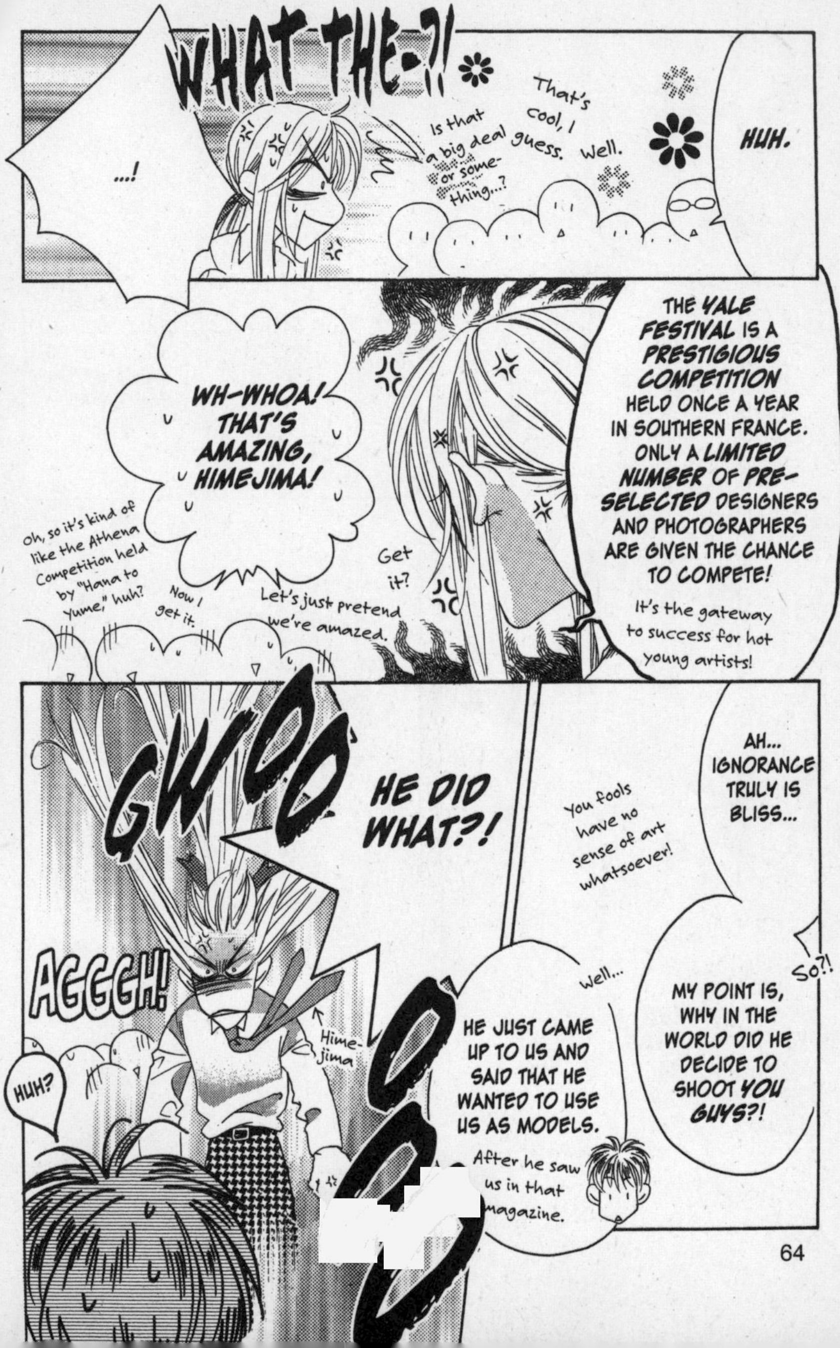
HUH.
Well.
That's cool, I guess.
Is that a big deal or some-thing...?
WHAT THE-?!
...!
THE YALE FESTIVAL IS A PRESTIGIOUS COMPETITION HELD ONCE A YEAR IN SOUTHERN FRANCE. ONLY A LIMITED NUMBER OF PRE-SELECTED DESIGNERS AND PHOTOGRAPHERS ARE GIVEN THE CHANCE TO COMPETE!
It's the gateway to success for hot young artists!
Get it?
Let's just pretend we're amazed.
WH-WHOA! THAT'S AMAZING, HIMEJIMA!
Now I get it.
Oh, so it's kind of like the Athena Competition held by "Hana to Yume," huh?
AH... IGNORANCE TRULY IS BLISS...
You fools have no sense of art whatsoever!
So?!
MY POINT IS, WHY IN THE WORLD DID HE DECIDE TO SHOOT YOU GUYS?!
Well...
HE JUST CAME UP TO US AND SAID THAT HE WANTED TO USE US AS MODELS.
After he saw us in that magazine.
HE DID WHAT?!
GWOOO
AGGGH!
Hime-jima
HUH?

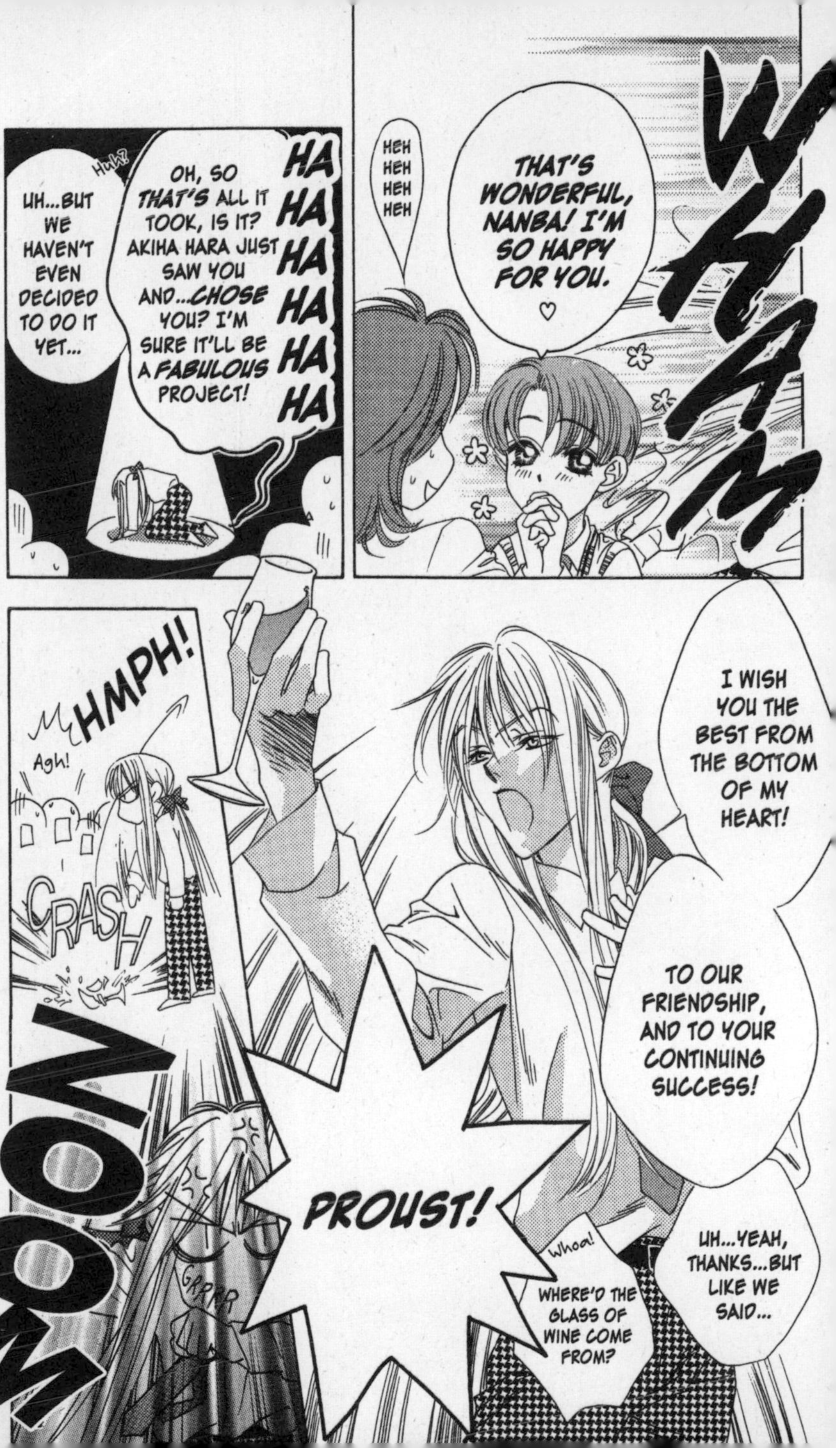
WHAM
THAT'S WONDERFUL, NANBA! I'M SO HAPPY FOR YOU.
HEH HEH HEH HEH
HA HA HA HA HA HA HA
OH, SO THAT'S ALL IT TOOK, IS IT? AKIHA HARA JUST SAW YOU AND...CHOSE YOU? I'M SURE IT'LL BE A FABULOUS PROJECT!
Huh?
UH...BUT WE HAVEN'T EVEN DECIDED TO DO IT YET...
I WISH YOU THE BEST FROM THE BOTTOM OF MY HEART!
TO OUR FRIENDSHIP, AND TO YOUR CONTINUING SUCCESS!
UH...YEAH, THANKS...BUT LIKE WE SAID...
Whoa!
WHERE'D THE GLASS OF WINE COME FROM?
PROUST!
HMPH!
Agh!
CRASH

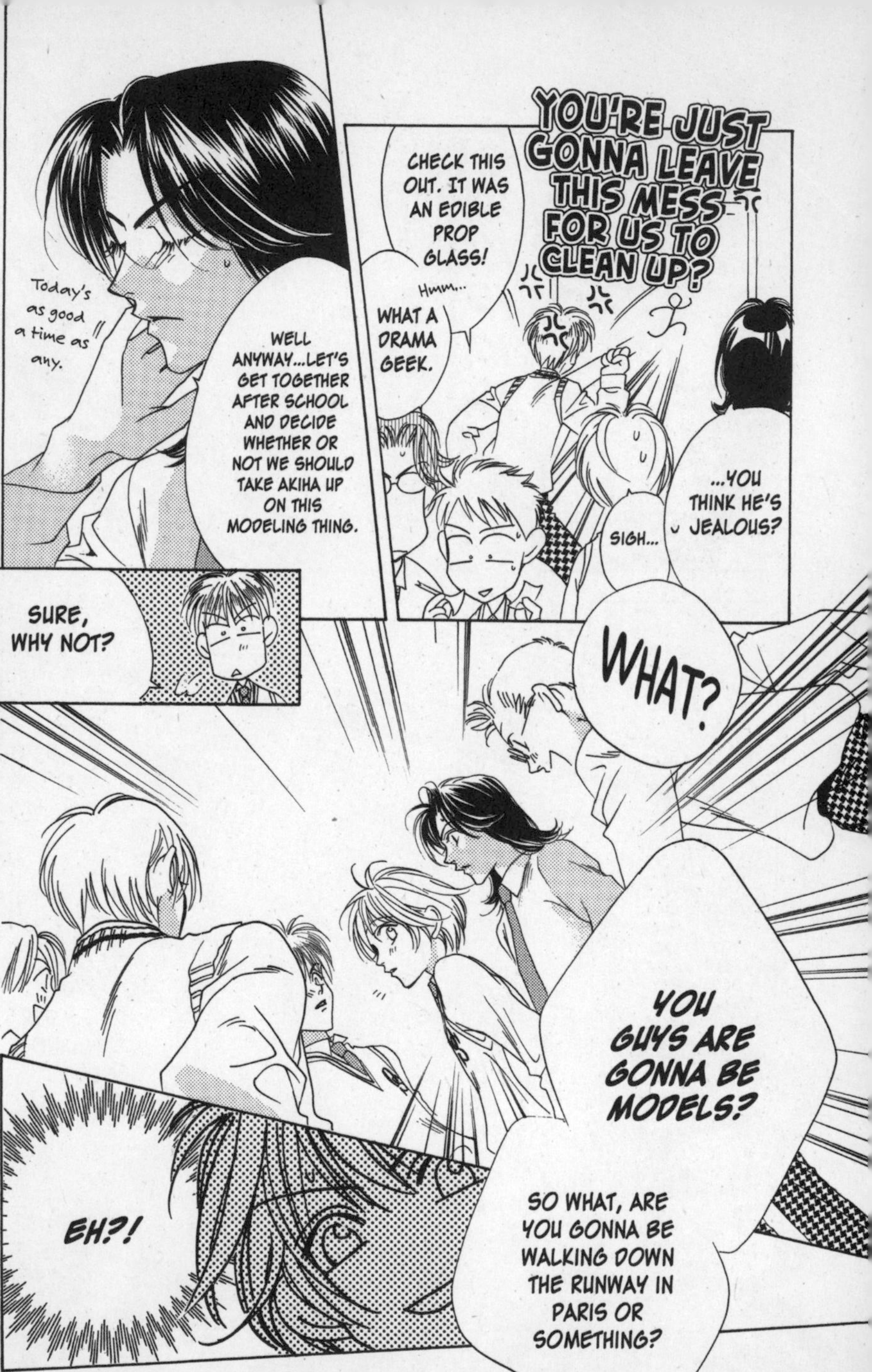
YOU'RE JUST GONNA LEAVE THIS MESS FOR US TO CLEAN UP?
CHECK THIS OUT. IT WAS AN EDIBLE PROP GLASS!
Hmm...
WHAT A DRAMA GEEK.
...YOU THINK HE'S JEALOUS?
SIGH...
WELL ANYWAY...LET'S GET TOGETHER AFTER SCHOOL AND DECIDE WHETHER OR NOT WE SHOULD TAKE AKIHA UP ON THIS MODELING THING.
Today's as good a time as any.
SURE, WHY NOT?
WHAT?
YOU GUYS ARE GONNA BE MODELS?
SO WHAT, ARE YOU GONNA BE WALKING DOWN THE RUNWAY IN PARIS OR SOMETHING?
EH?!

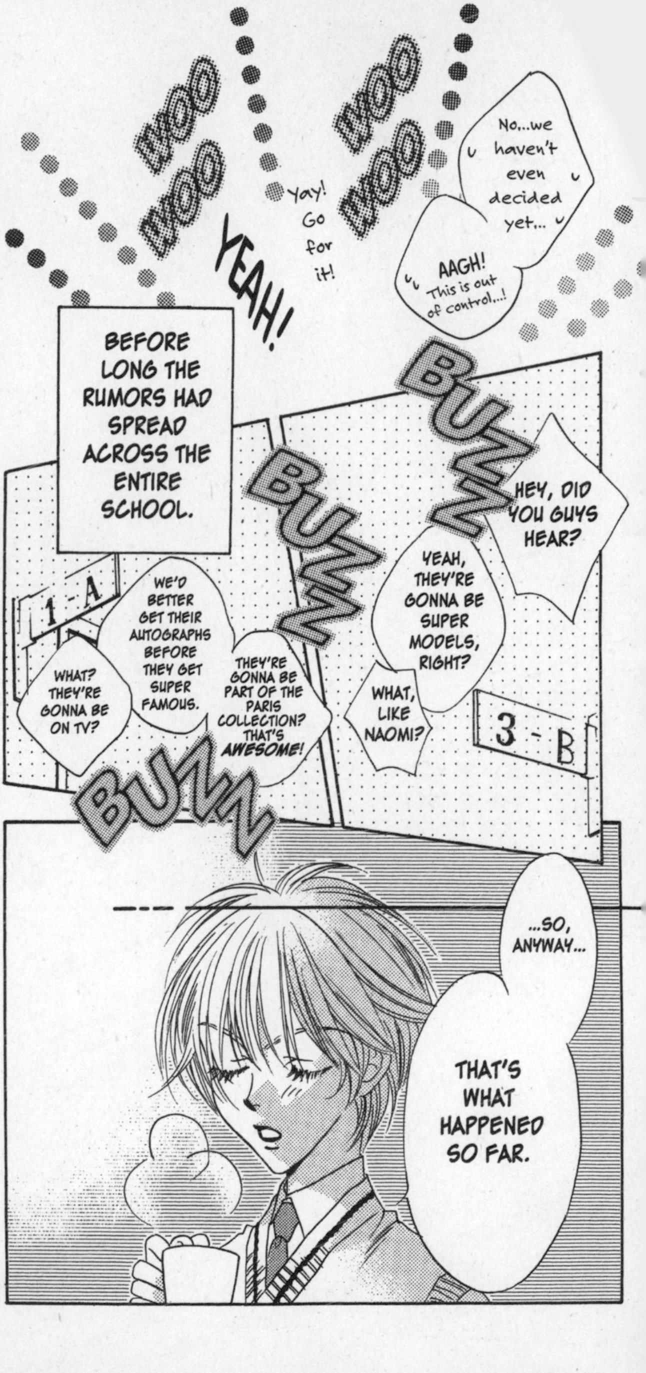
No...we haven't even decided yet...
AAGH! This is out of control...!
WOO WOO
Yay! Go for it!
WOO WOO
YEAH!
BEFORE LONG THE RUMORS HAD SPREAD ACROSS THE ENTIRE SCHOOL.
BUZZ
HEY, DID YOU GUYS HEAR?
YEAH, THEY'RE GONNA BE SUPER MODELS, RIGHT?
BUZZ
WHAT, LIKE NAOMI?
3-B
THEY'RE GONNA BE PART OF THE PARIS COLLECTION? THAT'S AWESOME!
WE'D BETTER GET THEIR AUTOGRAPHS BEFORE THEY GET SUPER FAMOUS.
WHAT? THEY'RE GONNA BE ON TV?
1-A
BUZZ
...SO, ANYWAY...
THAT'S WHAT HAPPENED SO FAR.

WHISPERED SECRETS

NOSTALGIC FLAVORS (2)

LET ME INTRODUCE MY FAVORITE WAY OF MAKING OKOMOMIYAKI. FIRST, I PREPARE THE FLOUR DOUGH, THEN MIX IT WITH BROTH, YAM, AN EGG, SLICED CABBAGE AND DEEP-FRIED TEMPURA BATTER. THEN, I PLACE THE DOUGH ON A 1.8 CM THICK GRILL, AND SPREAD IT OUT LIKE A PANCAKE. AFTER THAT, I PUT SLICED PORK ON TOP, THEN I FLIP IT AND GRILL THE OTHER SIDE. REMEMBER...NEVER TAP IT WITH YOUR SPATULA WHILE IT'S COOKING. WHEN IT'S READY, I PUT SAUCE, MAYONAISSE (NOT THE SOUR KIND), A LITTLE BIT OF MUSTARD AND BONITO FLAKES OVER IT, AND THAT'S IT! AH...IT'S SO DELICIOUS. ANYWAY, THIS IS HOW MY FAMILY COOKS OKONOMIYAKI, BUT I'M SURE EVERYBODY HAS THEIR OWN FAVORITE RECIPE. YOU JUST CAN'T BEAT THE OLD RECIPES YOU GREW UP WITH. THERE'S NO SENSE IN WORRYING ABOUT HOW YOU'RE "SUPPOSED" TO MAKE IT. JUST COOK IT UP THE WAY YOU LIKE IT.♡

SOME PURISTS SAY TRUE OKONOMIYAKI AFICIONADOS DON'T USE MAYO.

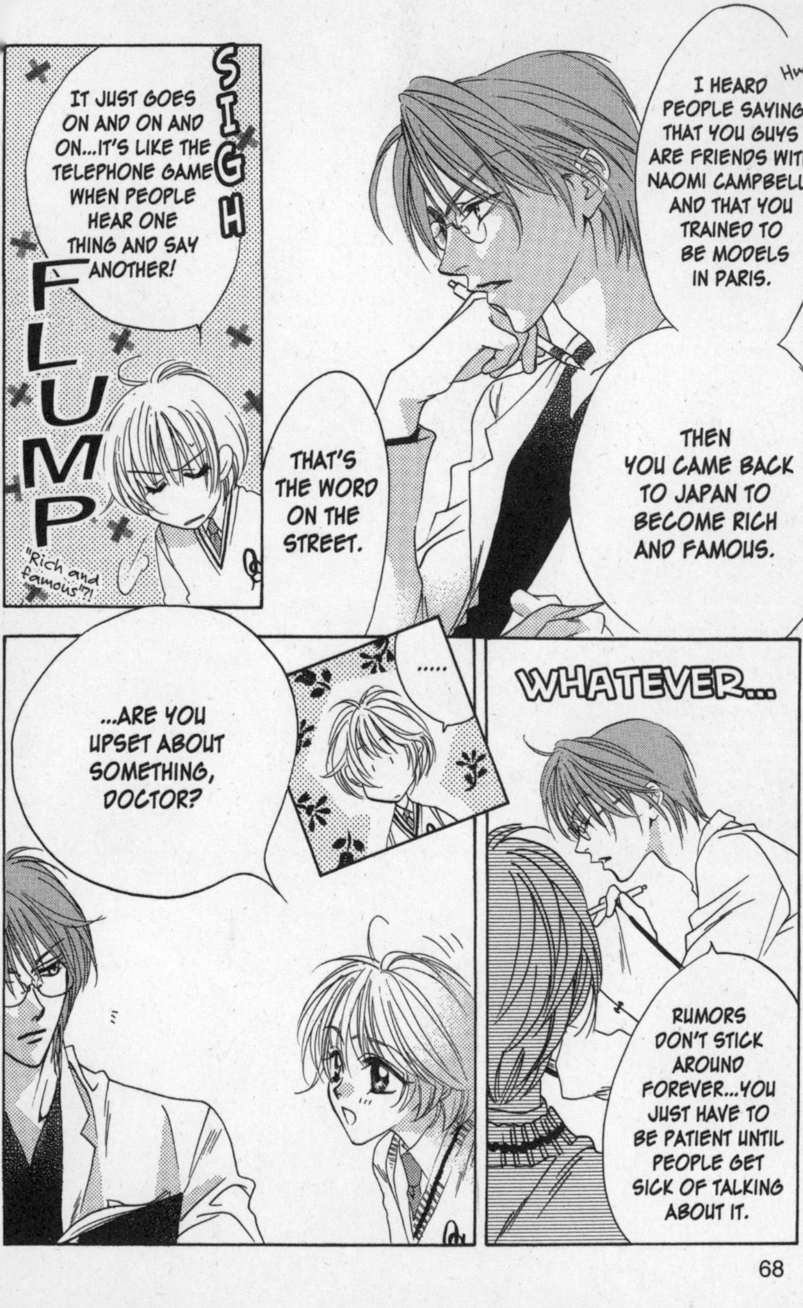
Hmm...
I HEARD PEOPLE SAYING THAT YOU GUYS ARE FRIENDS WITH NAOMI CAMPBELL, AND THAT YOU TRAINED TO BE MODELS IN PARIS.
THEN YOU CAME BACK TO JAPAN TO BECOME RICH AND FAMOUS.
THAT'S THE WORD ON THE STREET.
IT JUST GOES ON AND ON AND ON...IT'S LIKE THE TELEPHONE GAME WHEN PEOPLE HEAR ONE THING AND SAY ANOTHER!
SIGH
FLUMP
"Rich and famous"?!
WHATEVER...
RUMORS DON'T STICK AROUND FOREVER...YOU JUST HAVE TO BE PATIENT UNTIL PEOPLE GET SICK OF TALKING ABOUT IT.
.....
...ARE YOU UPSET ABOUT SOMETHING, DOCTOR?

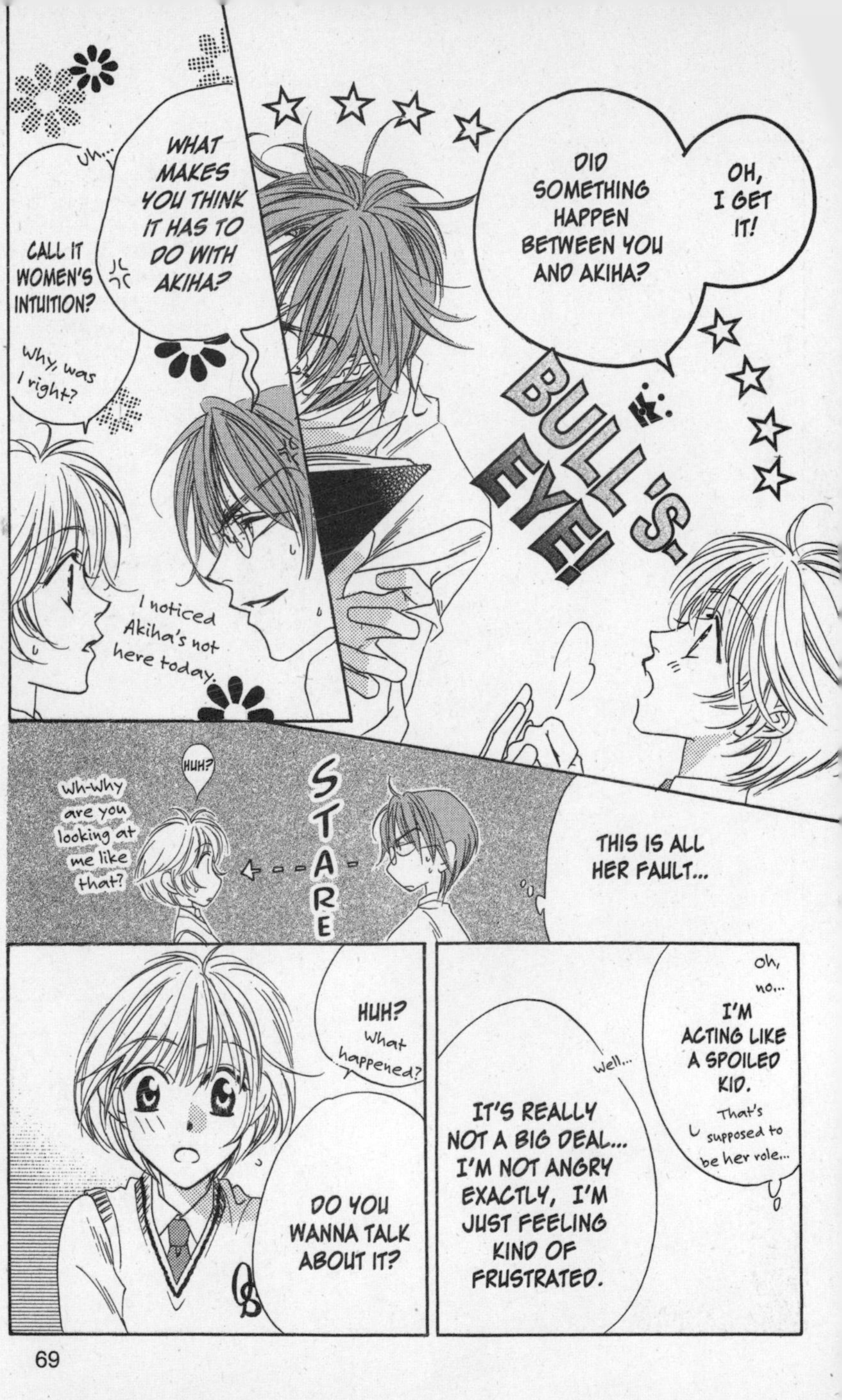
OH, I GET IT!
DID SOMETHING HAPPEN BETWEEN YOU AND AKIHA?
BULL'S-EYE!
WHAT MAKES YOU THINK IT HAS TO DO WITH AKIHA?
Uh...
CALL IT WOMEN'S INTUITION?
Why, was I right?
I noticed Akiha's not here today.
THIS IS ALL HER FAULT...
STARE
HUH?
Wh-Why are you looking at me like that?
Oh, no...
I'M ACTING LIKE A SPOILED KID.
That's supposed to be her role...
Well...
IT'S REALLY NOT A BIG DEAL... I'M NOT ANGRY EXACTLY, I'M JUST FEELING KIND OF FRUSTRATED.
HUH? What happened?
DO YOU WANNA TALK ABOUT IT?

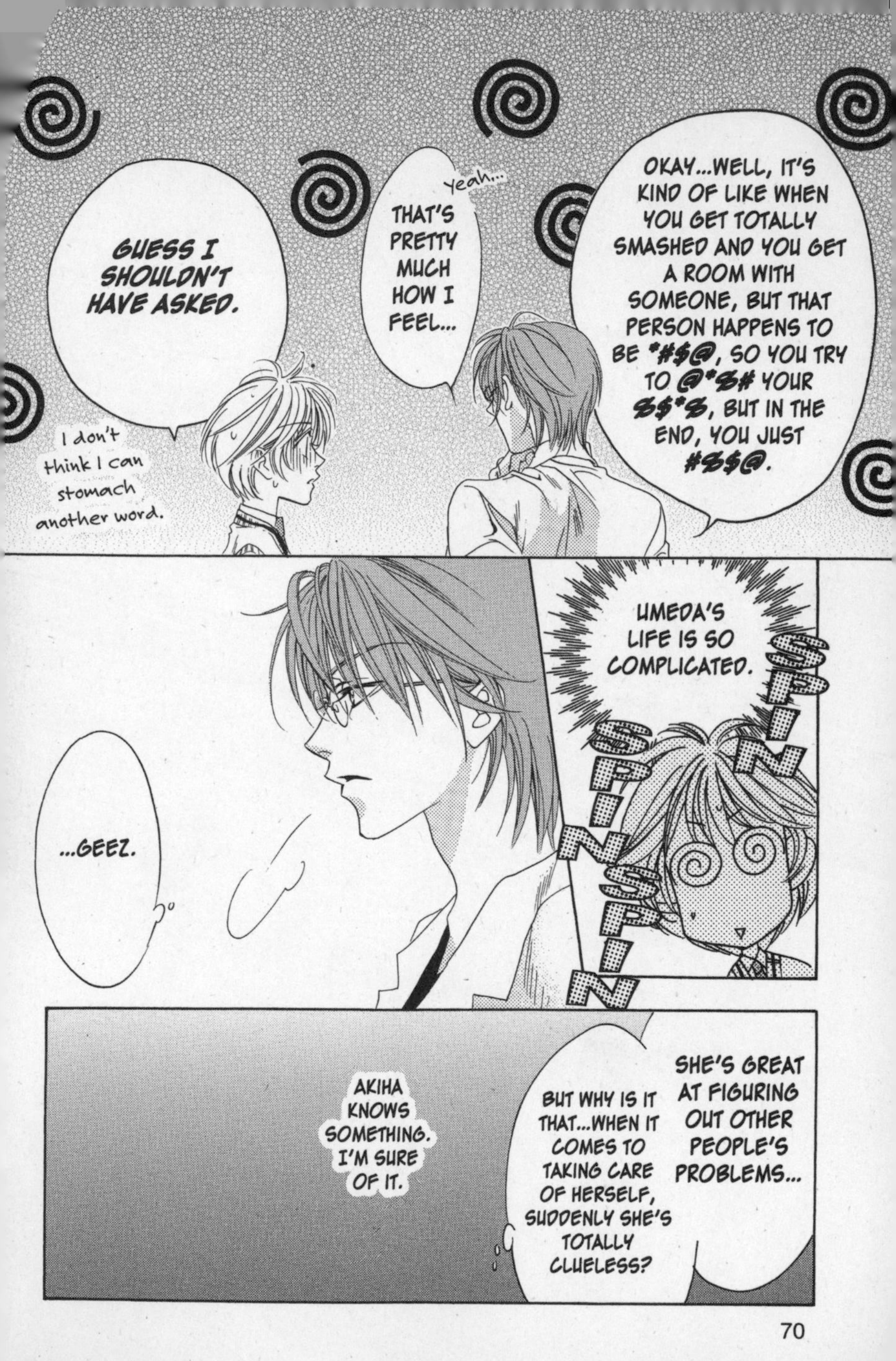
OKAY...WELL, IT'S KIND OF LIKE WHEN YOU GET TOTALLY SMASHED AND YOU GET A ROOM WITH SOMEONE, BUT THAT PERSON HAPPENS TO BE *#$@, SO YOU TRY TO @*$# YOUR $$*$, BUT IN THE END, YOU JUST #$$@.
yeah...
THAT'S PRETTY MUCH HOW I FEEL...
GUESS I SHOULDN'T HAVE ASKED.
I don't think I can stomach another word.
UMEDA'S LIFE IS SO COMPLICATED.
SPIN
SPIN
SPIN
...GEEZ.
SHE'S GREAT AT FIGURING OUT OTHER PEOPLE'S PROBLEMS...
BUT WHY IS IT THAT...WHEN IT COMES TO TAKING CARE OF HERSELF, SUDDENLY SHE'S TOTALLY CLUELESS?
AKIHA KNOWS SOMETHING. I'M SURE OF IT.

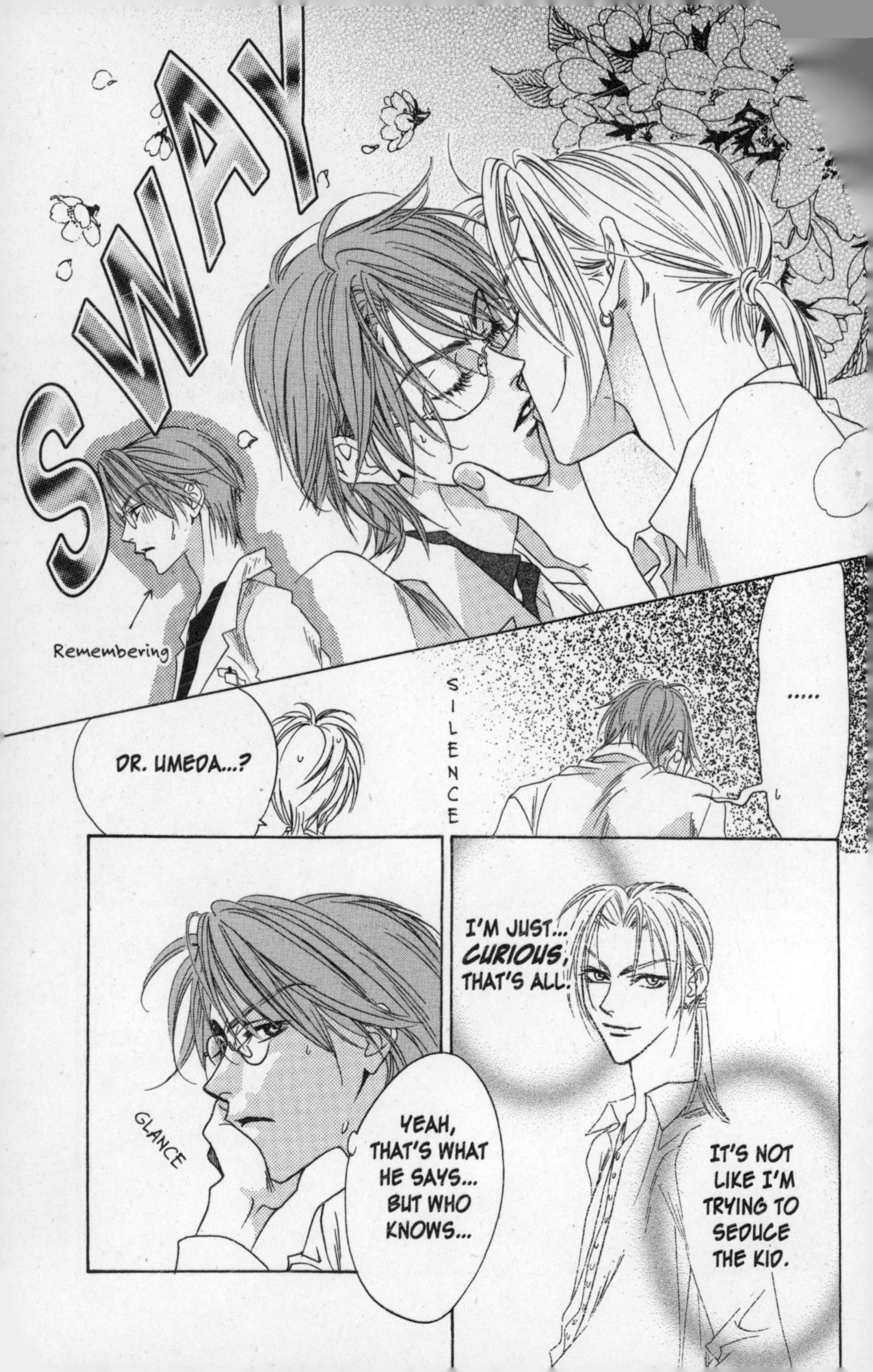
SWAY
Remembering
.....
SILENCE
DR. UMEDA...?
I'M JUST... CURIOUS, THAT'S ALL.
IT'S NOT LIKE I'M TRYING TO SEDUCE THE KID.
GLANCE
YEAH, THAT'S WHAT HE SAYS... BUT WHO KNOWS...

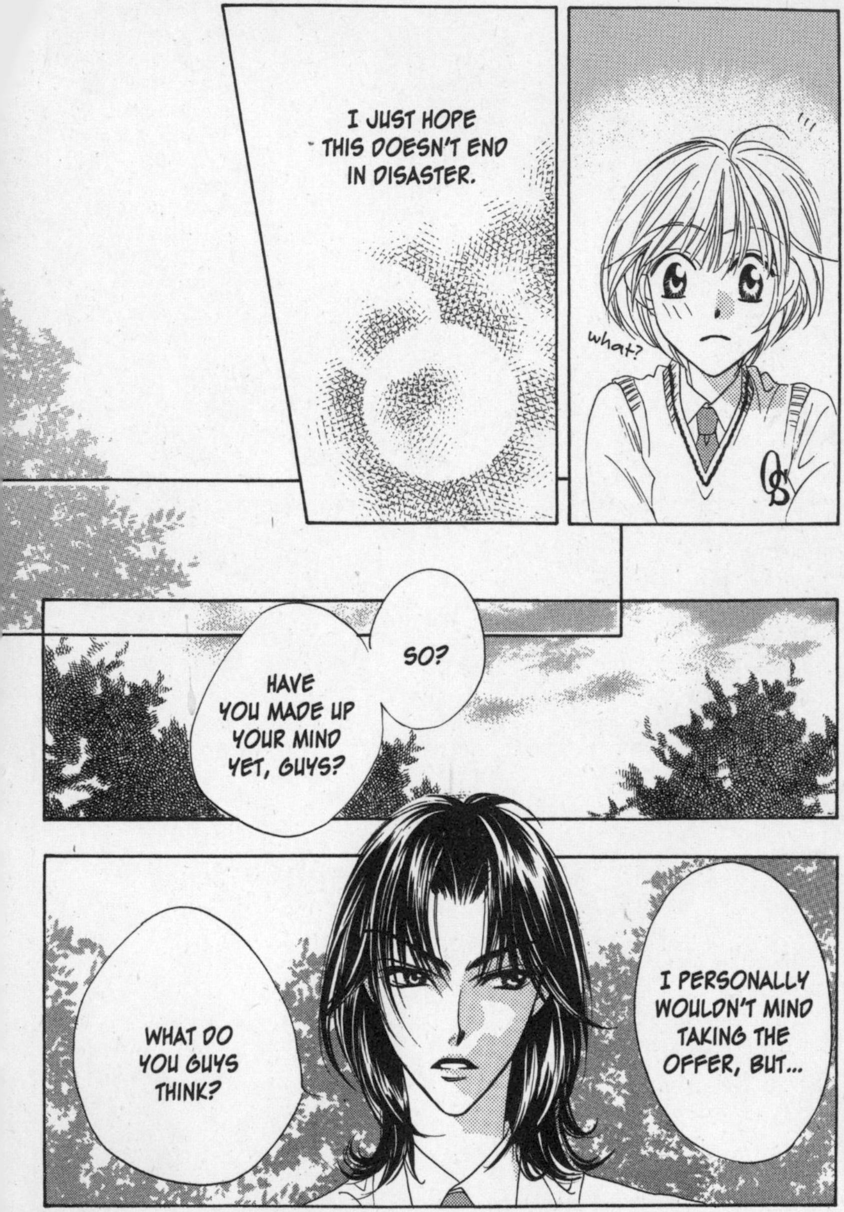
what?
I JUST HOPE THIS DOESN'T END IN DISASTER.
SO?
HAVE YOU MADE UP YOUR MIND YET, GUYS?
I PERSONALLY WOULDN'T MIND TAKING THE OFFER, BUT...
WHAT DO YOU GUYS THINK?

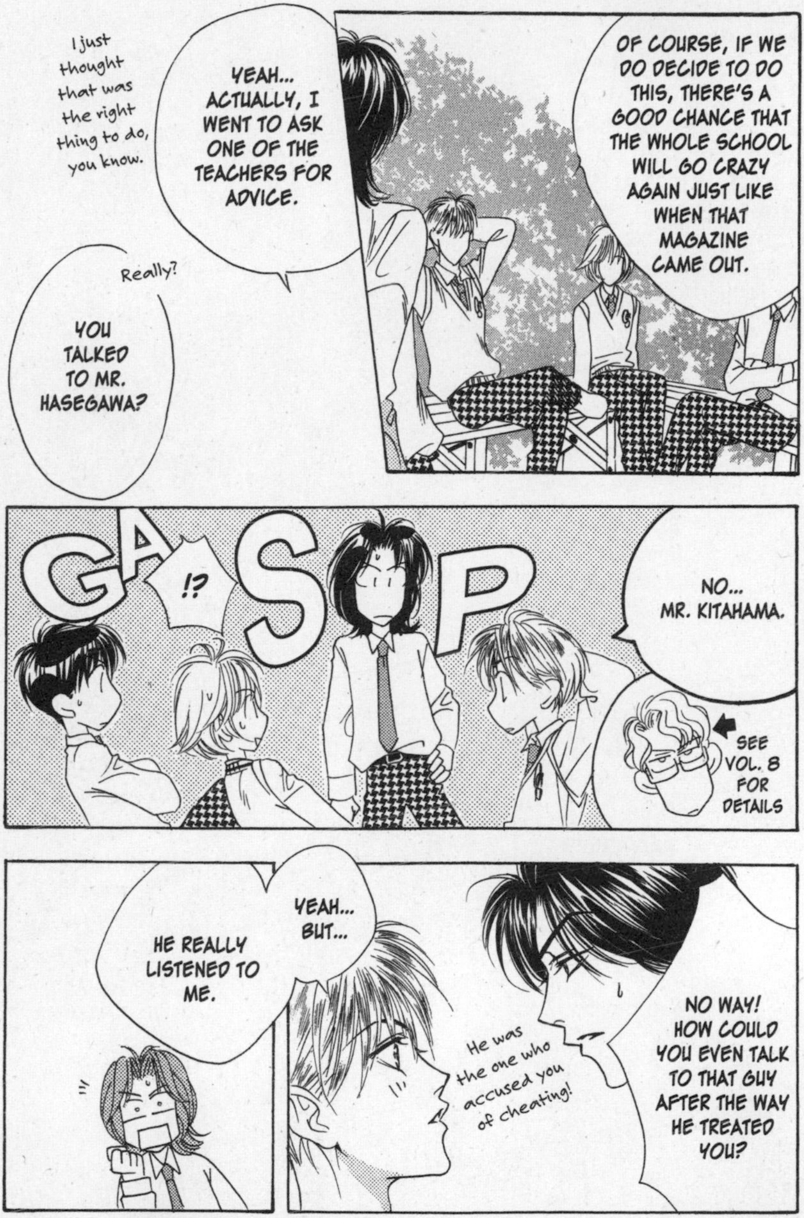
OF COURSE, IF WE DO DECIDE TO DO THIS, THERE'S A GOOD CHANCE THAT THE WHOLE SCHOOL WILL GO CRAZY AGAIN JUST LIKE WHEN THAT MAGAZINE CAME OUT.
YEAH... ACTUALLY, I WENT TO ASK ONE OF THE TEACHERS FOR ADVICE.
I just thought that was the right thing to do, you know.
Really?
YOU TALKED TO MR. HASEGAWA?
NO... MR. KITAHAMA.
SEE VOL. 8 FOR DETAILS
GASP
!?
NO WAY! HOW COULD YOU EVEN TALK TO THAT GUY AFTER THE WAY HE TREATED YOU?
He was the one who accused you of cheating!
YEAH... BUT...
HE REALLY LISTENED TO ME.

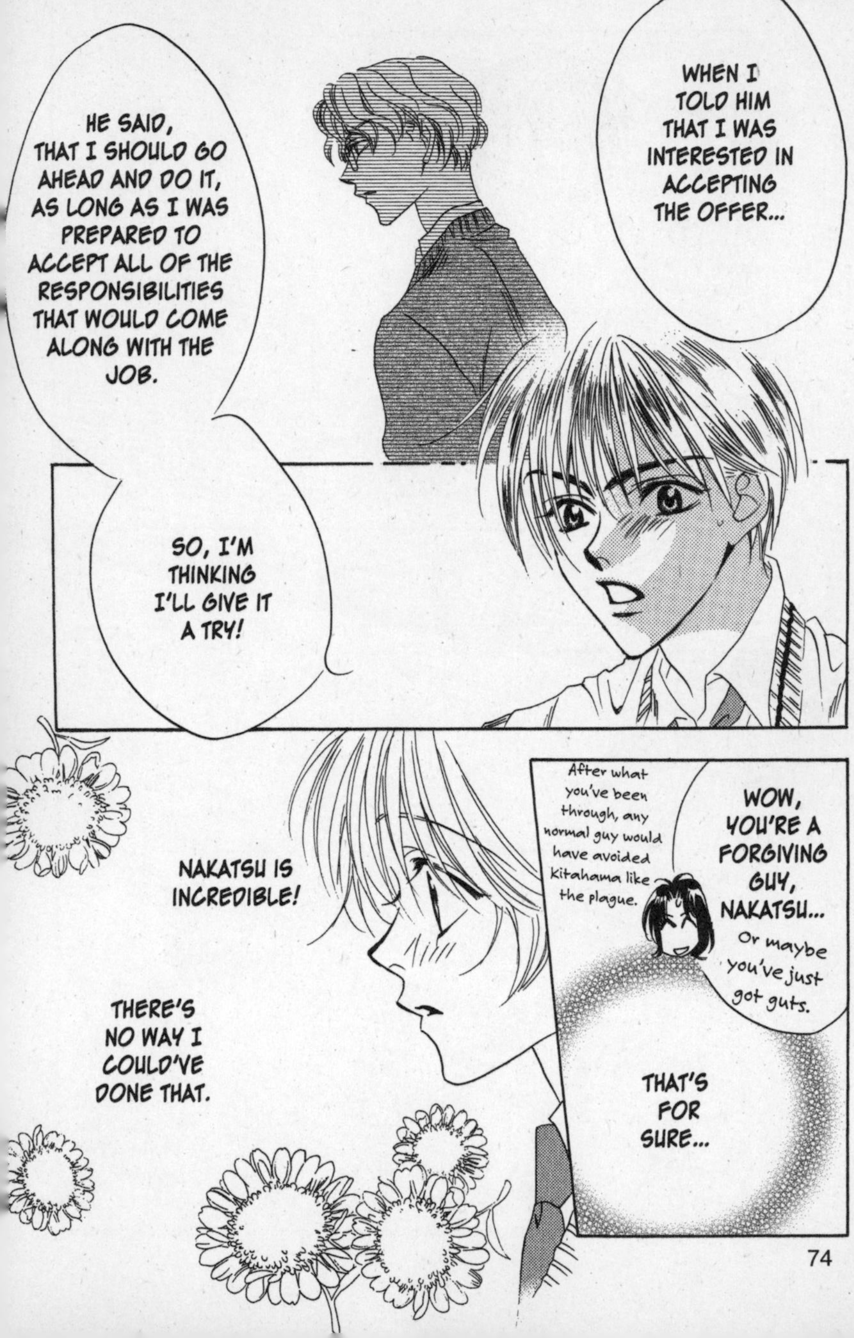
WHEN I TOLD HIM THAT I WAS INTERESTED IN ACCEPTING THE OFFER...
HE SAID, THAT I SHOULD GO AHEAD AND DO IT, AS LONG AS I WAS PREPARED TO ACCEPT ALL OF THE RESPONSIBILITIES THAT WOULD COME ALONG WITH THE JOB.
SO, I'M THINKING I'LL GIVE IT A TRY!
WOW, YOU'RE A FORGIVING GUY, NAKATSU...
Or maybe you've just got guts.
After what you've been through, any normal guy would have avoided Kitahama like the plague.
THAT'S FOR SURE...
NAKATSU IS INCREDIBLE!
THERE'S NO WAY I COULD'VE DONE THAT.

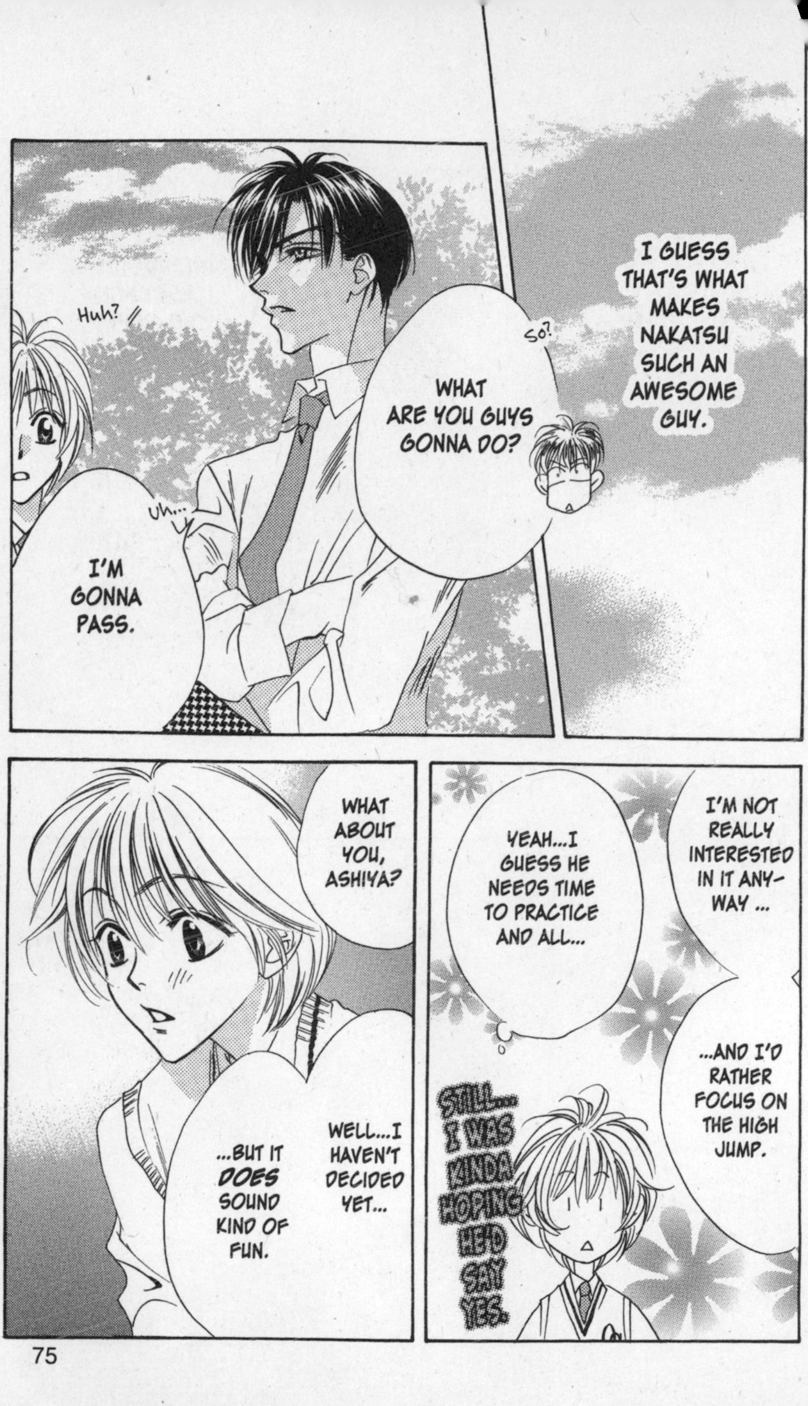
I GUESS THAT'S WHAT MAKES NAKATSU SUCH AN AWESOME GUY.
So?
WHAT ARE YOU GUYS GONNA DO?
Huh?
Uh...
I'M GONNA PASS.
I'M NOT REALLY INTERESTED IN IT ANY-WAY ...
...AND I'D RATHER FOCUS ON THE HIGH JUMP.
YEAH...I GUESS HE NEEDS TIME TO PRACTICE AND ALL...
STILL... I WAS KINDA HOPING HE'D SAY YES.
WHAT ABOUT YOU, ASHIYA?
WELL...I HAVEN'T DECIDED YET...
...BUT IT *DOES* SOUND KIND OF FUN.

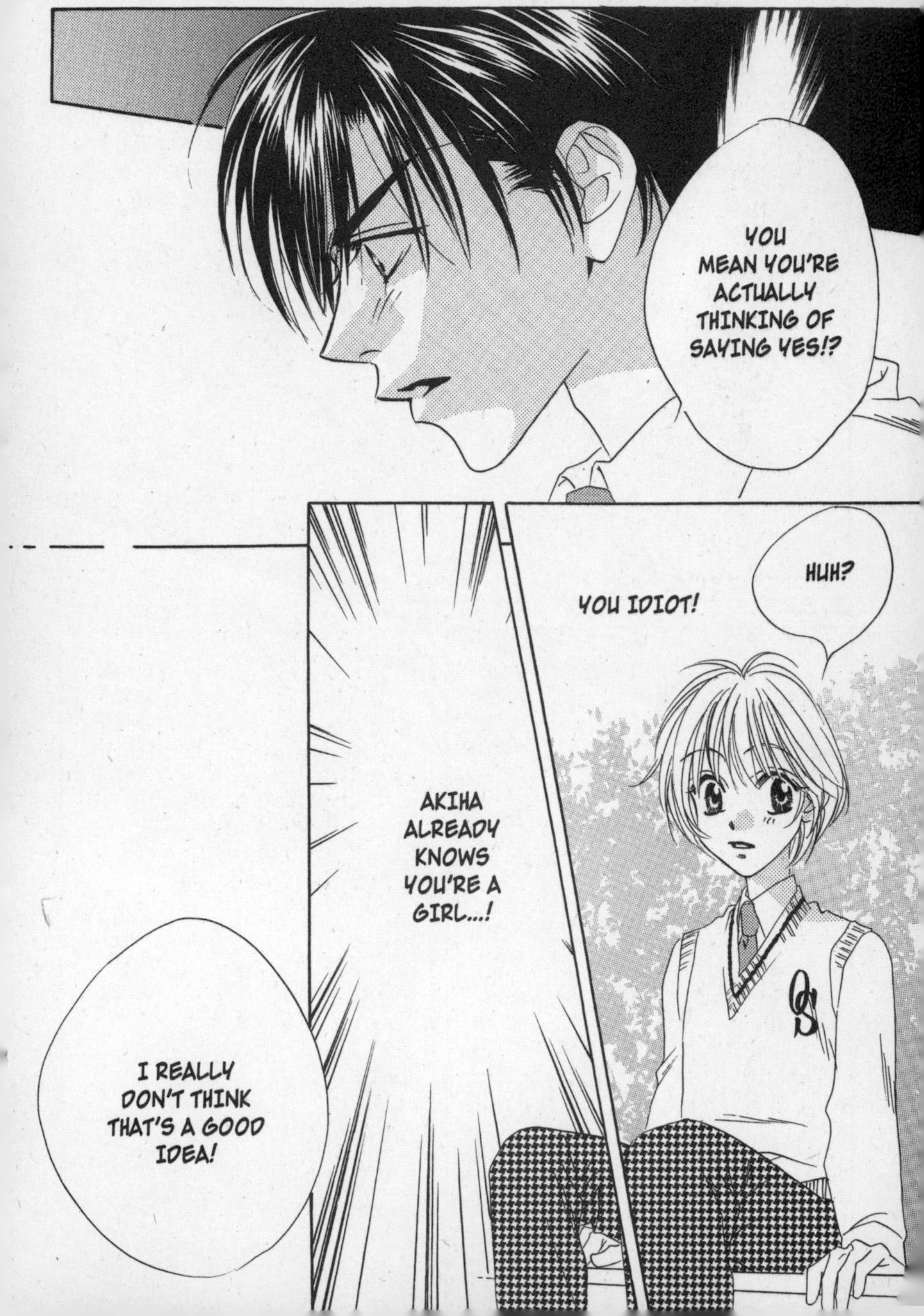
YOU MEAN YOU'RE ACTUALLY THINKING OF SAYING YES!?
HUH?
YOU IDIOT!
AKIHA ALREADY KNOWS YOU'RE A GIRL...!
I REALLY DON'T THINK THAT'S A GOOD IDEA!

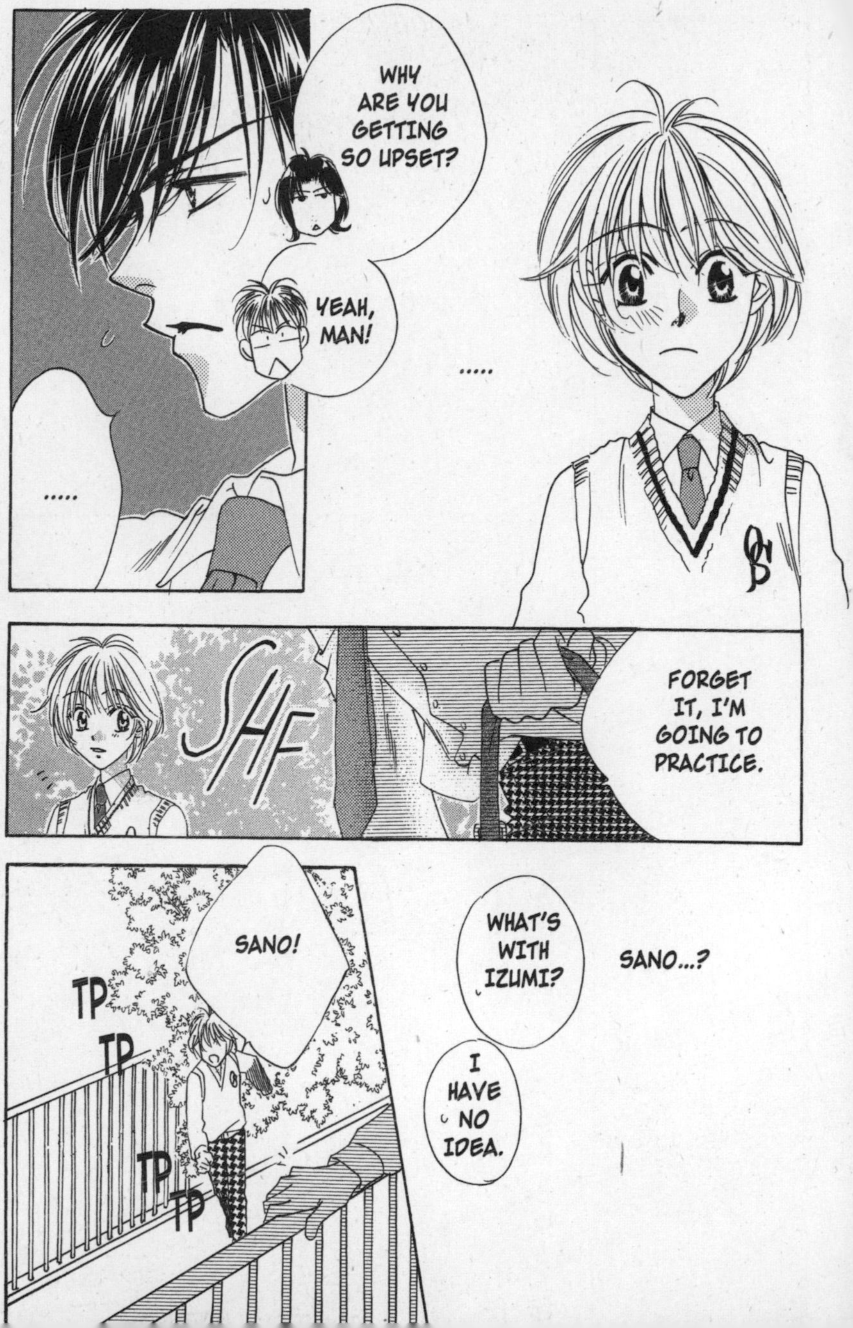
.....
WHY ARE YOU GETTING SO UPSET?
YEAH, MAN!
.....
FORGET IT, I'M GOING TO PRACTICE.
SHF
SANO...?
WHAT'S WITH IZUMI?
I HAVE NO IDEA.
SANO!
TP
TP
TP
TP

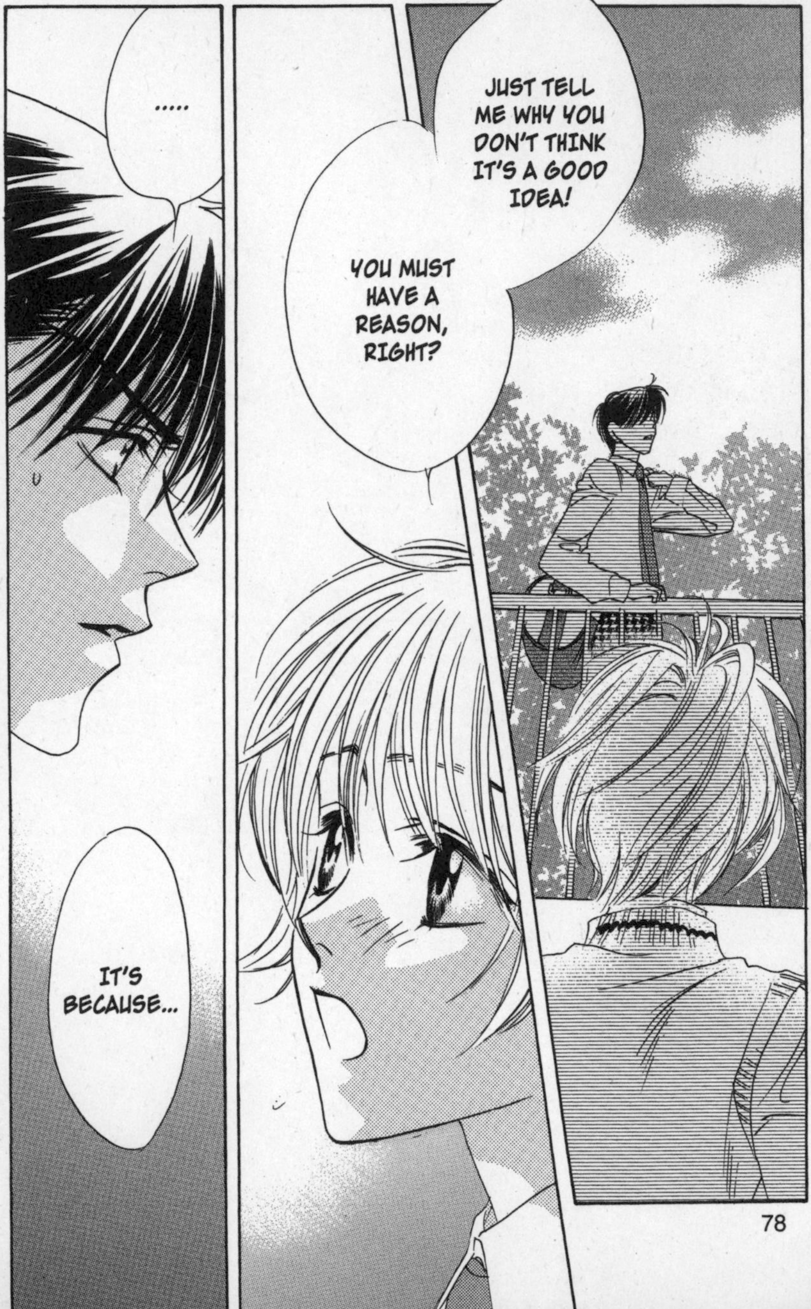
JUST TELL ME WHY YOU DON'T THINK IT'S A GOOD IDEA!
YOU MUST HAVE A REASON, RIGHT?
.....
IT'S BECAUSE...

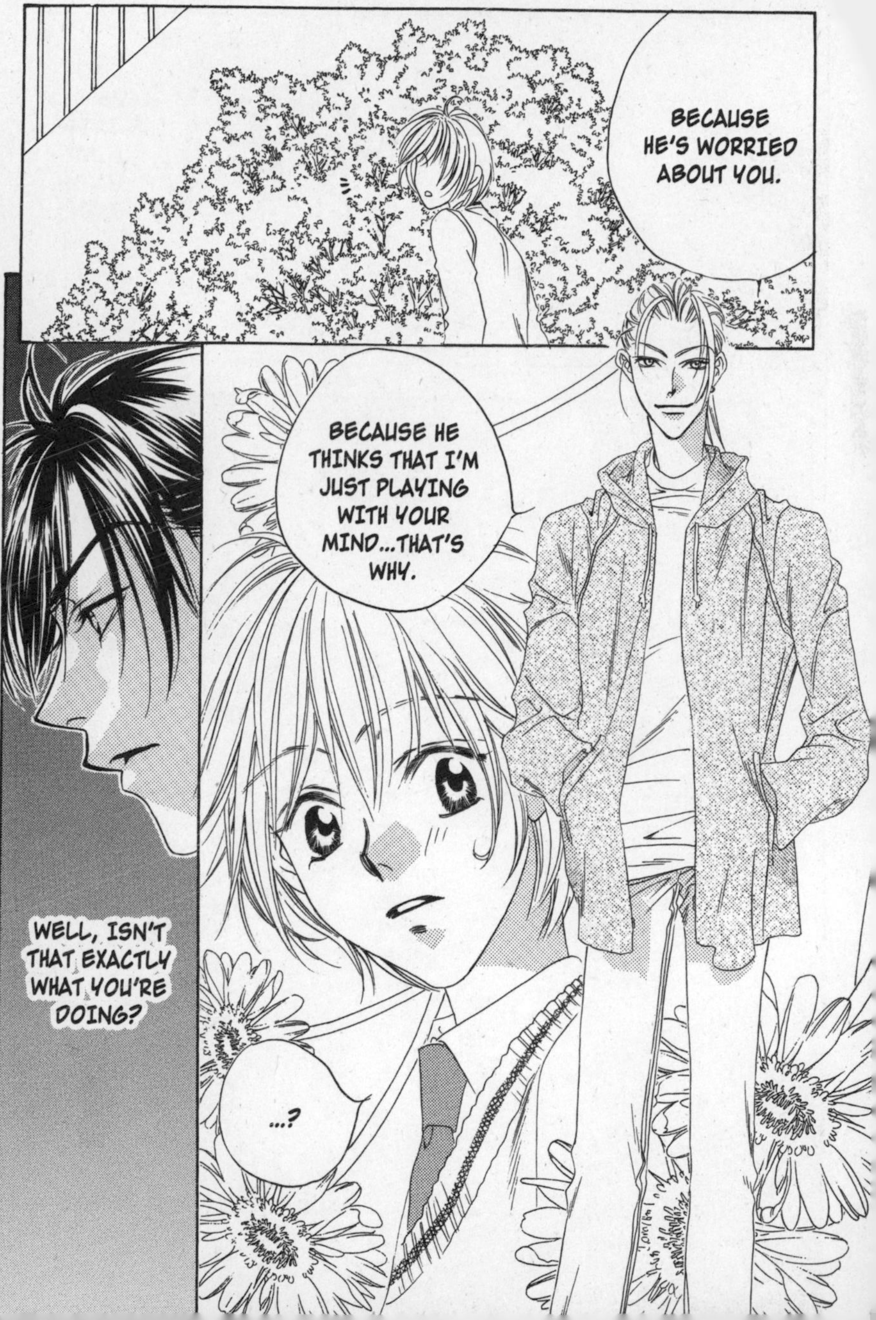
BECAUSE HE'S WORRIED ABOUT YOU.
BECAUSE HE THINKS THAT I'M JUST PLAYING WITH YOUR MIND...THAT'S WHY.
...?
WELL, ISN'T THAT EXACTLY WHAT YOU'RE DOING?

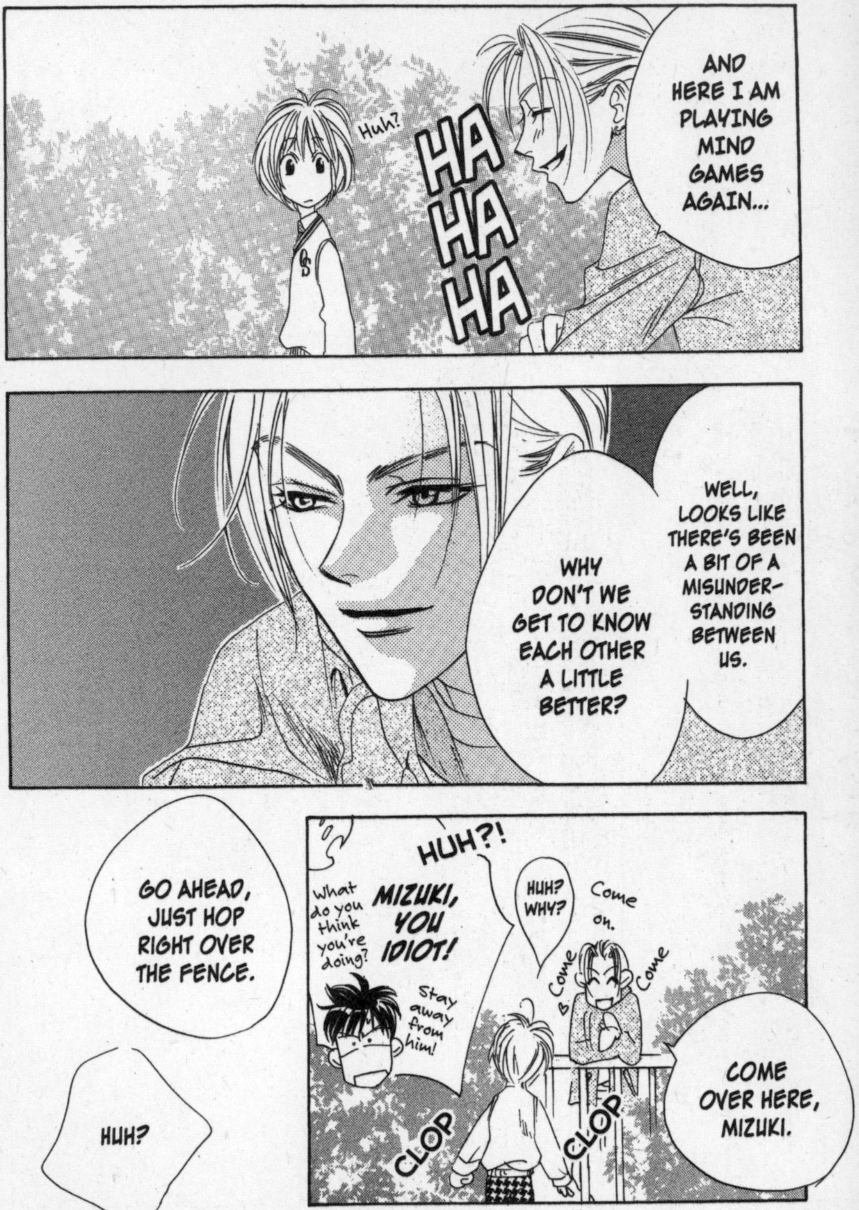
AND HERE I AM PLAYING MIND GAMES AGAIN...
HA HA HA
Huh?
WELL, LOOKS LIKE THERE'S BEEN A BIT OF A MISUNDER-STANDING BETWEEN US.
WHY DON'T WE GET TO KNOW EACH OTHER A LITTLE BETTER?
Come on.
HUH? WHY?
HUH?!
MIZUKI, YOU IDIOT!
What do you think you're doing?
Come Come
Stay away from him!
COME OVER HERE, MIZUKI.
CLOP CLOP
GO AHEAD, JUST HOP RIGHT OVER THE FENCE.
HUH?

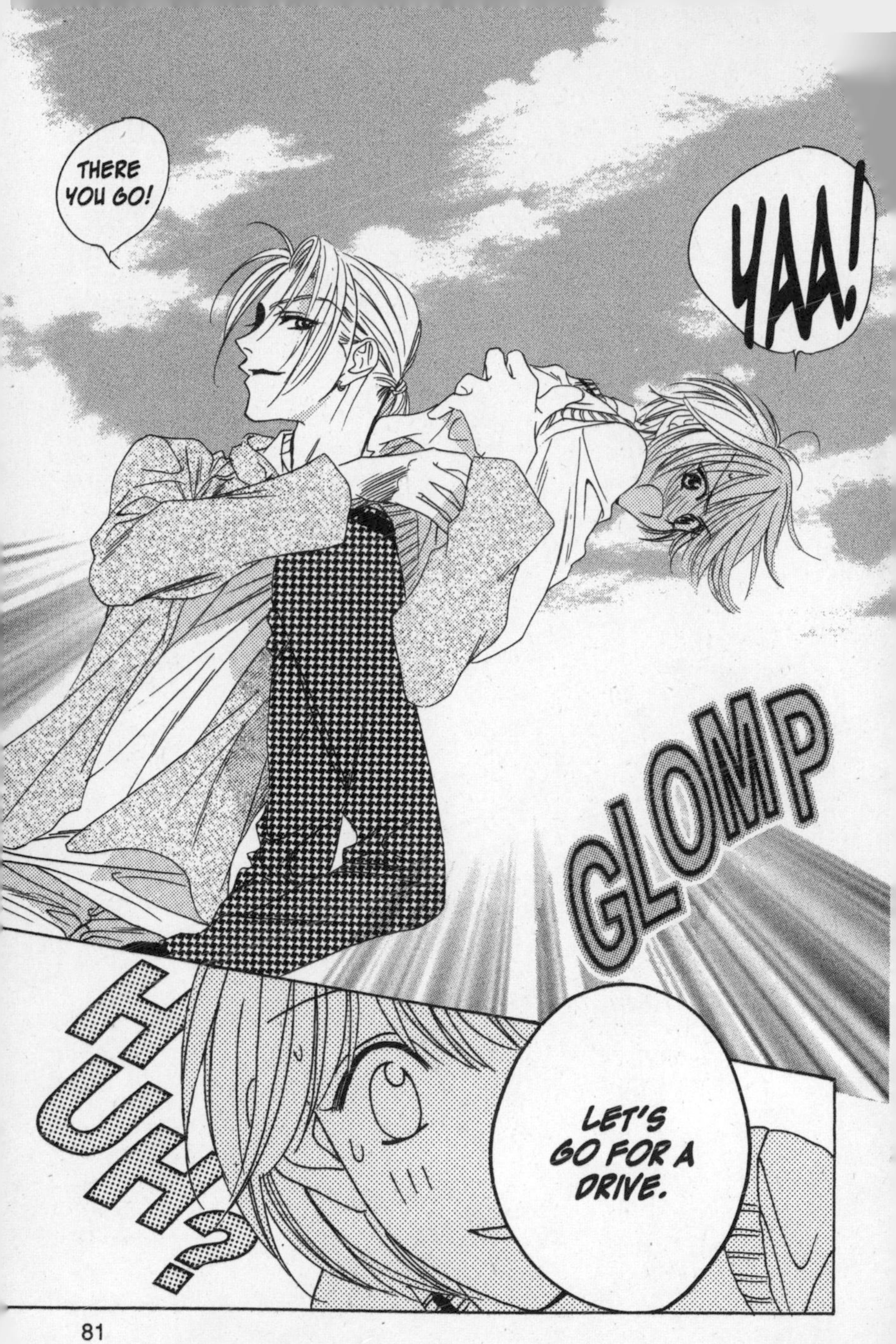
YAA!
THERE YOU GO!
GLOMP
LET'S GO FOR A DRIVE.
HUH?

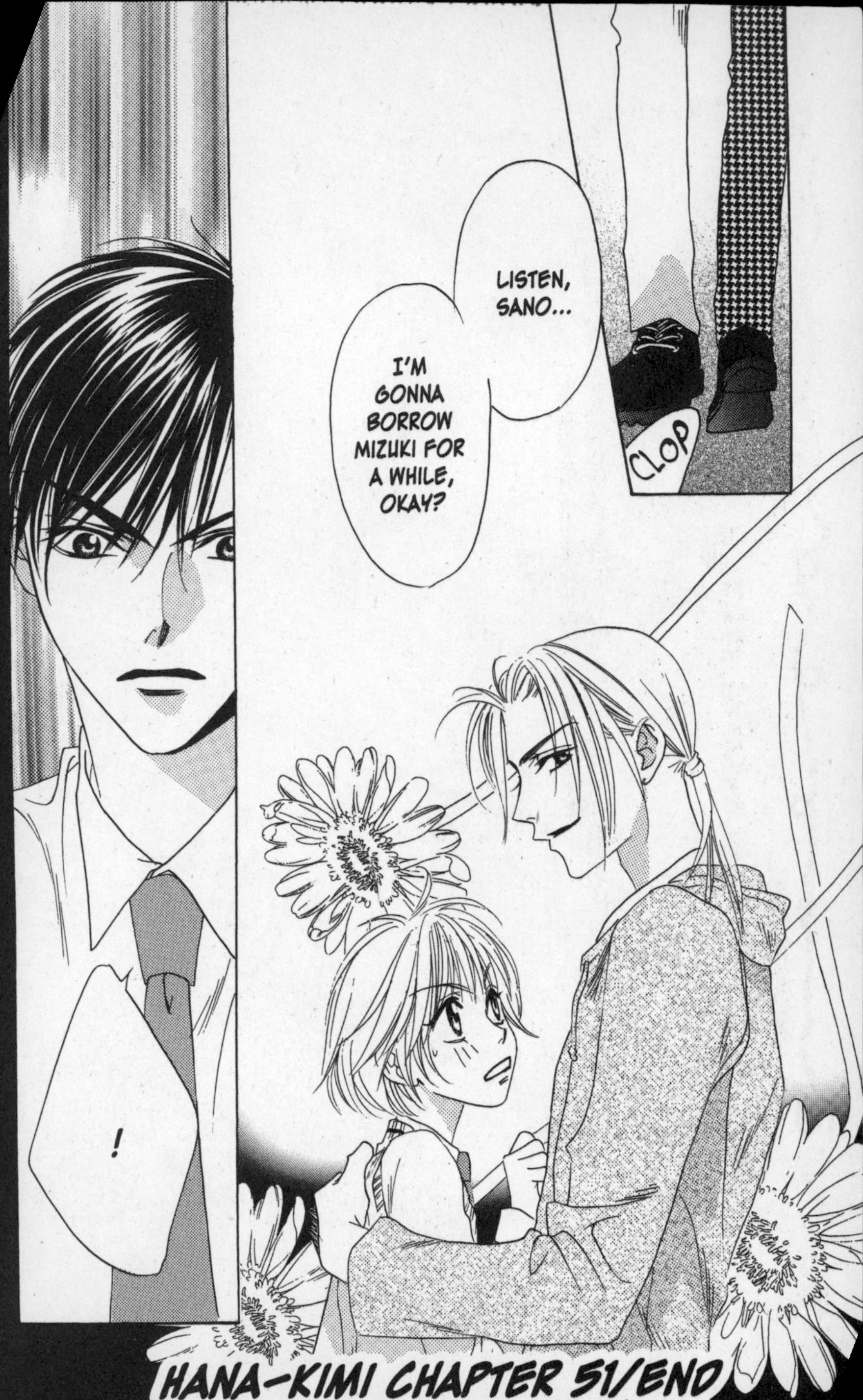
CLOP
LISTEN, SANO...
I'M GONNA BORROW MIZUKI FOR A WHILE, OKAY?
!
HANA-KIMI CHAPTER 51/END

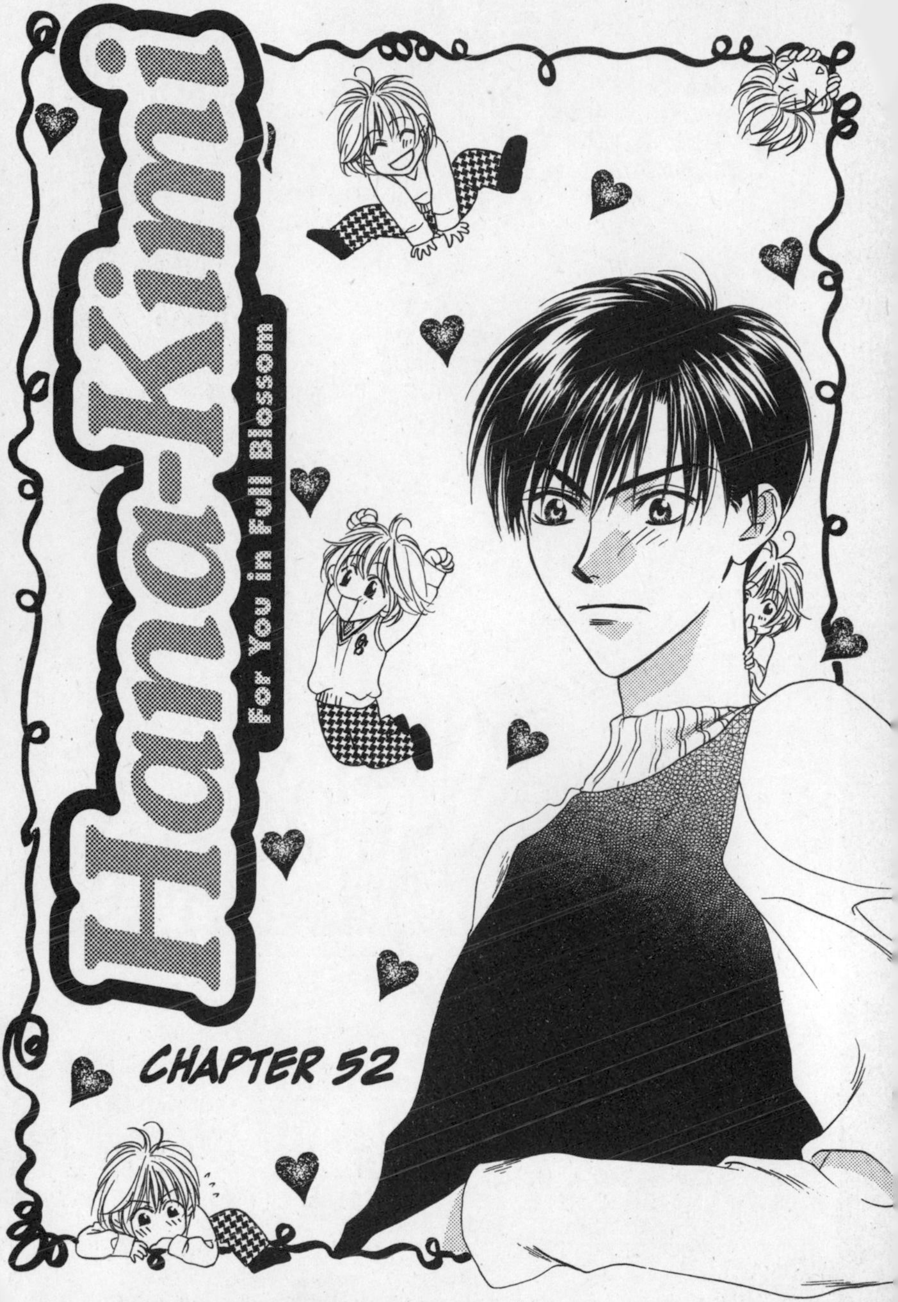
Hana-Kimi
For You in Full Blossom
CHAPTER 52

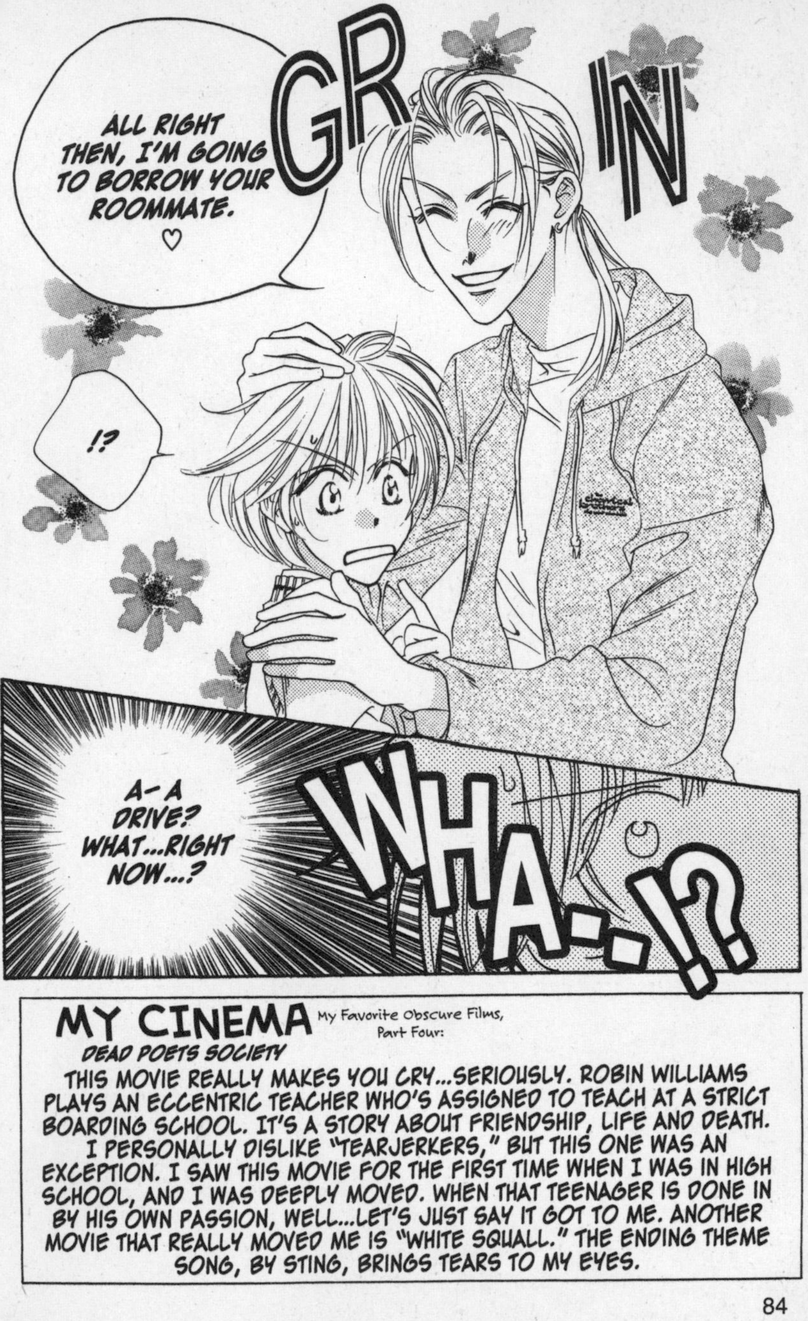
GRIN
ALL RIGHT THEN, I'M GOING TO BORROW YOUR ROOMMATE. ♡
!?
WHA...!?
A- A DRIVE? WHAT...RIGHT NOW...?

MY CINEMA

My Favorite Obscure Films, Part Four:

DEAD POETS SOCIETY

THIS MOVIE REALLY MAKES YOU CRY...SERIOUSLY. ROBIN WILLIAMS PLAYS AN ECCENTRIC TEACHER WHO'S ASSIGNED TO TEACH AT A STRICT BOARDING SCHOOL. IT'S A STORY ABOUT FRIENDSHIP, LIFE AND DEATH. I PERSONALLY DISLIKE "TEARJERKERS," BUT THIS ONE WAS AN EXCEPTION. I SAW THIS MOVIE FOR THE FIRST TIME WHEN I WAS IN HIGH SCHOOL, AND I WAS DEEPLY MOVED. WHEN THAT TEENAGER IS DONE IN BY HIS OWN PASSION, WELL...LET'S JUST SAY IT GOT TO ME. ANOTHER MOVIE THAT REALLY MOVED ME IS "WHITE SQUALL." THE ENDING THEME SONG, BY STING, BRINGS TEARS TO MY EYES.

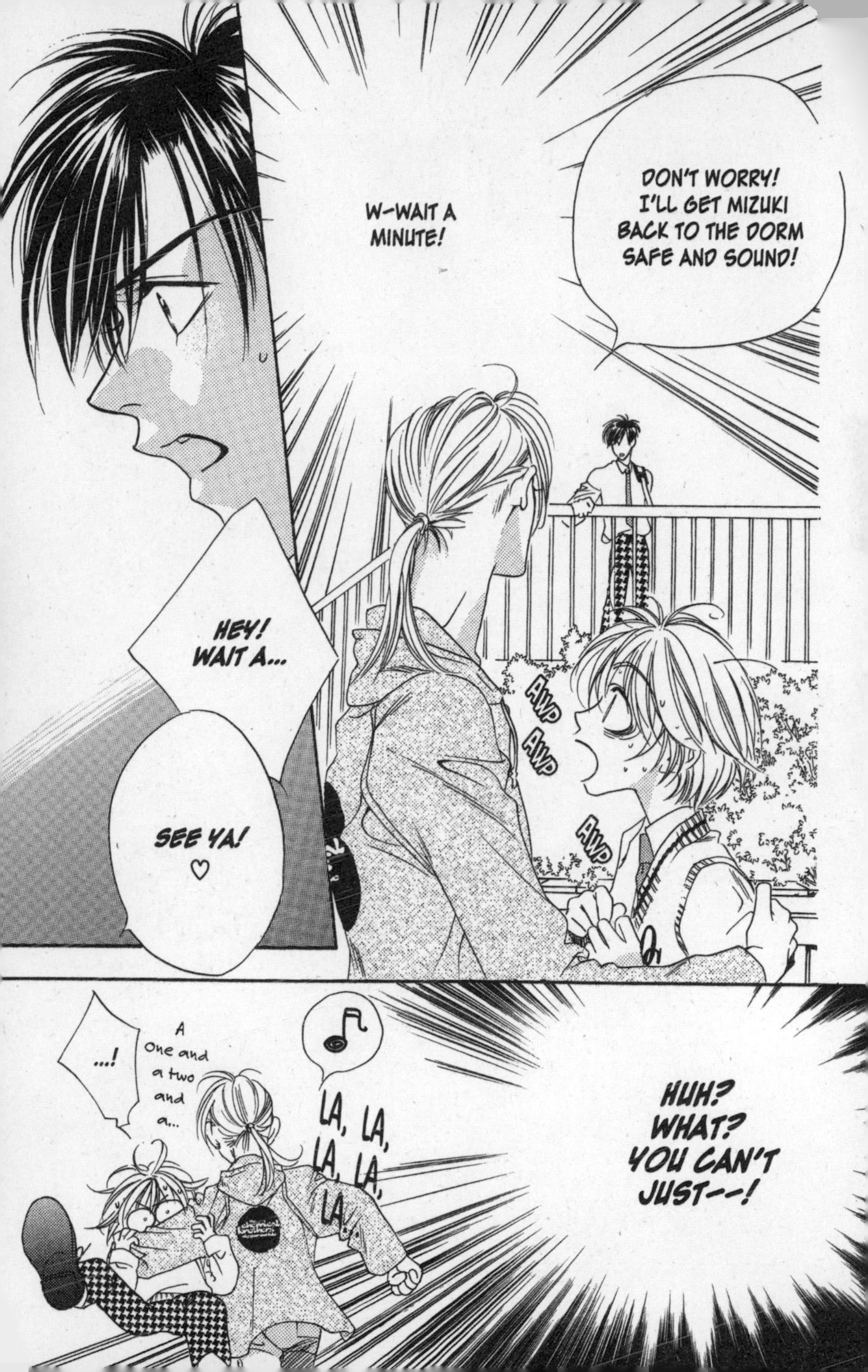
DON'T WORRY! I'LL GET MIZUKI BACK TO THE DORM SAFE AND SOUND!
W-WAIT A MINUTE!
AWP AWP AWP
HEY! WAIT A...
SEE YA! ♡
HUH? WHAT? YOU CAN'T JUST--!
LA, LA, LA, LA, LA...
♪
A one and a two and a...
...!

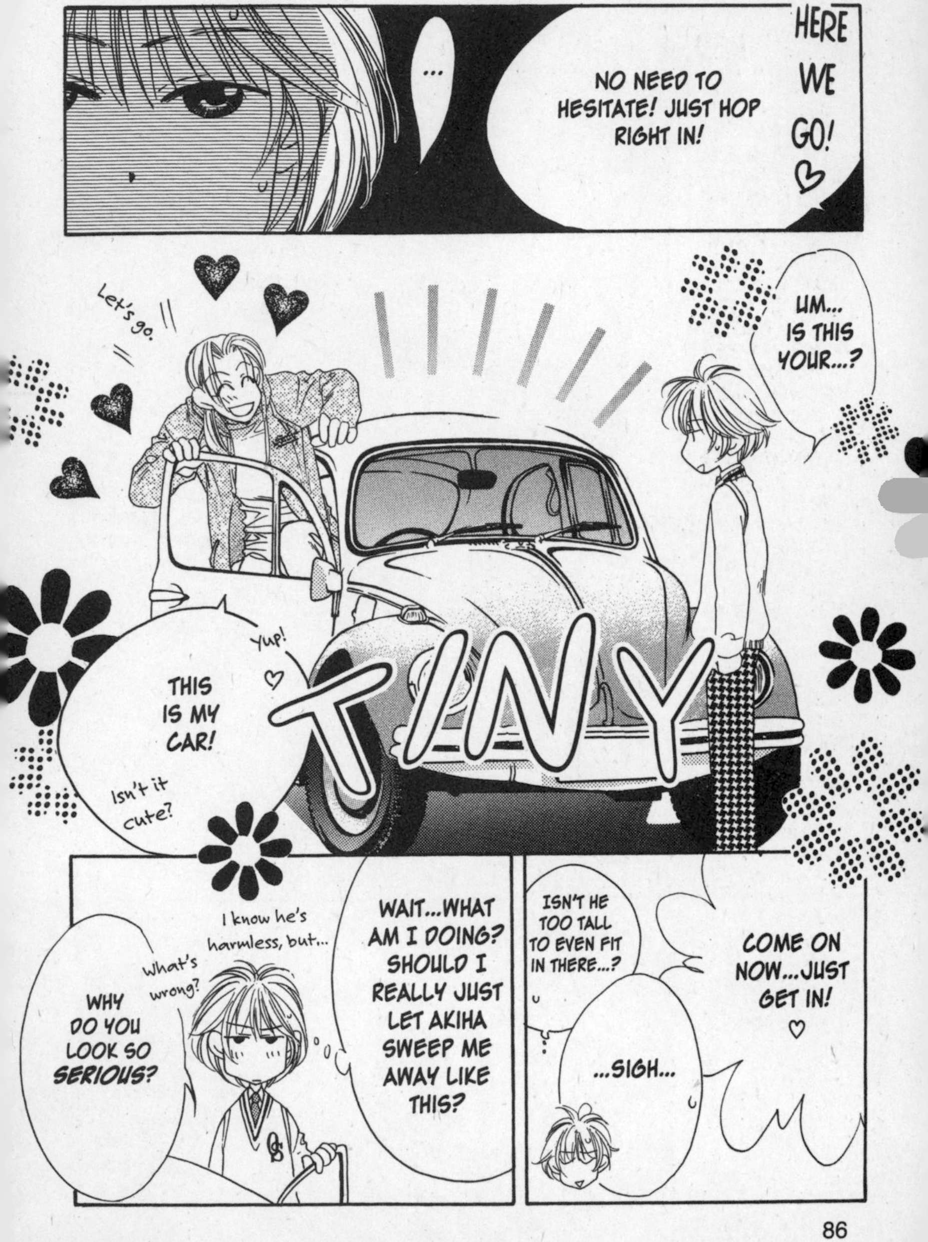
HERE WE GO! ♡
NO NEED TO HESITATE! JUST HOP RIGHT IN!
...
UM... IS THIS YOUR...?
TINY
Let's go.
Yup! ♡
THIS IS MY CAR!
Isn't it cute?
COME ON NOW...JUST GET IN! ♡
ISN'T HE TOO TALL TO EVEN FIT IN THERE...?
...SIGH...
WAIT...WHAT AM I DOING? SHOULD I REALLY JUST LET AKIHA SWEEP ME AWAY LIKE THIS?
I know he's harmless, but...
What's wrong?
WHY DO YOU LOOK SO SERIOUS?

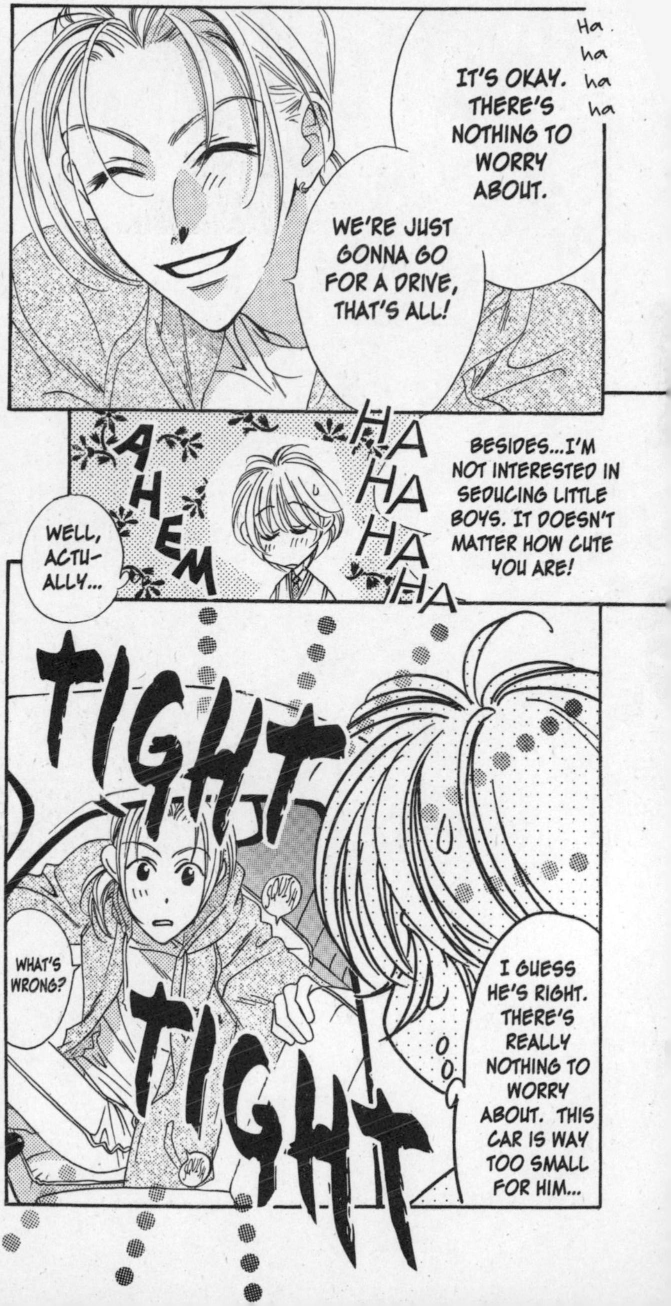
Ha ha ha ha
IT'S OKAY. THERE'S NOTHING TO WORRY ABOUT.
WE'RE JUST GONNA GO FOR A DRIVE, THAT'S ALL!
BESIDES...I'M NOT INTERESTED IN SEDUCING LITTLE BOYS. IT DOESN'T MATTER HOW CUTE YOU ARE!
HA HA HA HA HA
AHEM
WELL, ACTU-ALLY...
I GUESS HE'S RIGHT. THERE'S REALLY NOTHING TO WORRY ABOUT. THIS CAR IS WAY TOO SMALL FOR HIM...
TIGHT
SQUISH
WHAT'S WRONG?
TIGHT
SQUISH

WHISPERED SECRETS

THINGS I'M LOOKING FOR

THERE'S A MOVIE I SAW ON TV A LONG TIME AGO, BUT I CAN'T REMEMBER THE NAME. IT'S ABOUT A BEAUTIFUL LITTLE GIRL WHO COMMITS THESE HORRIBLE CRIMES, AND WHEN HER COUSIN FINDS OUT WHAT SHE'S DONE, SHE SETS HER UP AND TAKES REVENGE. I KNOW, IT'S SUCH A SIMPLE STORY, BUT I REALLY WANT TO SEE IT AGAIN... ANOTHER THING I'M LOOKING FOR IS A SONG TITLED "PILENTZE PEE" (OR MAYBE THAT'S THE TITLE OF THE ALBUM?) BY "BULGARIA VOICE." SEEMS LIKE IT'S OUT OF PRINT, AND I CAN'T FIND IT ANYWHERE... WAAH! IF ANYBODY CAN HELP, PLEASE LET ME KNOW!

I'm begging! Please! Please!

I'm really trying to dig up that "Bulgaria Voice" record. I've been looking all over the place!

Actually, I'm looking for anything related to "Bulgaria Voice".

THE RECORD NUMBER IS NIPPON COLUMBIA 304-1922.

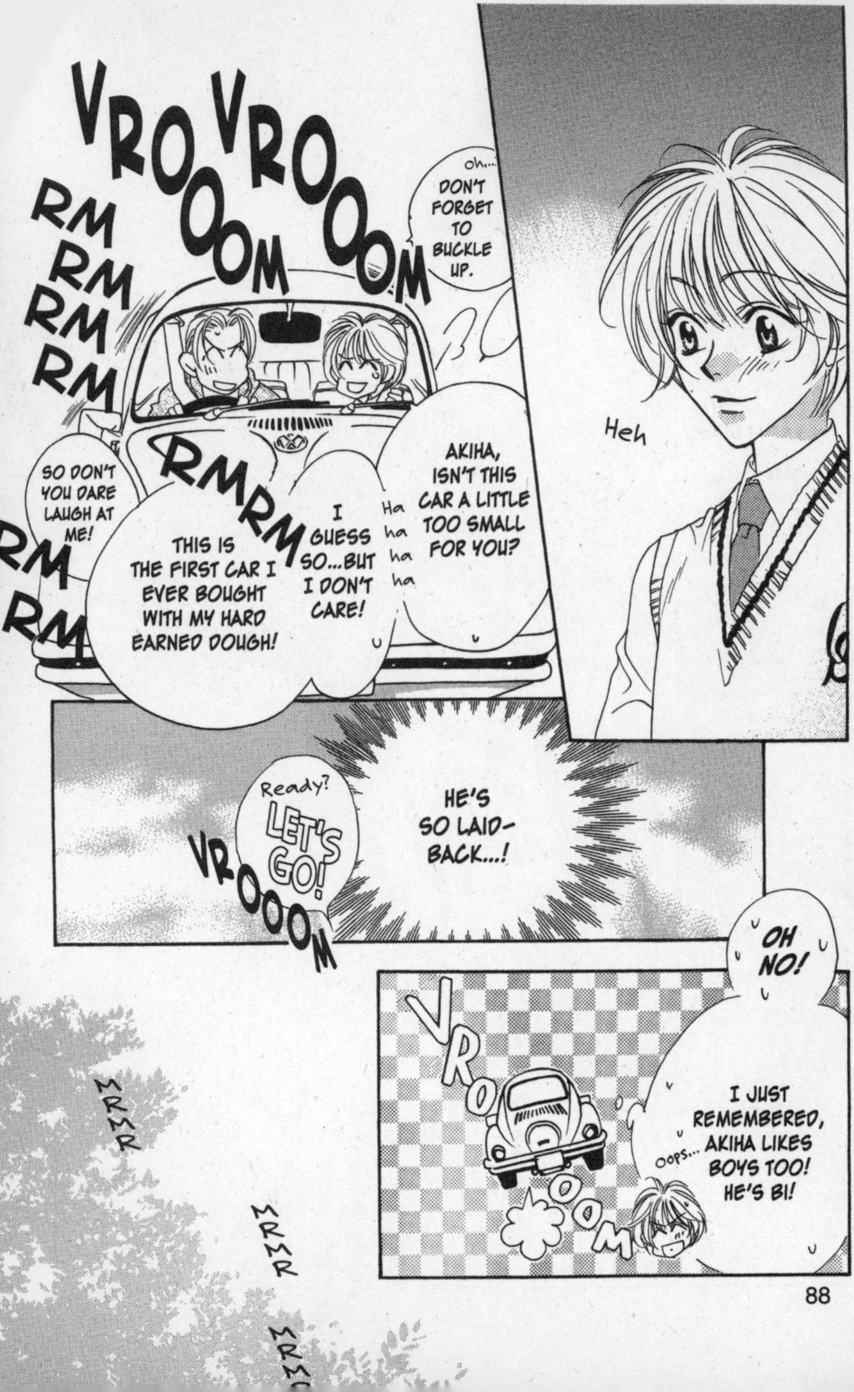
Heh
oh... DON'T FORGET TO BUCKLE UP.
VROOOM VROOOOM
AKIHA, ISN'T THIS CAR A LITTLE TOO SMALL FOR YOU?
Ha ha ha ha
I GUESS SO...BUT I DON'T CARE!
THIS IS THE FIRST CAR I EVER BOUGHT WITH MY HARD EARNED DOUGH!
SO DON'T YOU DARE LAUGH AT ME!
RMRM
RM RM RM RM RM RM
HE'S SO LAID-BACK...!
Ready? LET'S GO!
VROOOOM
OH NO!
I JUST REMEMBERED, AKIHA LIKES BOYS TOO! HE'S BI!
Oops...
VROOOOM
MRMR
MRMR
MRMR

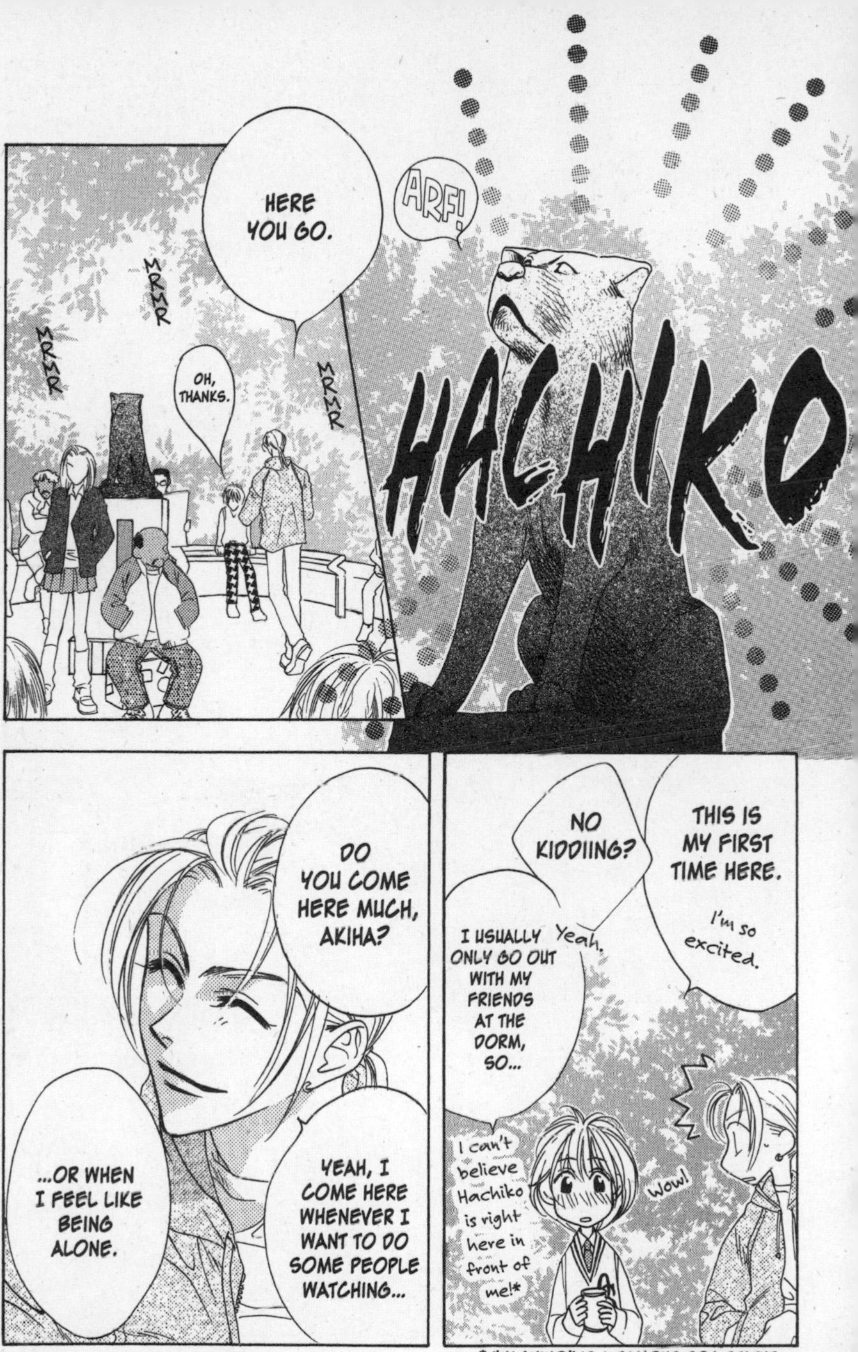
ARF!
HACHIKO
HERE YOU GO.
MRMR
MRMR
OH, THANKS.
MRMR
THIS IS MY FIRST TIME HERE.
I'm so excited.
NO KIDDIING?
Yeah.
I USUALLY ONLY GO OUT WITH MY FRIENDS AT THE DORM, SO...
Wow!
I can't believe Hachiko is right here in front of me!*
DO YOU COME HERE MUCH, AKIHA?
YEAH, I COME HERE WHENEVER I WANT TO DO SOME PEOPLE WATCHING...
...OR WHEN I FEEL LIKE BEING ALONE.

* "HACHIKO" IS A FAMOUS DOG STATUE IN FRONT OF TOKYO'S SHIBUYA STATION. IT'S A POPULAR MEETING PLACE.

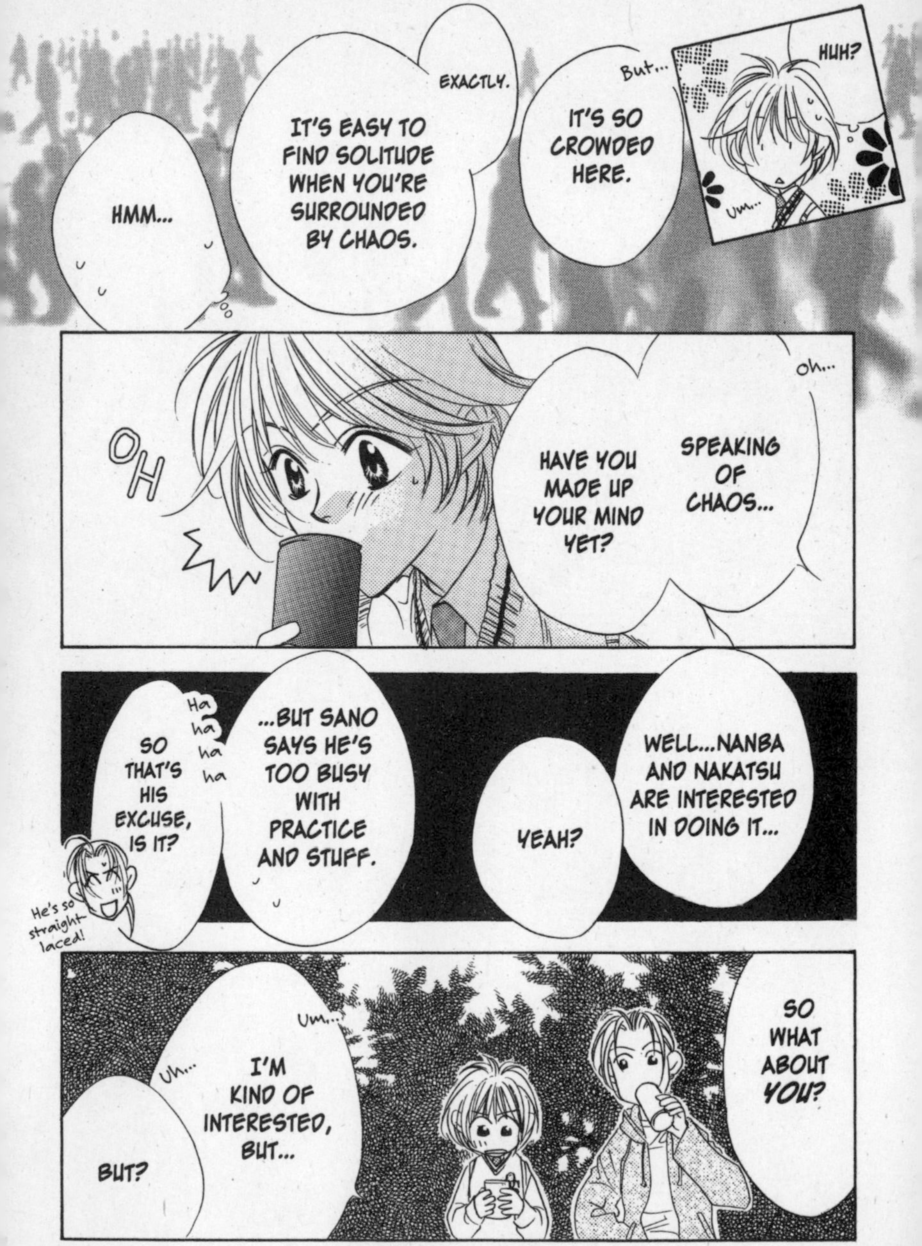
HUH?
Um...
But...
IT'S SO CROWDED HERE.
EXACTLY.
IT'S EASY TO FIND SOLITUDE WHEN YOU'RE SURROUNDED BY CHAOS.
HMM...
Oh...
SPEAKING OF CHAOS...
HAVE YOU MADE UP YOUR MIND YET?
OH
WELL...NANBA AND NAKATSU ARE INTERESTED IN DOING IT...
YEAH?
...BUT SANO SAYS HE'S TOO BUSY WITH PRACTICE AND STUFF.
Ha ha ha ha
SO THAT'S HIS EXCUSE, IS IT?
He's so straight-laced!
SO WHAT ABOUT *YOU?*
Um...
I'M KIND OF INTERESTED, BUT...
Uh...
BUT?

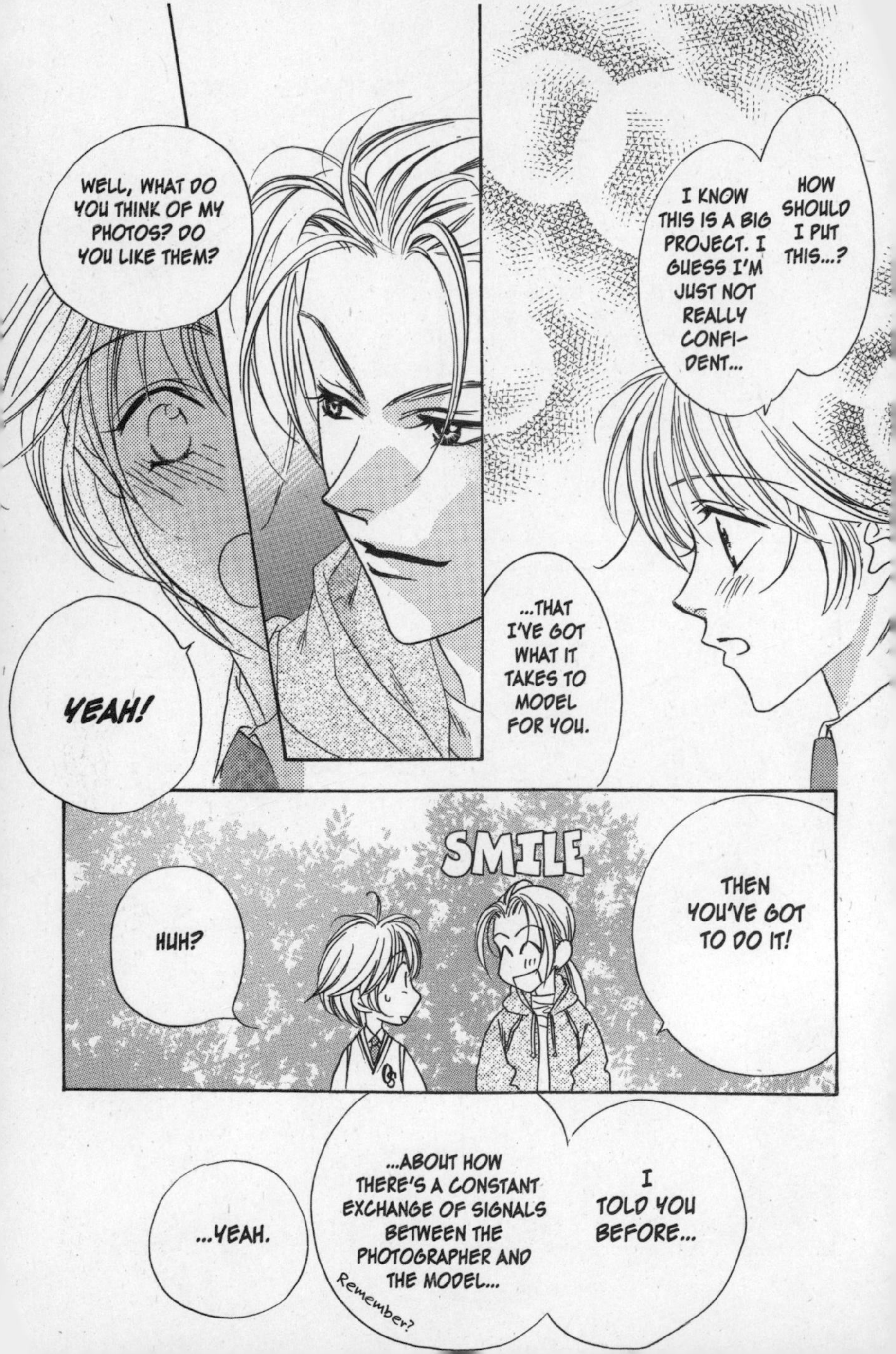
HOW SHOULD I PUT THIS...?
I KNOW THIS IS A BIG PROJECT. I GUESS I'M JUST NOT REALLY CONFI-DENT...
...THAT I'VE GOT WHAT IT TAKES TO MODEL FOR YOU.
WELL, WHAT DO YOU THINK OF MY PHOTOS? DO YOU LIKE THEM?
YEAH!
THEN YOU'VE GOT TO DO IT!
SMILE
HUH?
I TOLD YOU BEFORE...
...ABOUT HOW THERE'S A CONSTANT EXCHANGE OF SIGNALS BETWEEN THE PHOTOGRAPHER AND THE MODEL...
Remember?
...YEAH.

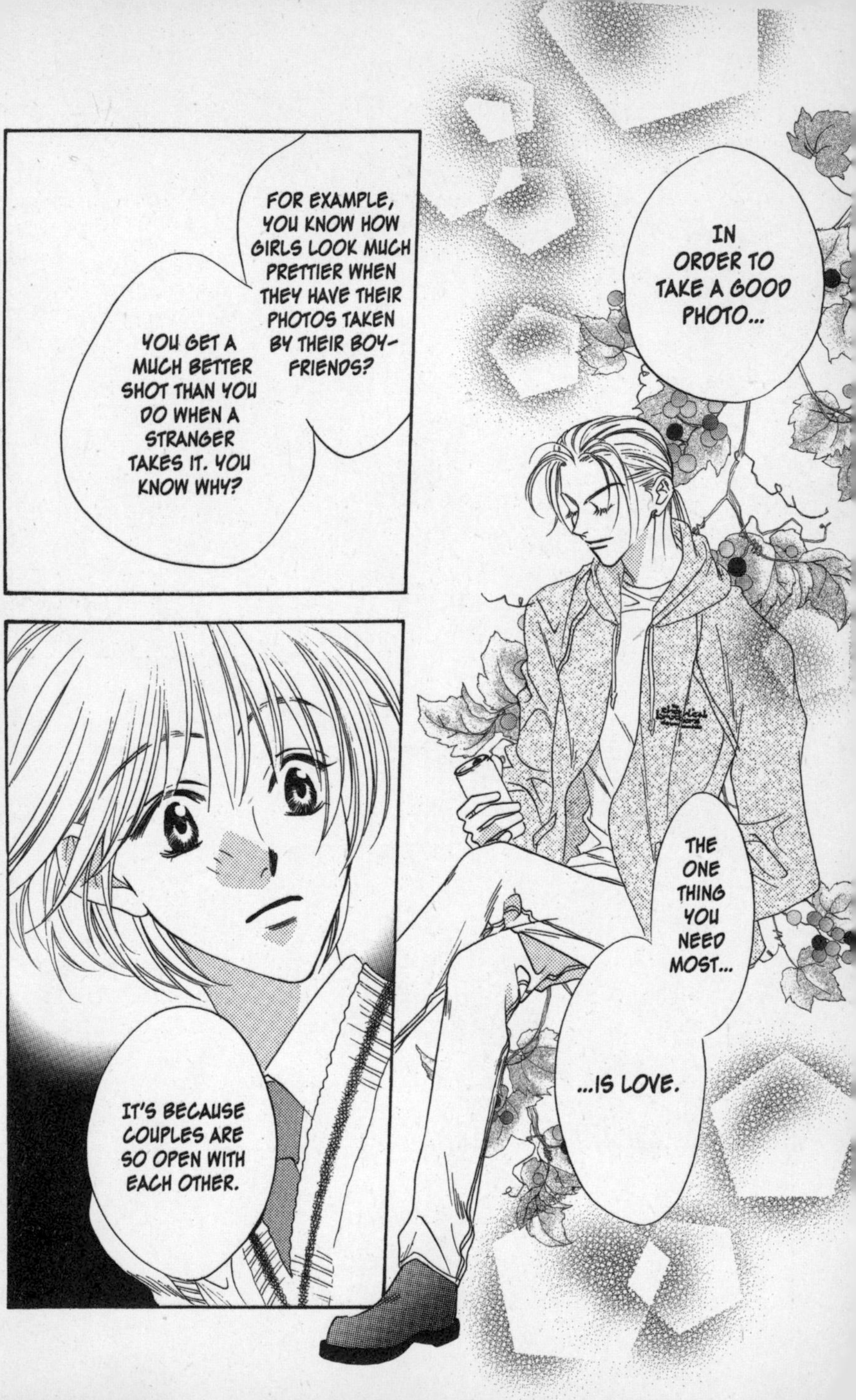
IN ORDER TO TAKE A GOOD PHOTO...
THE ONE THING YOU NEED MOST...
...IS LOVE.
FOR EXAMPLE, YOU KNOW HOW GIRLS LOOK MUCH PRETTIER WHEN THEY HAVE THEIR PHOTOS TAKEN BY THEIR BOY-FRIENDS?
YOU GET A MUCH BETTER SHOT THAN YOU DO WHEN A STRANGER TAKES IT. YOU KNOW WHY?
IT'S BECAUSE COUPLES ARE SO OPEN WITH EACH OTHER.

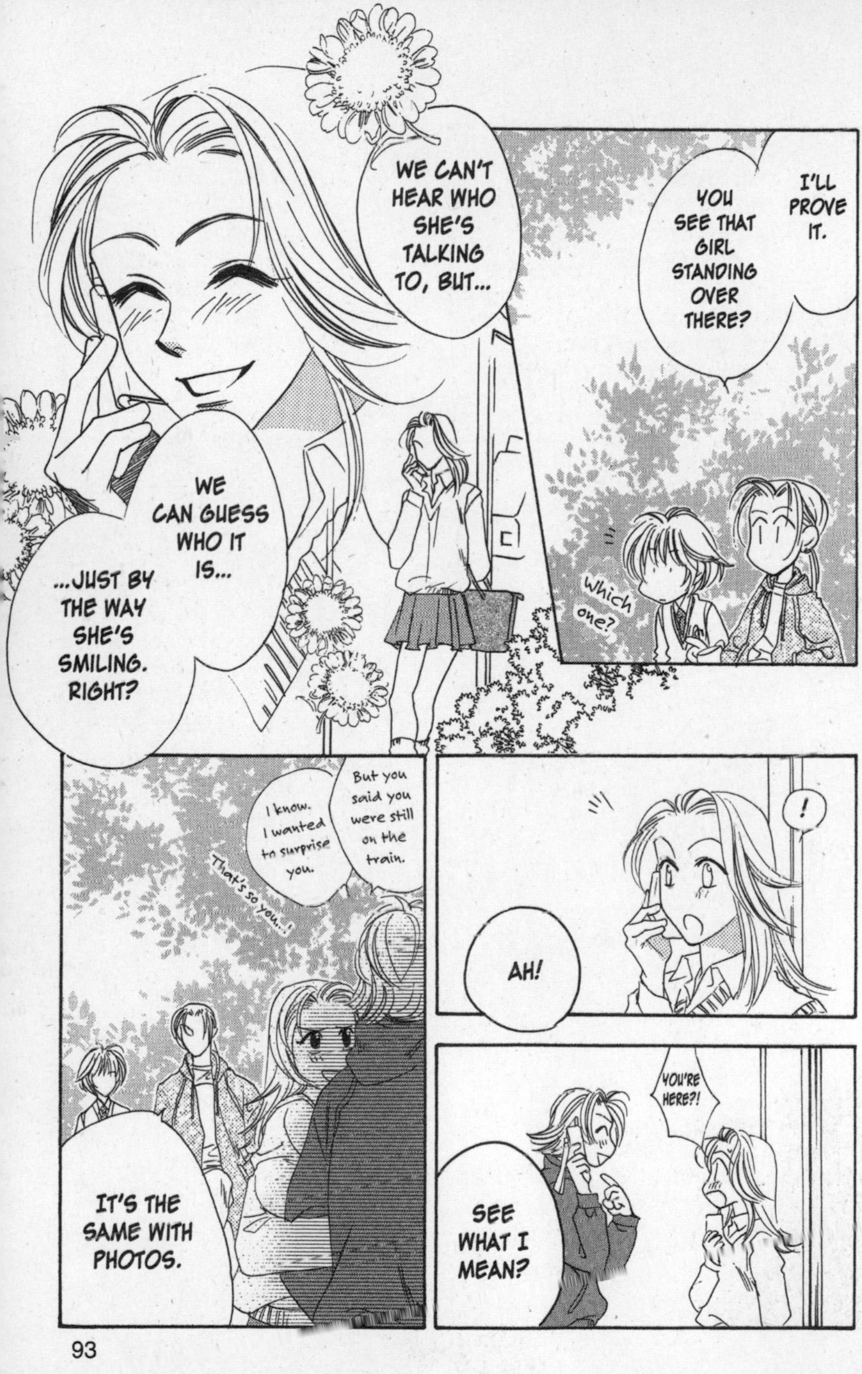
I'LL PROVE IT.
YOU SEE THAT GIRL STANDING OVER THERE?
Which one?
WE CAN'T HEAR WHO SHE'S TALKING TO, BUT...
WE CAN GUESS WHO IT IS...
...JUST BY THE WAY SHE'S SMILING. RIGHT?
!
AH!
YOU'RE HERE?!
SEE WHAT I MEAN?
But you said you were still on the train.
I know. I wanted to surprise you.
That's so you...!
IT'S THE SAME WITH PHOTOS.

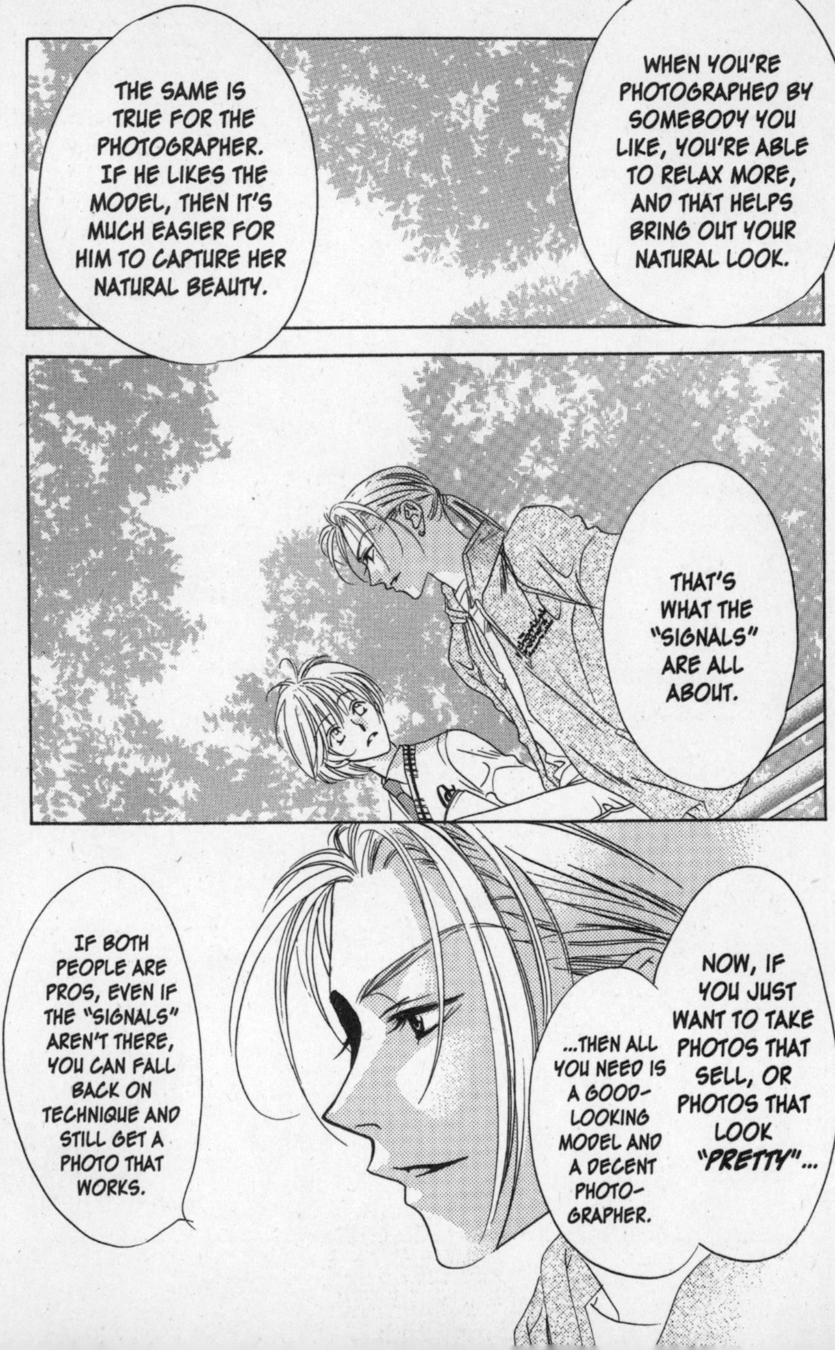
WHEN YOU'RE PHOTOGRAPHED BY SOMEBODY YOU LIKE, YOU'RE ABLE TO RELAX MORE, AND THAT HELPS BRING OUT YOUR NATURAL LOOK.
THE SAME IS TRUE FOR THE PHOTOGRAPHER. IF HE LIKES THE MODEL, THEN IT'S MUCH EASIER FOR HIM TO CAPTURE HER NATURAL BEAUTY.
THAT'S WHAT THE "SIGNALS" ARE ALL ABOUT.
NOW, IF YOU JUST WANT TO TAKE PHOTOS THAT SELL, OR PHOTOS THAT LOOK "*PRETTY*"...
...THEN ALL YOU NEED IS A GOOD-LOOKING MODEL AND A DECENT PHOTO-GRAPHER.
IF BOTH PEOPLE ARE PROS, EVEN IF THE "SIGNALS" AREN'T THERE, YOU CAN FALL BACK ON TECHNIQUE AND STILL GET A PHOTO THAT WORKS.

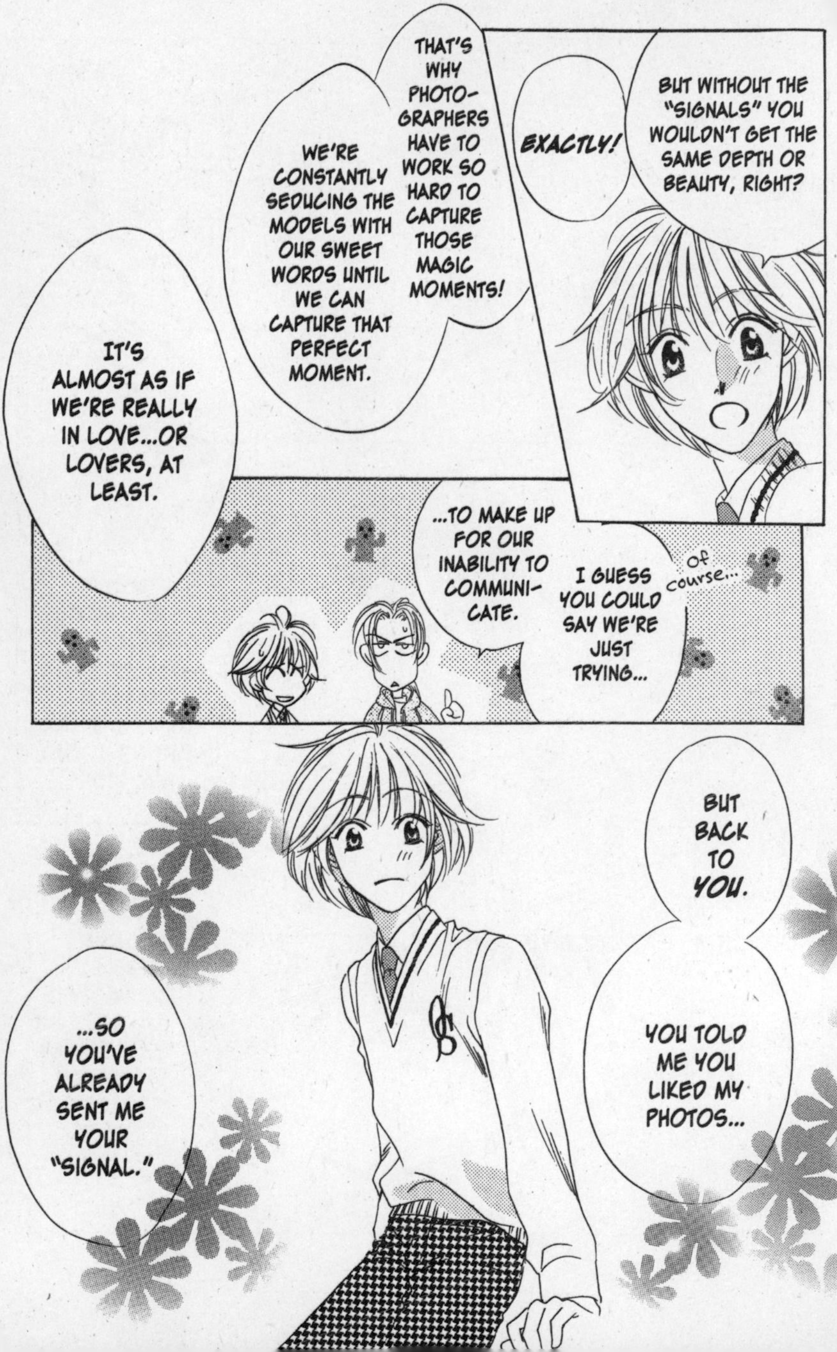
BUT WITHOUT THE "SIGNALS" YOU WOULDN'T GET THE SAME DEPTH OR BEAUTY, RIGHT?
EXACTLY!
THAT'S WHY PHOTOGRAPHERS HAVE TO WORK SO HARD TO CAPTURE THOSE MAGIC MOMENTS!
WE'RE CONSTANTLY SEDUCING THE MODELS WITH OUR SWEET WORDS UNTIL WE CAN CAPTURE THAT PERFECT MOMENT.
IT'S ALMOST AS IF WE'RE REALLY IN LOVE...OR LOVERS, AT LEAST.
I GUESS YOU COULD SAY WE'RE JUST TRYING...
Of course...
...TO MAKE UP FOR OUR INABILITY TO COMMUNICATE.
BUT BACK TO YOU.
YOU TOLD ME YOU LIKED MY PHOTOS...
...SO YOU'VE ALREADY SENT ME YOUR "SIGNAL."

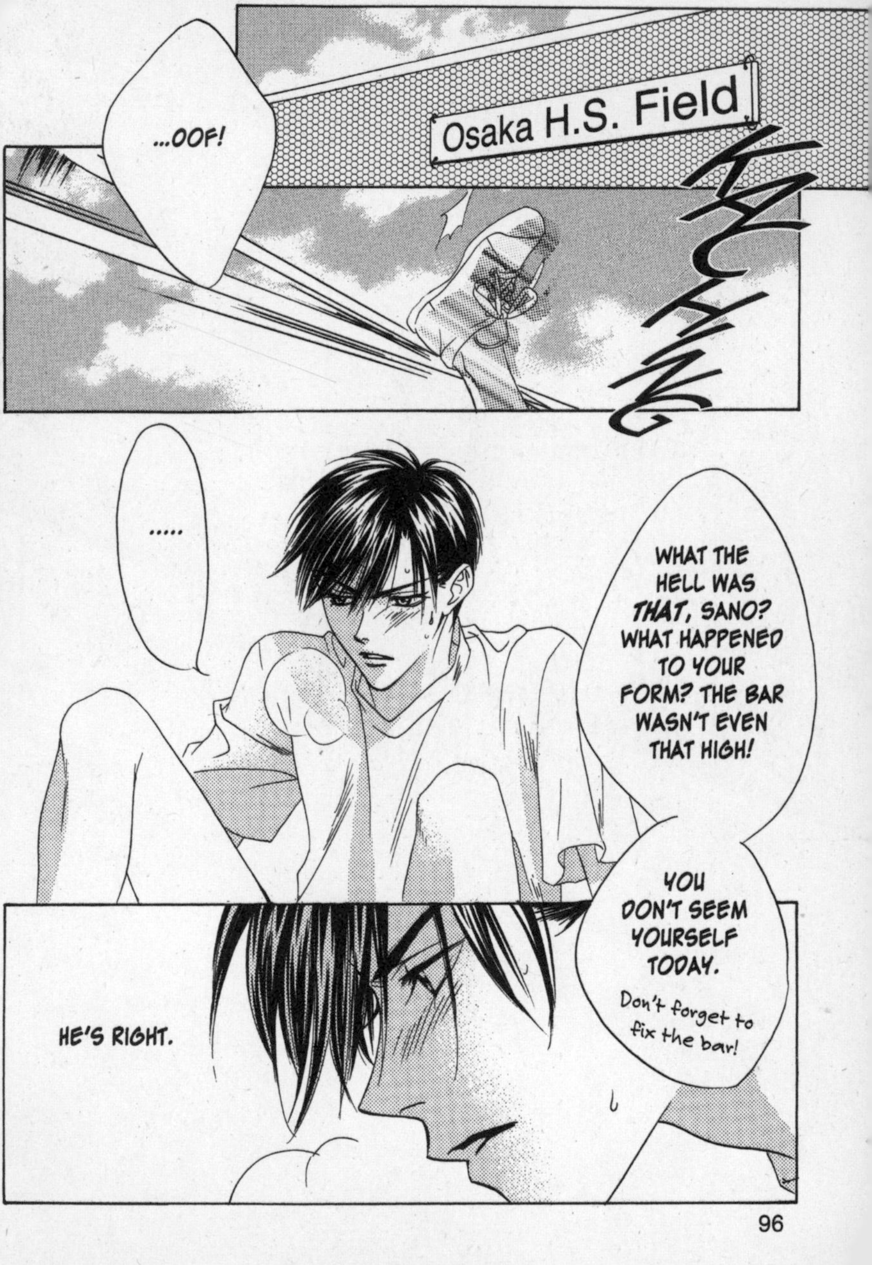
Osaka H.S. Field
KACHING
...OOF!
WHAT THE HELL WAS THAT, SANO? WHAT HAPPENED TO YOUR FORM? THE BAR WASN'T EVEN THAT HIGH!
.....
YOU DON'T SEEM YOURSELF TODAY.
Don't forget to fix the bar!
HE'S RIGHT.

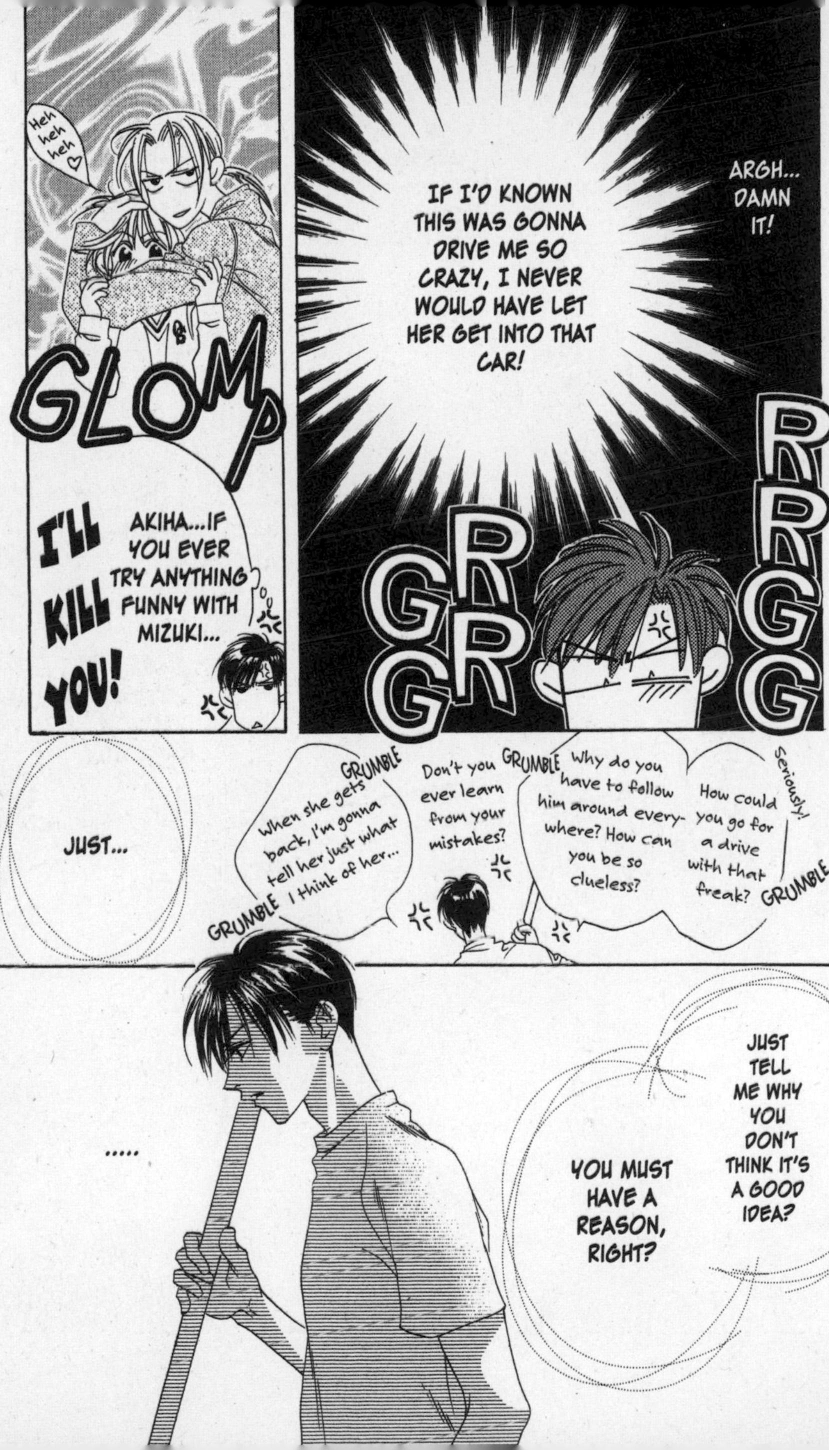

ARGH... DAMN IT!
IF I'D KNOWN THIS WAS GONNA DRIVE ME SO CRAZY, I NEVER WOULD HAVE LET HER GET INTO THAT CAR!
RRRGG
GRRGRG
Heh heh heh ♡
GLOMP
AKIHA...IF YOU EVER TRY ANYTHING FUNNY WITH MIZUKI...
I'LL KILL YOU!
Seriously!
How could you go for a drive with that freak?
GRUMBLE
Why do you have to follow him around every-where? How can you be so clueless?
GRUMBLE
Don't you ever learn from your mistakes?
GRUMBLE
When she gets back, I'm gonna tell her just what I think of her...
GRUMBLE
JUST...
JUST TELL ME WHY YOU DON'T THINK IT'S A GOOD IDEA?
YOU MUST HAVE A REASON, RIGHT?
.....

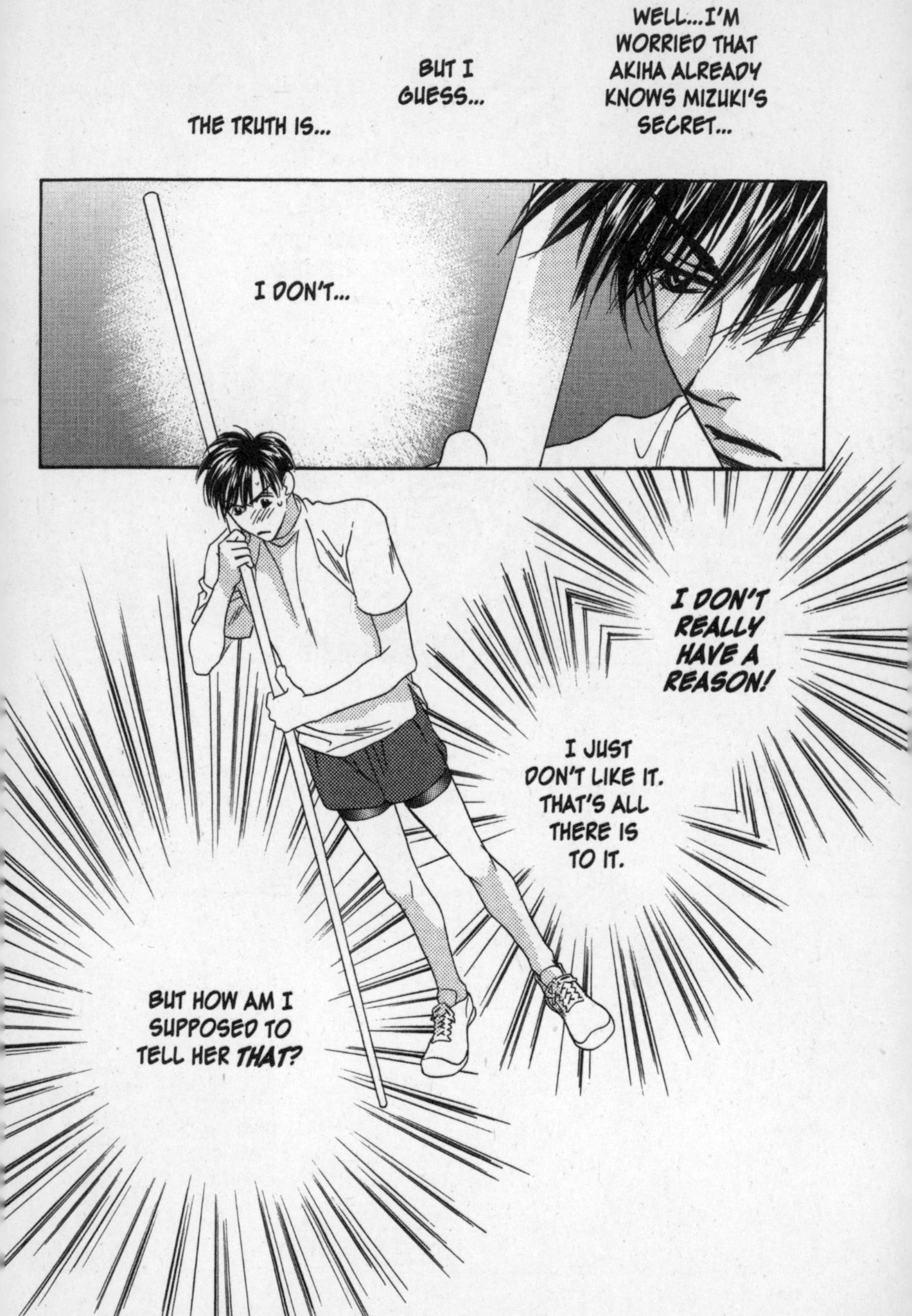
WELL...I'M WORRIED THAT AKIHA ALREADY KNOWS MIZUKI'S SECRET...
BUT I GUESS...
THE TRUTH IS...
I DON'T...
I DON'T REALLY HAVE A REASON!
I JUST DON'T LIKE IT. THAT'S ALL THERE IS TO IT.
BUT HOW AM I SUPPOSED TO TELL HER *THAT*?

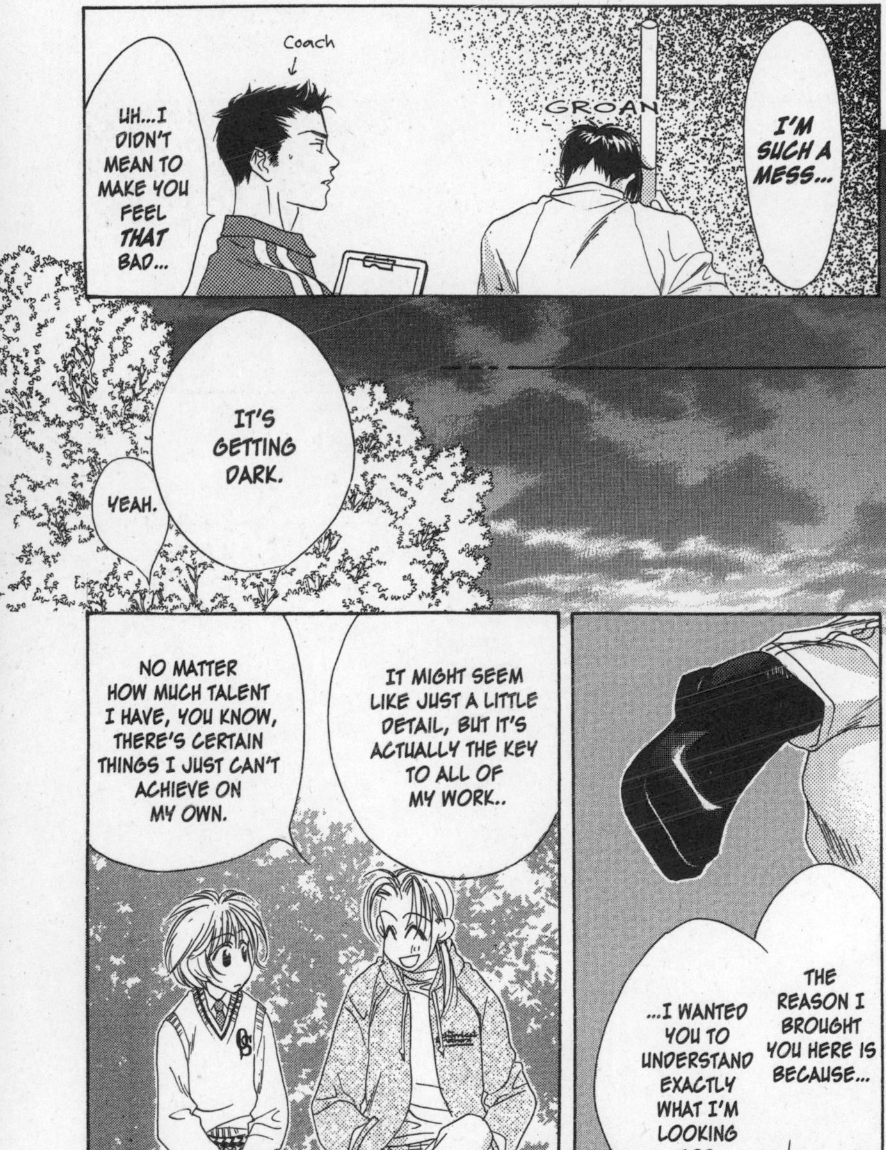
I'M SUCH A MESS...
GROAN
Coach
UH...I DIDN'T MEAN TO MAKE YOU FEEL *THAT* BAD...
IT'S GETTING DARK.
YEAH.
THE REASON I BROUGHT YOU HERE IS BECAUSE...
...I WANTED YOU TO UNDERSTAND EXACTLY WHAT I'M LOOKING FOR.
IT MIGHT SEEM LIKE JUST A LITTLE DETAIL, BUT IT'S ACTUALLY THE KEY TO ALL OF MY WORK..
NO MATTER HOW MUCH TALENT I HAVE, YOU KNOW, THERE'S CERTAIN THINGS I JUST CAN'T ACHIEVE ON MY OWN.

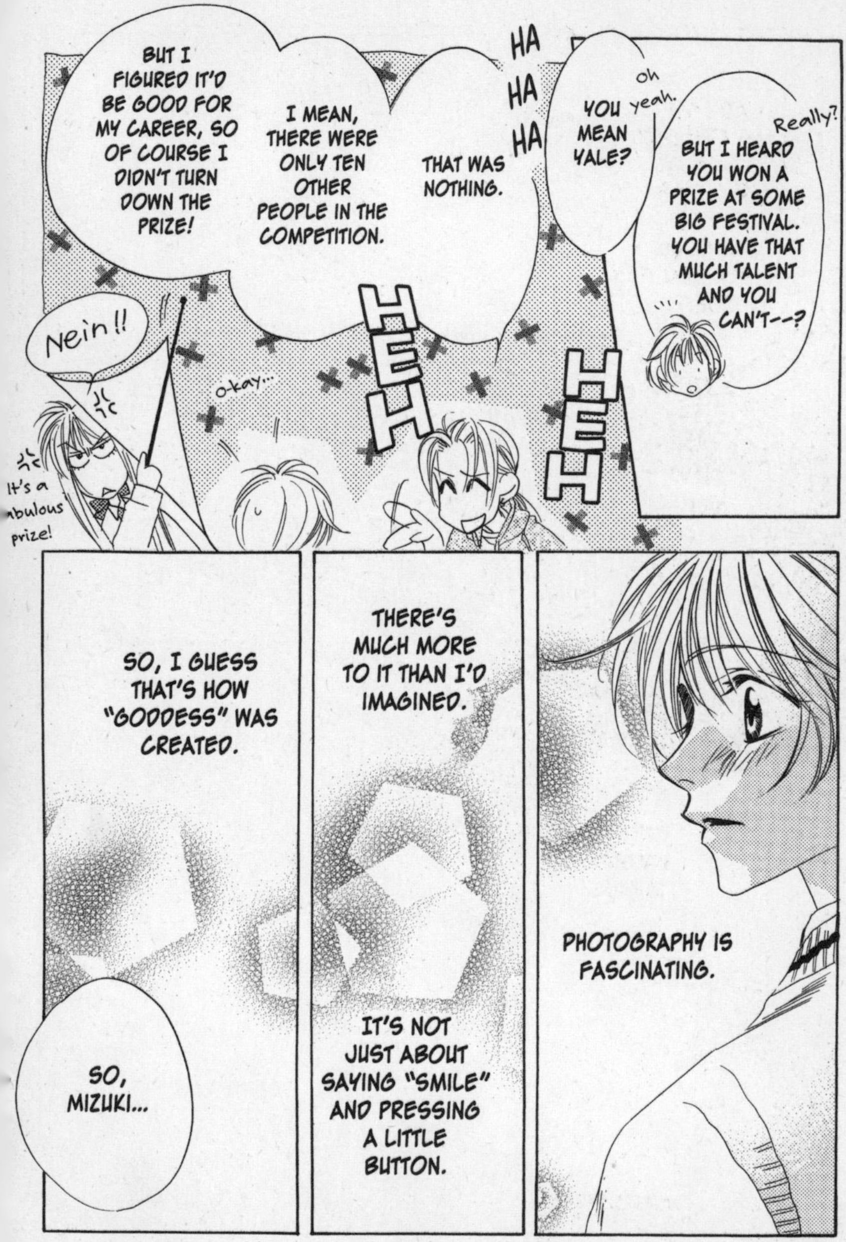
Really?
BUT I HEARD YOU WON A PRIZE AT SOME BIG FESTIVAL. YOU HAVE THAT MUCH TALENT AND YOU CAN'T--?
Oh yeah.
YOU MEAN YALE?
HA HA HA
THAT WAS NOTHING.
I MEAN, THERE WERE ONLY TEN OTHER PEOPLE IN THE COMPETITION.
BUT I FIGURED IT'D BE GOOD FOR MY CAREER, SO OF COURSE I DIDN'T TURN DOWN THE PRIZE!
HEH HEH
HEH HEH
o-kay...
Nein!!
It's a abulous prize!
PHOTOGRAPHY IS FASCINATING.
THERE'S MUCH MORE TO IT THAN I'D IMAGINED.
IT'S NOT JUST ABOUT SAYING "SMILE" AND PRESSING A LITTLE BUTTON.
SO, I GUESS THAT'S HOW "GODDESS" WAS CREATED.
SO, MIZUKI...

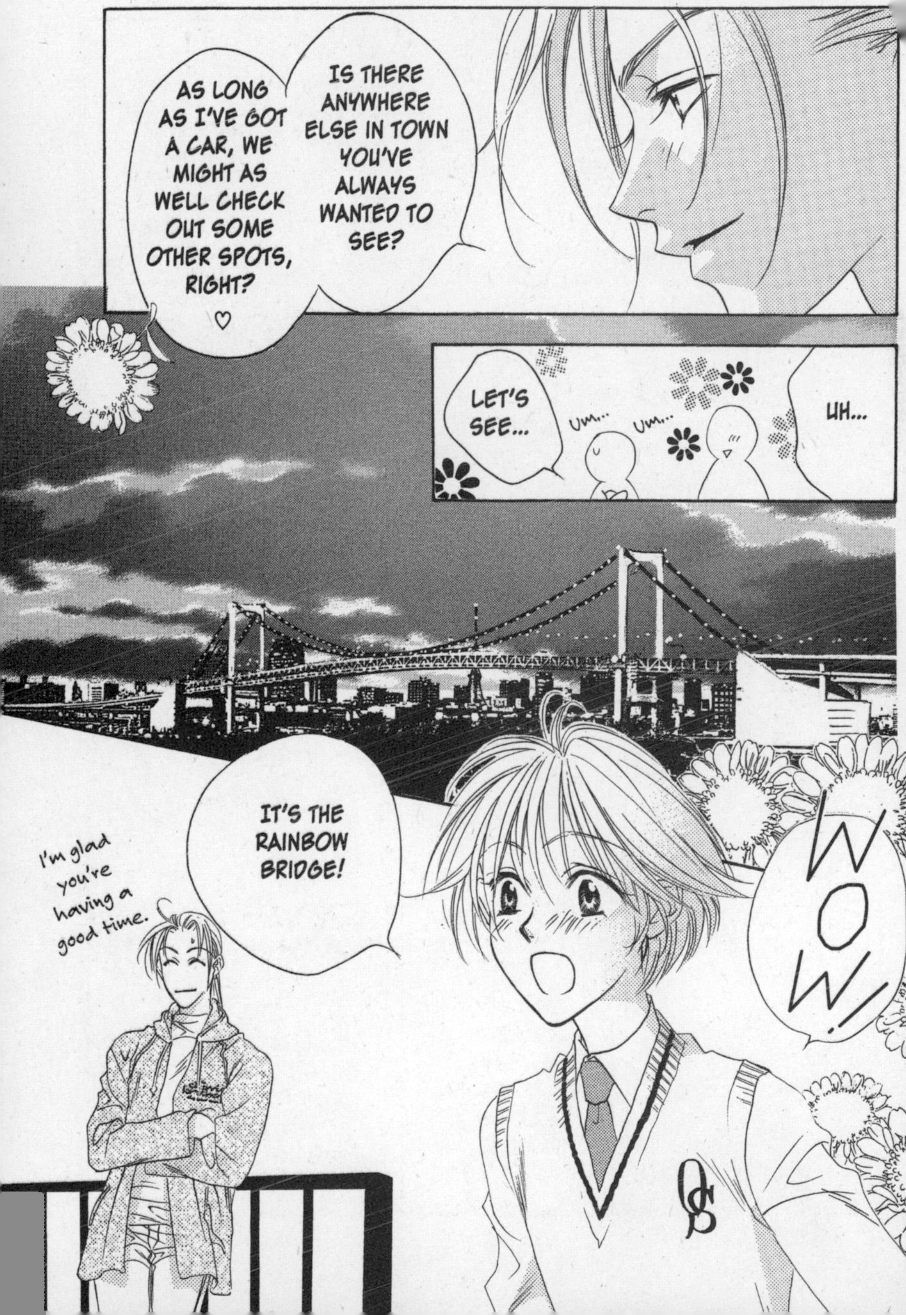
IS THERE ANYWHERE ELSE IN TOWN YOU'VE ALWAYS WANTED TO SEE?
AS LONG AS I'VE GOT A CAR, WE MIGHT AS WELL CHECK OUT SOME OTHER SPOTS, RIGHT? ♡
UH...
Um...
Um...
LET'S SEE...
WOW!
IT'S THE RAINBOW BRIDGE!
I'm glad you're having a good time.

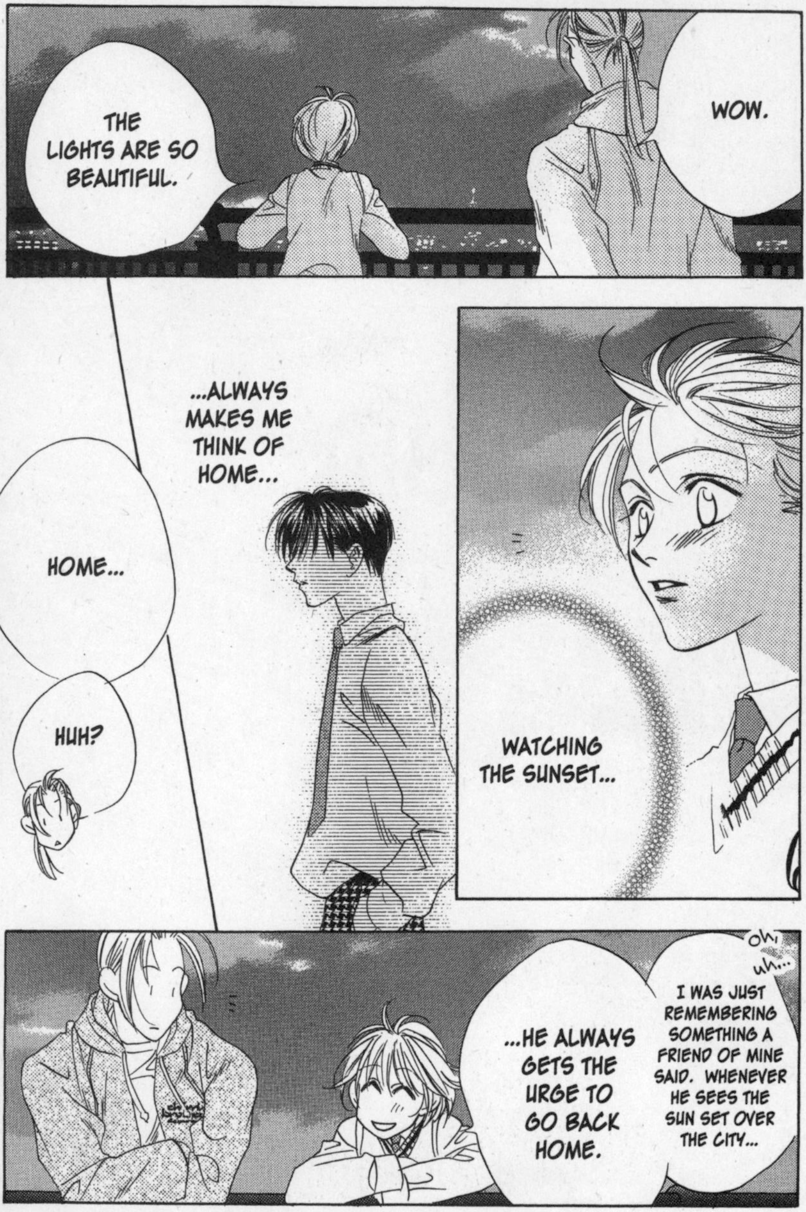
WOW.
THE LIGHTS ARE SO BEAUTIFUL.
WATCHING THE SUNSET...
...ALWAYS MAKES ME THINK OF HOME...
HOME...
HUH?
oh, uh...
I WAS JUST REMEMBERING SOMETHING A FRIEND OF MINE SAID. WHENEVER HE SEES THE SUN SET OVER THE CITY...
...HE ALWAYS GETS THE URGE TO GO BACK HOME.

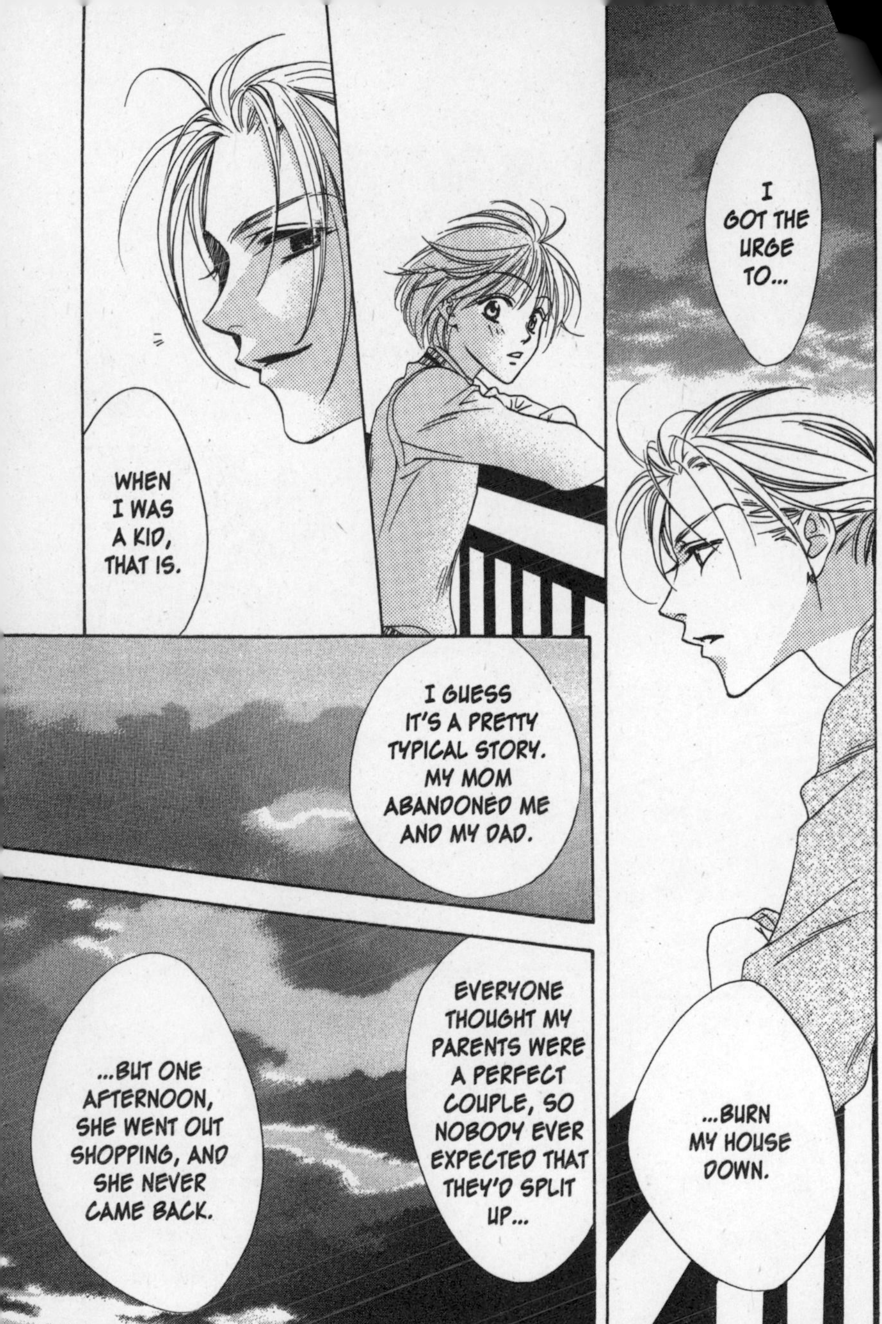
I GOT THE URGE TO...
...BURN MY HOUSE DOWN.
WHEN I WAS A KID, THAT IS.
I GUESS IT'S A PRETTY TYPICAL STORY. MY MOM ABANDONED ME AND MY DAD.
EVERYONE THOUGHT MY PARENTS WERE A PERFECT COUPLE, SO NOBODY EVER EXPECTED THAT THEY'D SPLIT UP...
...BUT ONE AFTERNOON, SHE WENT OUT SHOPPING, AND SHE NEVER CAME BACK.

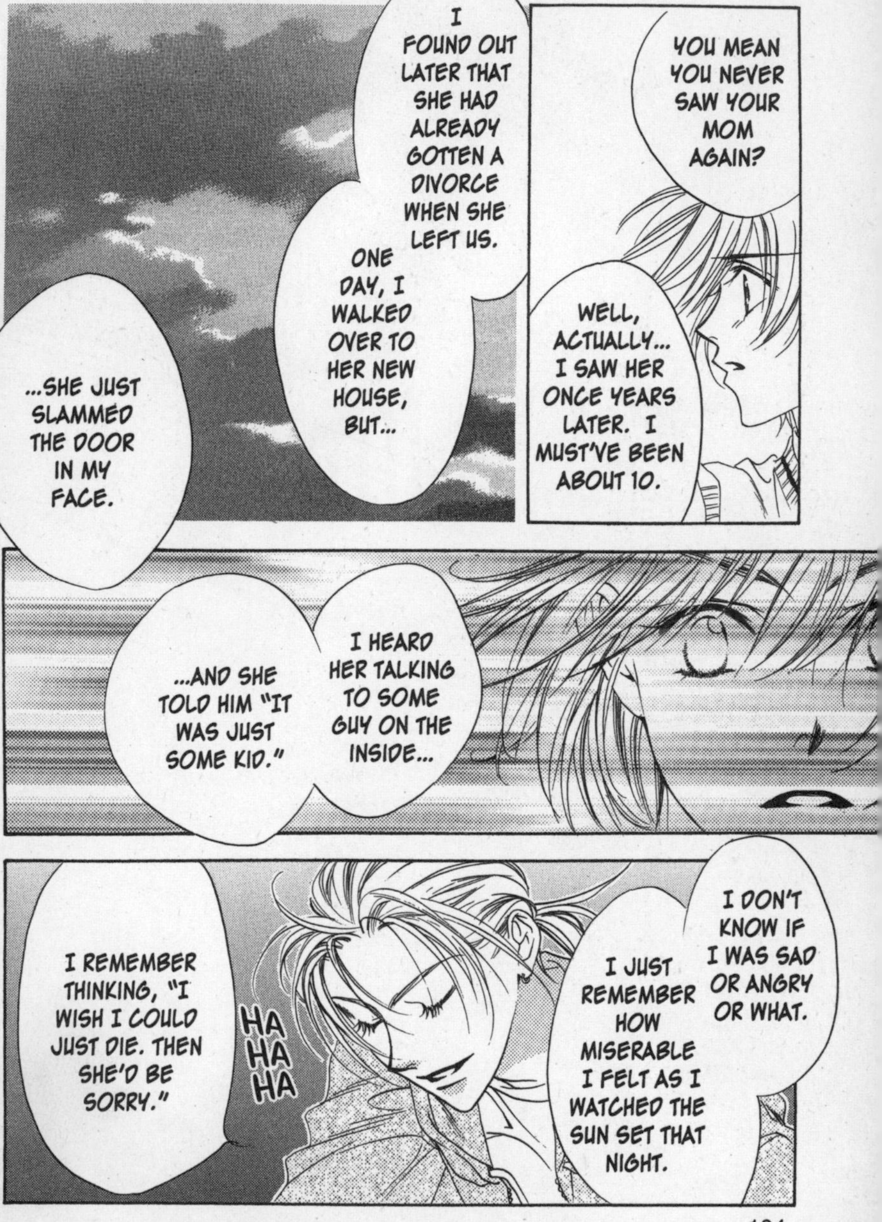
YOU MEAN YOU NEVER SAW YOUR MOM AGAIN?
WELL, ACTUALLY... I SAW HER ONCE YEARS LATER. I MUST'VE BEEN ABOUT 10.
I FOUND OUT LATER THAT SHE HAD ALREADY GOTTEN A DIVORCE WHEN SHE LEFT US.
ONE DAY, I WALKED OVER TO HER NEW HOUSE, BUT...
...SHE JUST SLAMMED THE DOOR IN MY FACE.
I HEARD HER TALKING TO SOME GUY ON THE INSIDE...
...AND SHE TOLD HIM "IT WAS JUST SOME KID."
I DON'T KNOW IF I WAS SAD OR ANGRY OR WHAT.
I JUST REMEMBER HOW MISERABLE I FELT AS I WATCHED THE SUN SET THAT NIGHT.
HA HA HA
I REMEMBER THINKING, "I WISH I COULD JUST DIE. THEN SHE'D BE SORRY."

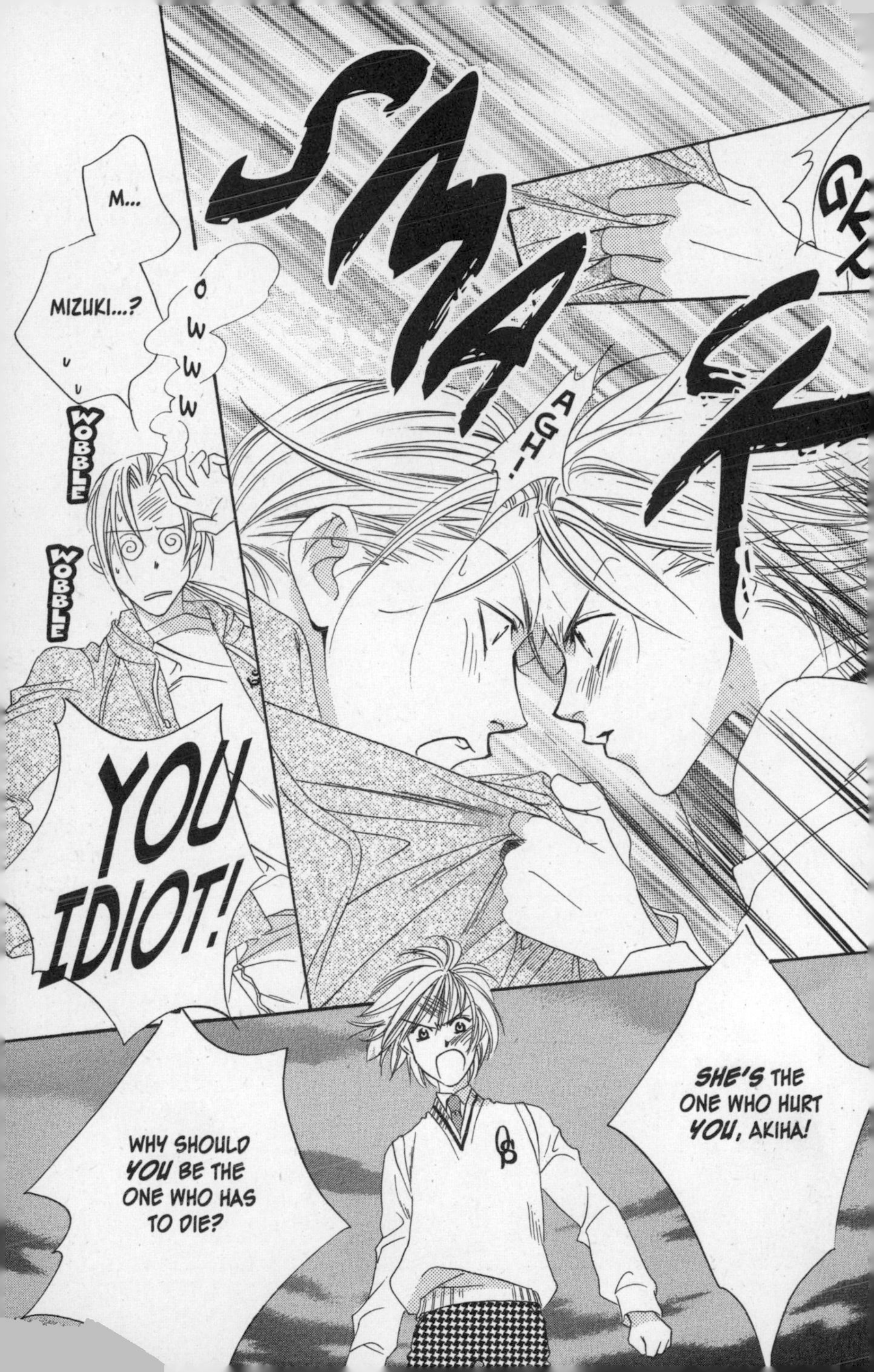

GK
SMACK
AGH!
M...
MIZUKI...?
OWWWW
WOBBLE
WOBBLE
YOU IDIOT!
SHE'S THE ONE WHO HURT ***YOU***, AKIHA!
WHY SHOULD ***YOU*** BE THE ONE WHO HAS TO DIE?

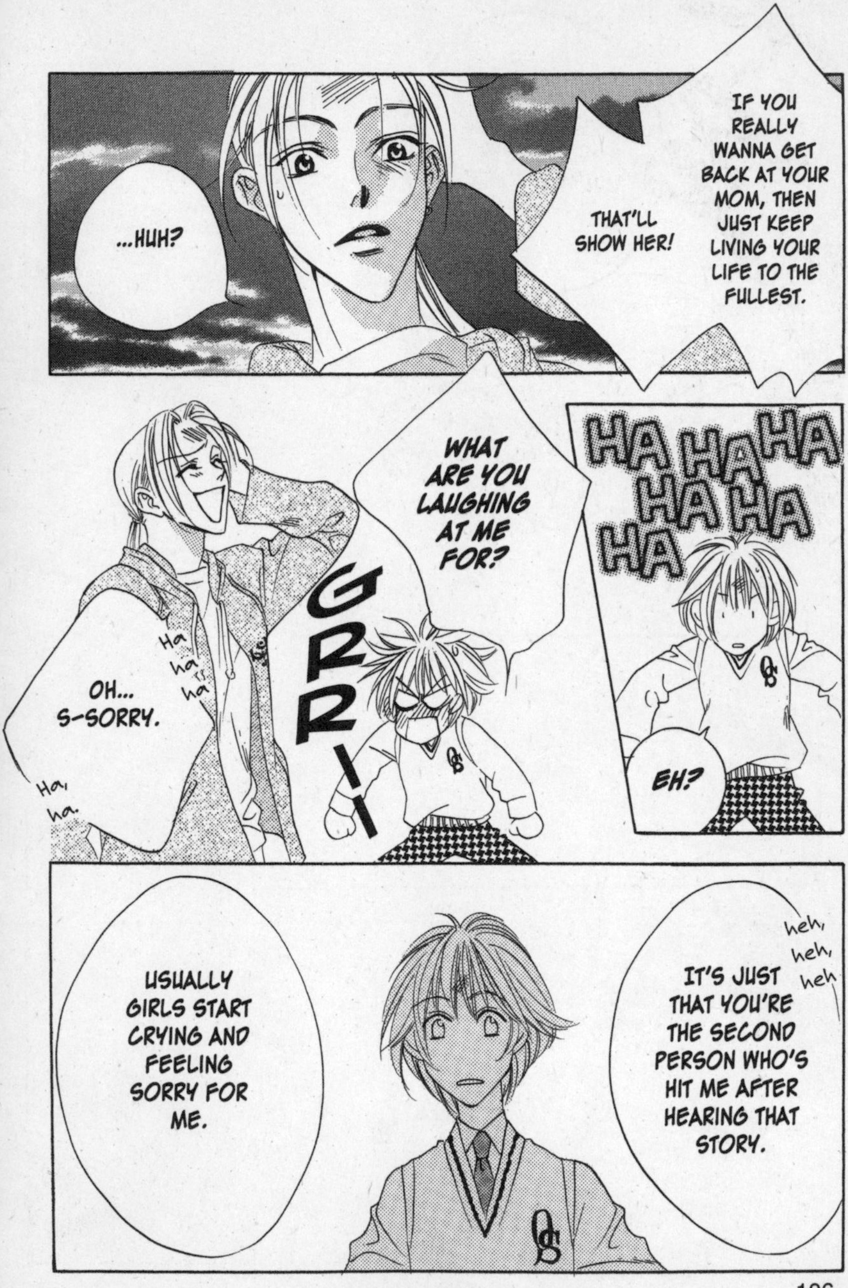
IF YOU REALLY WANNA GET BACK AT YOUR MOM, THEN JUST KEEP LIVING YOUR LIFE TO THE FULLEST.
THAT'LL SHOW HER!
...HUH?
HA HA HA HA HA HA
EH?
WHAT ARE YOU LAUGHING AT ME FOR?
GRR!!
Ha ha ha
OH... S-SORRY.
Ha, ha.
heh, heh, heh
IT'S JUST THAT YOU'RE THE SECOND PERSON WHO'S HIT ME AFTER HEARING THAT STORY.
USUALLY GIRLS START CRYING AND FEELING SORRY FOR ME.

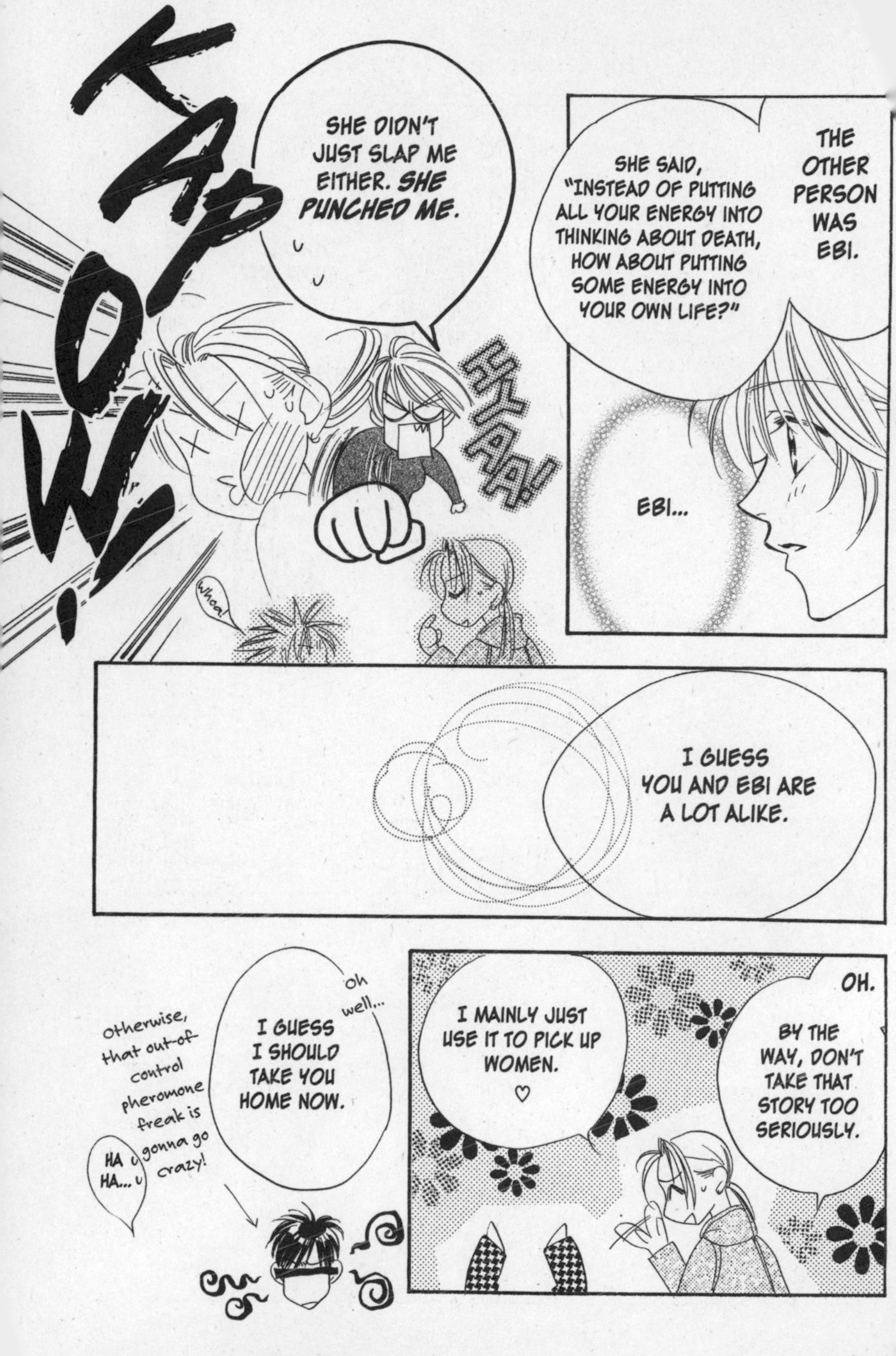
THE OTHER PERSON WAS EBI.
SHE SAID, "INSTEAD OF PUTTING ALL YOUR ENERGY INTO THINKING ABOUT DEATH, HOW ABOUT PUTTING SOME ENERGY INTO YOUR OWN LIFE?"
EBI...
KAPOW!!
SHE DIDN'T JUST SLAP ME EITHER. *SHE PUNCHED ME.*
HIYAA!
Whoa!
I GUESS YOU AND EBI ARE A LOT ALIKE.
OH.
BY THE WAY, DON'T TAKE THAT STORY TOO SERIOUSLY.
I MAINLY JUST USE IT TO PICK UP WOMEN. ♡
oh well...
I GUESS I SHOULD TAKE YOU HOME NOW.
Otherwise, that out-of-control pheromone freak is gonna go crazy!
HA HA...

* KEMI BRA=CHEMICAL BROTHERS, CIRCUS=THE CIRCUS, PUROJII=PRODIGY, RECCHIRI=RED HOT CHILI PEPPERS

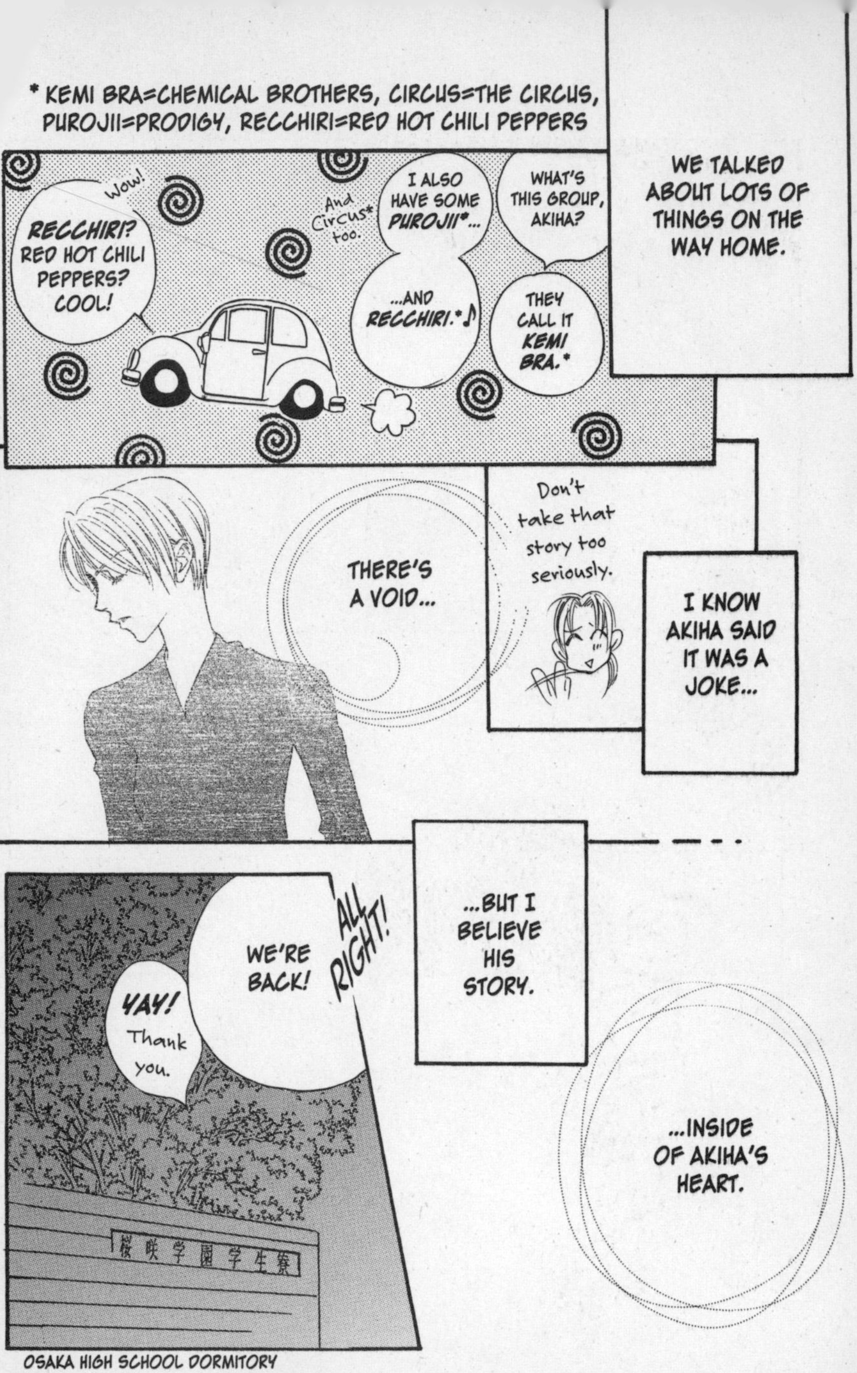
WE TALKED ABOUT LOTS OF THINGS ON THE WAY HOME.
WHAT'S THIS GROUP, AKIHA?
THEY CALL IT KEMI BRA.*
I ALSO HAVE SOME PUROJII*...
...AND RECCHIRI.*♪
And Circus* too.
Wow!
RECCHIRI? RED HOT CHILI PEPPERS? COOL!
I KNOW AKIHA SAID IT WAS A JOKE...
Don't take that story too seriously.
THERE'S A VOID...
...BUT I BELIEVE HIS STORY.
...INSIDE OF AKIHA'S HEART.
ALL RIGHT!
WE'RE BACK!
YAY! Thank you.
桜咲学園学生寮
OSAKA HIGH SCHOOL DORMITORY

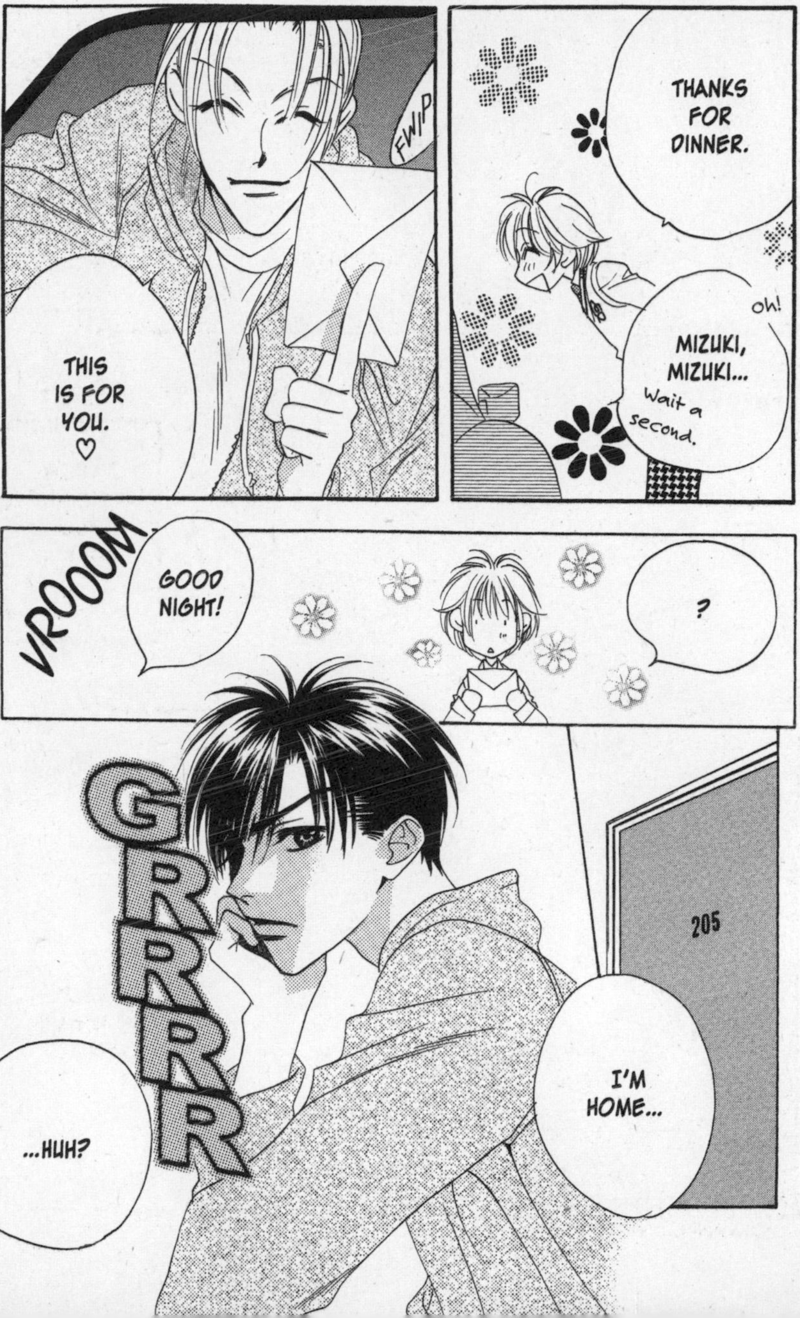
THANKS FOR DINNER.
Oh!
MIZUKI, MIZUKI... Wait a second.
FWIP
THIS IS FOR YOU. ♡
?
VROOOM
GOOD NIGHT!
205
I'M HOME...
GRRRR
...HUH?

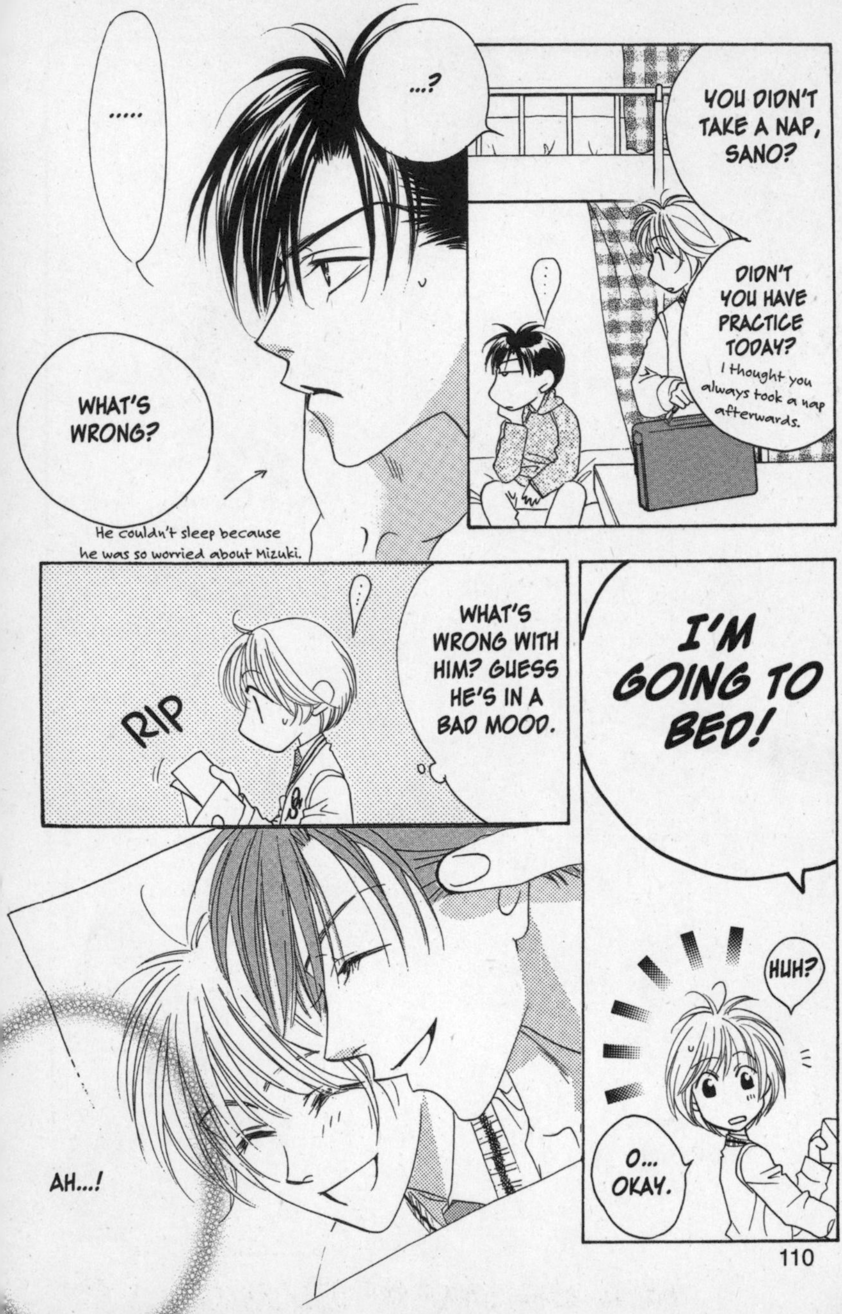
YOU DIDN'T TAKE A NAP, SANO?
DIDN'T YOU HAVE PRACTICE TODAY?
I thought you always took a nap afterwards.
...?
......
WHAT'S WRONG?
He couldn't sleep because he was so worried about Mizuki.
I'M GOING TO BED!
HUH?
O... OKAY.
WHAT'S WRONG WITH HIM? GUESS HE'S IN A BAD MOOD.
RIP
AH...!

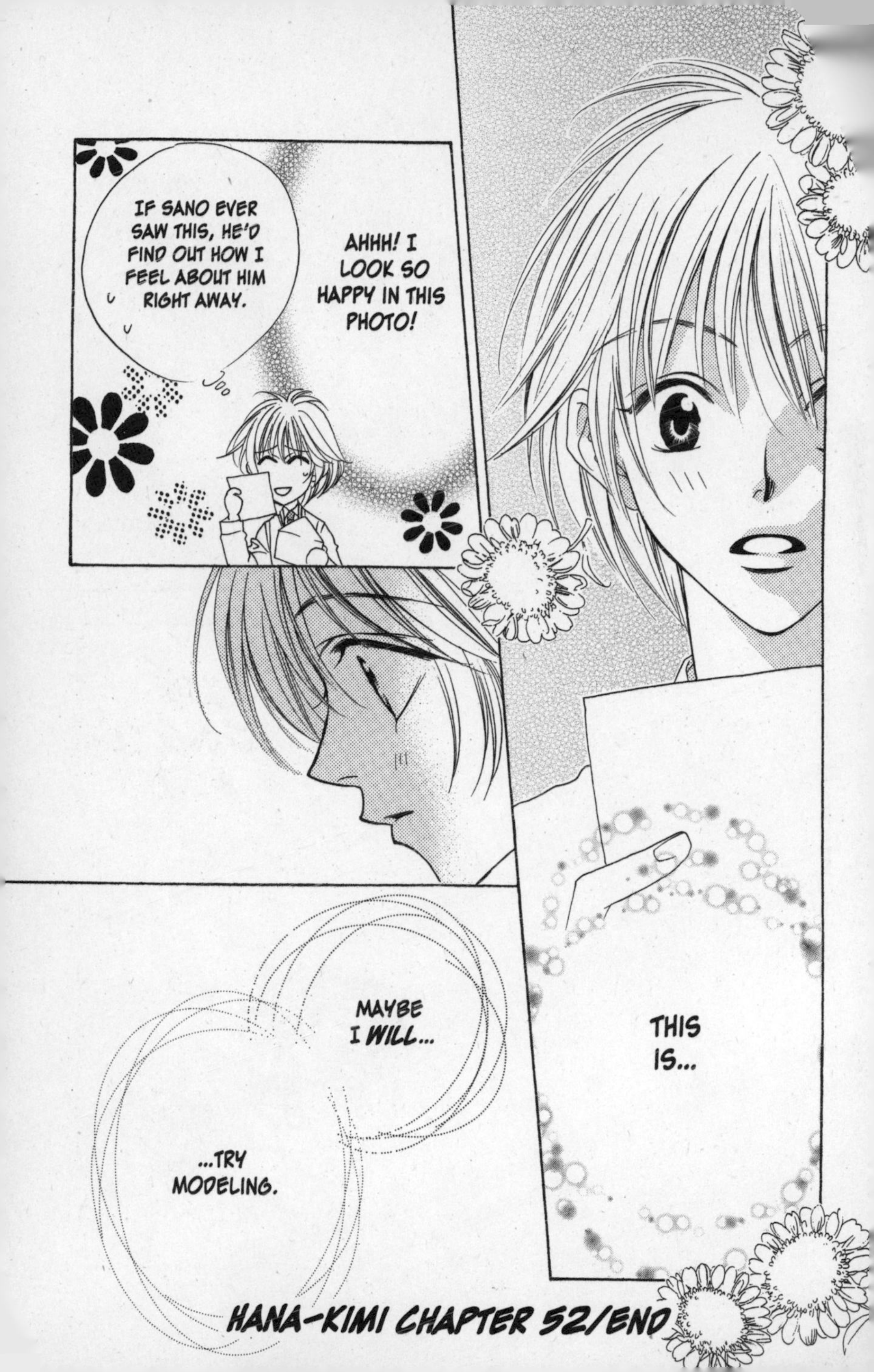
THIS IS...
AHHH! I LOOK SO HAPPY IN THIS PHOTO!
IF SANO EVER SAW THIS, HE'D FIND OUT HOW I FEEL ABOUT HIM RIGHT AWAY.
MAYBE I WILL...
...TRY MODELING.
HANA-KIMI CHAPTER 52/END

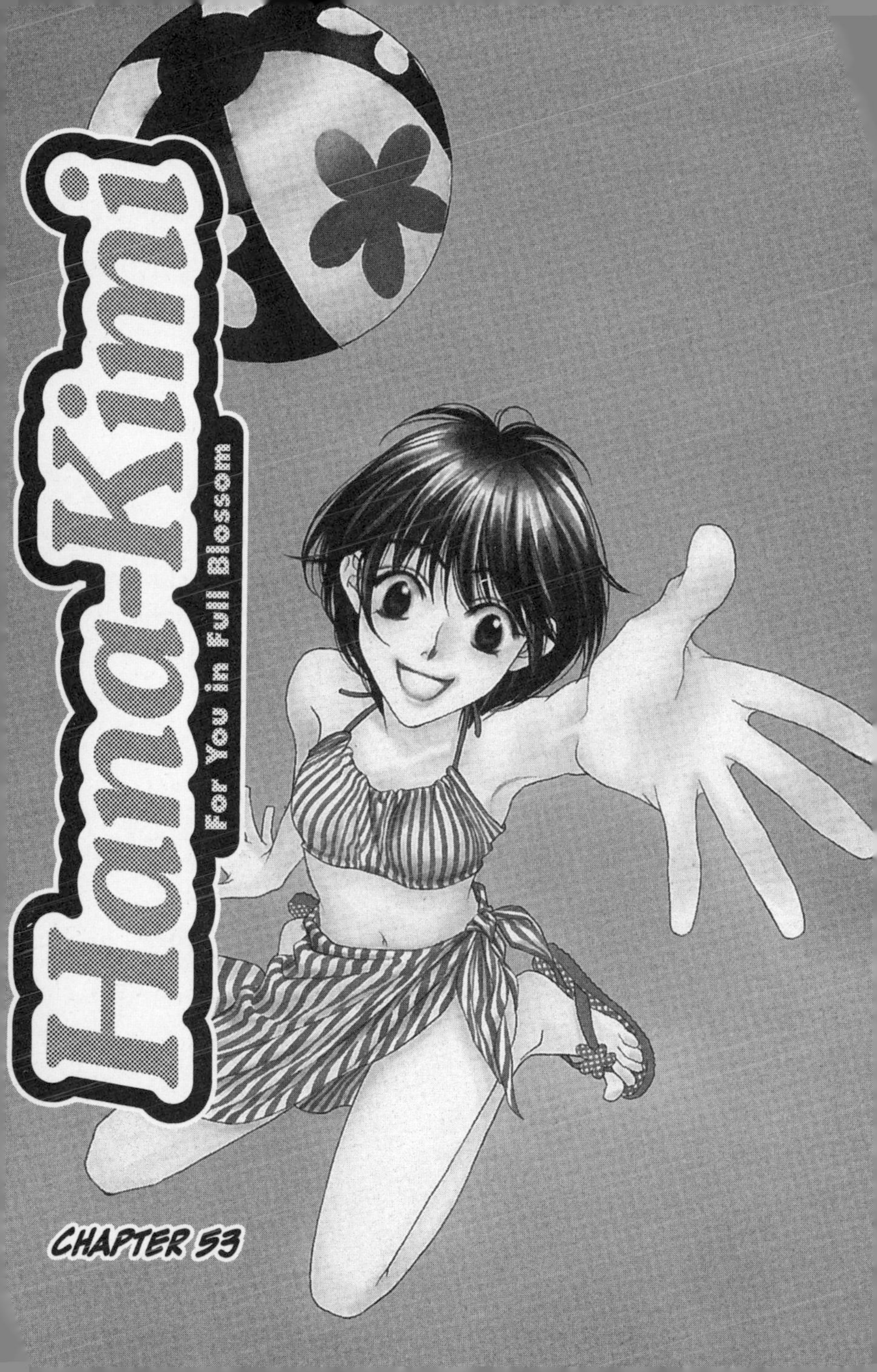
Hana-Kimi
For You in Full Blossom
CHAPTER 53

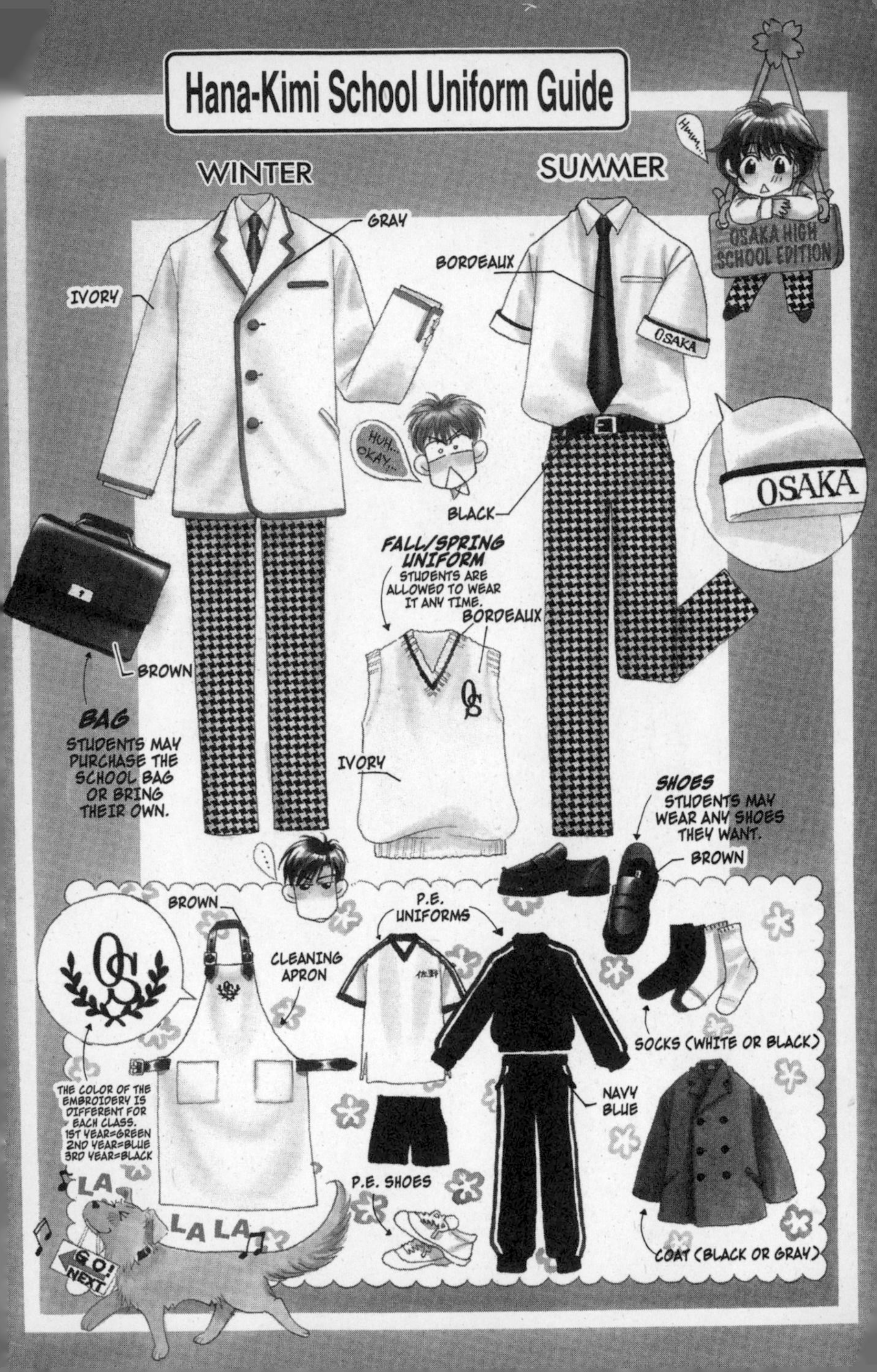
Hana-Kimi School Uniform Guide
Hmm...
OSAKA HIGH SCHOOL EDITION
WINTER
SUMMER
GRAY
IVORY
BORDEAUX
OSAKA
HUH... OKAY...
OSAKA
BLACK
FALL/SPRING UNIFORM
STUDENTS ARE ALLOWED TO WEAR IT ANY TIME.
BORDEAUX
BROWN
BAG
STUDENTS MAY PURCHASE THE SCHOOL BAG OR BRING THEIR OWN.
IVORY
SHOES
STUDENTS MAY WEAR ANY SHOES THEY WANT.
BROWN
BROWN
P.E. UNIFORMS
CLEANING APRON
SOCKS (WHITE OR BLACK)
THE COLOR OF THE EMBROIDERY IS DIFFERENT FOR EACH CLASS.
1ST YEAR=GREEN
2ND YEAR=BLUE
3RD YEAR=BLACK
NAVY BLUE
LA
LA LA
P.E. SHOES
GO! NEXT
COAT (BLACK OR GRAY)

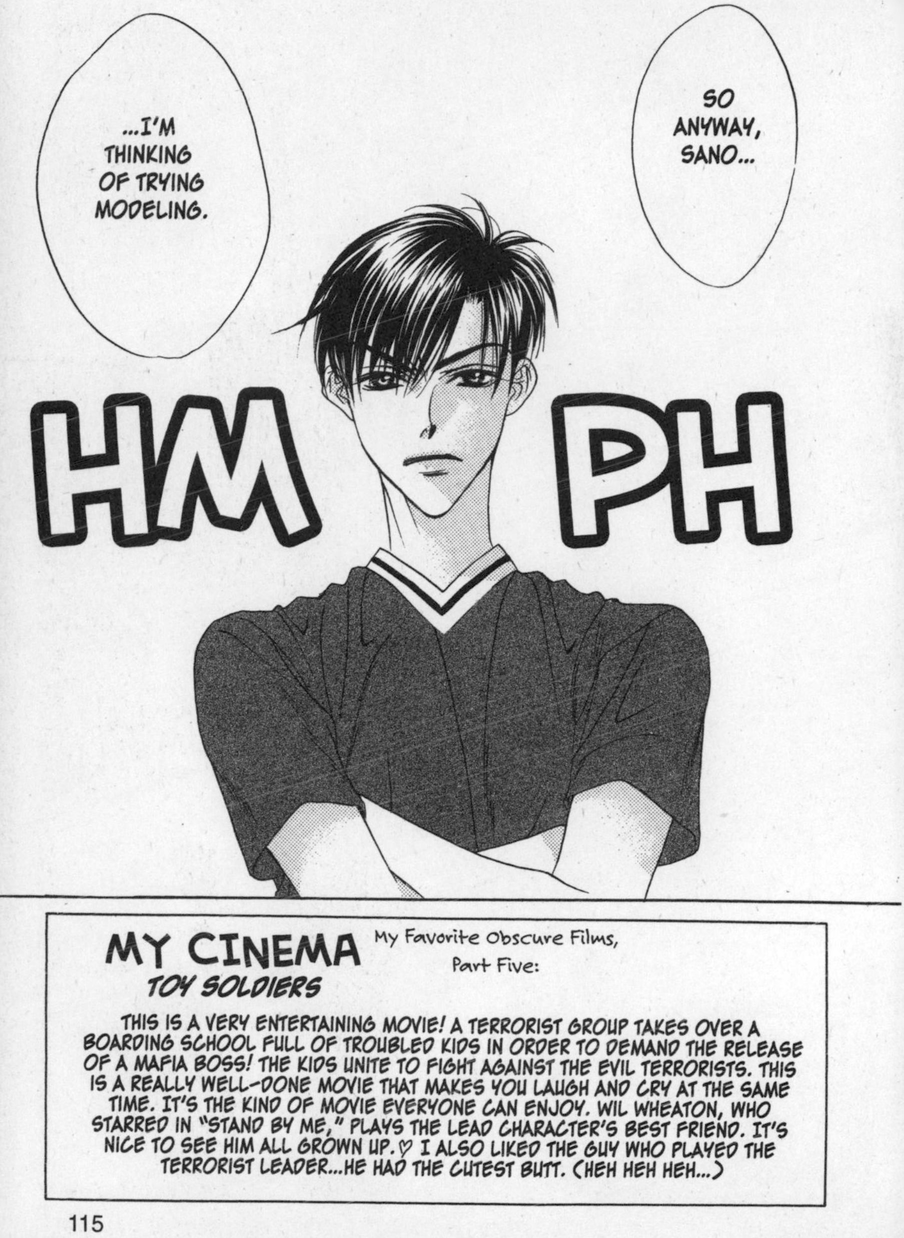
SO ANYWAY, SANO...
...I'M THINKING OF TRYING MODELING.
HMPH

MY CINEMA

My Favorite Obscure Films, Part Five:

TOY SOLDIERS

THIS IS A VERY ENTERTAINING MOVIE! A TERRORIST GROUP TAKES OVER A BOARDING SCHOOL FULL OF TROUBLED KIDS IN ORDER TO DEMAND THE RELEASE OF A MAFIA BOSS! THE KIDS UNITE TO FIGHT AGAINST THE EVIL TERRORISTS. THIS IS A REALLY WELL-DONE MOVIE THAT MAKES YOU LAUGH AND CRY AT THE SAME TIME. IT'S THE KIND OF MOVIE EVERYONE CAN ENJOY. WIL WHEATON, WHO STARRED IN "STAND BY ME," PLAYS THE LEAD CHARACTER'S BEST FRIEND. IT'S NICE TO SEE HIM ALL GROWN UP.♡ I ALSO LIKED THE GUY WHO PLAYED THE TERRORIST LEADER...HE HAD THE CUTEST BUTT. (HEH HEH HEH...)

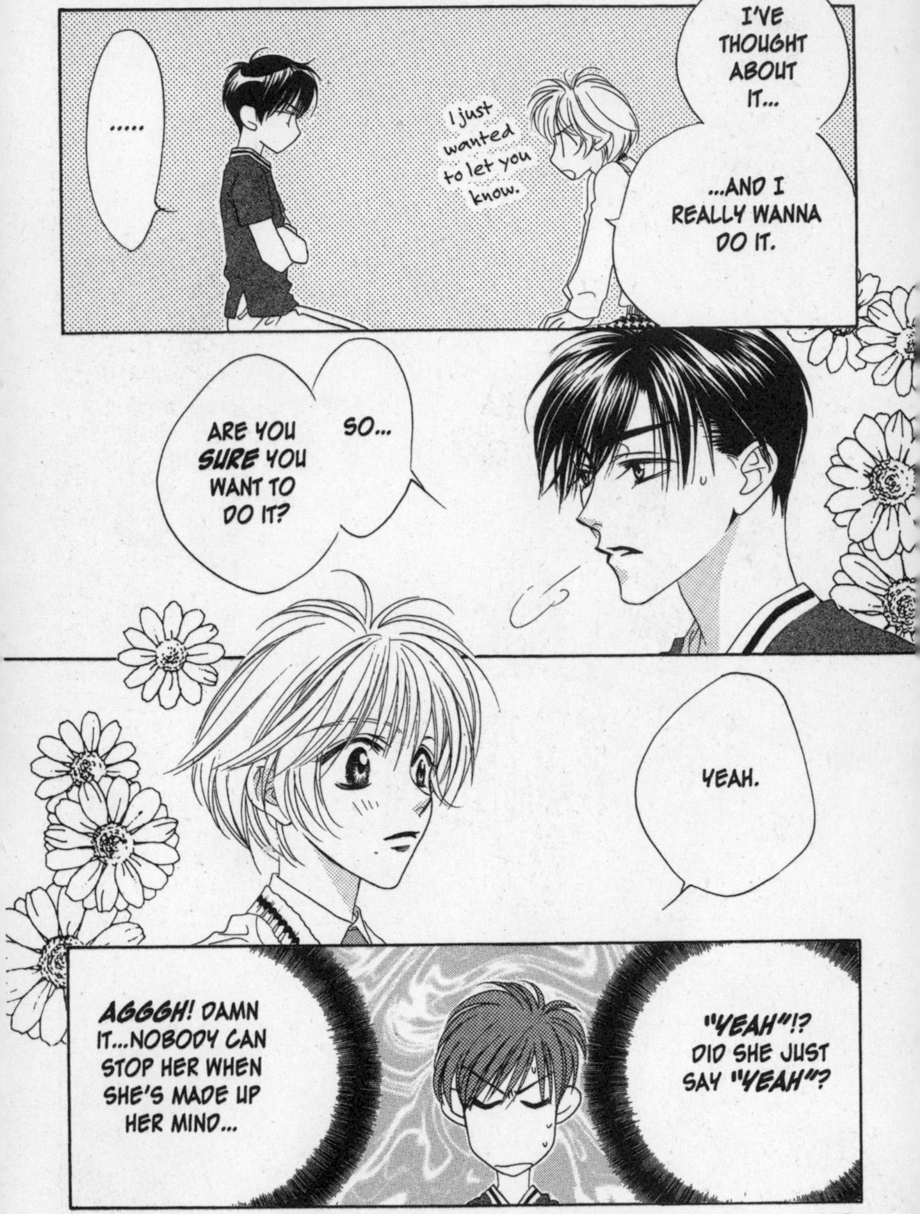
I'VE THOUGHT ABOUT IT...
...AND I REALLY WANNA DO IT.
I just wanted to let you know.
.....
SO...
ARE YOU **SURE** YOU WANT TO DO IT?
YEAH.
"YEAH"!? DID SHE JUST SAY "YEAH"?
AGGGH! DAMN IT...NOBODY CAN STOP HER WHEN SHE'S MADE UP HER MIND...

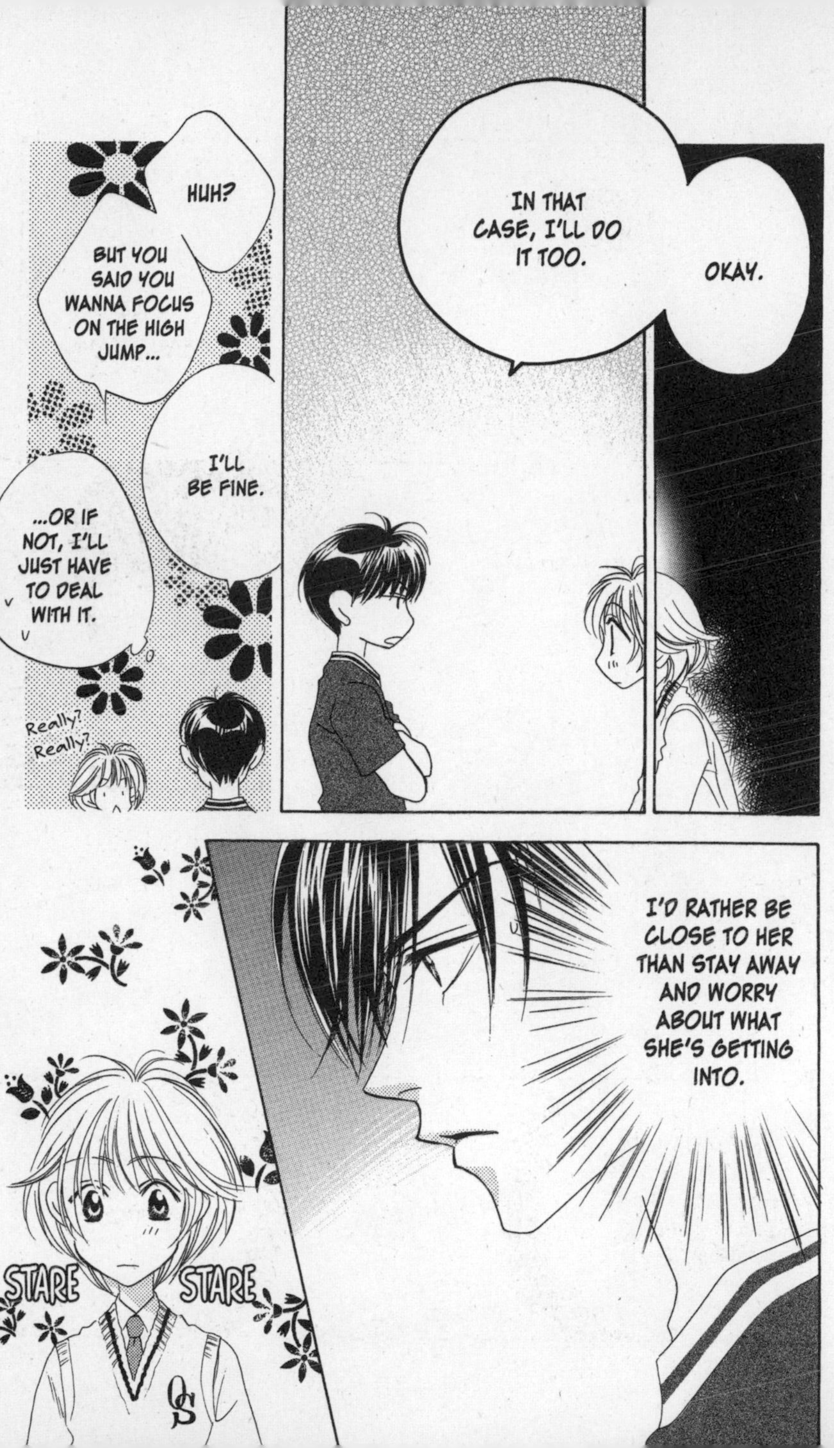
IN THAT CASE, I'LL DO IT TOO.
OKAY.
HUH?
BUT YOU SAID YOU WANNA FOCUS ON THE HIGH JUMP...
I'LL BE FINE.
...OR IF NOT, I'LL JUST HAVE TO DEAL WITH IT.
Really? Really?
I'D RATHER BE CLOSE TO HER THAN STAY AWAY AND WORRY ABOUT WHAT SHE'S GETTING INTO.
STARE STARE

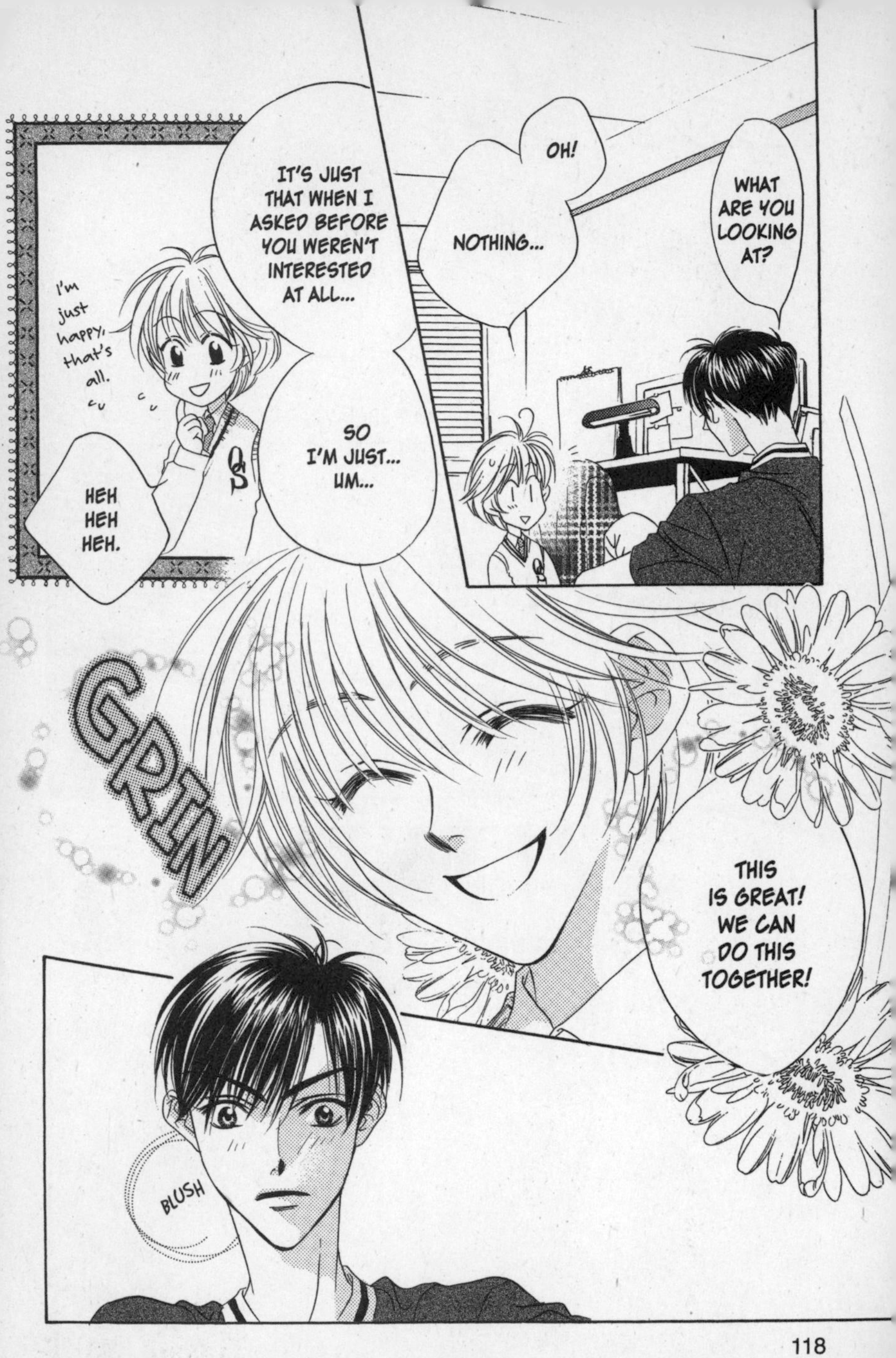
WHAT ARE YOU LOOKING AT?
OH!
NOTHING...
IT'S JUST THAT WHEN I ASKED BEFORE YOU WEREN'T INTERESTED AT ALL...
SO I'M JUST... UM...
I'm just happy, that's all.
HEH HEH HEH.
THIS IS GREAT! WE CAN DO THIS TOGETHER!
GRIN
BLUSH

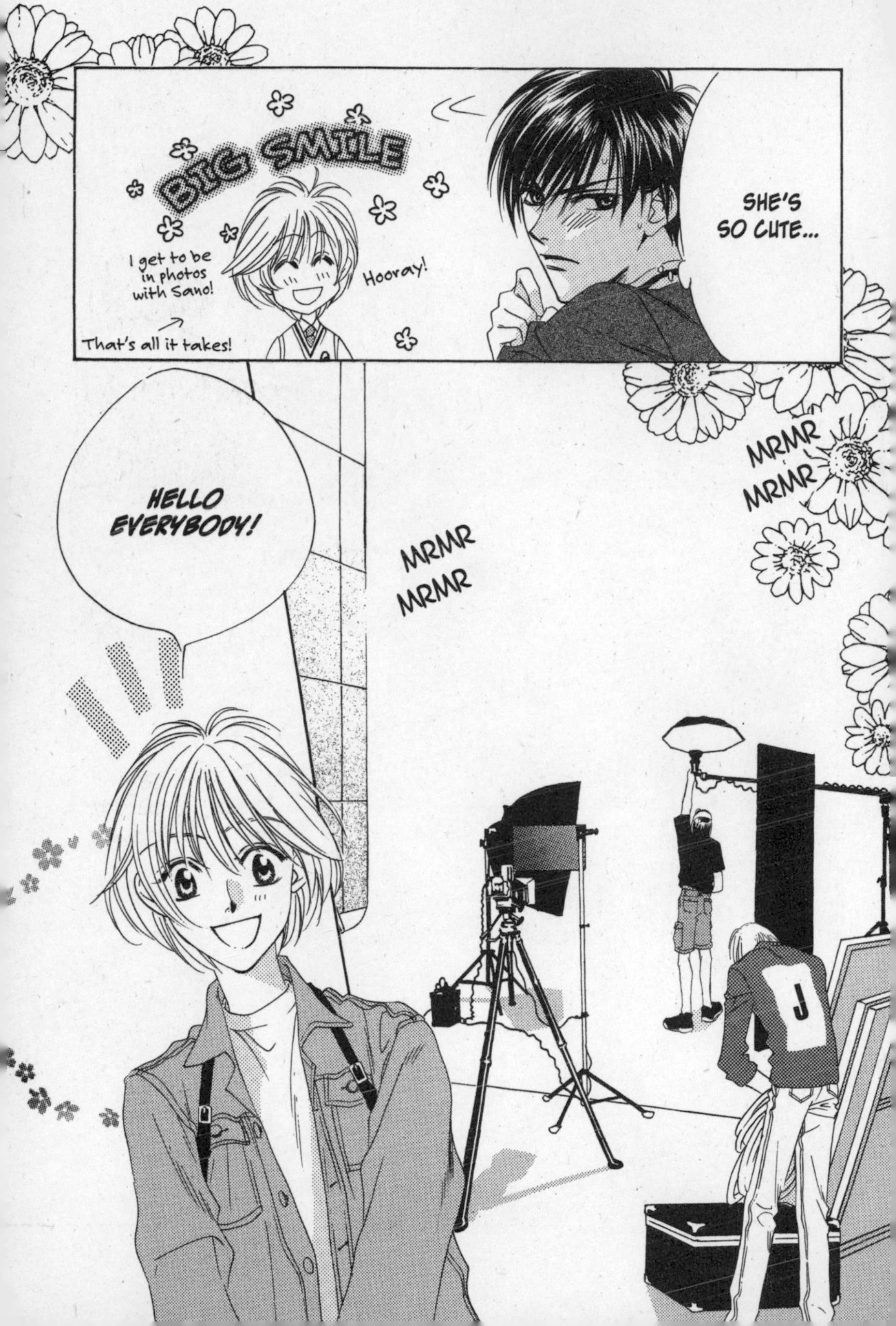
SHE'S SO CUTE...
BIG SMILE
Hooray!
I get to be in photos with Sano!
That's all it takes!
MRMR MRMR
MRMR MRMR
HELLO EVERYBODY!

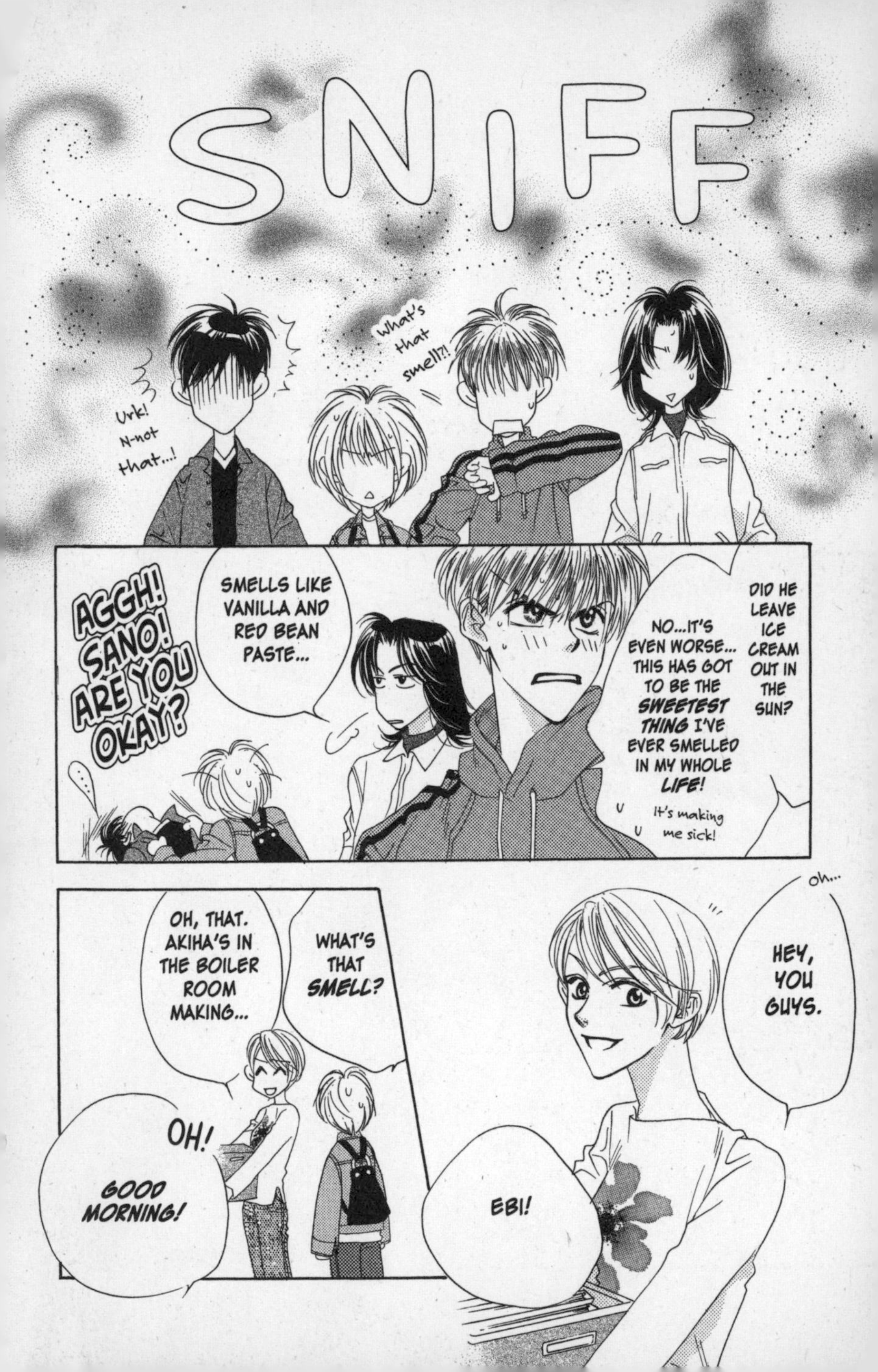
SNIFF
What's that smell!?!
Urk! N-not that...!
DID HE LEAVE ICE CREAM OUT IN THE SUN?
NO...IT'S EVEN WORSE... THIS HAS GOT TO BE THE *SWEETEST THING* I'VE EVER SMELLED IN MY WHOLE *LIFE!*
It's making me sick!
SMELLS LIKE VANILLA AND RED BEAN PASTE...
AGGH! SANO! ARE YOU OKAY?
oh...
HEY, YOU GUYS.
EBI!
OH! GOOD MORNING!
WHAT'S THAT *SMELL?*
OH, THAT. AKIHA'S IN THE BOILER ROOM MAKING...

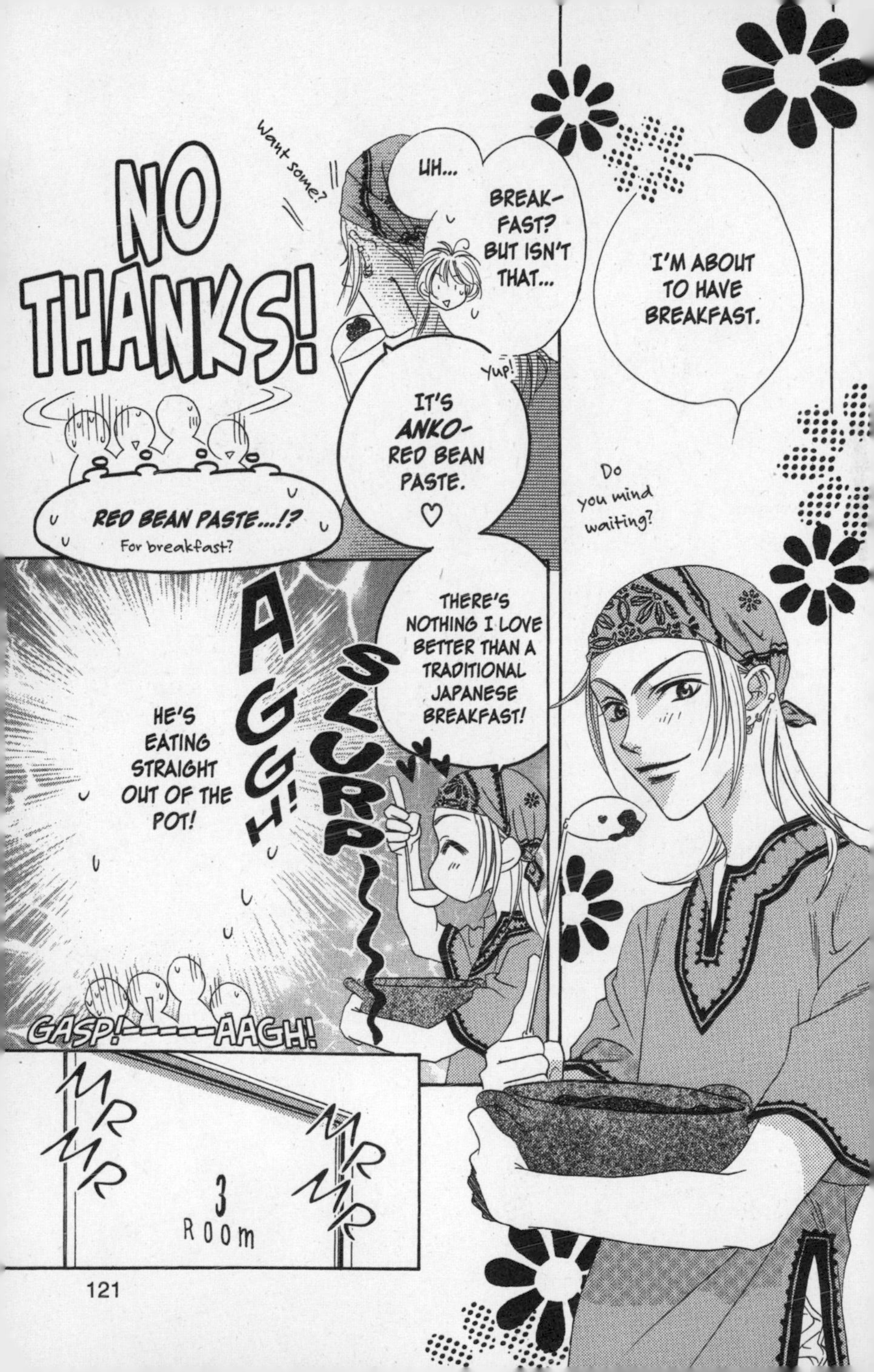

I'M ABOUT TO HAVE BREAKFAST.
Do you mind waiting?
UH...
BREAKFAST? BUT ISN'T THAT...
Want some?
Yup!
IT'S ANKO-RED BEAN PASTE. ♡
NO THANKS!
RED BEAN PASTE...!?
For breakfast?
THERE'S NOTHING I LOVE BETTER THAN A TRADITIONAL JAPANESE BREAKFAST!
SLURP
AGGH!
HE'S EATING STRAIGHT OUT OF THE POT!
GASP!-----AAGH!
MR MR
MR MR
3 Room

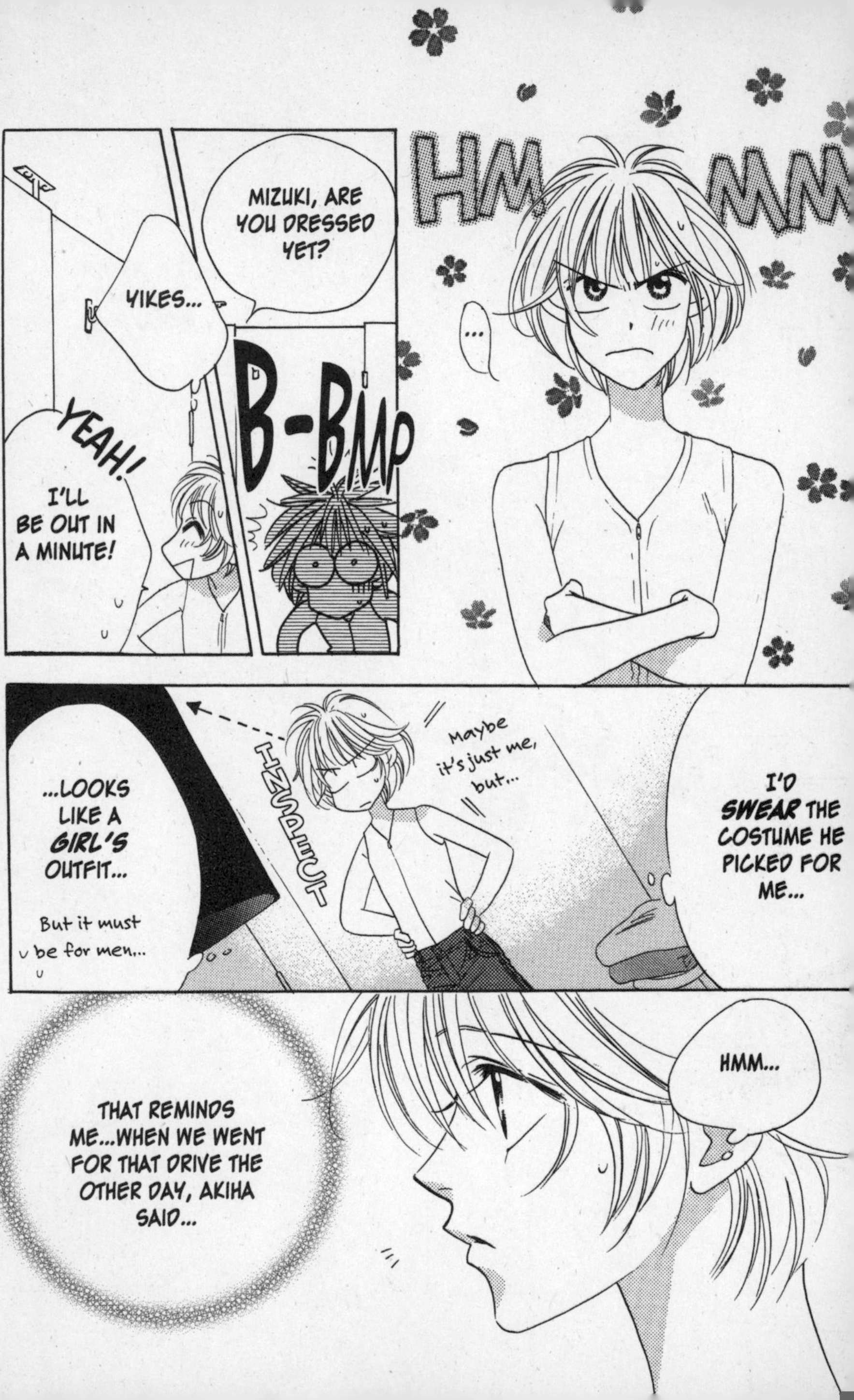
HMMMM
...
MIZUKI, ARE YOU DRESSED YET?
B-BMP
YIKES...
YEAH! I'LL BE OUT IN A MINUTE!
I'D SWEAR THE COSTUME HE PICKED FOR ME...
Maybe it's just me, but...
INSPECT
...LOOKS LIKE A GIRL'S OUTFIT...
But it must be for men...
HMM...
THAT REMINDS ME...WHEN WE WENT FOR THAT DRIVE THE OTHER DAY, AKIHA SAID...

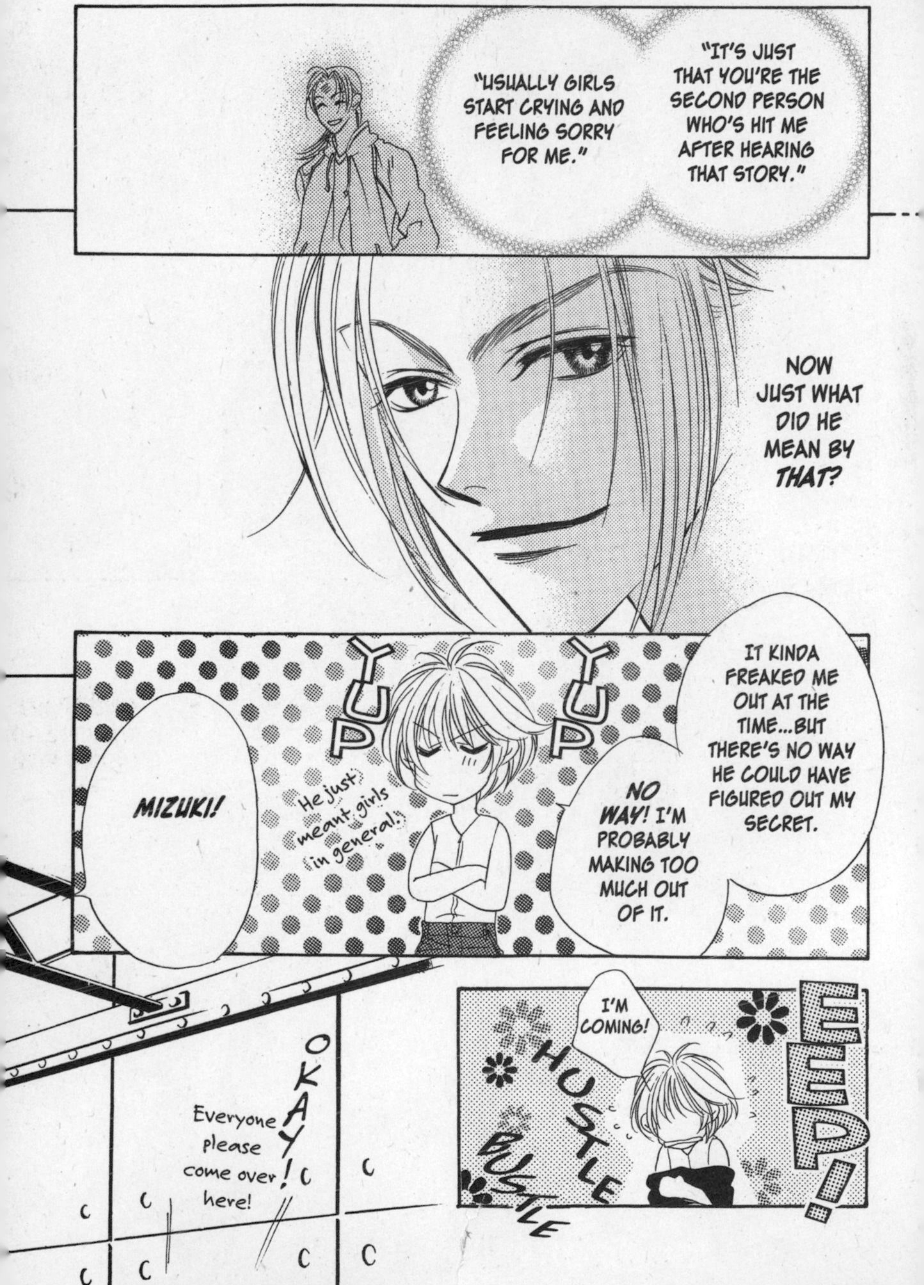
"IT'S JUST THAT YOU'RE THE SECOND PERSON WHO'S HIT ME AFTER HEARING THAT STORY."
"USUALLY GIRLS START CRYING AND FEELING SORRY FOR ME."
NOW JUST WHAT DID HE MEAN BY *THAT?*
YUP YUP
IT KINDA FREAKED ME OUT AT THE TIME...BUT THERE'S NO WAY HE COULD HAVE FIGURED OUT MY SECRET.
NO WAY! I'M PROBABLY MAKING TOO MUCH OUT OF IT.
He just meant girls in general.
MIZUKI!
EEP!
I'M COMING!
HUSTLE BUSTLE
OKAY!
Everyone please come over here!

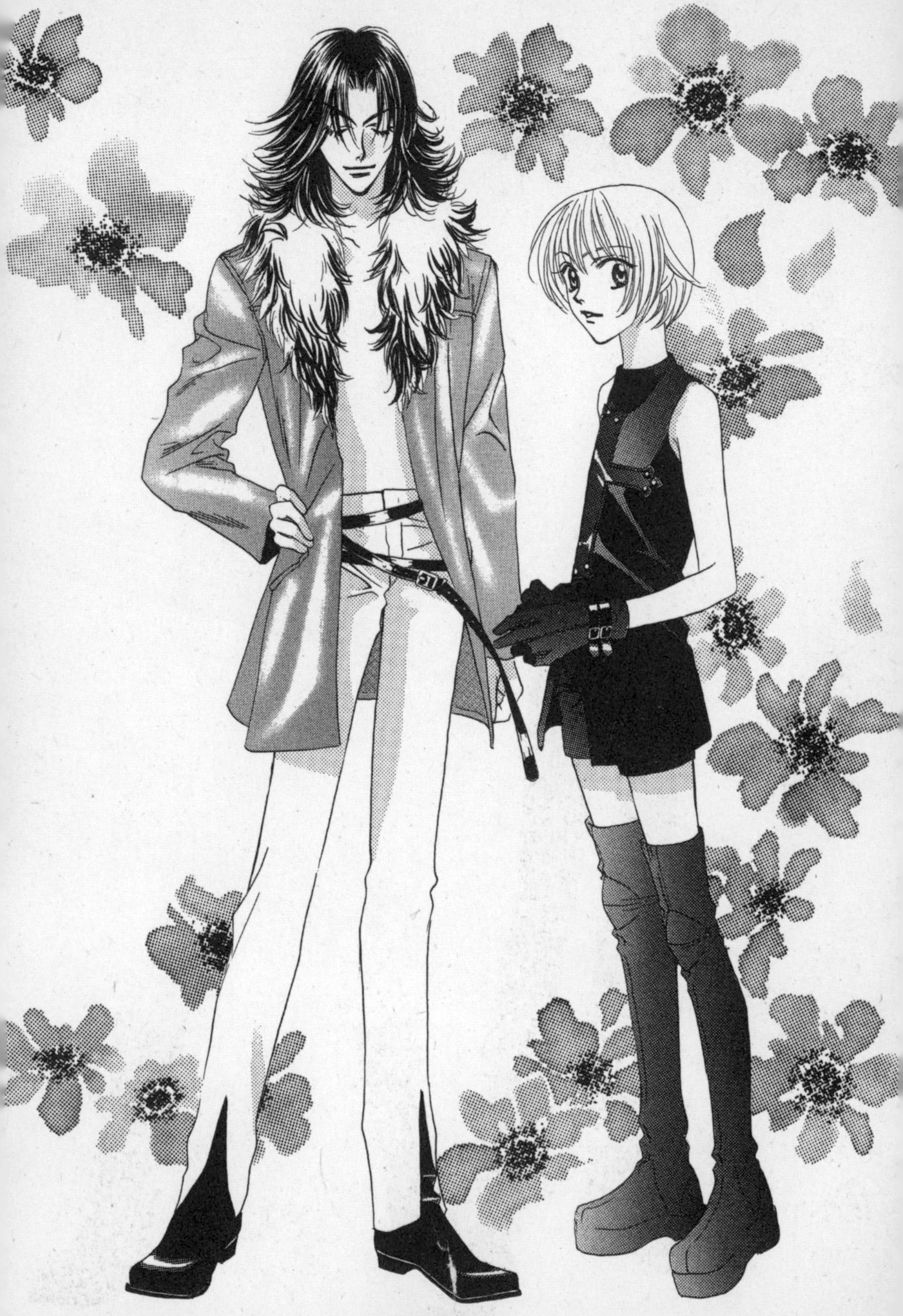

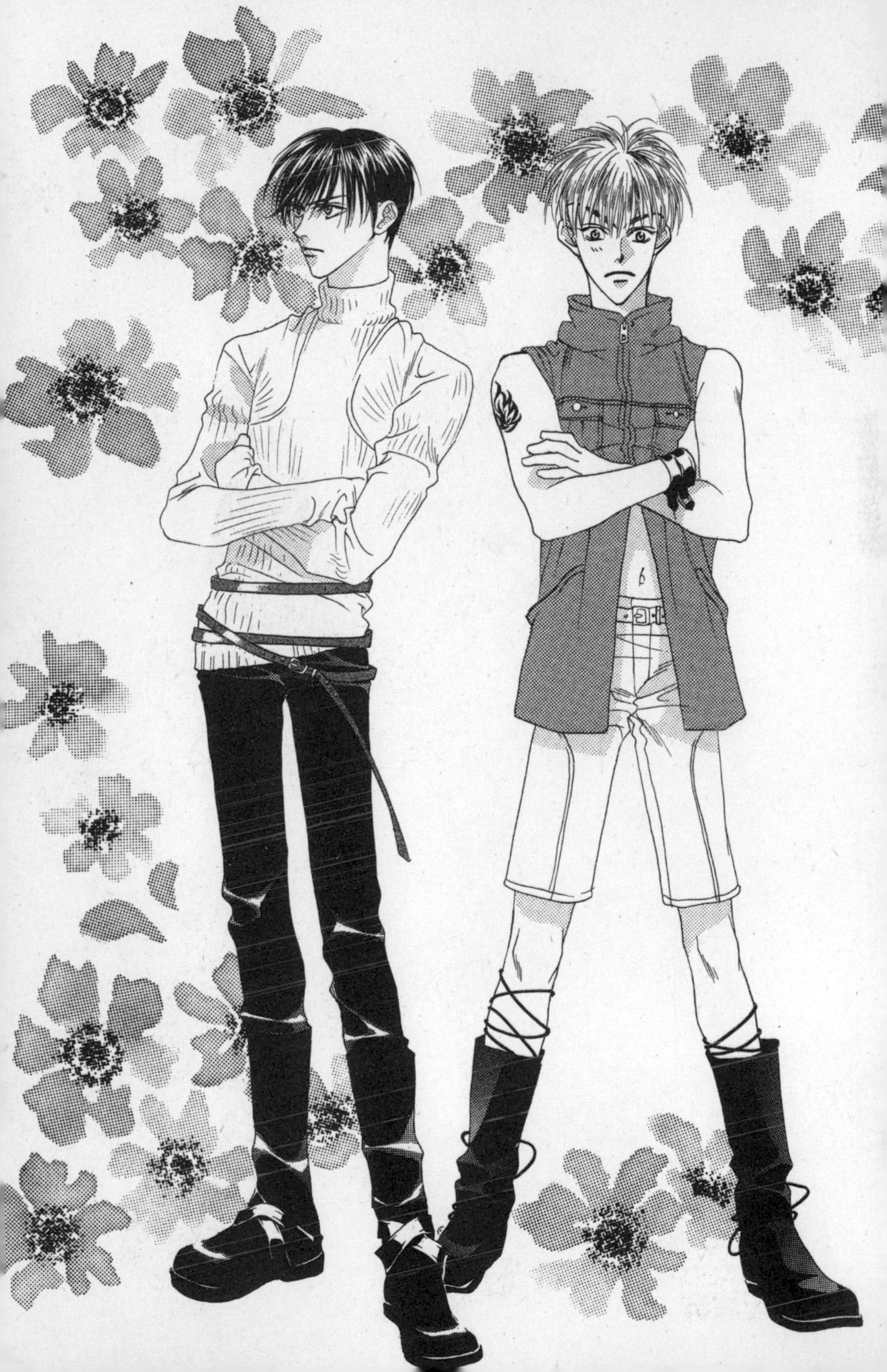

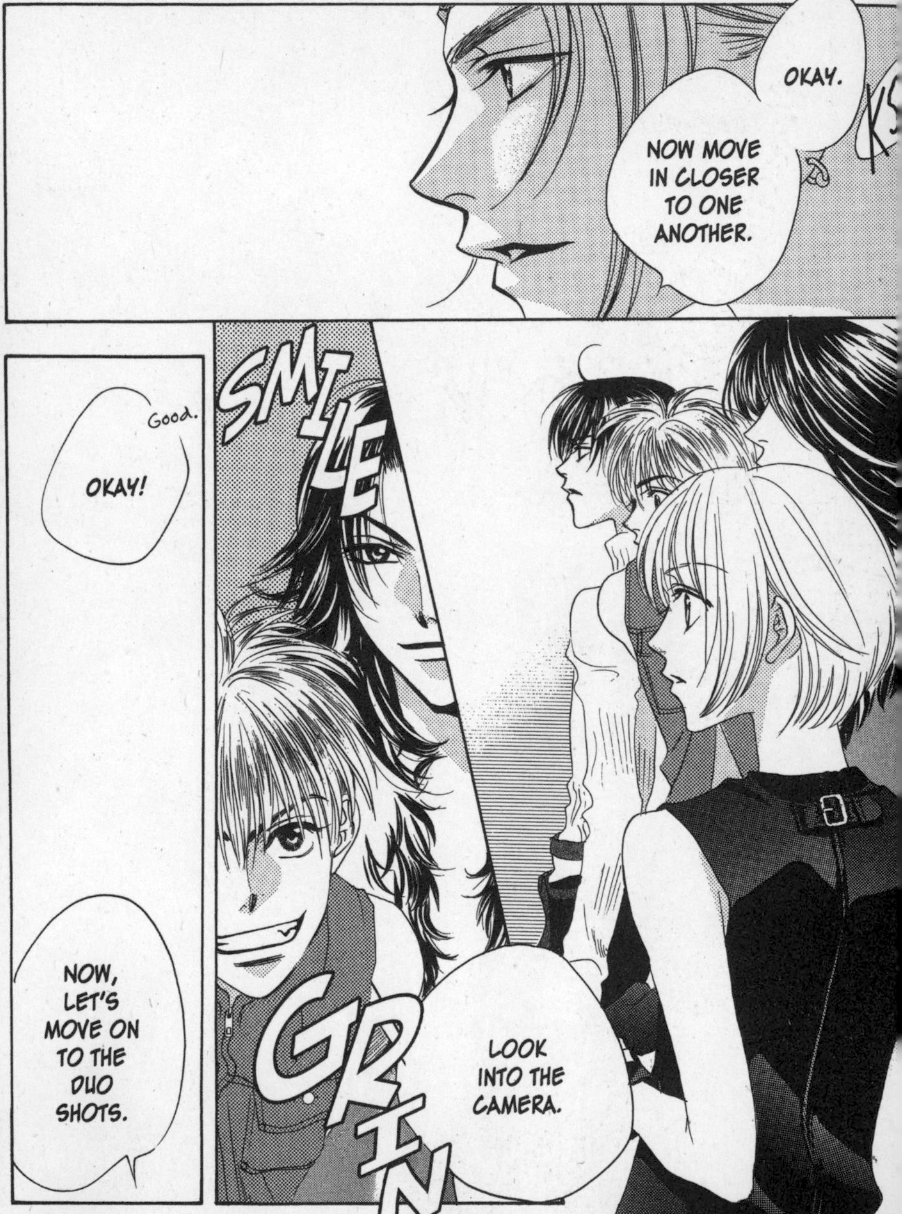

OKAY.
NOW MOVE IN CLOSER TO ONE ANOTHER.
LOOK INTO THE CAMERA.
SMILE
GRIN
Good.
OKAY!
NOW, LET'S MOVE ON TO THE DUO SHOTS.

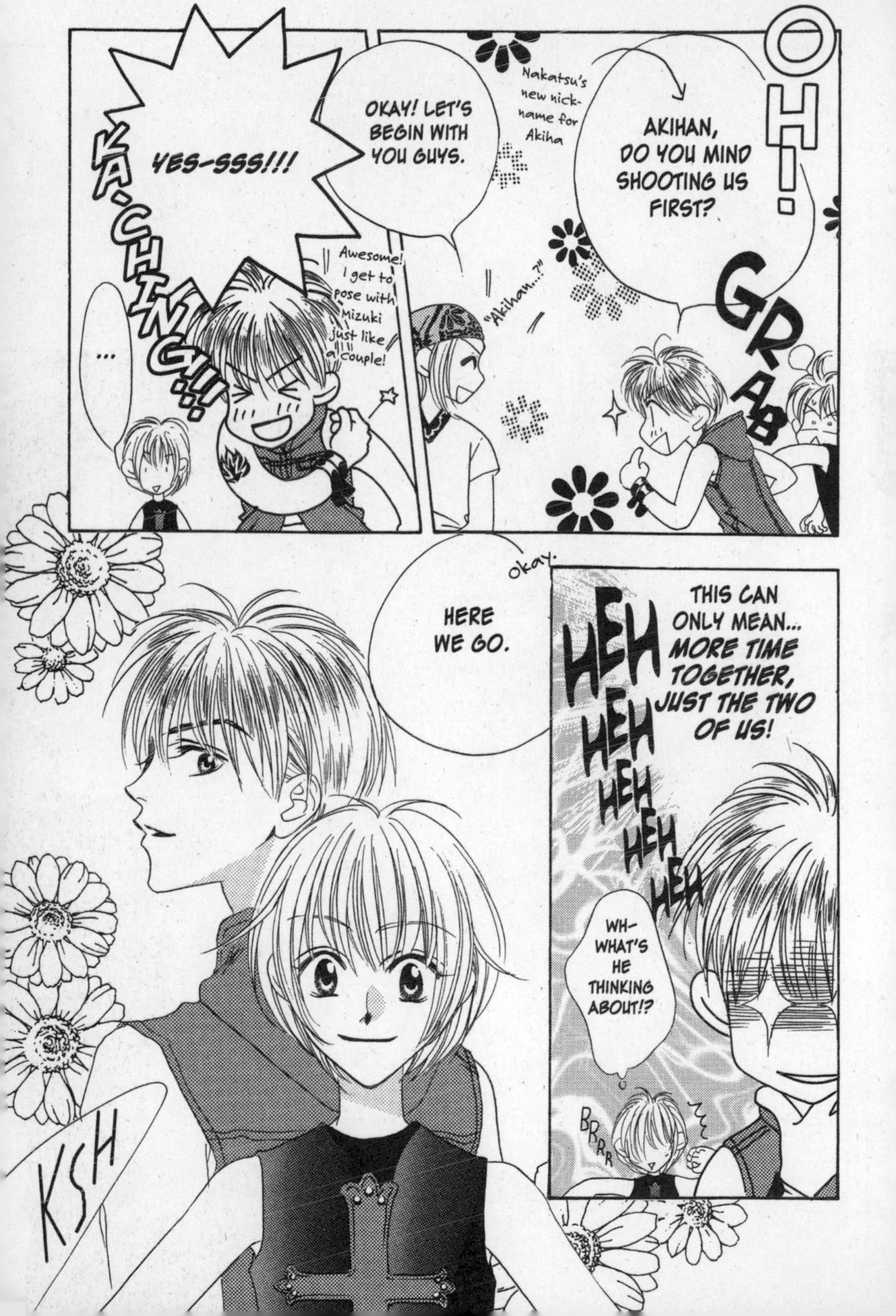
OH!
AKIHAN, DO YOU MIND SHOOTING US FIRST?
Nakatsu's new nick-name for Akiha
GRAB
"Akihan...?"
OKAY! LET'S BEGIN WITH YOU GUYS.
YES-SSS!!!
KA-CHING!!!
Awesome! I get to pose with Mizuki just like a couple!
...
THIS CAN ONLY MEAN... MORE TIME TOGETHER, JUST THE TWO OF US!
HEH HEH HEH HEH HEH
WH-WHAT'S HE THINKING ABOUT!?
BRRR
Okay.
HERE WE GO.
KSH

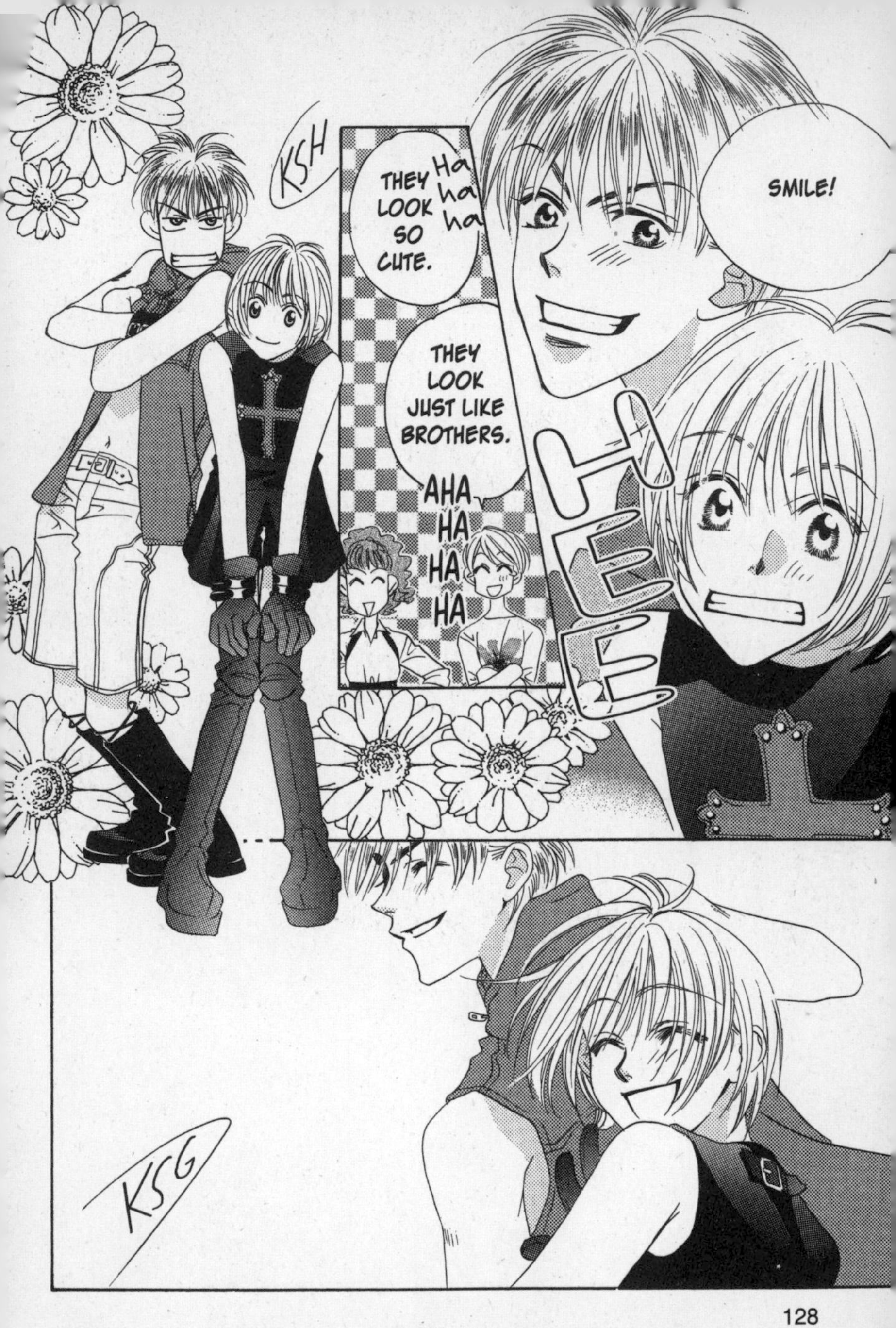
SMILE!
HEE
THEY LOOK SO CUTE.
Ha ha ha
THEY LOOK JUST LIKE BROTHERS.
AHA HA HA HA
KSH
KSG

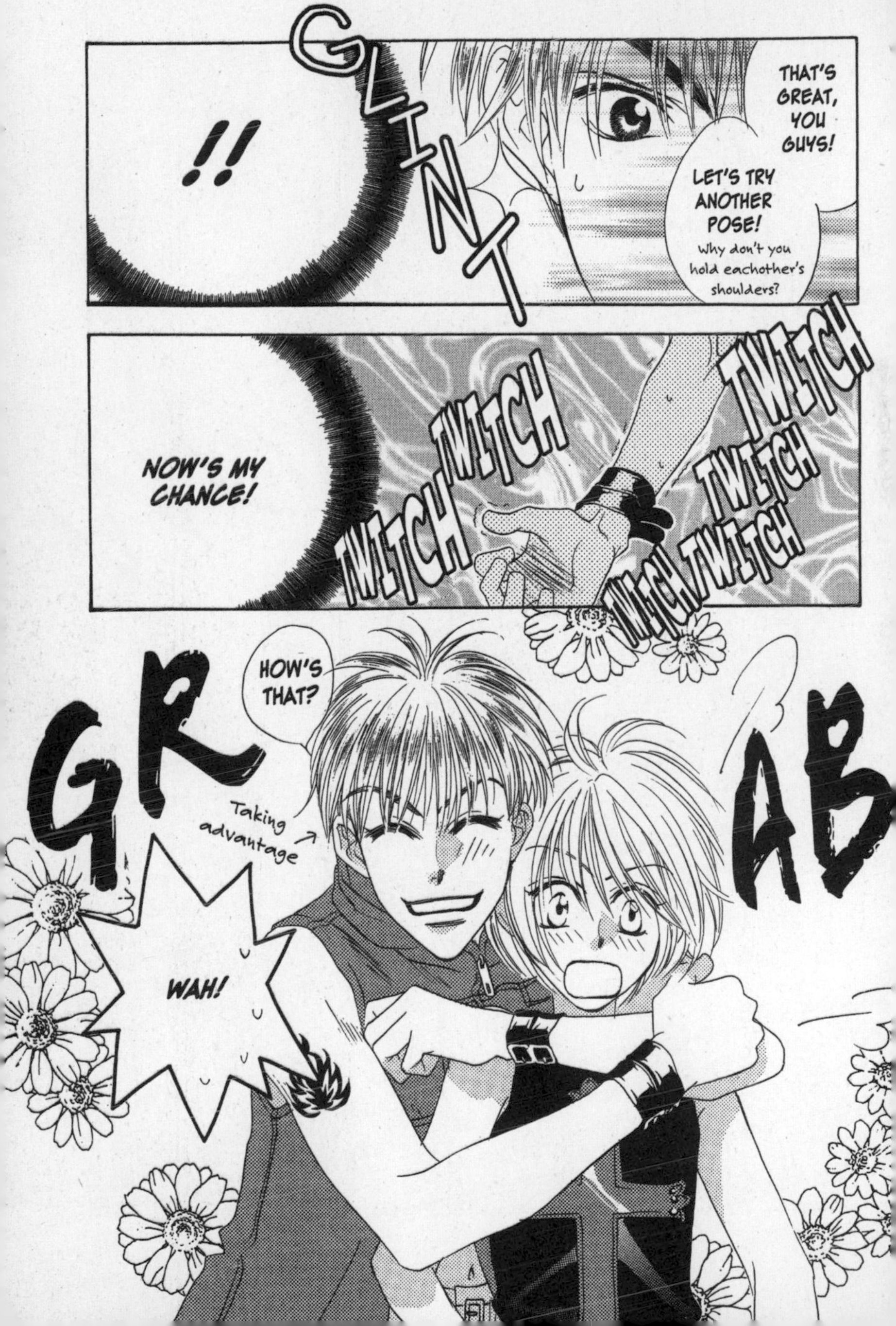
THAT'S GREAT, YOU GUYS!
LET'S TRY ANOTHER POSE!
Why don't you hold eachother's shoulders?
GLINT
!!
TWITCH TWITCH
TWITCH TWITCH TWITCH TWITCH
TWITCH TWITCH
NOW'S MY CHANCE!
GRAB
HOW'S THAT?
Taking advantage
WAH!

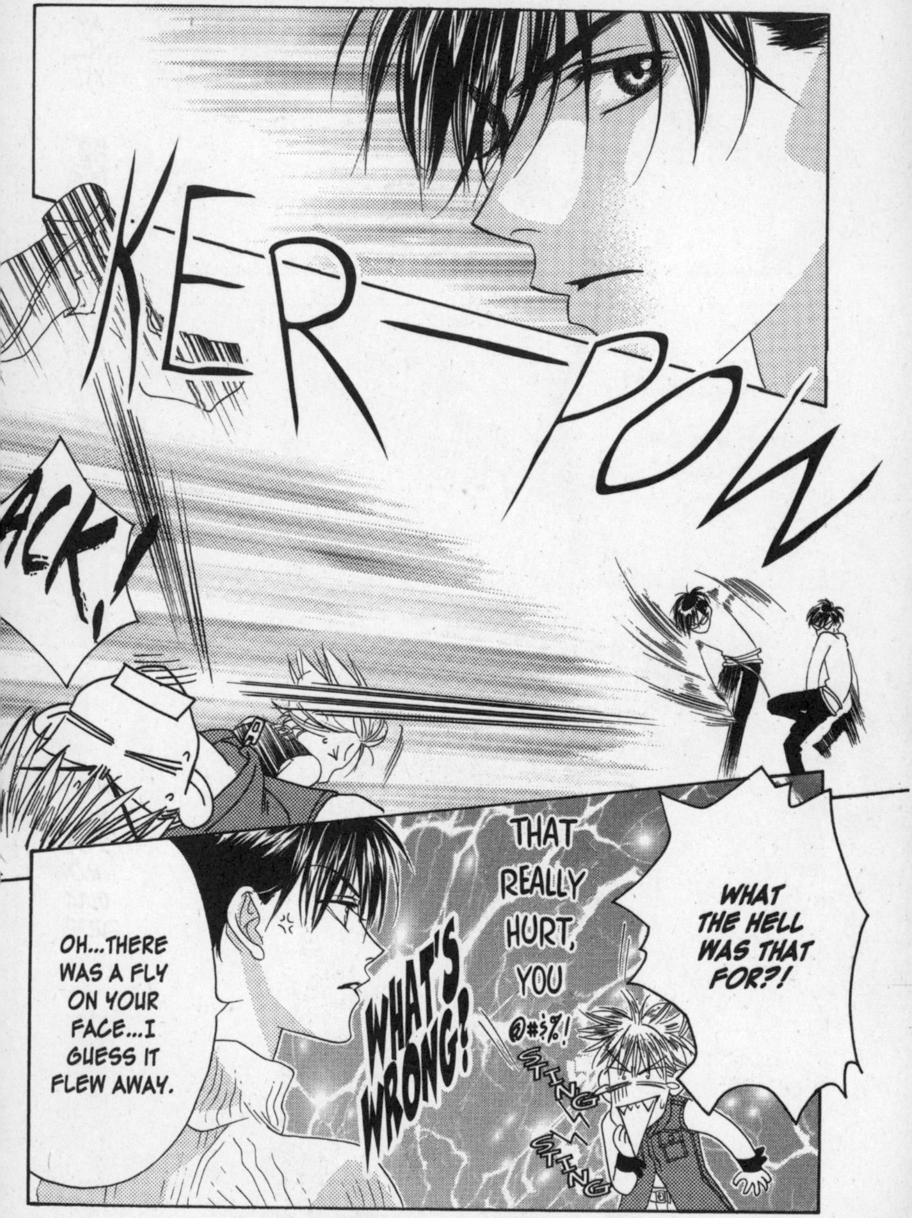
KER—POW
ACK!
WHAT THE HELL WAS THAT FOR?!
THAT REALLY HURT, YOU @#$%!
STING STING
WHAT'S WRONG!
OH...THERE WAS A FLY ON YOUR FACE...I GUESS IT FLEW AWAY.

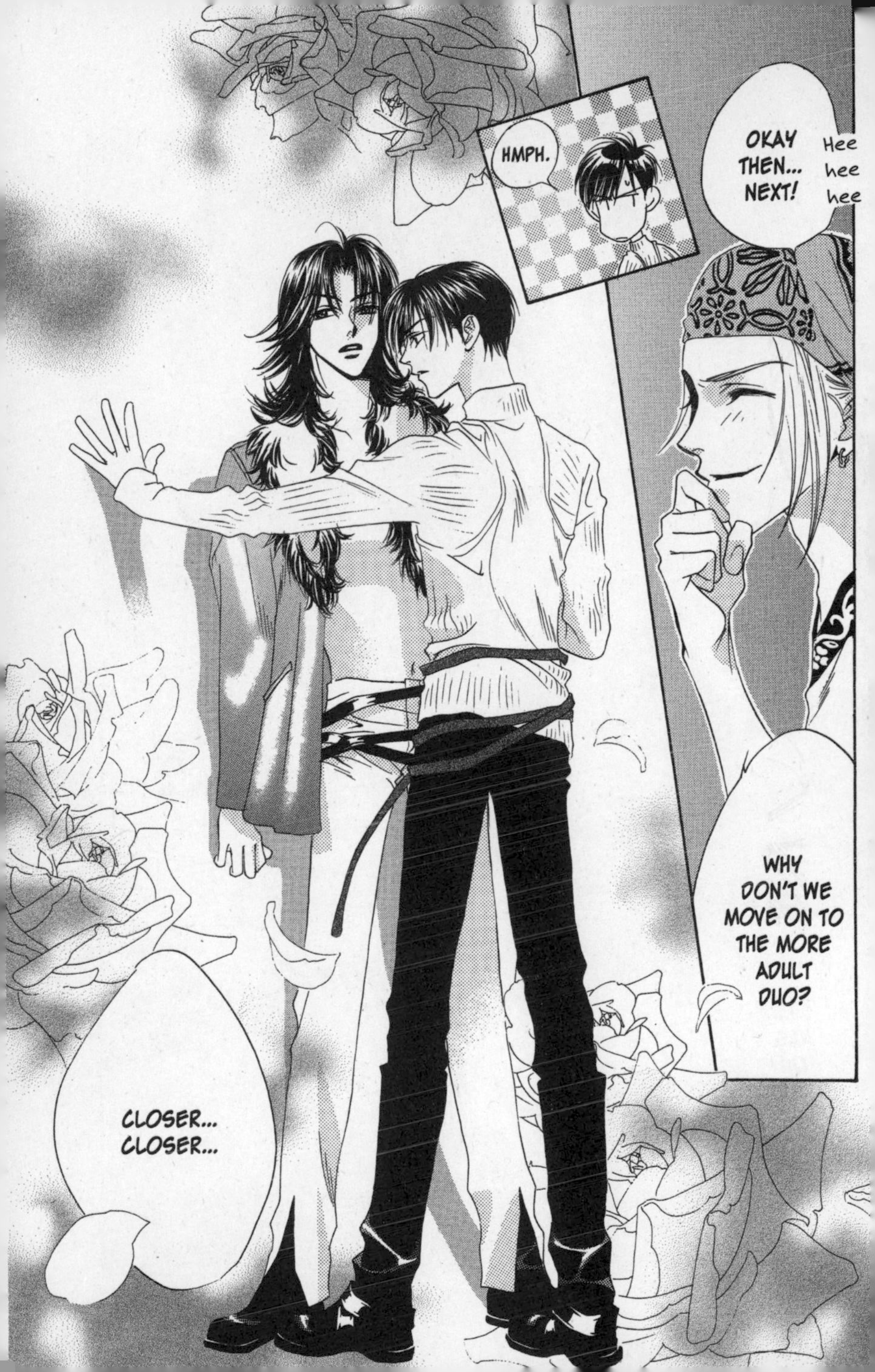
OKAY THEN... NEXT!
Hee hee hee
WHY DON'T WE MOVE ON TO THE MORE ADULT DUO?
HMPH.
CLOSER... CLOSER...

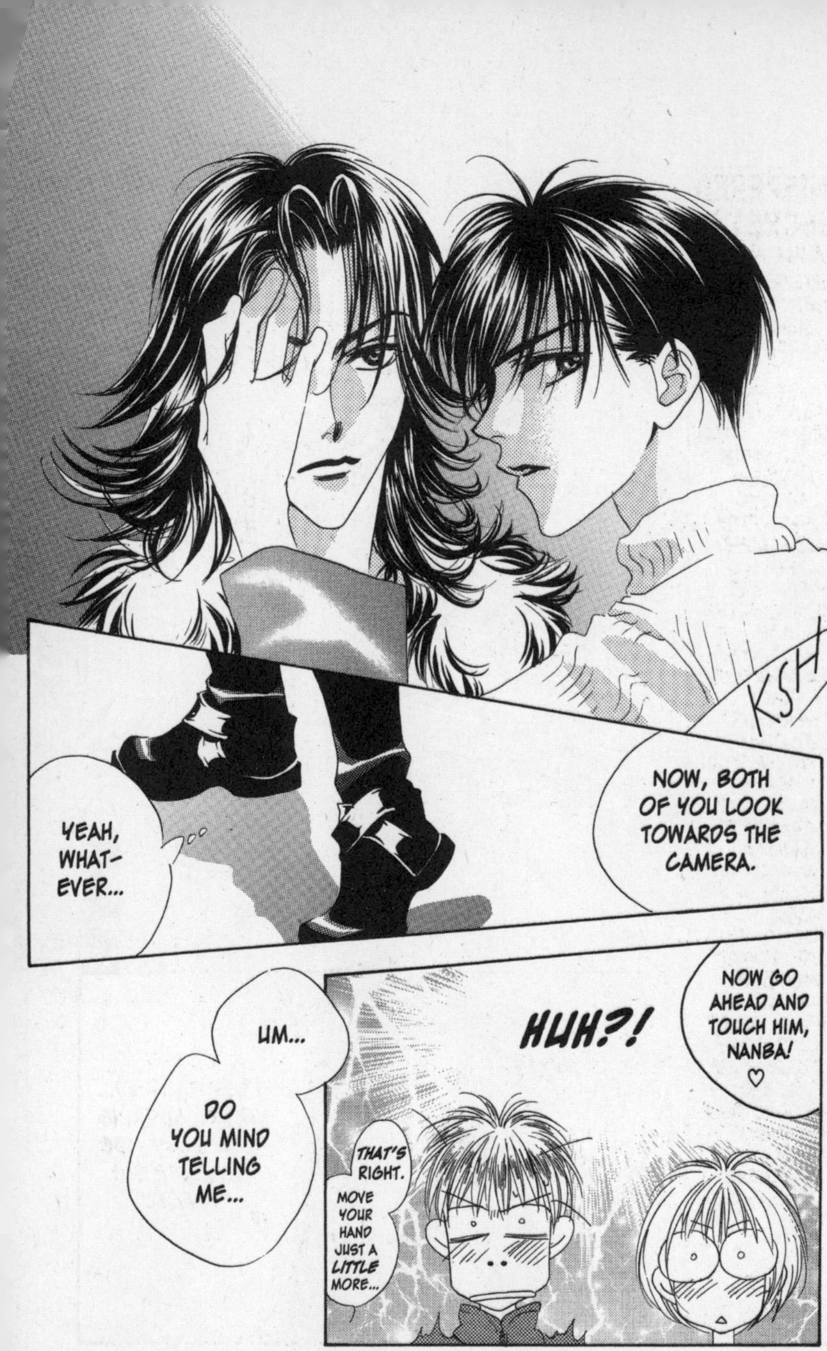
KSH
NOW, BOTH OF YOU LOOK TOWARDS THE CAMERA.
YEAH, WHAT-EVER...
NOW GO AHEAD AND TOUCH HIM, NANBA! ♡
HUH?!
THAT'S RIGHT. MOVE YOUR HAND JUST A LITTLE MORE...
UM...
DO YOU MIND TELLING ME...

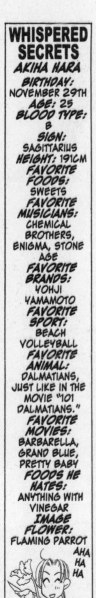

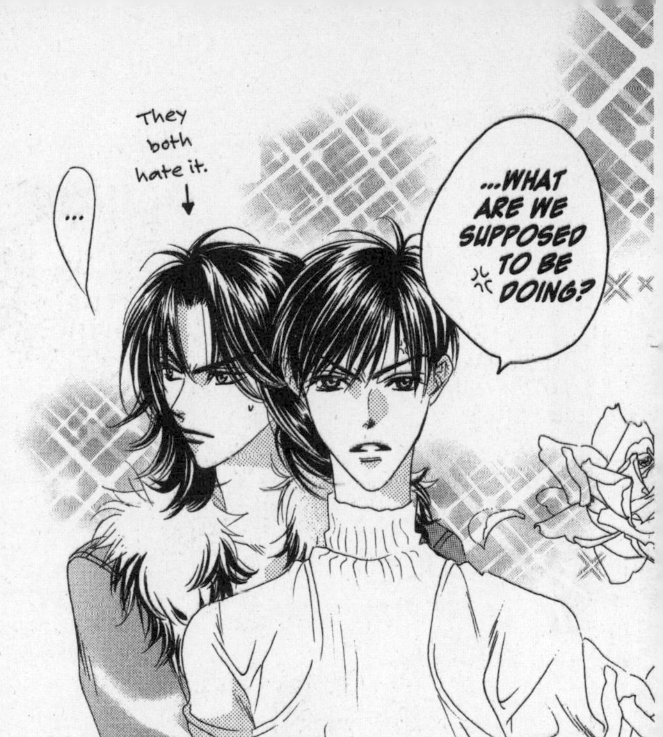
...WHAT ARE WE SUPPOSED TO BE DOING?
They both hate it.
...

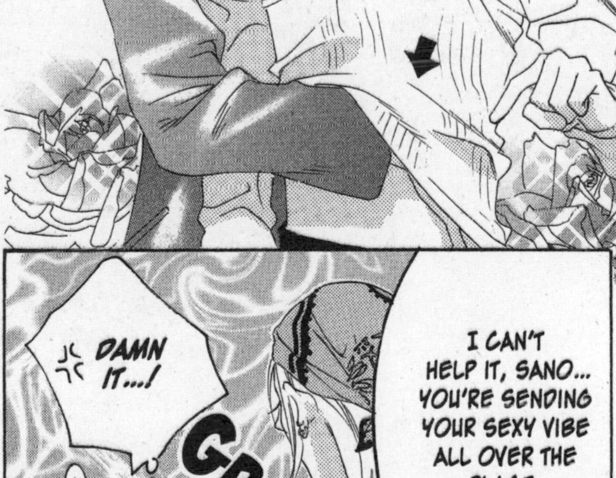
I CAN'T HELP IT, SANO... YOU'RE SENDING YOUR SEXY VIBE ALL OVER THE PLACE.
DAMN IT...!
GRRR
Why?!
Why do they all say that?!
......

WHISPERED SECRETS

AKIHA HARA

BIRTHDAY: NOVEMBER 29TH

AGE: 25

BLOOD TYPE: B

SIGN: SAGITTARIUS

HEIGHT: 191CM

FAVORITE FOODS: SWEETS

FAVORITE MUSICIANS: CHEMICAL BROTHERS, ENIGMA, STONE AGE

FAVORITE BRANDS: YOHJI YAMAMOTO

FAVORITE SPORT: BEACH VOLLEYBALL

FAVORITE ANIMAL: DALMATIANS, JUST LIKE IN THE MOVIE "101 DALMATIANS."

FAVORITE MOVIES: BARBARELLA, GRAND BLUE, PRETTY BABY

FOODS HE HATES: ANYTHING WITH VINEGAR

IMAGE FLOWER: FLAMING PARROT

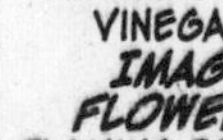
AHA HA HA

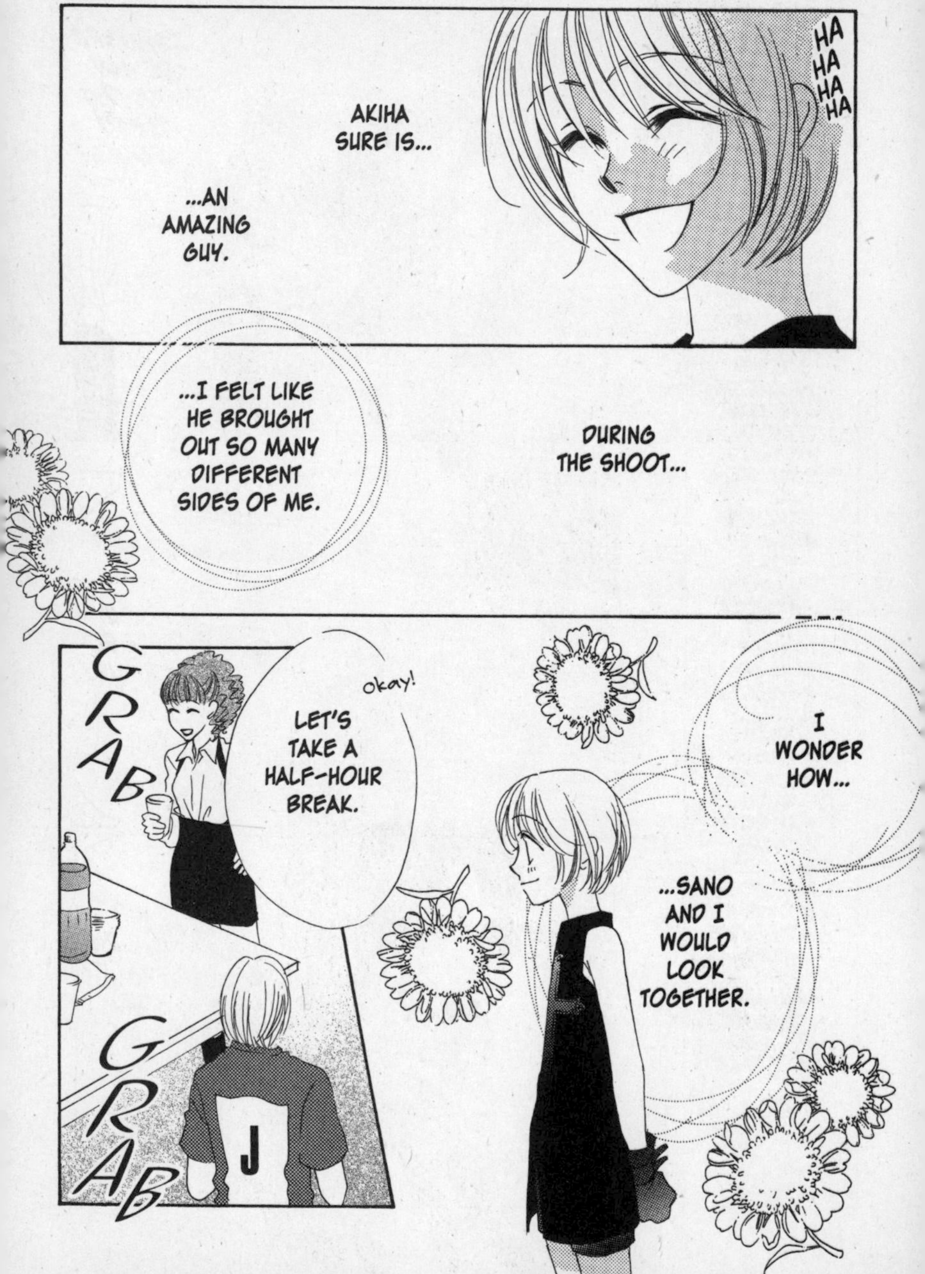
HA HA HA HA
AKIHA SURE IS...
...AN AMAZING GUY.
DURING THE SHOOT...
...I FELT LIKE HE BROUGHT OUT SO MANY DIFFERENT SIDES OF ME.
I WONDER HOW...
...SANO AND I WOULD LOOK TOGETHER.
okay!
LET'S TAKE A HALF-HOUR BREAK.
GRAB
GRAB
J

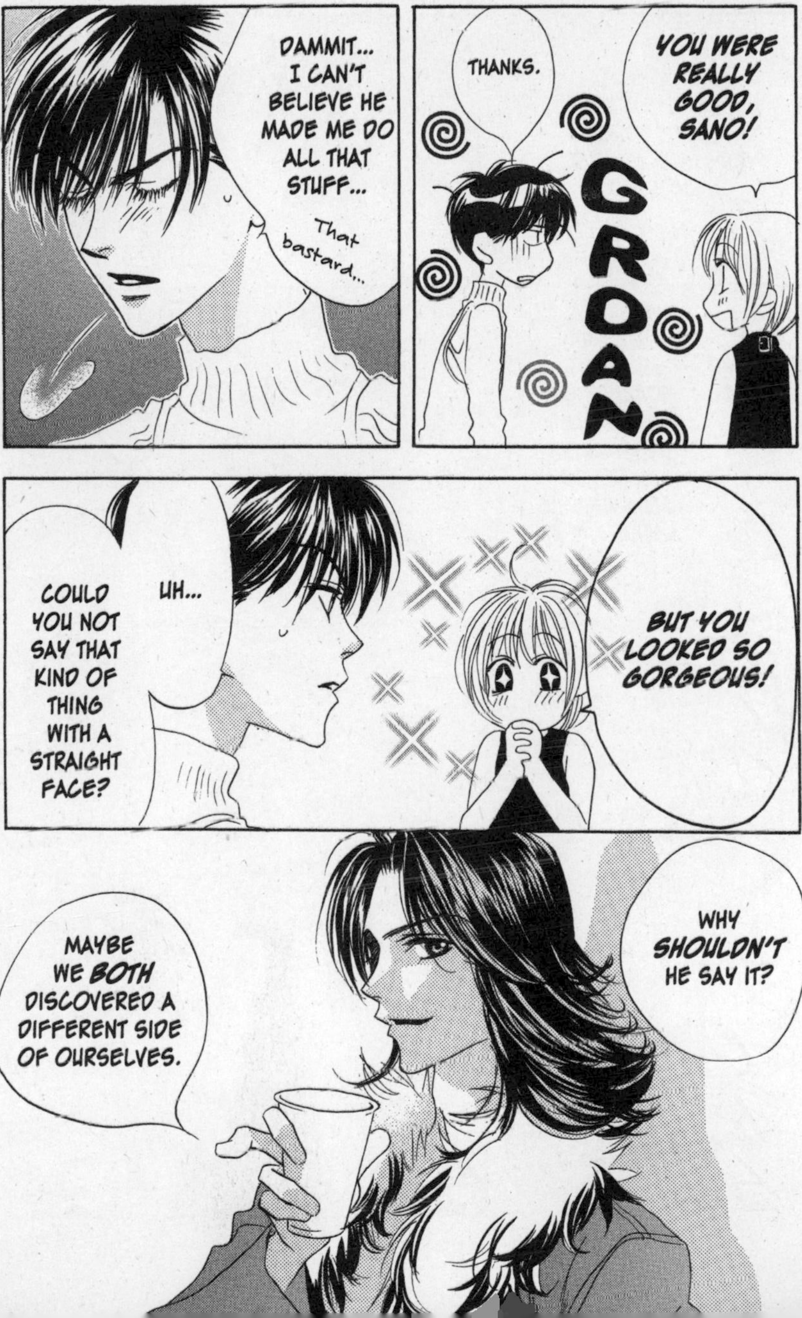
YOU WERE REALLY GOOD, SANO!
THANKS.
GROAN
DAMMIT... I CAN'T BELIEVE HE MADE ME DO ALL THAT STUFF...
That bastard...
BUT YOU LOOKED SO GORGEOUS!
UH...
COULD YOU NOT SAY THAT KIND OF THING WITH A STRAIGHT FACE?
WHY SHOULDN'T HE SAY IT?
MAYBE WE BOTH DISCOVERED A DIFFERENT SIDE OF OURSELVES.

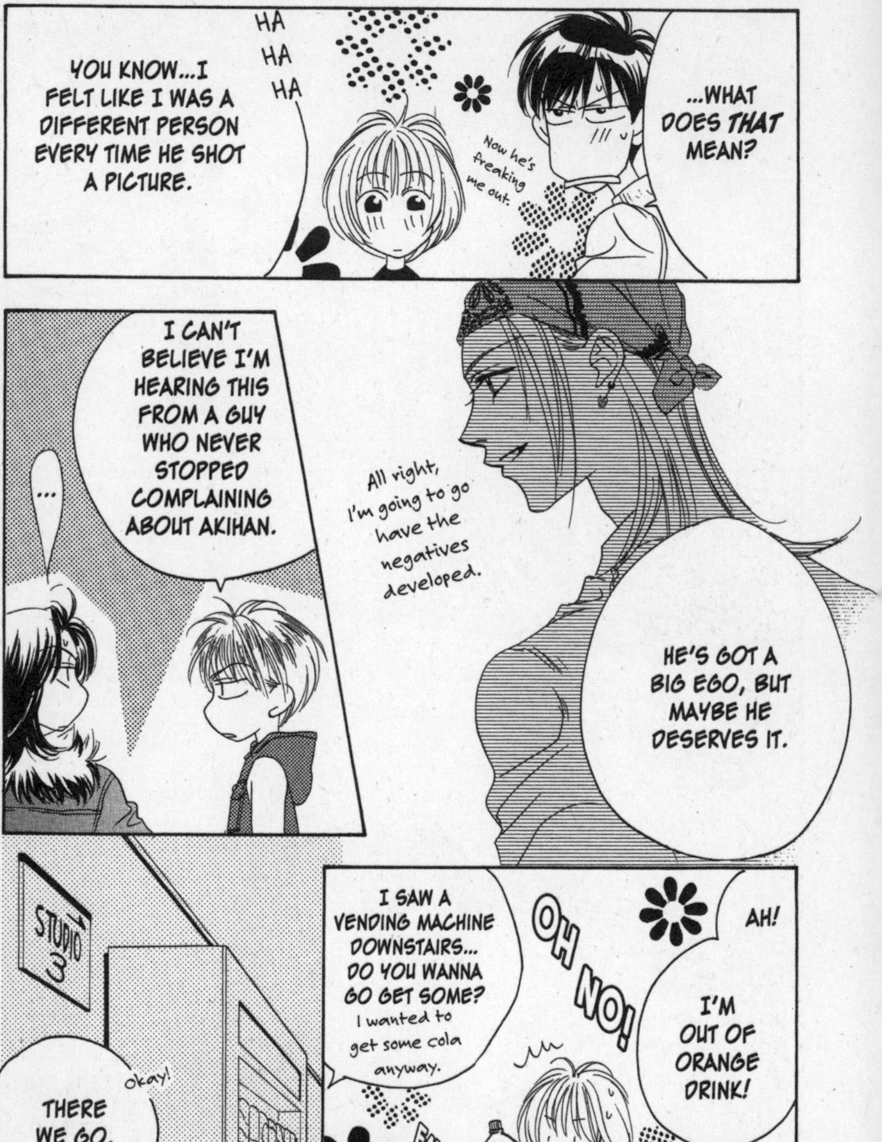
...WHAT DOES *THAT* MEAN?
Now he's freaking me out.
HA HA HA
YOU KNOW...I FELT LIKE I WAS A DIFFERENT PERSON EVERY TIME HE SHOT A PICTURE.
All right, I'm going to go have the negatives developed.
HE'S GOT A BIG EGO, BUT MAYBE HE DESERVES IT.
I CAN'T BELIEVE I'M HEARING THIS FROM A GUY WHO NEVER STOPPED COMPLAINING ABOUT AKIHAN.
...
AH!
I'M OUT OF ORANGE DRINK!
OH NO!
I SAW A VENDING MACHINE DOWNSTAIRS... DO YOU WANNA GO GET SOME?
I wanted to get some cola anyway.
EMPTY
NAN-CHAN
STUDIO 3
okay!
THERE WE GO.

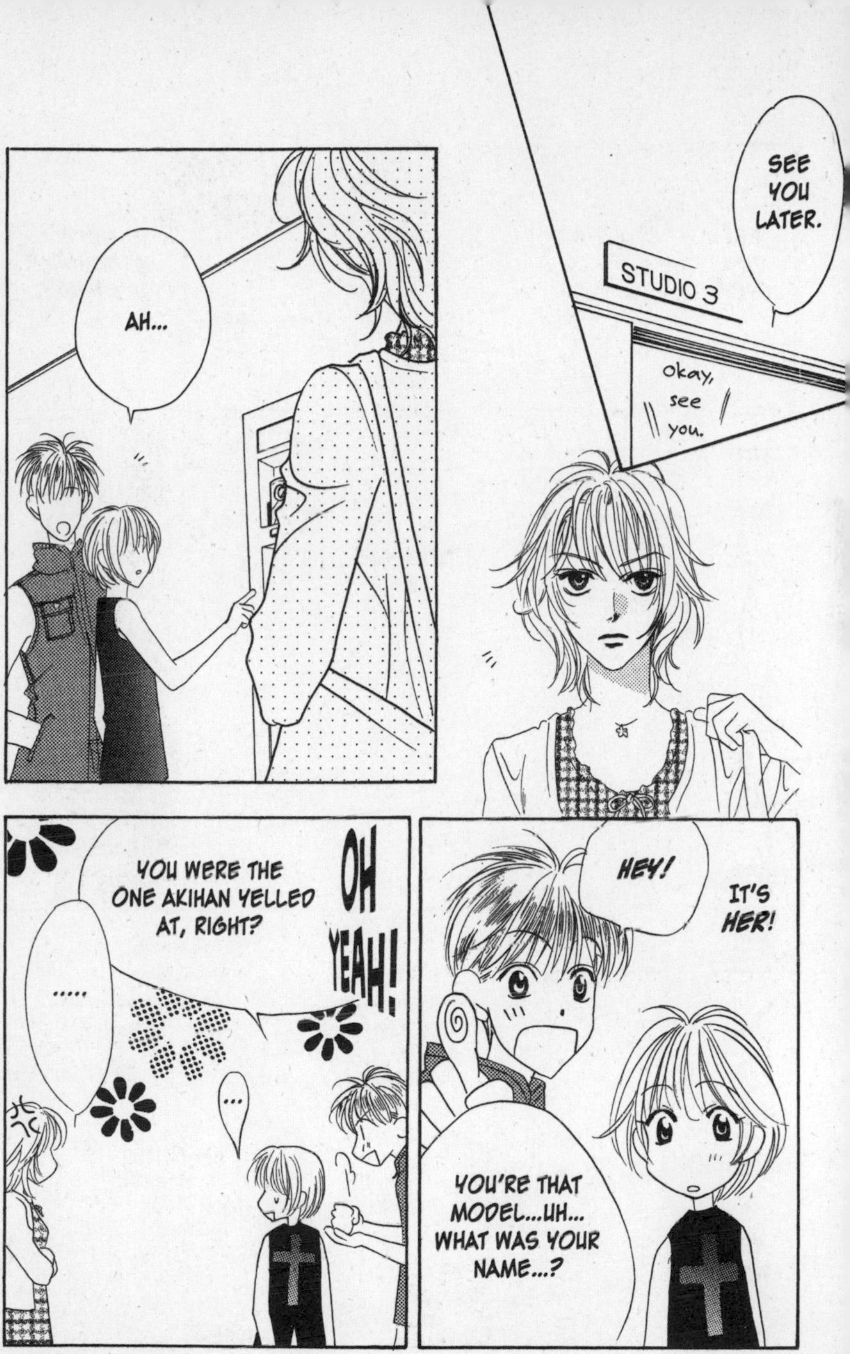
SEE YOU LATER.
STUDIO 3
okay, see you.
AH...
HEY!
IT'S HER!
YOU'RE THAT MODEL...UH... WHAT WAS YOUR NAME...?
OH YEAH!
YOU WERE THE ONE AKIHAN YELLED AT, RIGHT?
.....
...

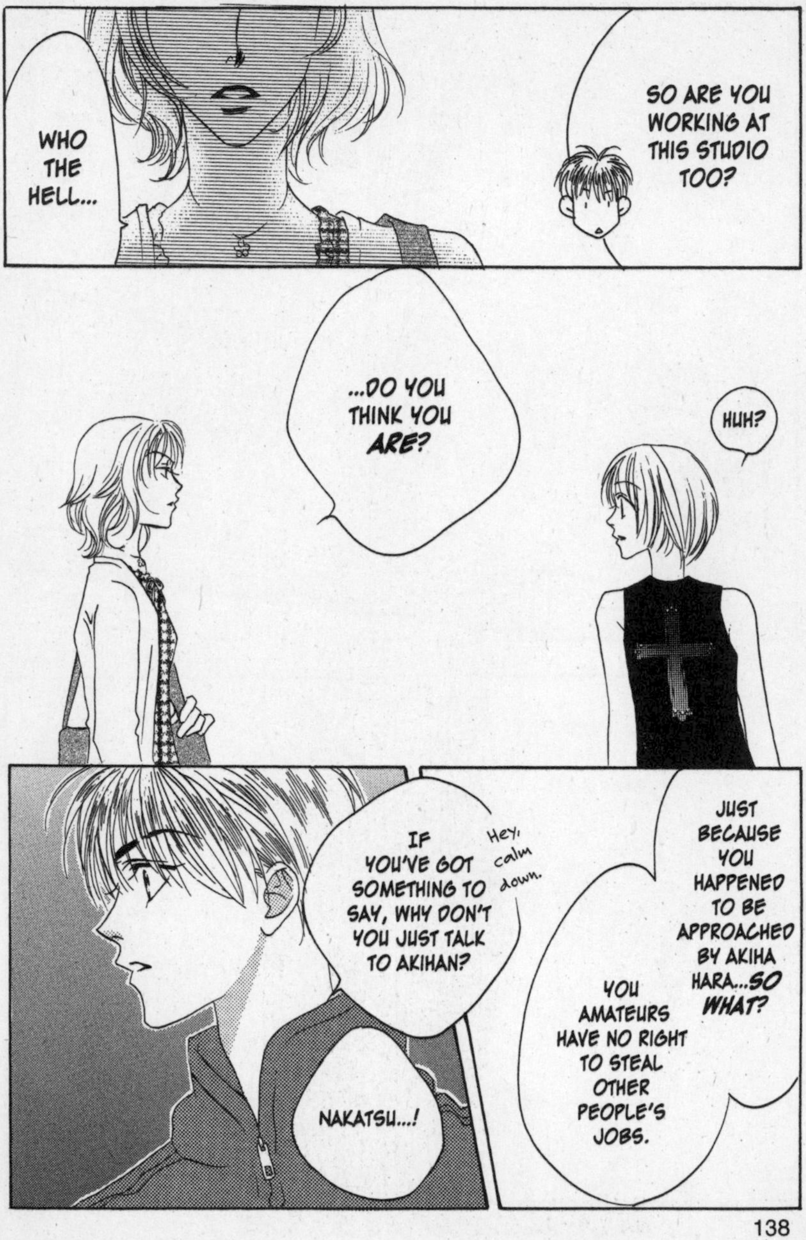
SO ARE YOU WORKING AT THIS STUDIO TOO?
WHO THE HELL...
HUH?
...DO YOU THINK YOU ARE?
JUST BECAUSE YOU HAPPENED TO BE APPROACHED BY AKIHA HARA...SO WHAT?
YOU AMATEURS HAVE NO RIGHT TO STEAL OTHER PEOPLE'S JOBS.
IF YOU'VE GOT SOMETHING TO SAY, WHY DON'T YOU JUST TALK TO AKIHAN?
Hey, calm down.
NAKATSU...!

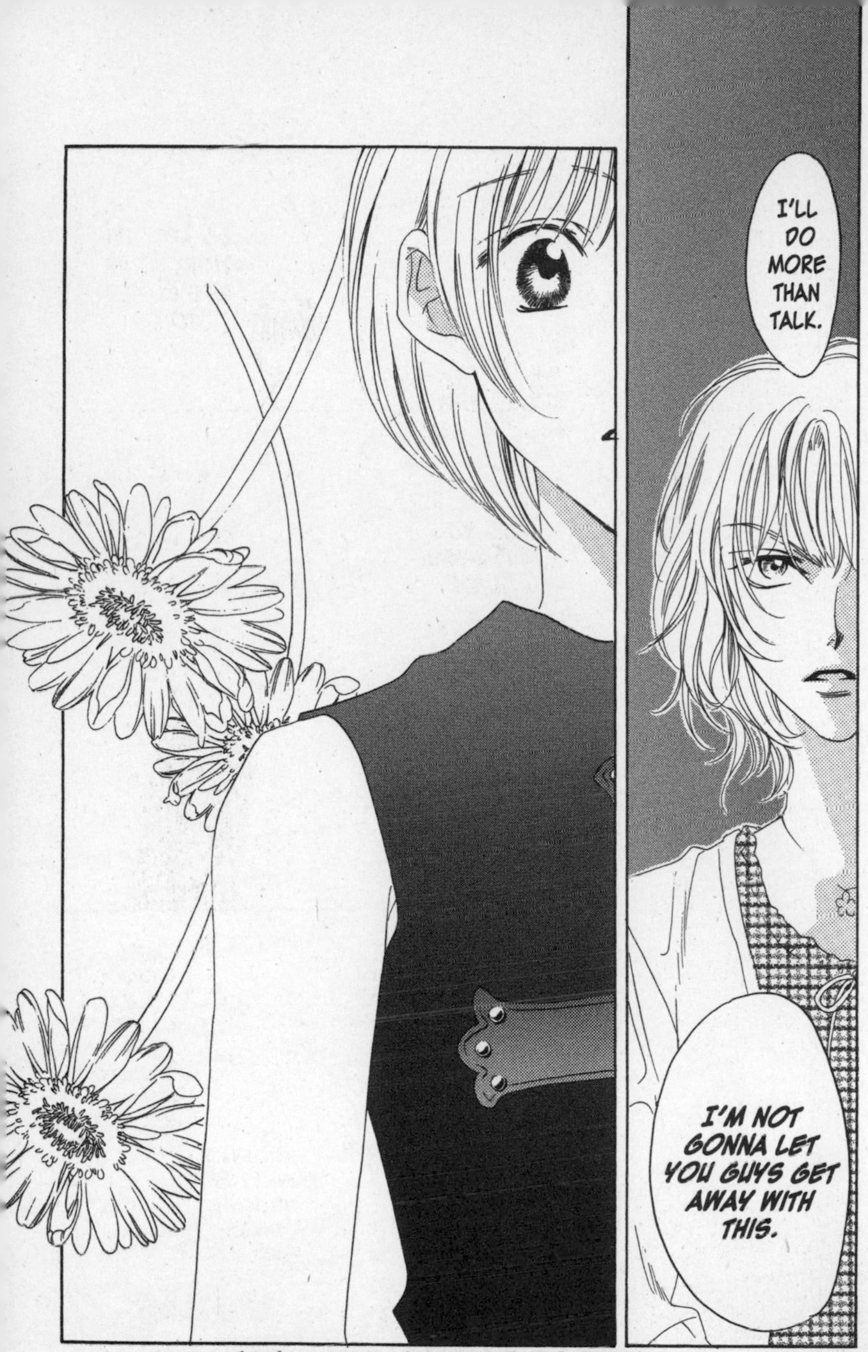
I'LL DO MORE THAN TALK.
I'M NOT GONNA LET YOU GUYS GET AWAY WITH THIS.

HANA-KIMI CHAPTER 53/END

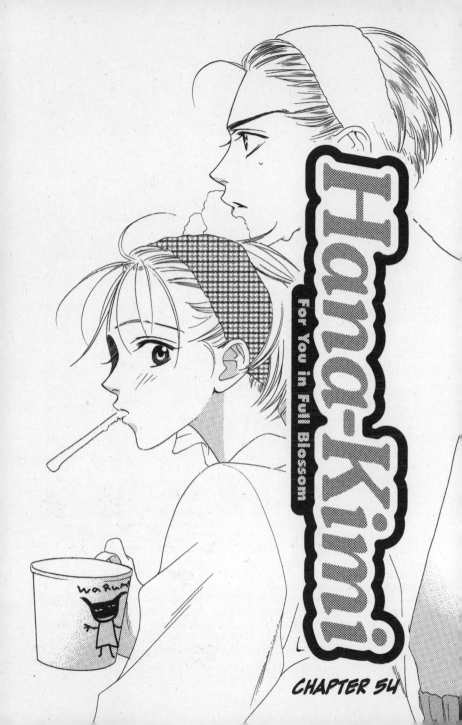

Hana-Kimi

For You in Full Blossom

CHAPTER 54

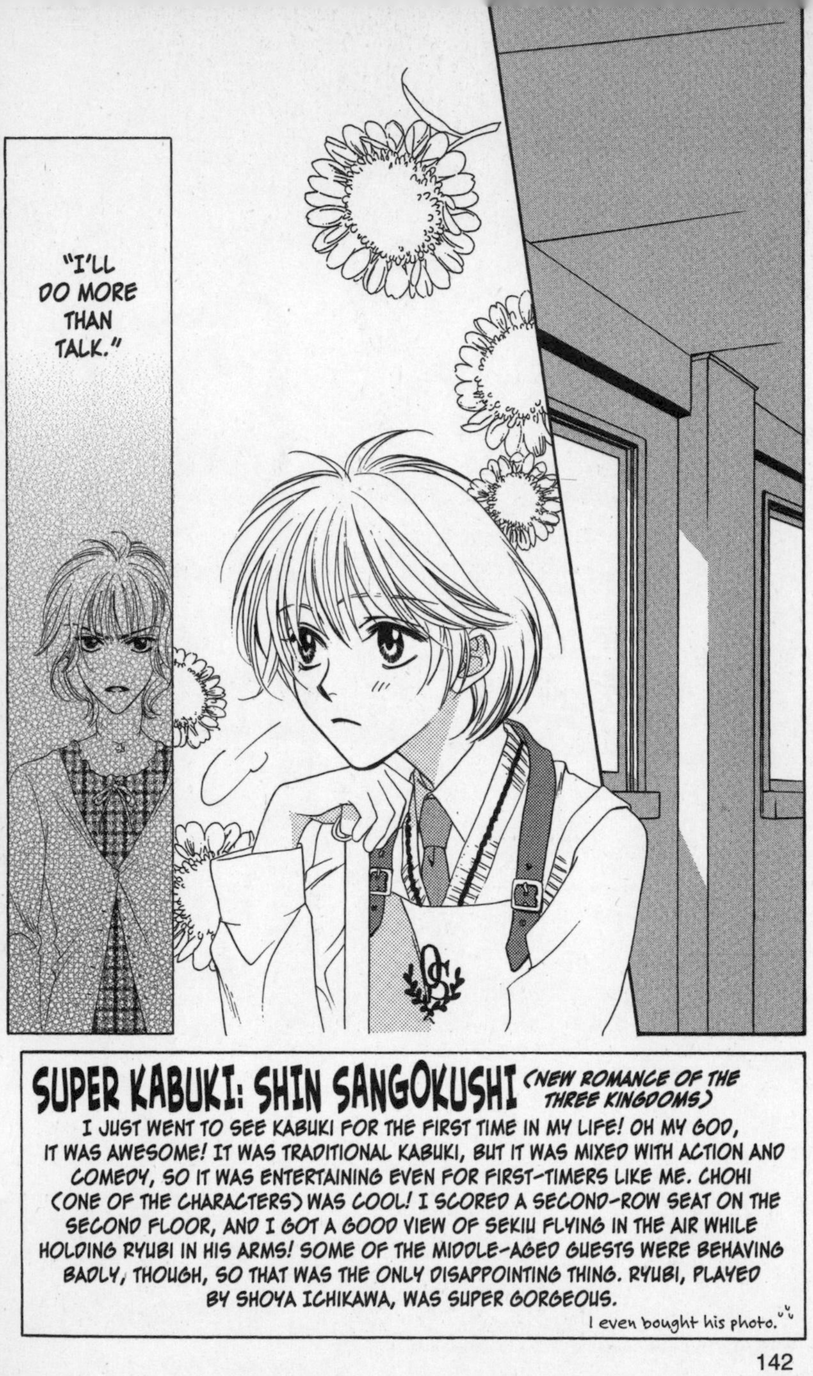
"I'LL DO MORE THAN TALK."

SUPER KABUKI: SHIN SANGOKUSHI (NEW ROMANCE OF THE THREE KINGDOMS)

I JUST WENT TO SEE KABUKI FOR THE FIRST TIME IN MY LIFE! OH MY GOD, IT WAS AWESOME! IT WAS TRADITIONAL KABUKI, BUT IT WAS MIXED WITH ACTION AND COMEDY, SO IT WAS ENTERTAINING EVEN FOR FIRST-TIMERS LIKE ME. CHOHI (ONE OF THE CHARACTERS) WAS COOL! I SCORED A SECOND-ROW SEAT ON THE SECOND FLOOR, AND I GOT A GOOD VIEW OF SEKIU FLYING IN THE AIR WHILE HOLDING RYUBI IN HIS ARMS! SOME OF THE MIDDLE-AGED GUESTS WERE BEHAVING BADLY, THOUGH, SO THAT WAS THE ONLY DISAPPOINTING THING. RYUBI, PLAYED BY SHOYA ICHIKAWA, WAS SUPER GORGEOUS.

I even bought his photo.

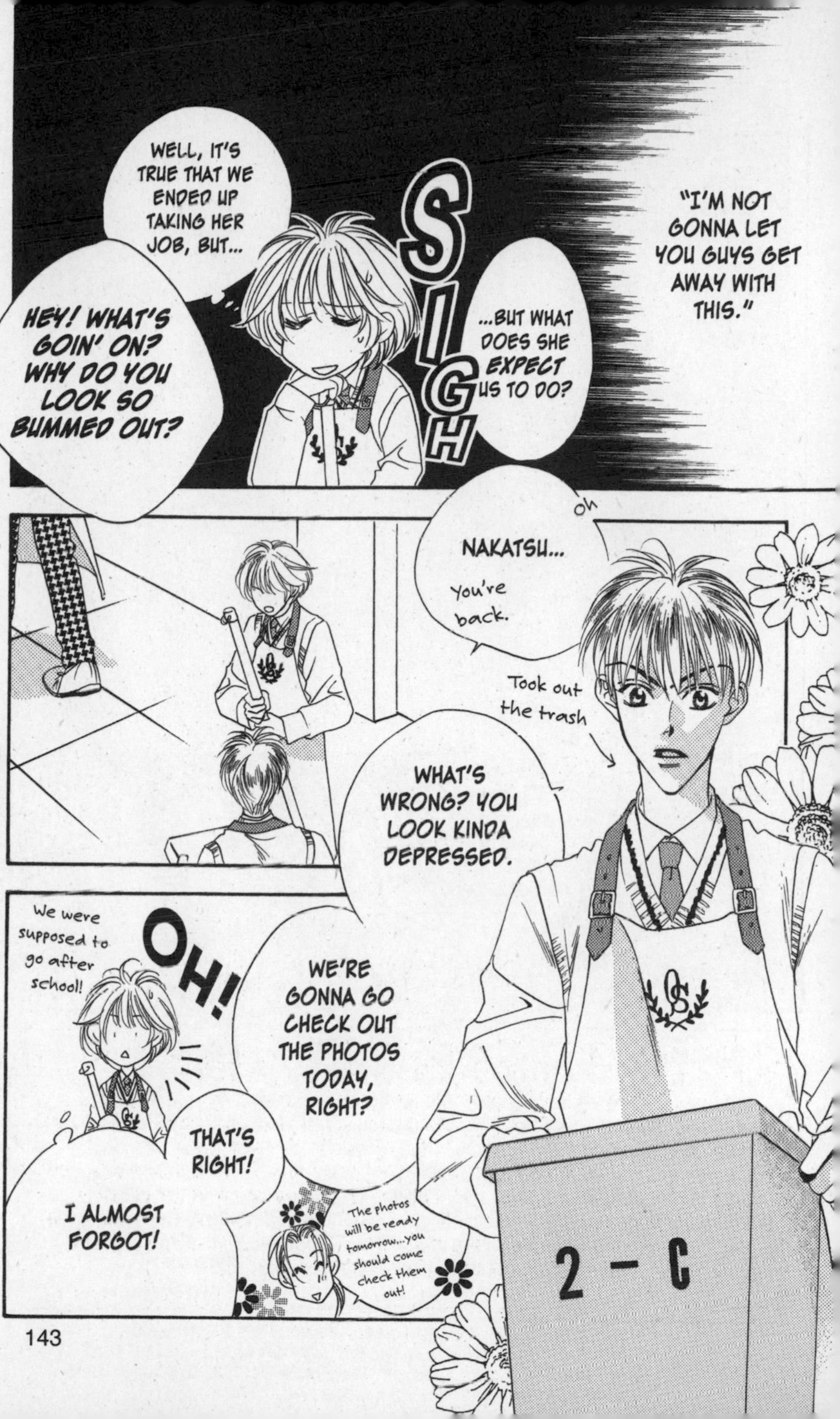
"I'M NOT GONNA LET YOU GUYS GET AWAY WITH THIS."
WELL, IT'S TRUE THAT WE ENDED UP TAKING HER JOB, BUT...
...BUT WHAT DOES SHE EXPECT US TO DO?
SIGH
HEY! WHAT'S GOIN' ON? WHY DO YOU LOOK SO BUMMED OUT?
CLEANING TIME
Oh
NAKATSU...
You're back.
Took out the trash
WHAT'S WRONG? YOU LOOK KINDA DEPRESSED.
2 – C
WE'RE GONNA GO CHECK OUT THE PHOTOS TODAY, RIGHT?
OH!
We were supposed to go after school!
THAT'S RIGHT!
I ALMOST FORGOT!
The photos will be ready tomorrow...you should come check them out!

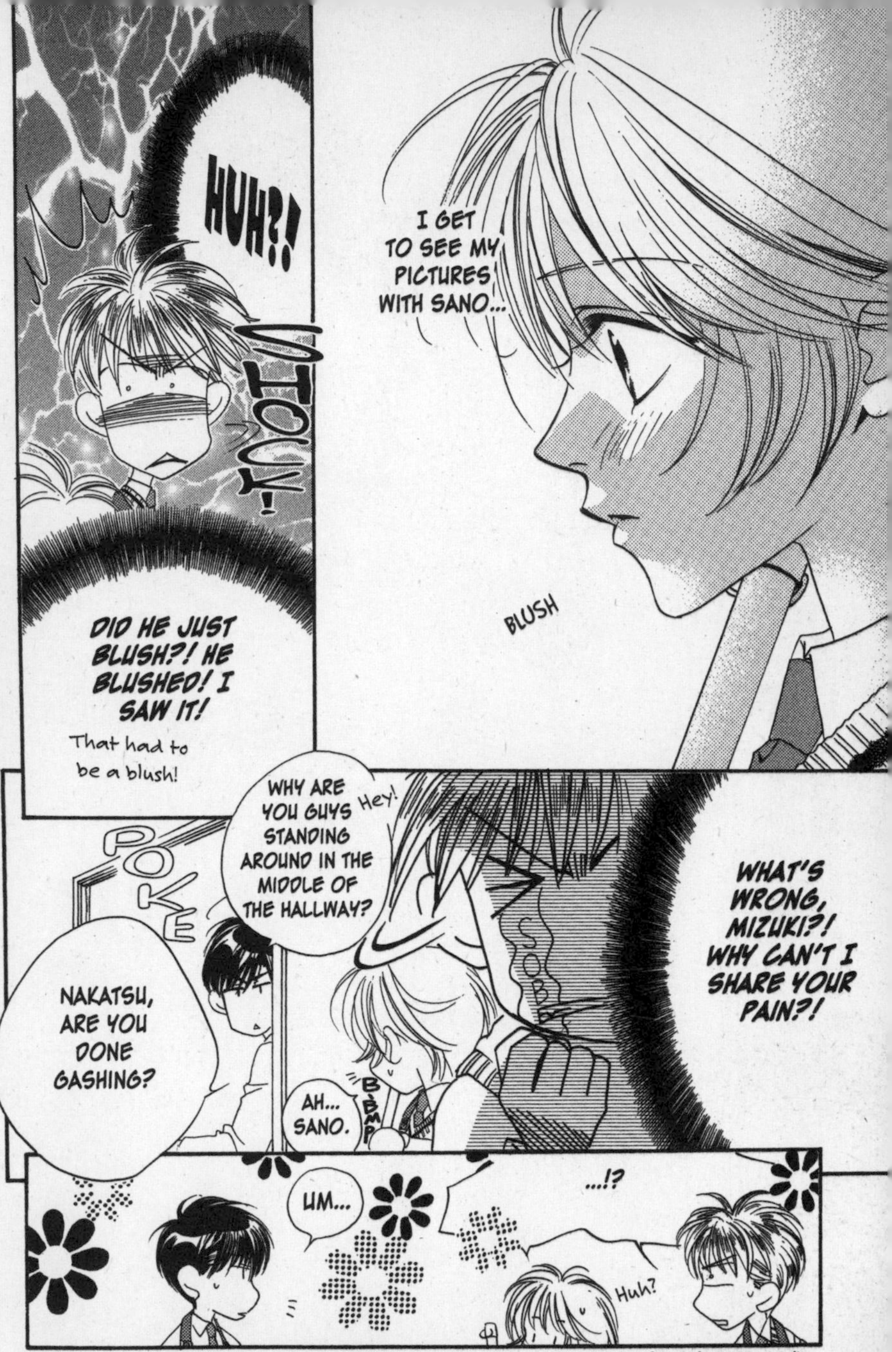

I GET TO SEE MY PICTURES WITH SANO...
BLUSH
HUH?!
SHOCK!
DID HE JUST BLUSH?! HE BLUSHED! I SAW IT!
That had to be a blush!
WHAT'S WRONG, MIZUKI?! WHY CAN'T I SHARE YOUR PAIN?!
SOB
WHY ARE YOU GUYS STANDING AROUND IN THE MIDDLE OF THE HALLWAY?
Hey!
POKE
AH... SANO.
BUMP
NAKATSU, ARE YOU DONE GASHING?
...!?
Huh?
UM...

IN THE ORIGINAL JAPANESE, SANO SAYS "GOMI NAGERU," MEANING "TO THROW (AWAY) GARBAGE." THE USUAL TERM IS "GOMI SUTERU," MEANING "TO DUMP GARBAGE." NAKATSU SAYS "(GOMI) HOKASU", MEANING "TO RELEASE/SET ASIDE GARBAGE." THE ENGLISH REWRITE USES BRITISH AND NEW YORK TERMS FOR GARBAGE.

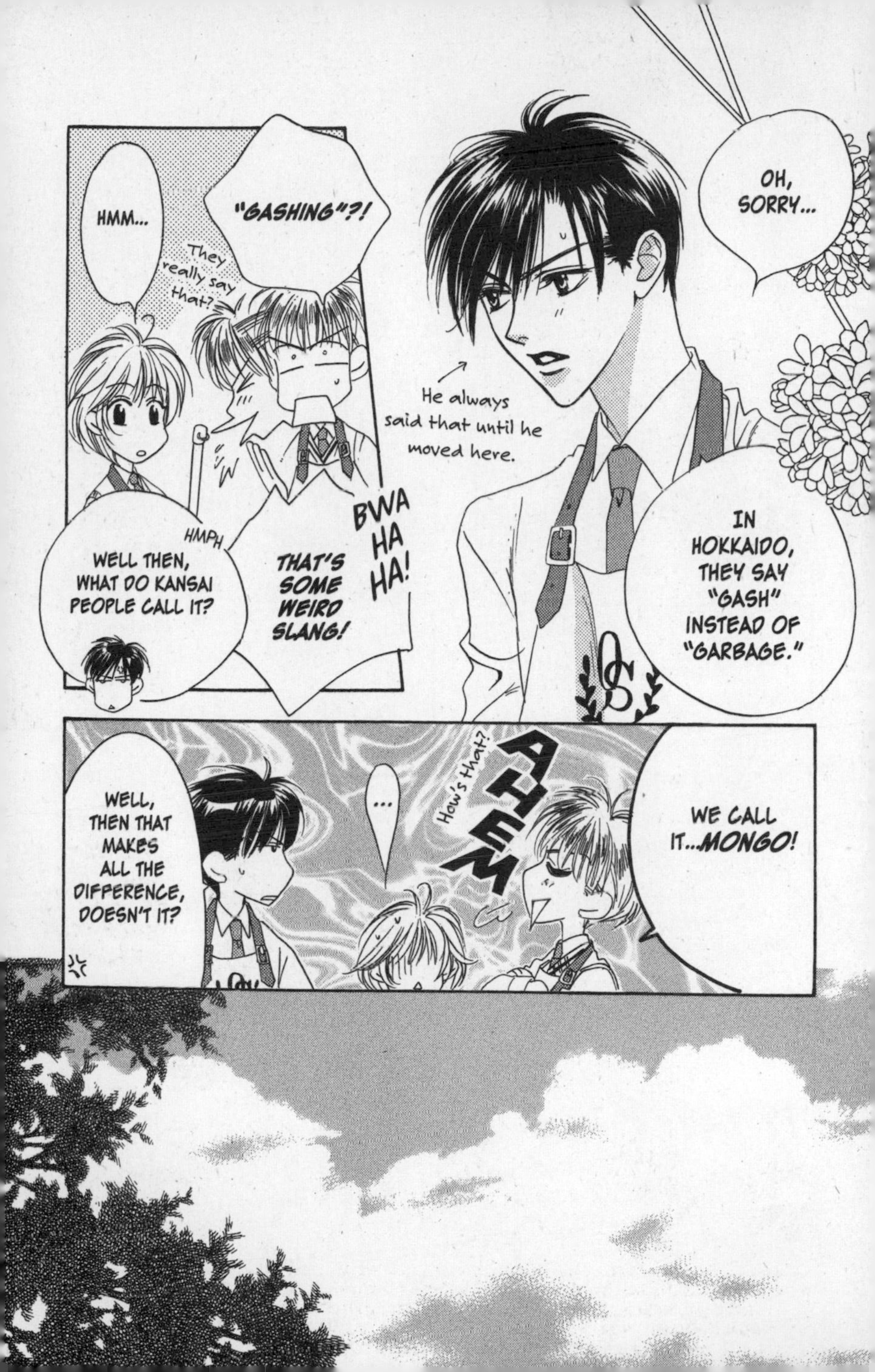
OH, SORRY...
He always said that until he moved here.
IN HOKKAIDO, THEY SAY "GASH" INSTEAD OF "GARBAGE."
"GASHING"?!
They really say that?
HMM...
BWA HA HA!
THAT'S SOME WEIRD SLANG!
HMPH
WELL THEN, WHAT DO KANSAI PEOPLE CALL IT?
WE CALL IT...MONGO!
AHEM
How's that?
...
WELL, THEN THAT MAKES ALL THE DIFFERENCE, DOESN'T IT?

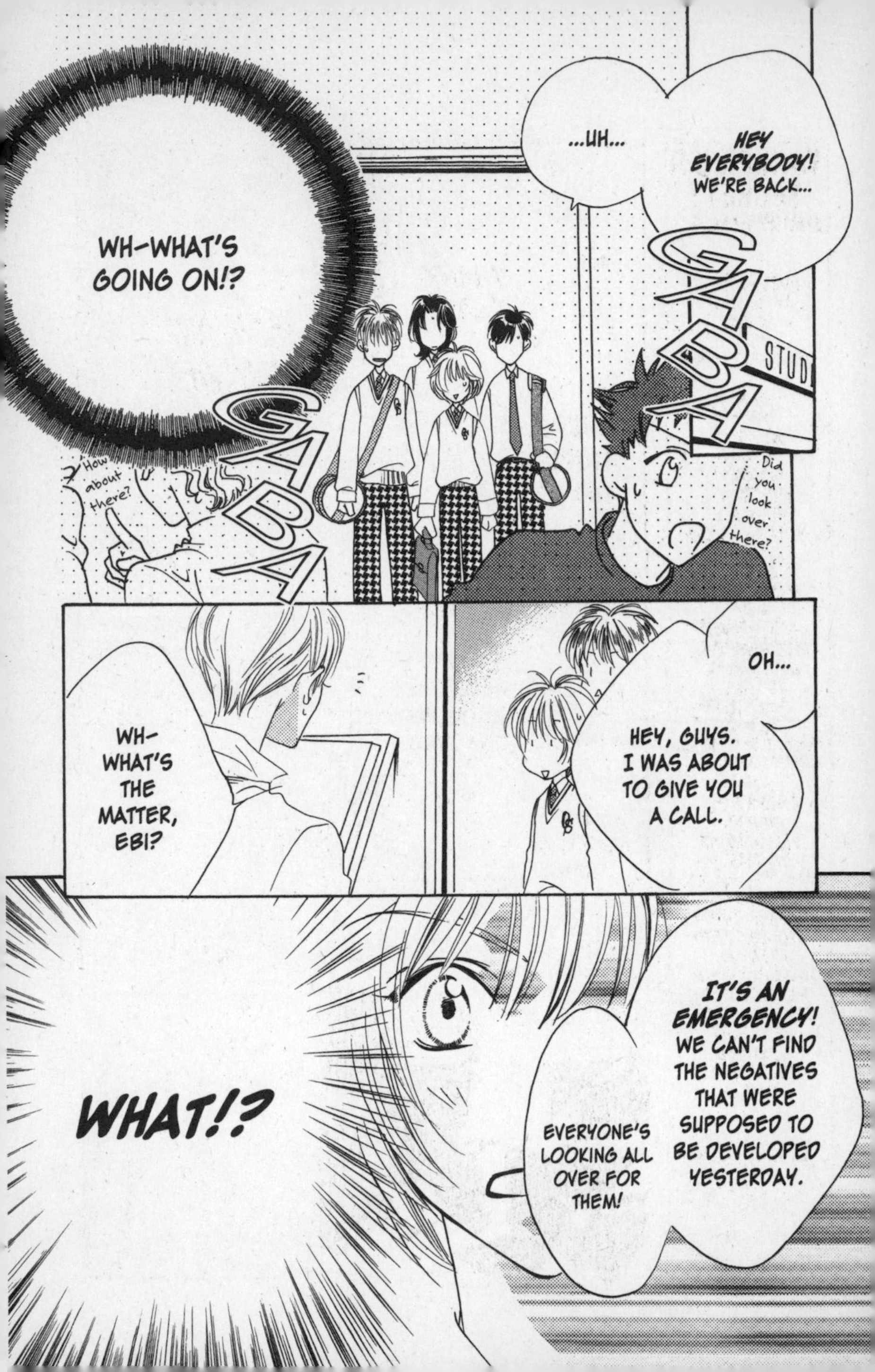
HEY EVERYBODY! WE'RE BACK...
...UH...
GABA
GABA
STUD
Did you look over there?
How about there?
WH-WHAT'S GOING ON!?
OH...
HEY, GUYS. I WAS ABOUT TO GIVE YOU A CALL.
WH-WHAT'S THE MATTER, EBI?
IT'S AN EMERGENCY! WE CAN'T FIND THE NEGATIVES THAT WERE SUPPOSED TO BE DEVELOPED YESTERDAY.
EVERYONE'S LOOKING ALL OVER FOR THEM!
WHAT!?

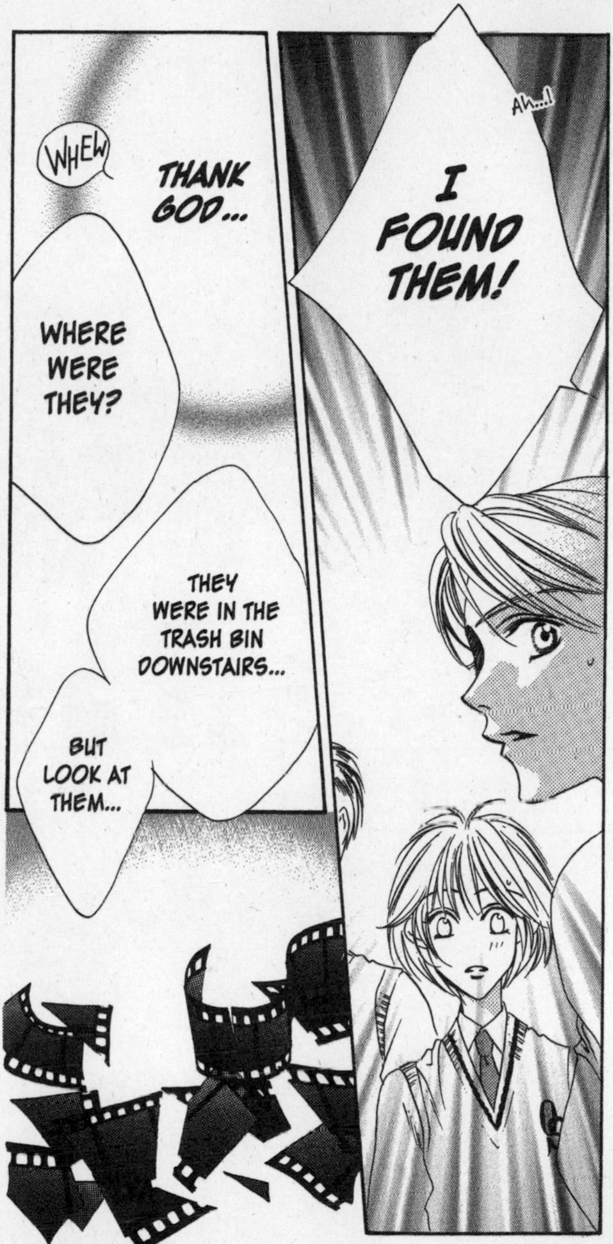
Ah...!
I FOUND THEM!
THANK GOD...
WHEW
WHERE WERE THEY?
THEY WERE IN THE TRASH BIN DOWNSTAIRS...
BUT LOOK AT THEM...

WHISPERED SECRETS

SENRI NAKAO

BIRTHDAY: APRIL 3RD
AGE: 17
BLOOD TYPE: A
SIGN: ARIES
HEIGHT: 164CM
FAVORITE FOODS: PUDDING, STEAMED EGG CUSTARD
FAVORITE MUSICIAN: GLAY
FAVORITE DESIGNERS: CARL HELM, NICOLE
FAVORITE MOVIE: INTERVIEW WITH THE VAMPIRE
LOVE INTEREST: NANBA
FOODS HE HATES: PICKLES, SALADS WITH VINEGAR, ANYTHING CHEWY
CHARACTER-ISTICS: UNDERGOES A PERSONALITY CHANGE WHEN HE'S MAD
IMAGE FLOWER: DAHLIA

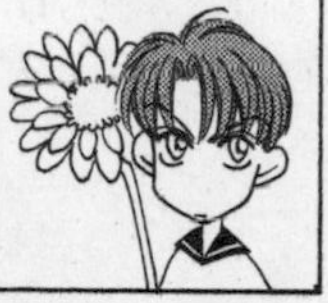

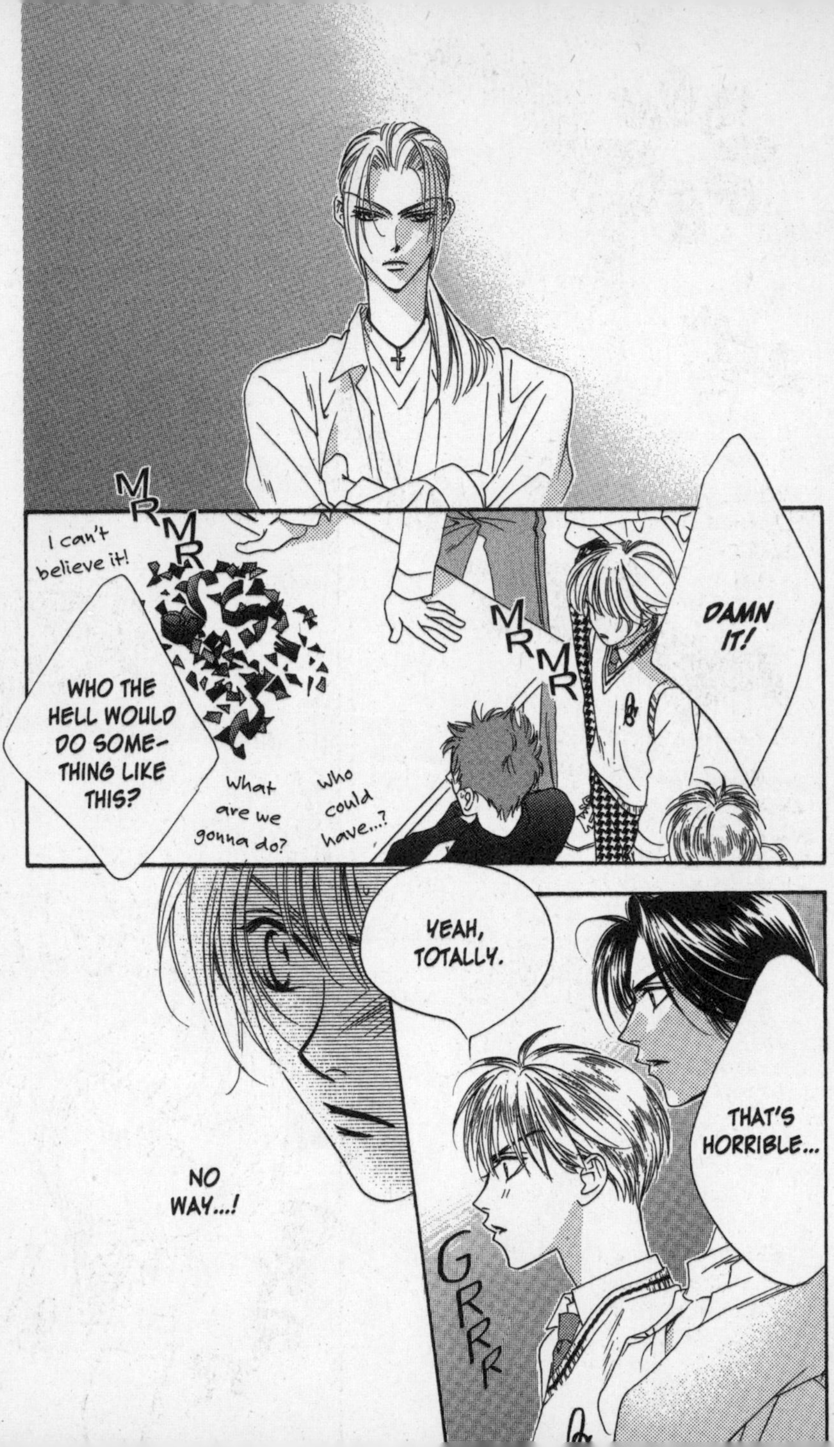
DAMN IT!
MRMR
who could have...?
What are we gonna do?
I can't believe it!
MRMR
WHO THE HELL WOULD DO SOME-THING LIKE THIS?
THAT'S HORRIBLE...
YEAH, TOTALLY.
GRRR
NO WAY...!

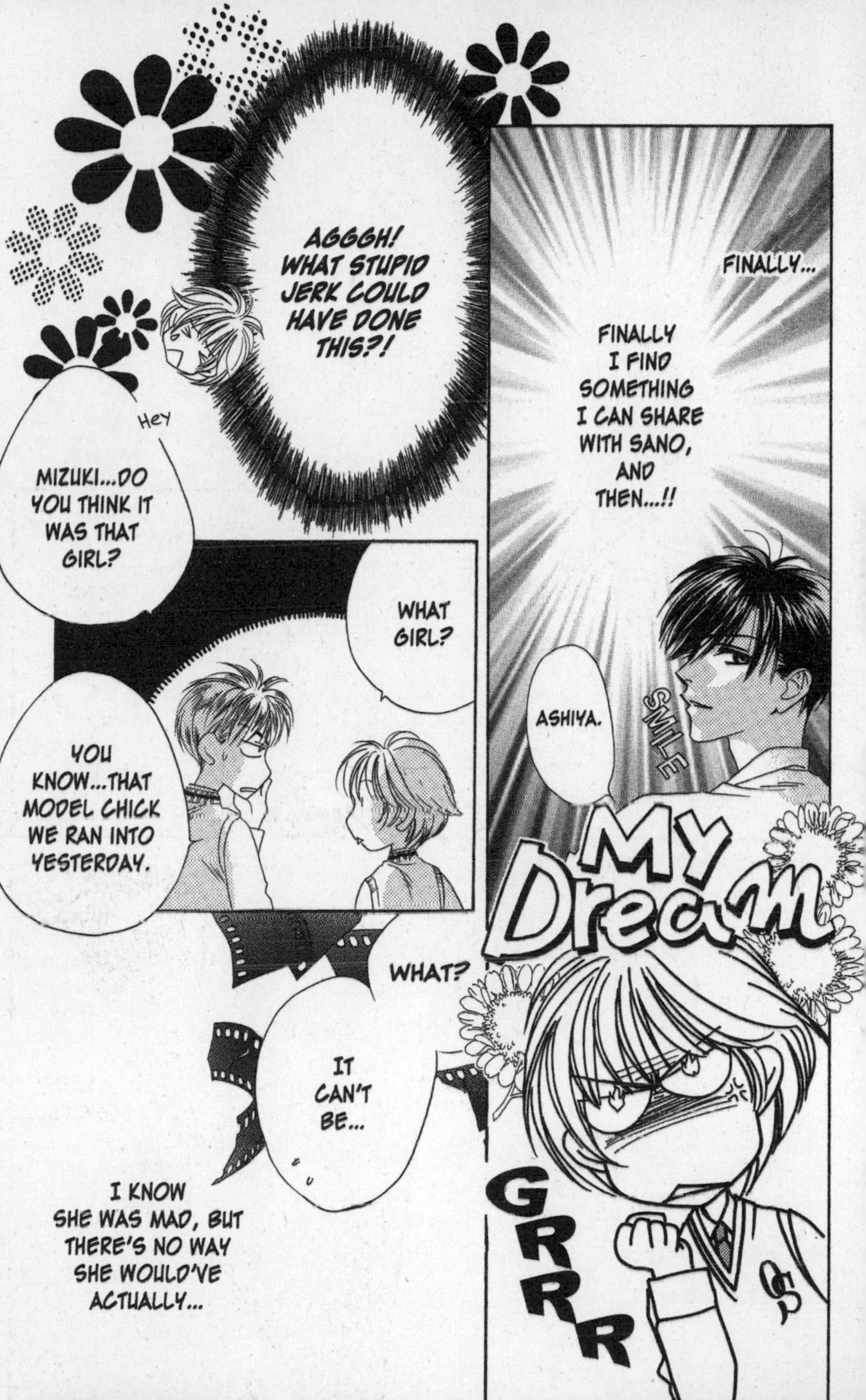
FINALLY...
FINALLY I FIND SOMETHING I CAN SHARE WITH SANO, AND THEN...!!
ASHIYA.
SMILE
MY Dream
GRRR
AGGGH! WHAT STUPID JERK COULD HAVE DONE THIS?!
Hey
MIZUKI...DO YOU THINK IT WAS THAT GIRL?
WHAT GIRL?
YOU KNOW...THAT MODEL CHICK WE RAN INTO YESTERDAY.
WHAT?
IT CAN'T BE...
I KNOW SHE WAS MAD, BUT THERE'S NO WAY SHE WOULD'VE ACTUALLY...

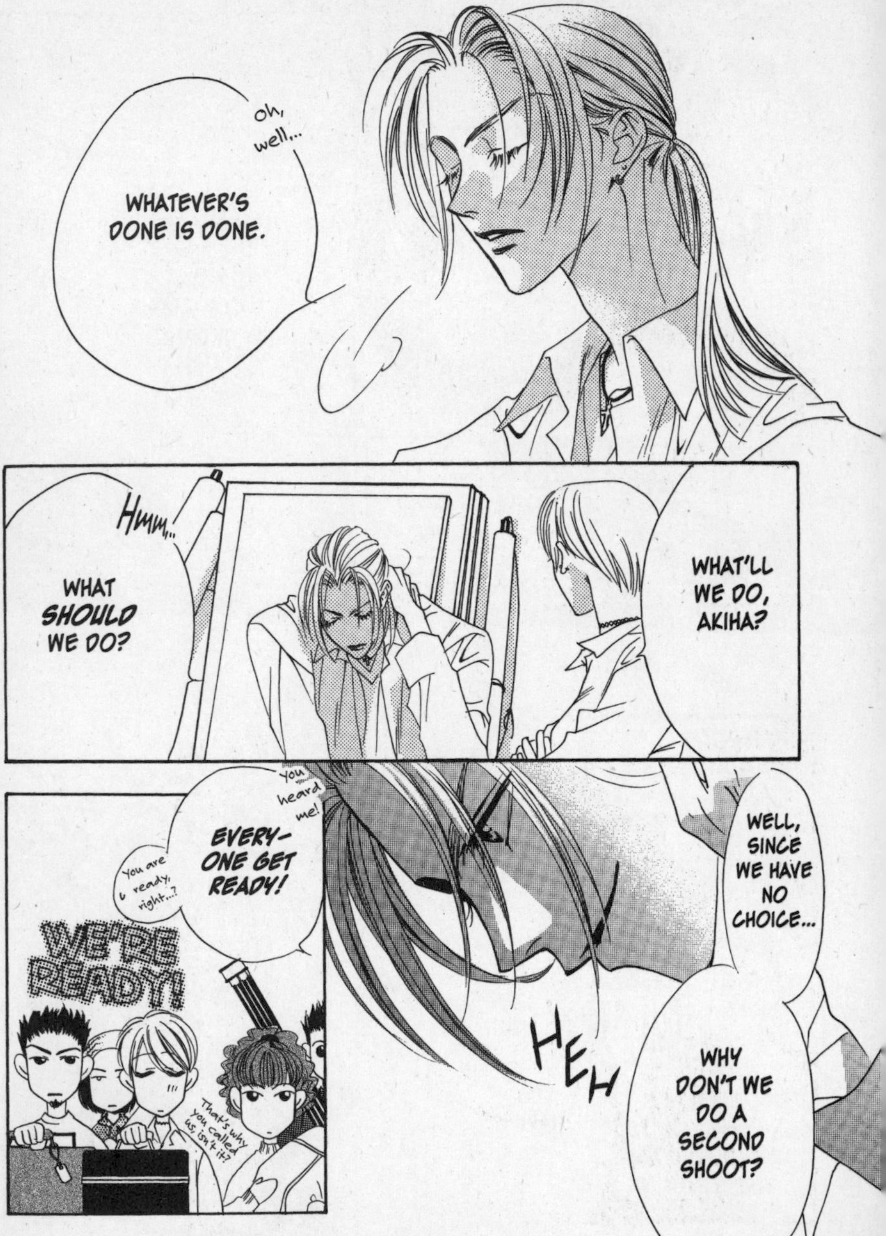
Oh, well...
WHATEVER'S DONE IS DONE.
WHAT'LL WE DO, AKIHA?
Hmm...
WHAT SHOULD WE DO?
WELL, SINCE WE HAVE NO CHOICE...
HEH
WHY DON'T WE DO A SECOND SHOOT?
You heard me!
EVERY-ONE GET READY!
You are ready, right...?
WE'RE READY!
That's why you called us, isn't it?

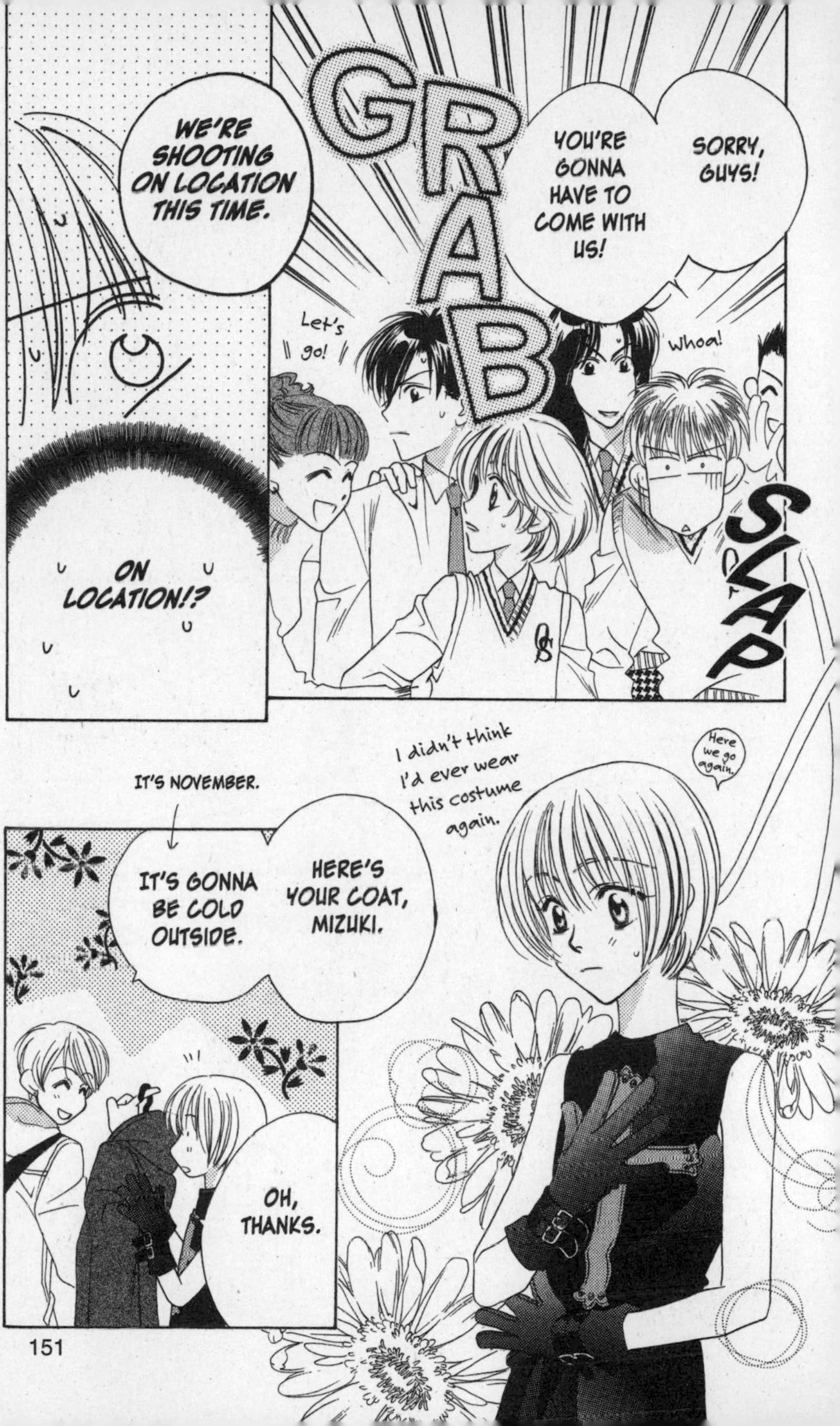
GRAB
SORRY, GUYS!
YOU'RE GONNA HAVE TO COME WITH US!
Whoa!
Let's go!
SLAP
WE'RE SHOOTING ON LOCATION THIS TIME.
ON LOCATION!?
Here we go again.
I didn't think I'd ever wear this costume again.
HERE'S YOUR COAT, MIZUKI.
IT'S GONNA BE COLD OUTSIDE.
IT'S NOVEMBER.
OH, THANKS.

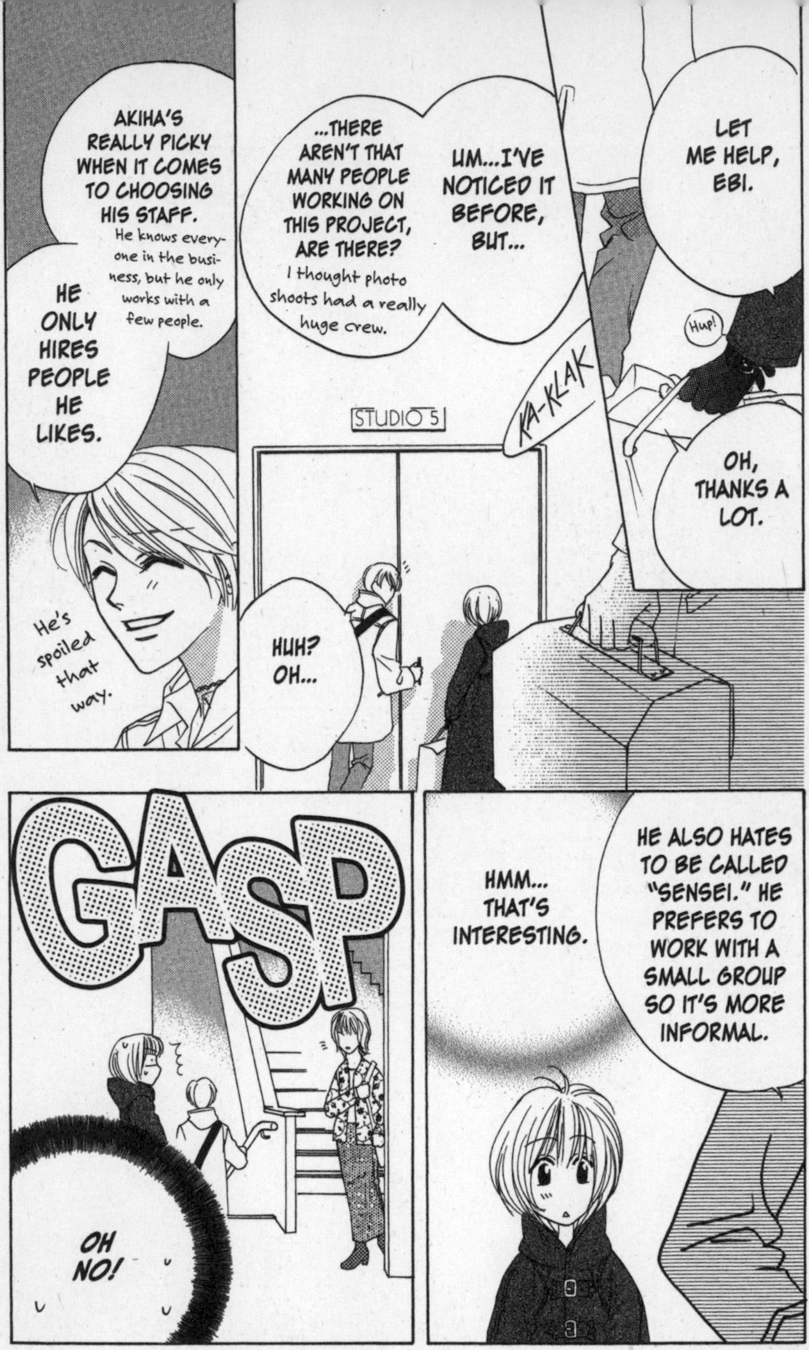
LET ME HELP, EBI.
Hup!
KA-KLAK
OH, THANKS A LOT.
UM...I'VE NOTICED IT BEFORE, BUT...
...THERE AREN'T THAT MANY PEOPLE WORKING ON THIS PROJECT, ARE THERE?
I thought photo shoots had a really huge crew.
STUDIO 5
HUH? OH...
AKIHA'S REALLY PICKY WHEN IT COMES TO CHOOSING HIS STAFF.
He knows everyone in the business, but he only works with a few people.
HE ONLY HIRES PEOPLE HE LIKES.
He's spoiled that way.
HE ALSO HATES TO BE CALLED "SENSEI." HE PREFERS TO WORK WITH A SMALL GROUP SO IT'S MORE INFORMAL.
HMM... THAT'S INTERESTING.
GASP
OH NO!

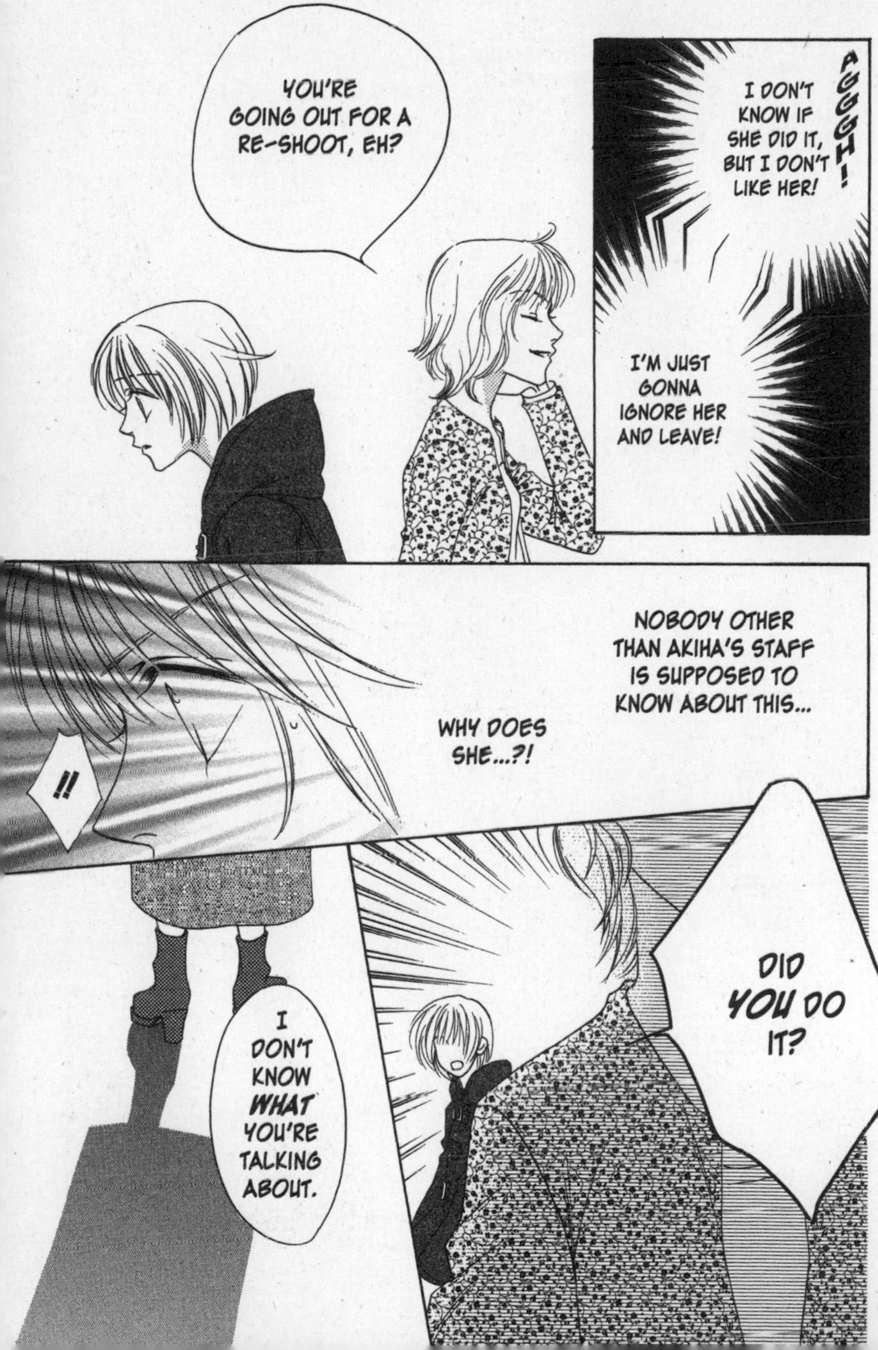
AGGGH!
I DON'T KNOW IF SHE DID IT, BUT I DON'T LIKE HER!
I'M JUST GONNA IGNORE HER AND LEAVE!
YOU'RE GOING OUT FOR A RE-SHOOT, EH?
NOBODY OTHER THAN AKIHA'S STAFF IS SUPPOSED TO KNOW ABOUT THIS...
WHY DOES SHE...?!
!!
DID *YOU* DO IT?
I DON'T KNOW *WHAT* YOU'RE TALKING ABOUT.

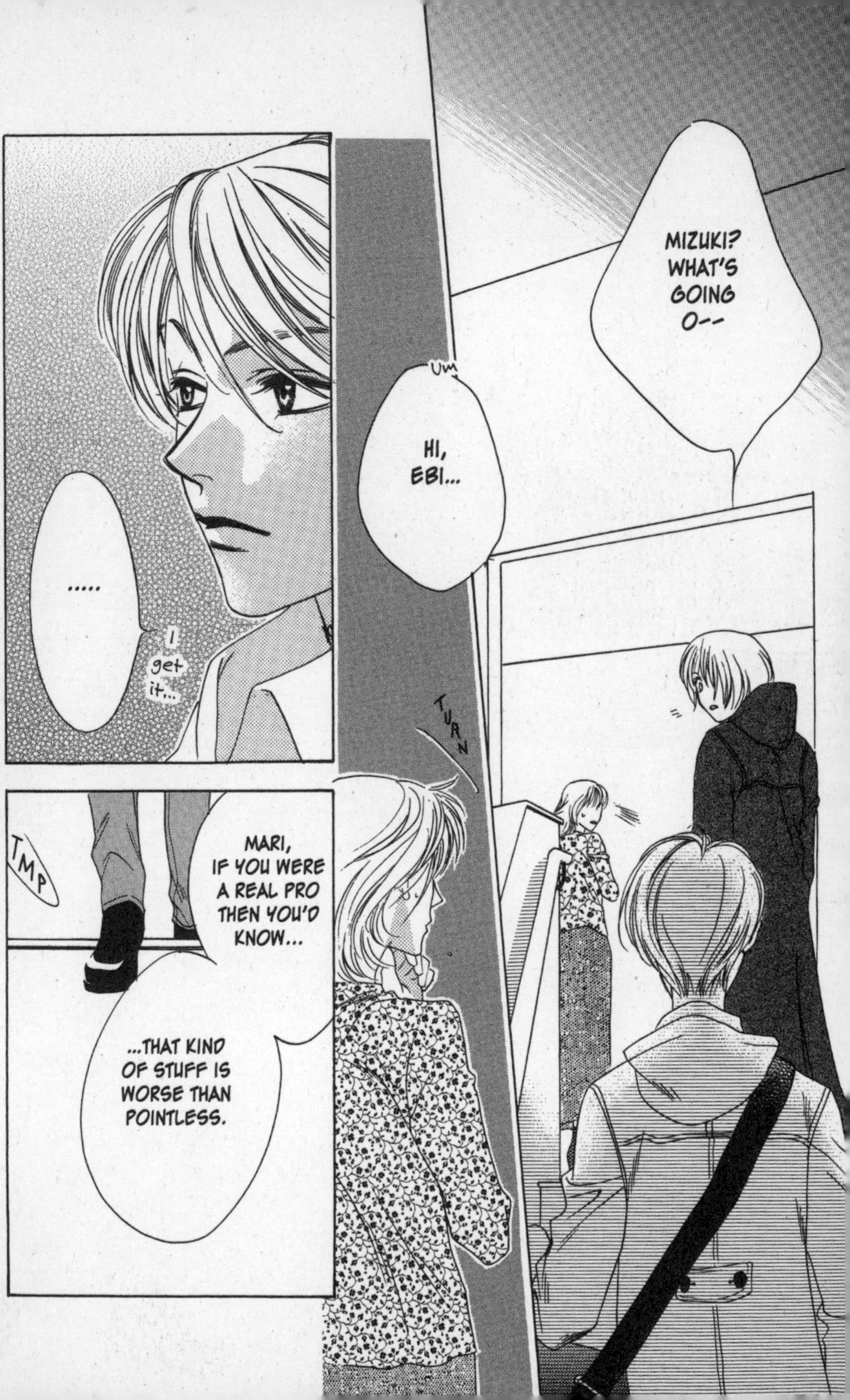
MIZUKI? WHAT'S GOING O--
UM
HI, EBI...
TURN
.....
I get it...
TMP
MARI, IF YOU WERE A REAL PRO THEN YOU'D KNOW...
...THAT KIND OF STUFF IS WORSE THAN POINTLESS.

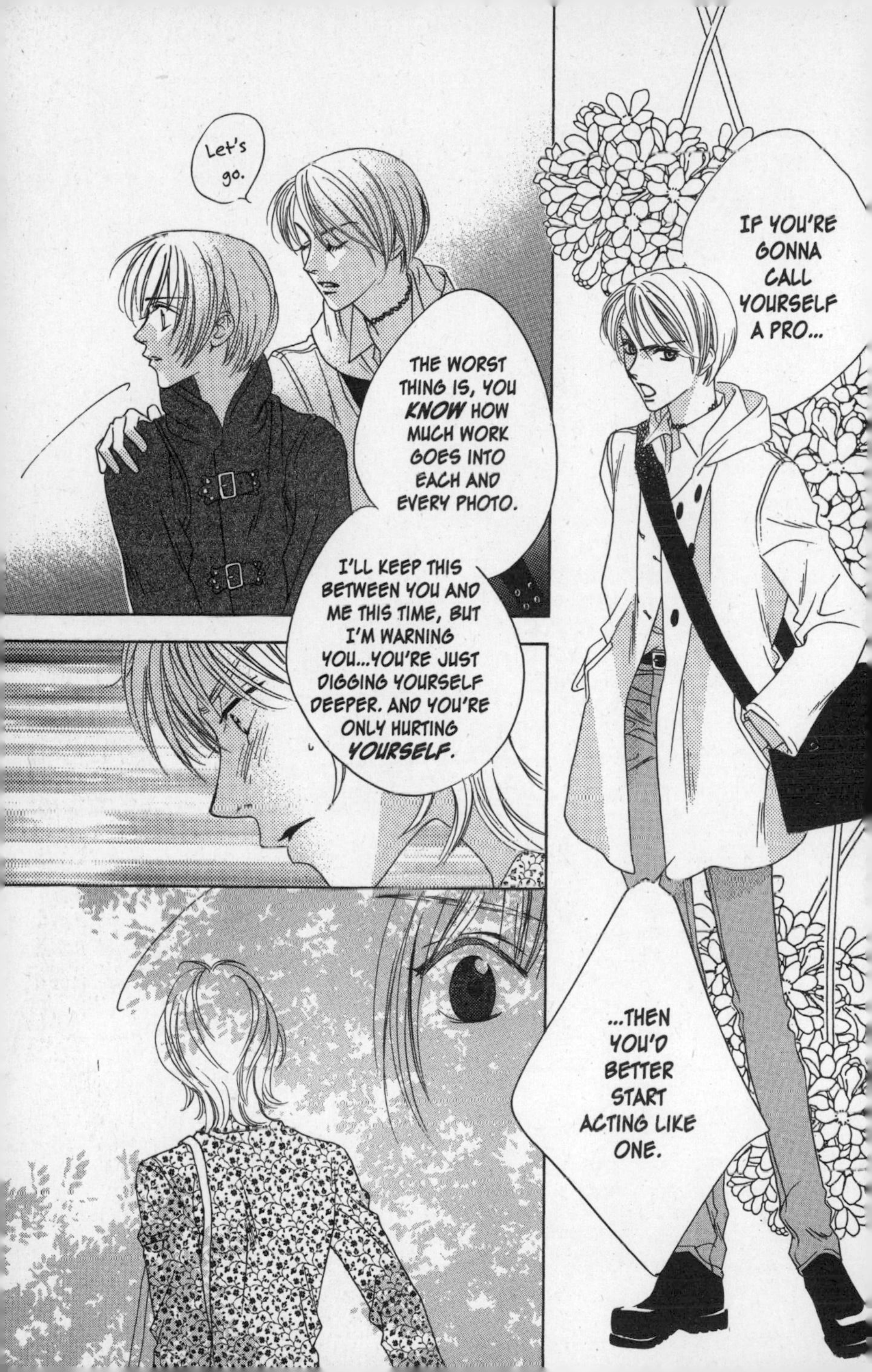
IF YOU'RE GONNA CALL YOURSELF A PRO...
...THEN YOU'D BETTER START ACTING LIKE ONE.
THE WORST THING IS, YOU *KNOW* HOW MUCH WORK GOES INTO EACH AND EVERY PHOTO.
I'LL KEEP THIS BETWEEN YOU AND ME THIS TIME, BUT I'M WARNING YOU...YOU'RE JUST DIGGING YOURSELF DEEPER. AND YOU'RE ONLY HURTING *YOURSELF*.
Let's go.

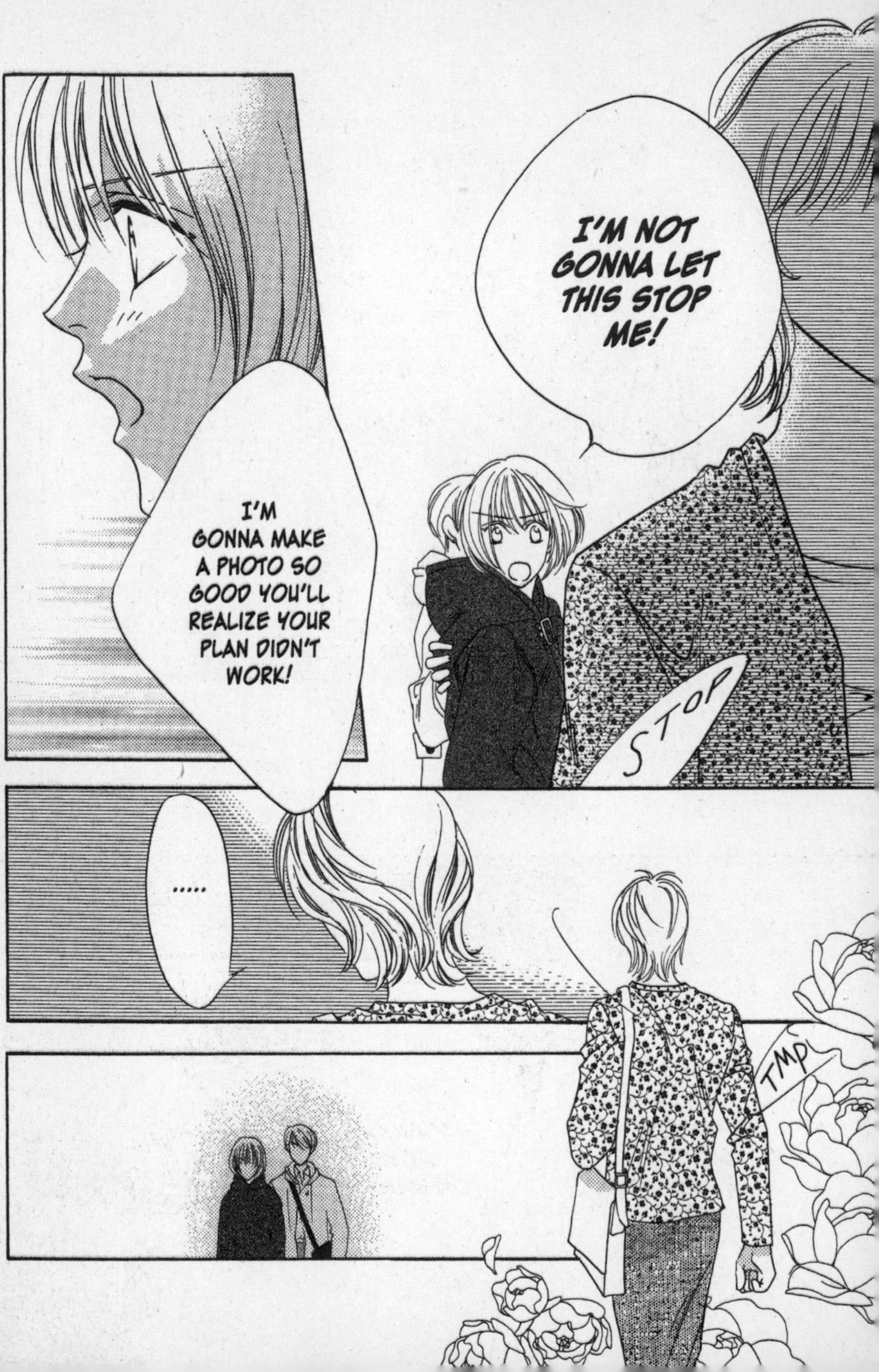
I'M NOT GONNA LET THIS STOP ME!
STOP
I'M GONNA MAKE A PHOTO SO GOOD YOU'LL REALIZE YOUR PLAN DIDN'T WORK!
.....
TMP

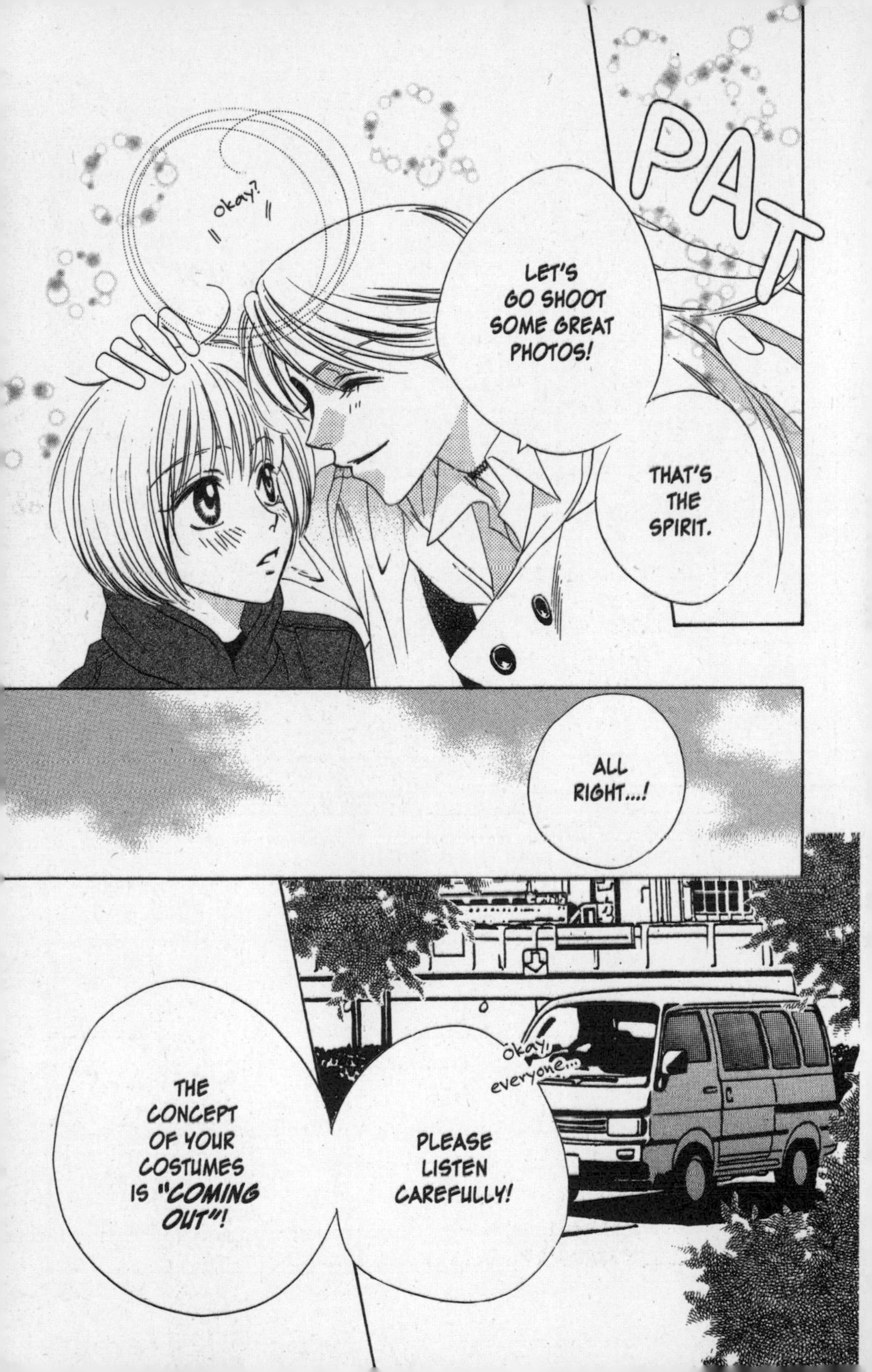
PAT
LET'S GO SHOOT SOME GREAT PHOTOS!
THAT'S THE SPIRIT.
okay?
ALL RIGHT...!
okay, everyone...
PLEASE LISTEN CAREFULLY!
THE CONCEPT OF YOUR COSTUMES IS "COMING OUT"!

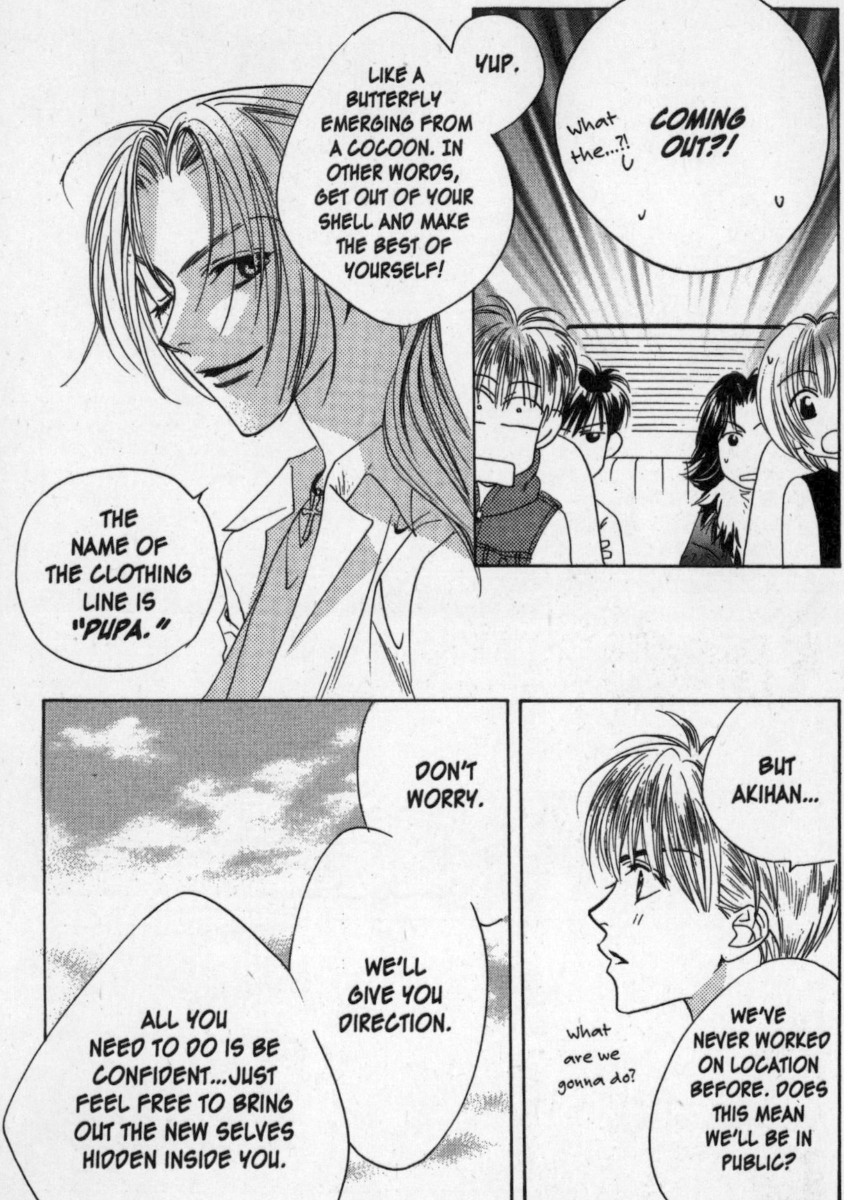
COMING OUT?!
What the...?!
YUP.
LIKE A BUTTERFLY EMERGING FROM A COCOON. IN OTHER WORDS, GET OUT OF YOUR SHELL AND MAKE THE BEST OF YOURSELF!
THE NAME OF THE CLOTHING LINE IS "PUPA."
BUT AKIHAN...
WE'VE NEVER WORKED ON LOCATION BEFORE. DOES THIS MEAN WE'LL BE IN PUBLIC?
What are we gonna do?
DON'T WORRY.
WE'LL GIVE YOU DIRECTION.
ALL YOU NEED TO DO IS BE CONFIDENT...JUST FEEL FREE TO BRING OUT THE NEW SELVES HIDDEN INSIDE YOU.

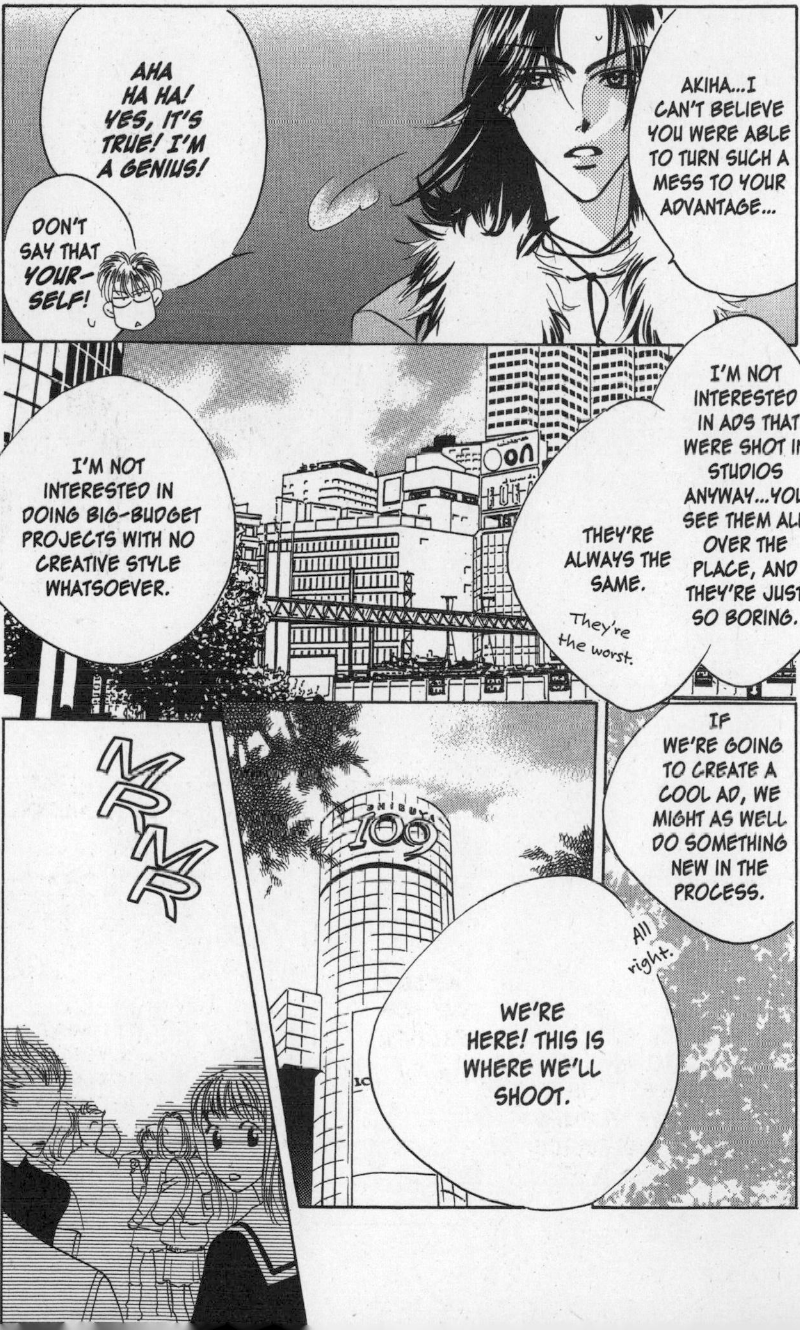
AKIHA...I CAN'T BELIEVE YOU WERE ABLE TO TURN SUCH A MESS TO YOUR ADVANTAGE...
AHA HA HA! YES, IT'S TRUE! I'M A GENIUS!
DON'T SAY THAT YOURSELF!
I'M NOT INTERESTED IN ADS THAT WERE SHOT IN STUDIOS ANYWAY...YOU SEE THEM ALL OVER THE PLACE, AND THEY'RE JUST SO BORING.
THEY'RE ALWAYS THE SAME.
They're the worst.
I'M NOT INTERESTED IN DOING BIG-BUDGET PROJECTS WITH NO CREATIVE STYLE WHATSOEVER.
IF WE'RE GOING TO CREATE A COOL AD, WE MIGHT AS WELL DO SOMETHING NEW IN THE PROCESS.
All right.
WE'RE HERE! THIS IS WHERE WE'LL SHOOT.
MRMR

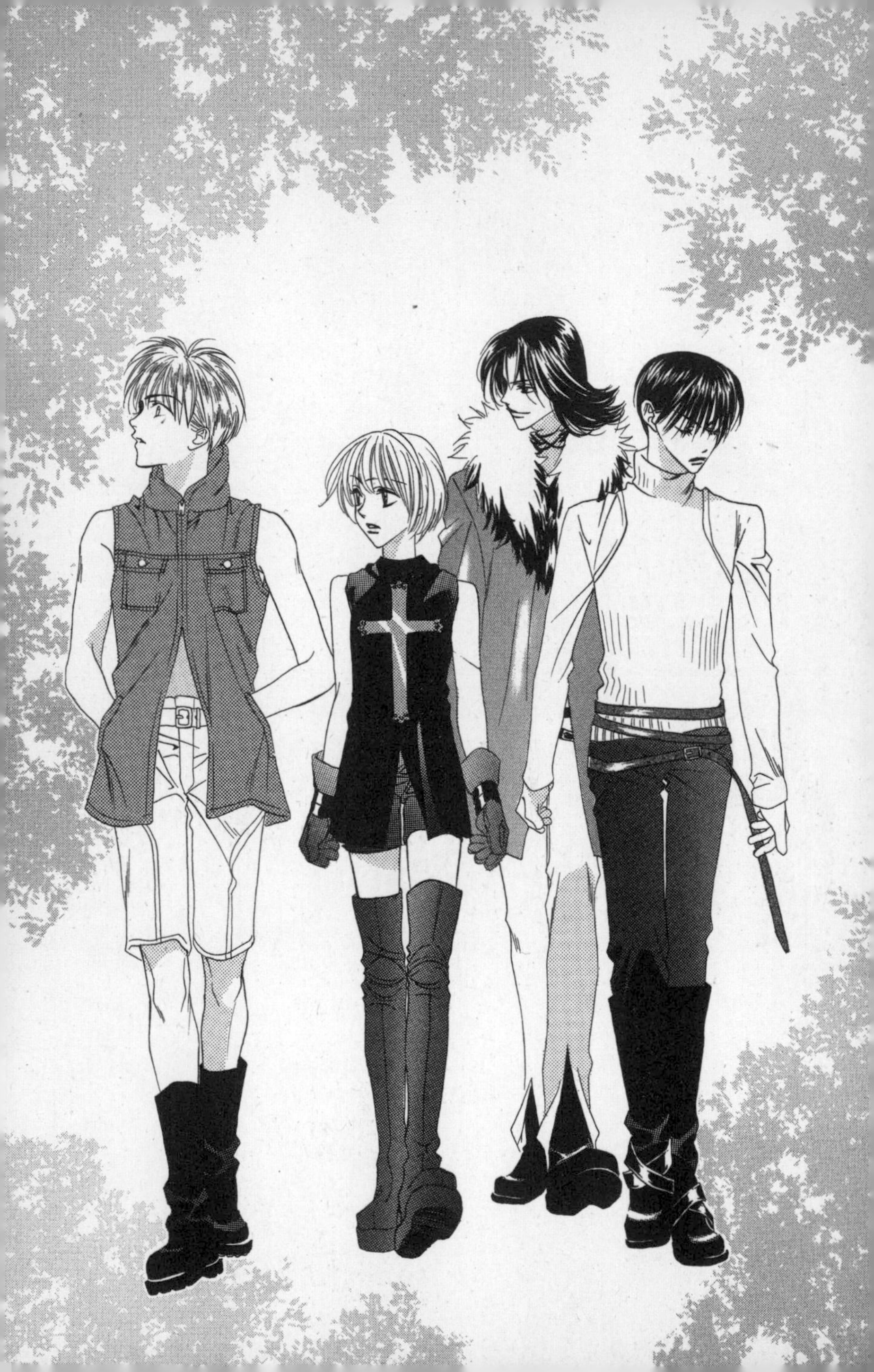

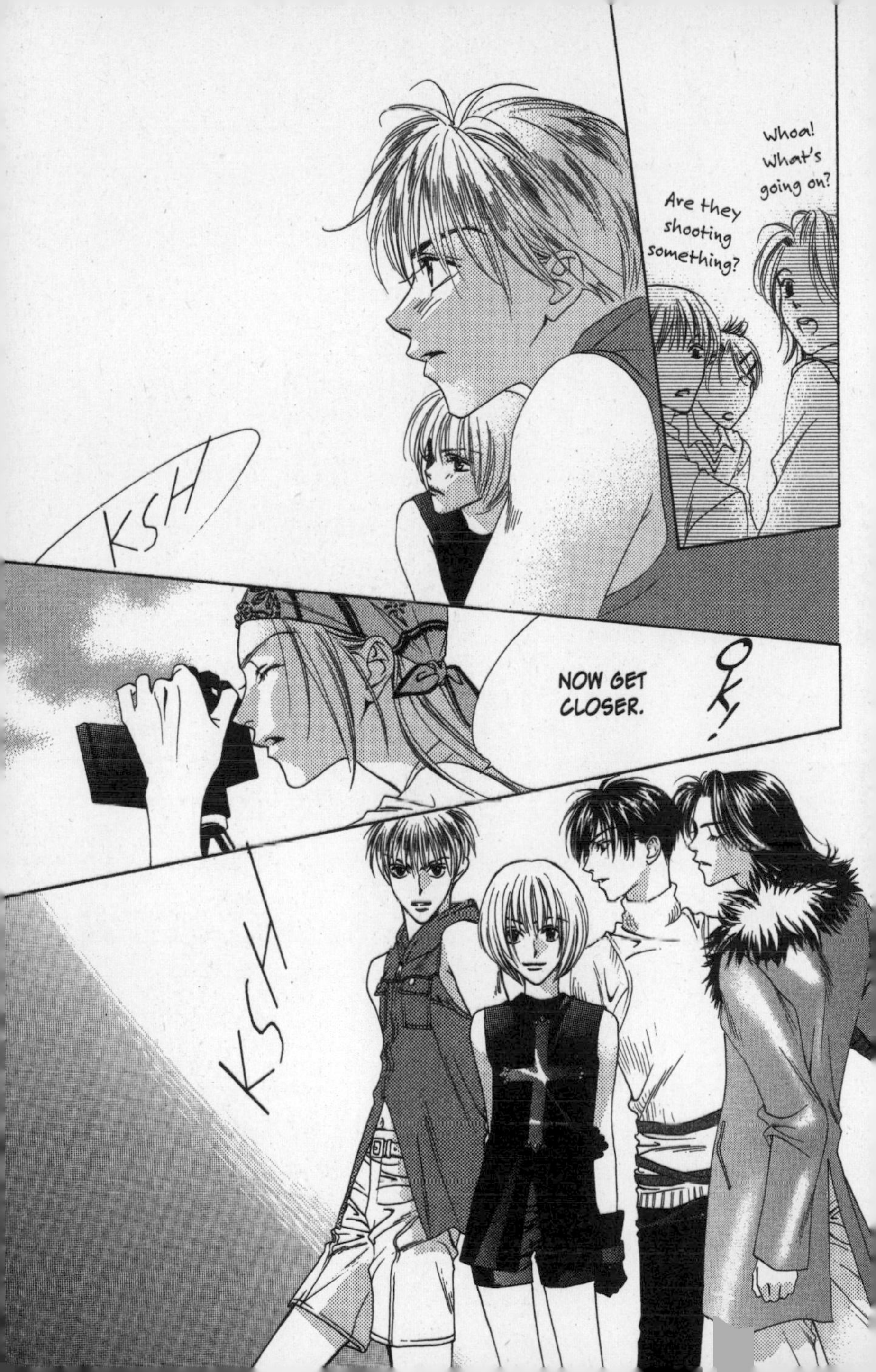
Whoa! What's going on?
Are they shooting something?
KSH
OK!
NOW GET CLOSER.
KSH

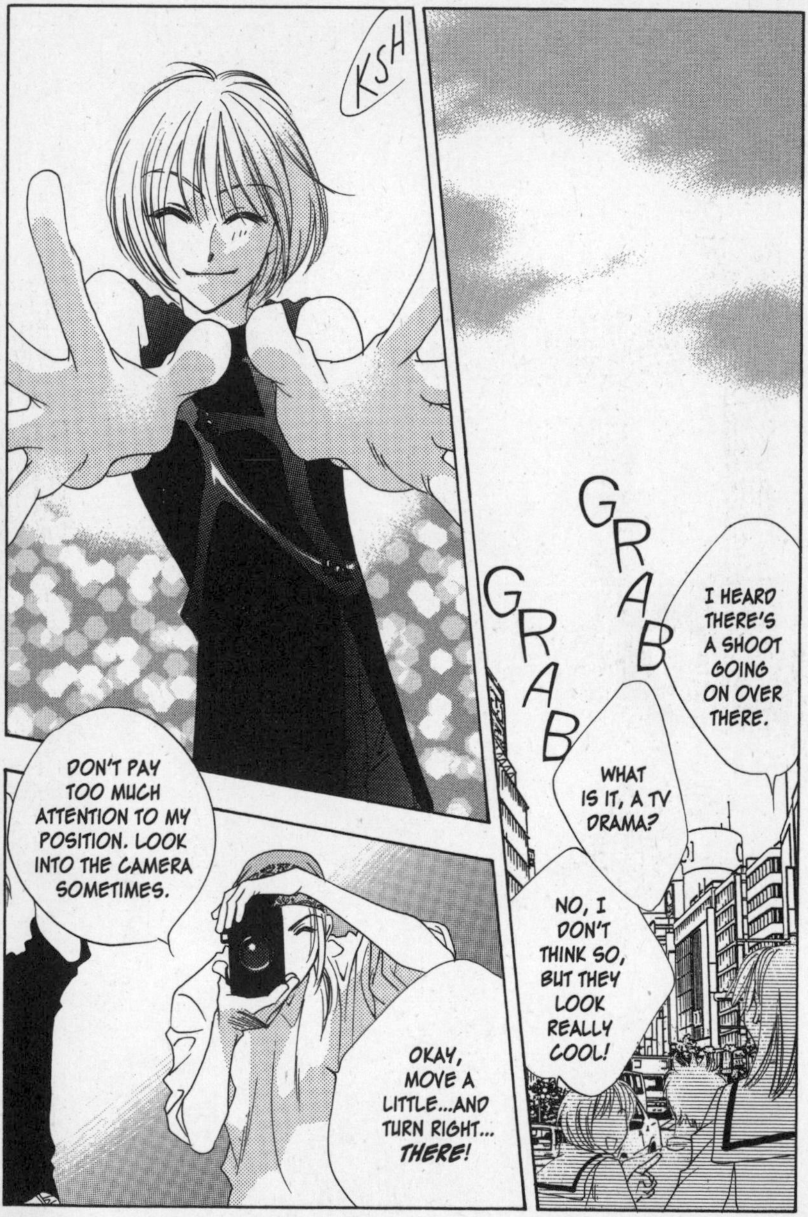
GRAB GRAB
I HEARD THERE'S A SHOOT GOING ON OVER THERE.
WHAT IS IT, A TV DRAMA?
NO, I DON'T THINK SO, BUT THEY LOOK REALLY COOL!
KSH
DON'T PAY TOO MUCH ATTENTION TO MY POSITION. LOOK INTO THE CAMERA SOMETIMES.
OKAY, MOVE A LITTLE...AND TURN RIGHT... *THERE!*

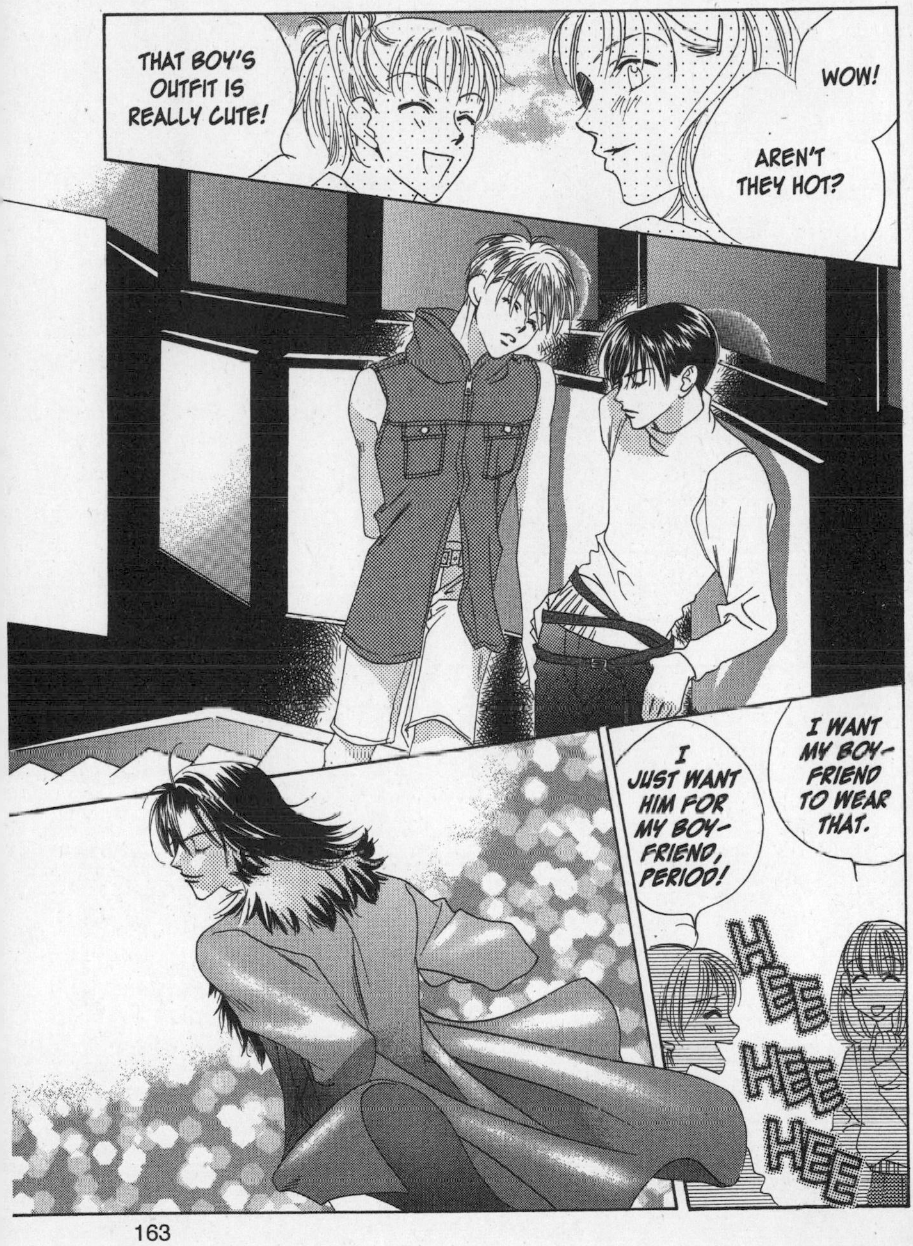
WOW!
AREN'T THEY HOT?
THAT BOY'S OUTFIT IS REALLY CUTE!
I WANT MY BOY-FRIEND TO WEAR THAT.
I JUST WANT HIM FOR MY BOY-FRIEND, PERIOD!
HEE HEE HEE

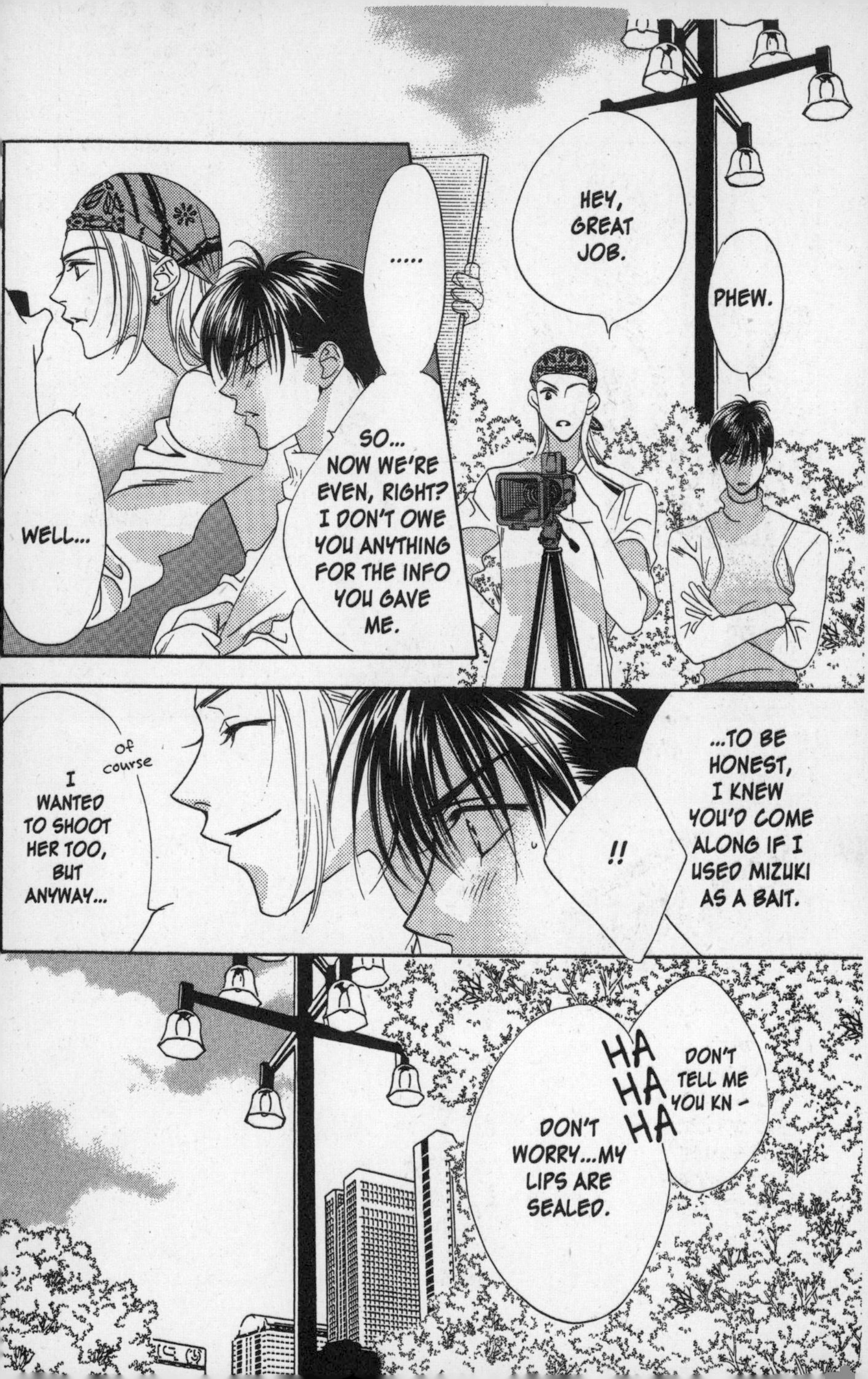
HEY, GREAT JOB.
PHEW.
.....
SO... NOW WE'RE EVEN, RIGHT? I DON'T OWE YOU ANYTHING FOR THE INFO YOU GAVE ME.
WELL...
...TO BE HONEST, I KNEW YOU'D COME ALONG IF I USED MIZUKI AS A BAIT.
!!
I WANTED TO SHOOT HER TOO, BUT ANYWAY...
of course
DON'T TELL ME YOU KN-
HA HA HA
DON'T WORRY...MY LIPS ARE SEALED.

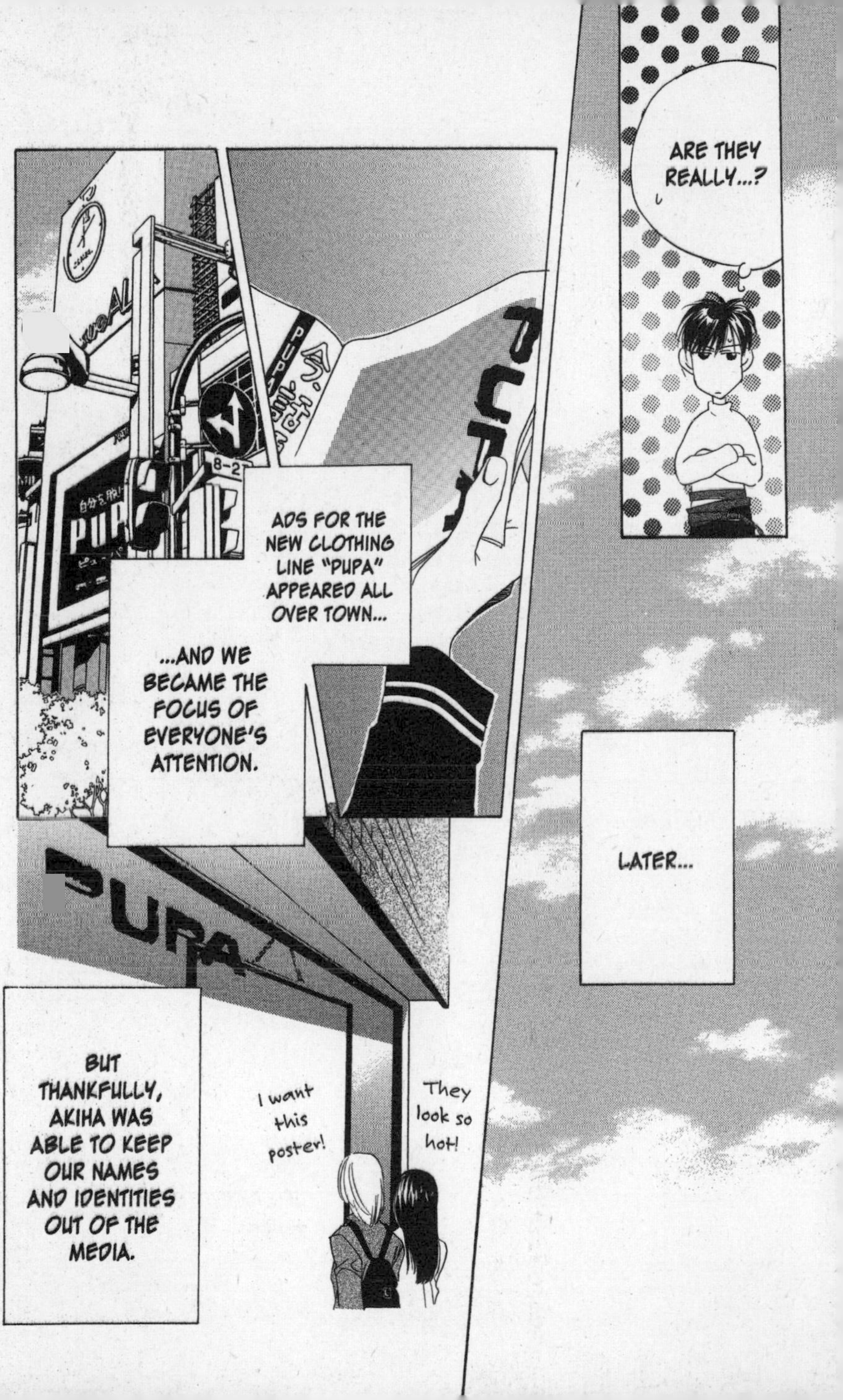
ADS FOR THE NEW CLOTHING LINE "PUPA" APPEARED ALL OVER TOWN...
...AND WE BECAME THE FOCUS OF EVERYONE'S ATTENTION.
PUPA
8-2
PUPA
BUT THANKFULLY, AKIHA WAS ABLE TO KEEP OUR NAMES AND IDENTITIES OUT OF THE MEDIA.
They look so hot!
I want this poster!
ARE THEY REALLY...?
LATER...

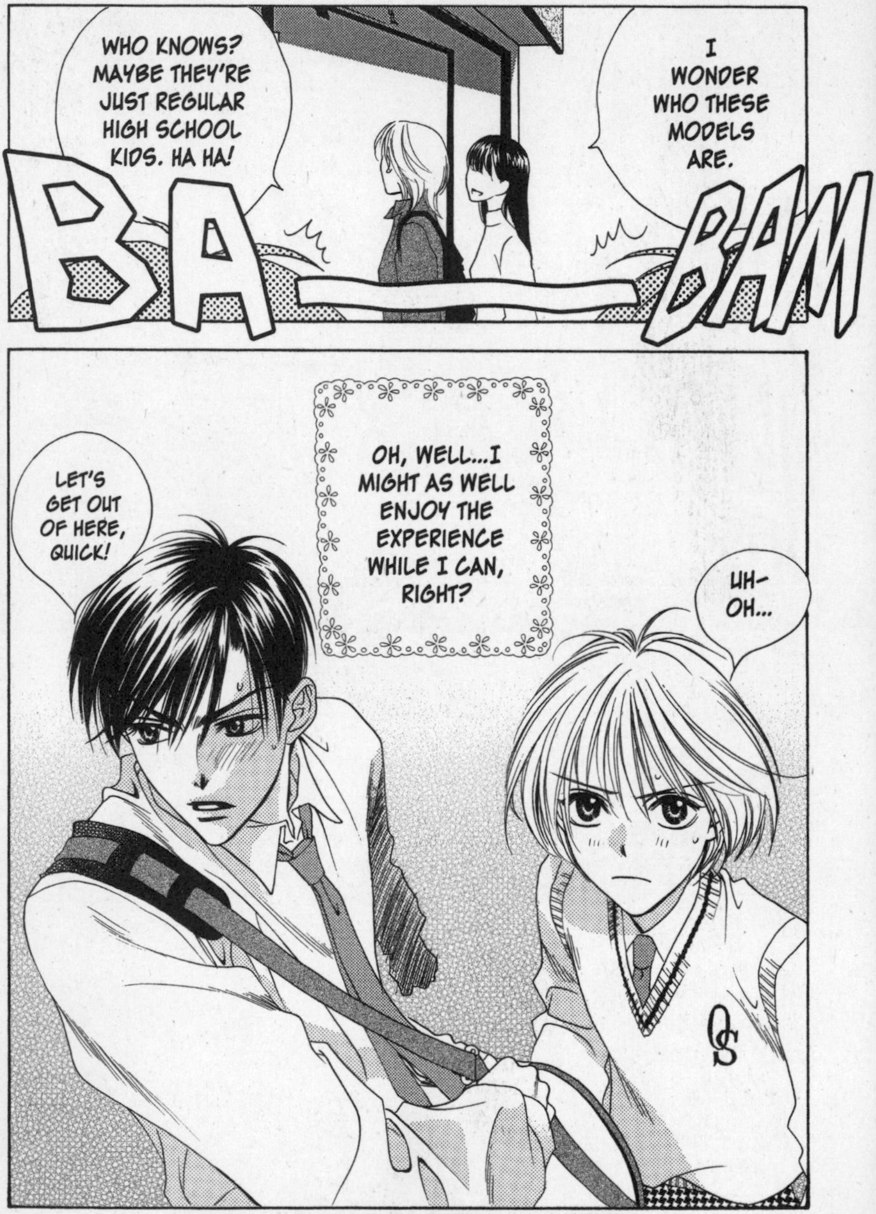
I WONDER WHO THESE MODELS ARE.
WHO KNOWS? MAYBE THEY'RE JUST REGULAR HIGH SCHOOL KIDS. HA HA!
BA—BAM
OH, WELL...I MIGHT AS WELL ENJOY THE EXPERIENCE WHILE I CAN, RIGHT?
UH-OH...
LET'S GET OUT OF HERE, QUICK!
OS

HANA-KIMI CHAPTER 54/END

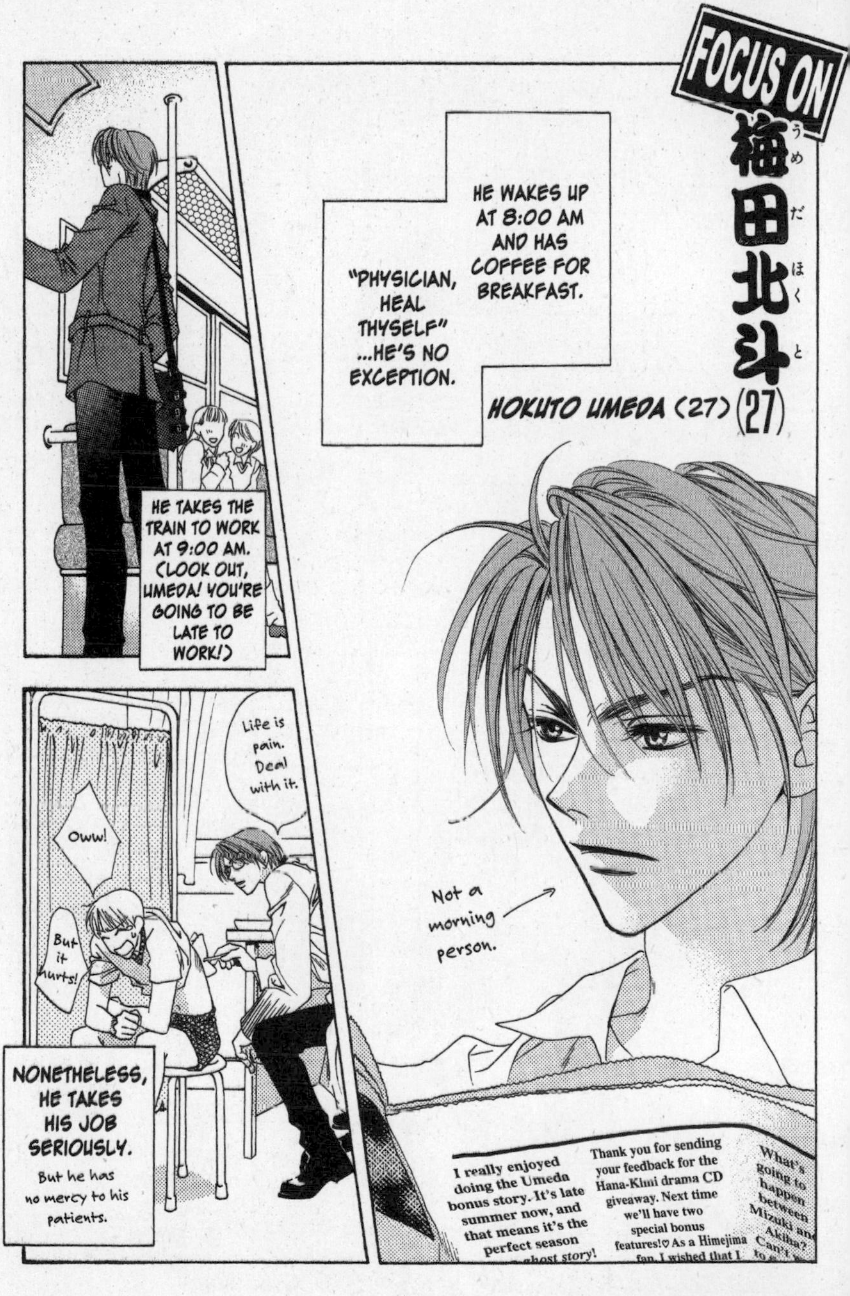
FOCUS ON
梅田北斗(27)
うめだほくと
HE WAKES UP AT 8:00 AM AND HAS COFFEE FOR BREAKFAST.
"PHYSICIAN, HEAL THYSELF" ...HE'S NO EXCEPTION.
HOKUTO UMEDA (27)
Not a morning person.
I really enjoyed doing the Umeda bonus story. It's late summer now, and that means it's the perfect season
ghost story!
Thank you for sending your feedback for the Hana-Kimi drama CD giveaway. Next time we'll have two special bonus features!♡ As a Himejima fan, I wished that I
What's going to happen between Mizuki and Akiha?
HE TAKES THE TRAIN TO WORK AT 9:00 AM. (LOOK OUT, UMEDA! YOU'RE GOING TO BE LATE TO WORK!)
Life is pain. Deal with it.
Oww!
But it hurts!
NONETHELESS, HE TAKES HIS JOB SERIOUSLY.
But he has no mercy to his patients.

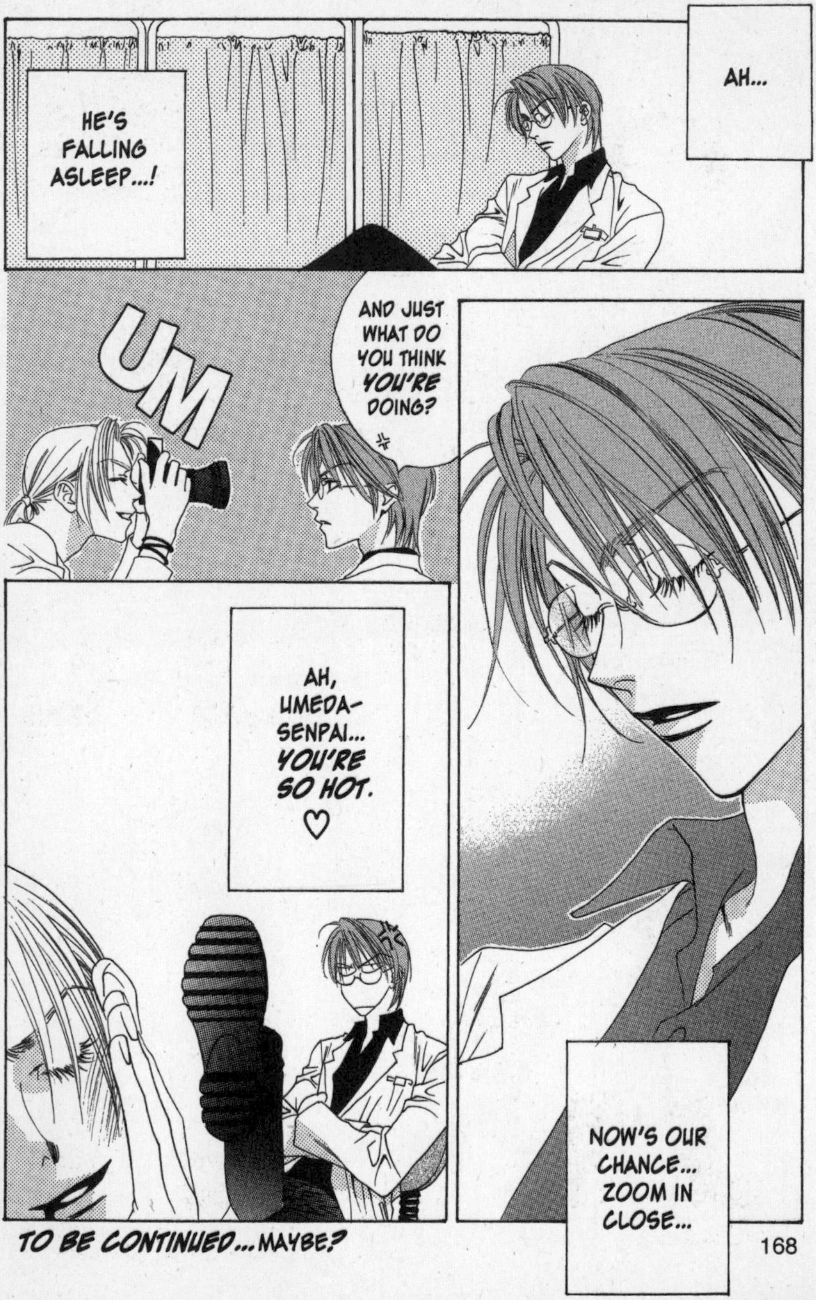
AH...
HE'S FALLING ASLEEP...!
NOW'S OUR CHANCE... ZOOM IN CLOSE...
AND JUST WHAT DO YOU THINK *YOU'RE* DOING?
UM
AH, UMEDA-SENPAI... *YOU'RE SO HOT.* ♡

TO BE CONTINUED... MAYBE?

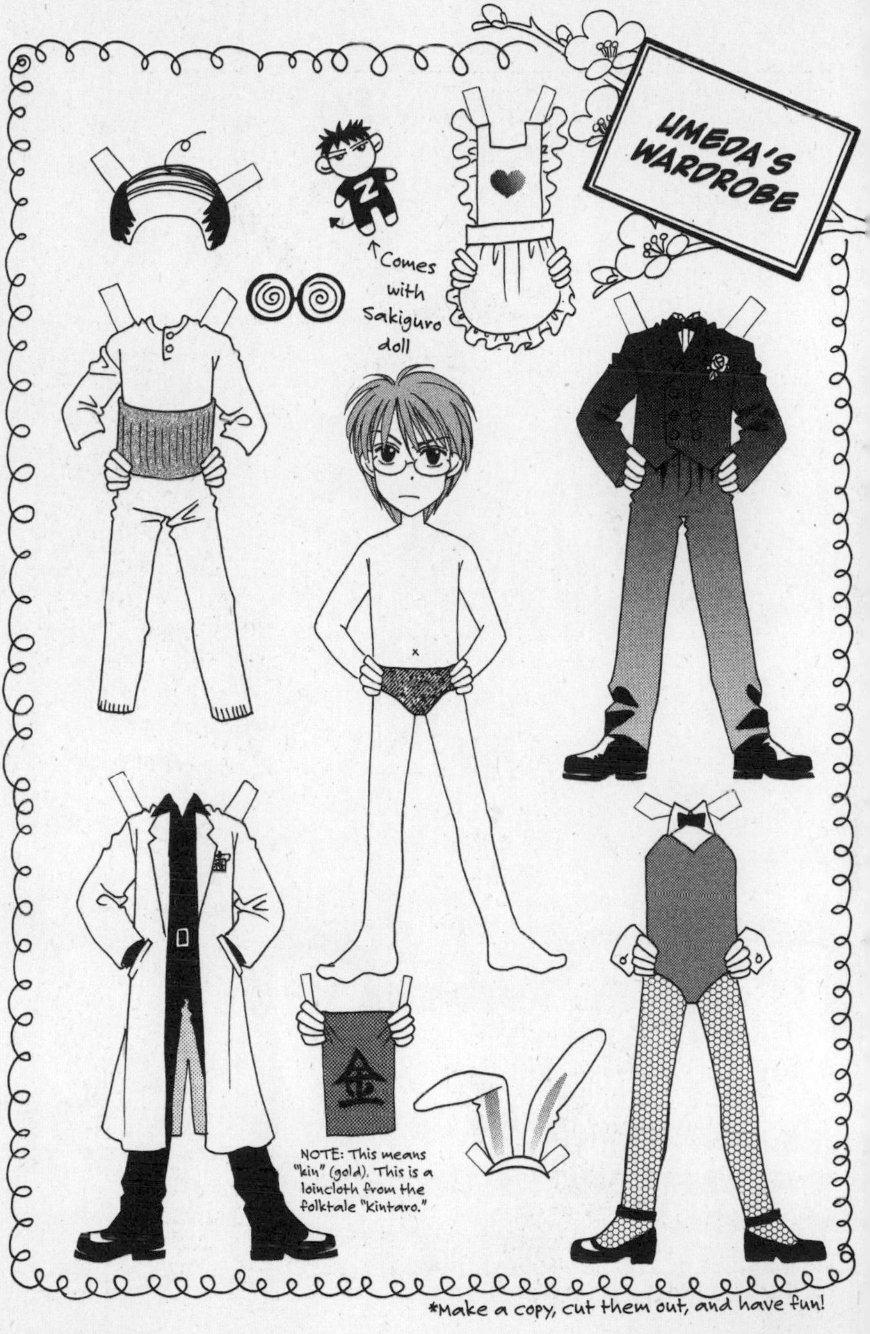
UMEDA'S WARDROBE
Comes with Sakiguro doll
金
NOTE: This means "kin" (gold). This is a loincloth from the folktale "Kintaro."

*Make a copy, cut them out, and have fun!

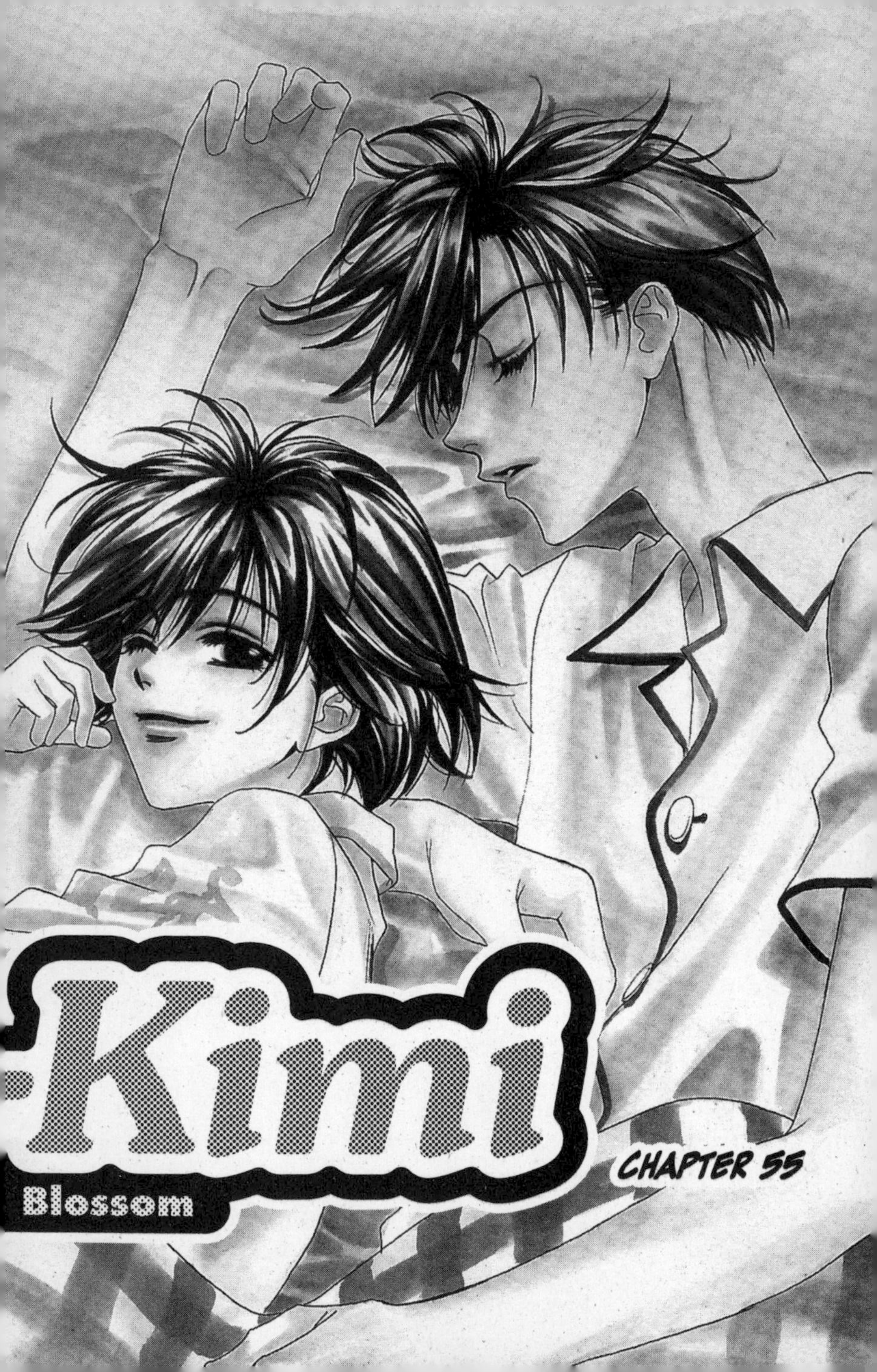
Kimi
Blossom
CHAPTER 55

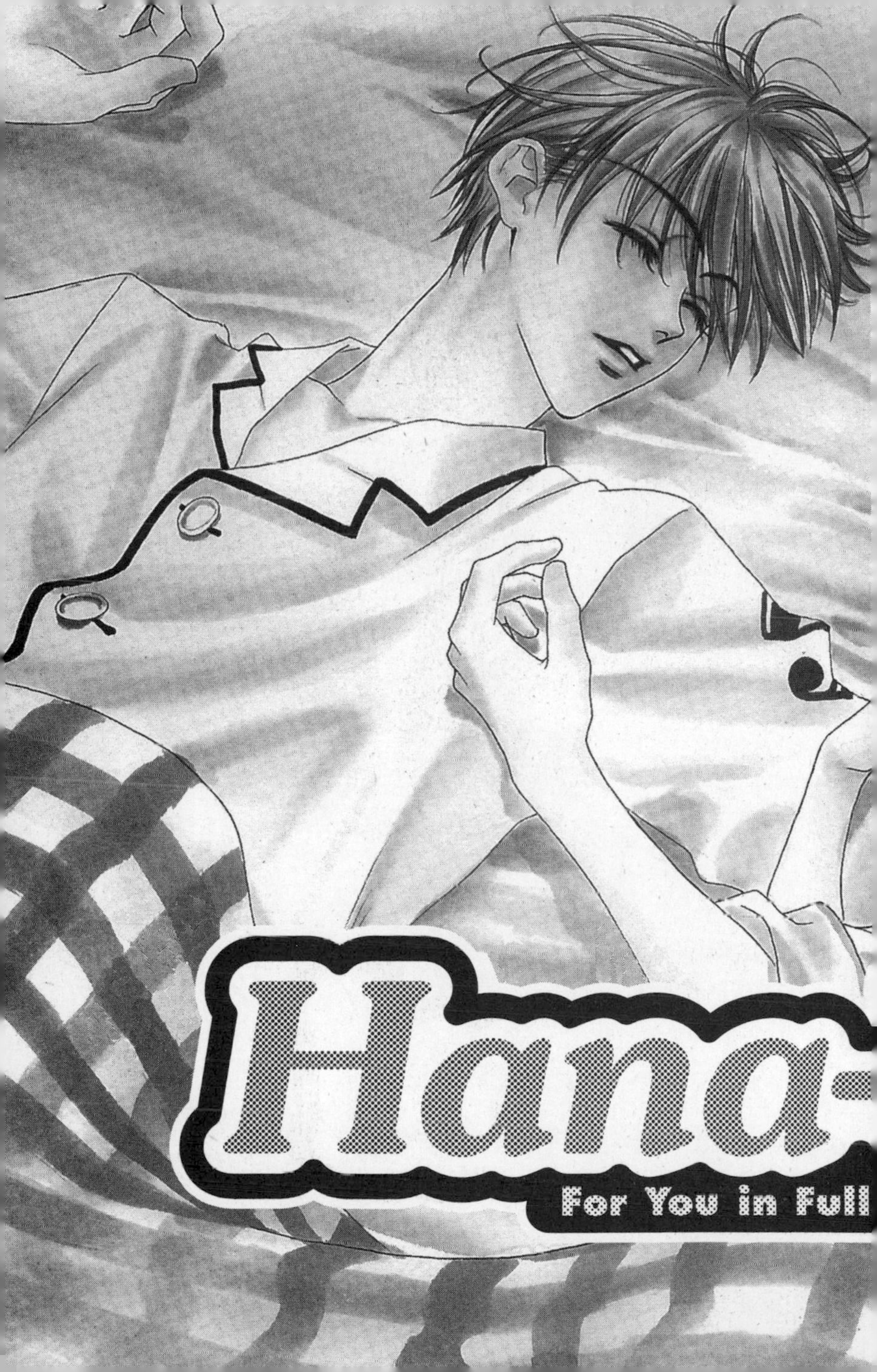
Hana-
For You in Full

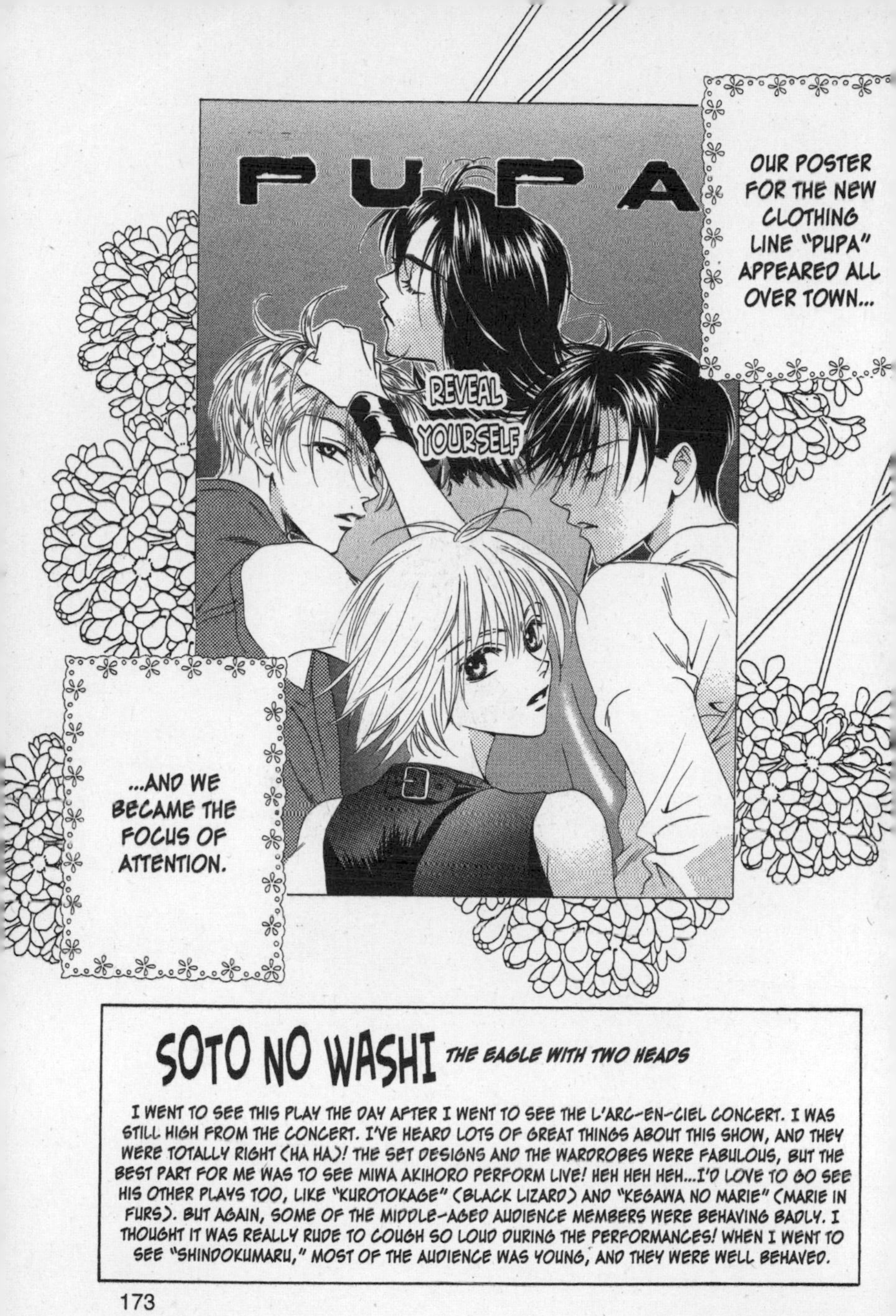
OUR POSTER FOR THE NEW CLOTHING LINE "PUPA" APPEARED ALL OVER TOWN...
PUPA
REVEAL YOURSELF
...AND WE BECAME THE FOCUS OF ATTENTION.

SOTO NO WASHI *THE EAGLE WITH TWO HEADS*

I WENT TO SEE THIS PLAY THE DAY AFTER I WENT TO SEE THE L'ARC-EN-CIEL CONCERT. I WAS STILL HIGH FROM THE CONCERT. I'VE HEARD LOTS OF GREAT THINGS ABOUT THIS SHOW, AND THEY WERE TOTALLY RIGHT (HA HA)! THE SET DESIGNS AND THE WARDROBES WERE FABULOUS, BUT THE BEST PART FOR ME WAS TO SEE MIWA AKIHORO PERFORM LIVE! HEH HEH HEH...I'D LOVE TO GO SEE HIS OTHER PLAYS TOO, LIKE "KUROTOKAGE" (BLACK LIZARD) AND "KEGAWA NO MARIE" (MARIE IN FURS). BUT AGAIN, SOME OF THE MIDDLE-AGED AUDIENCE MEMBERS WERE BEHAVING BADLY. I THOUGHT IT WAS REALLY RUDE TO COUGH SO LOUD DURING THE PERFORMANCES! WHEN I WENT TO SEE "SHINDOKUMARU," MOST OF THE AUDIENCE WAS YOUNG, AND THEY WERE WELL BEHAVED.

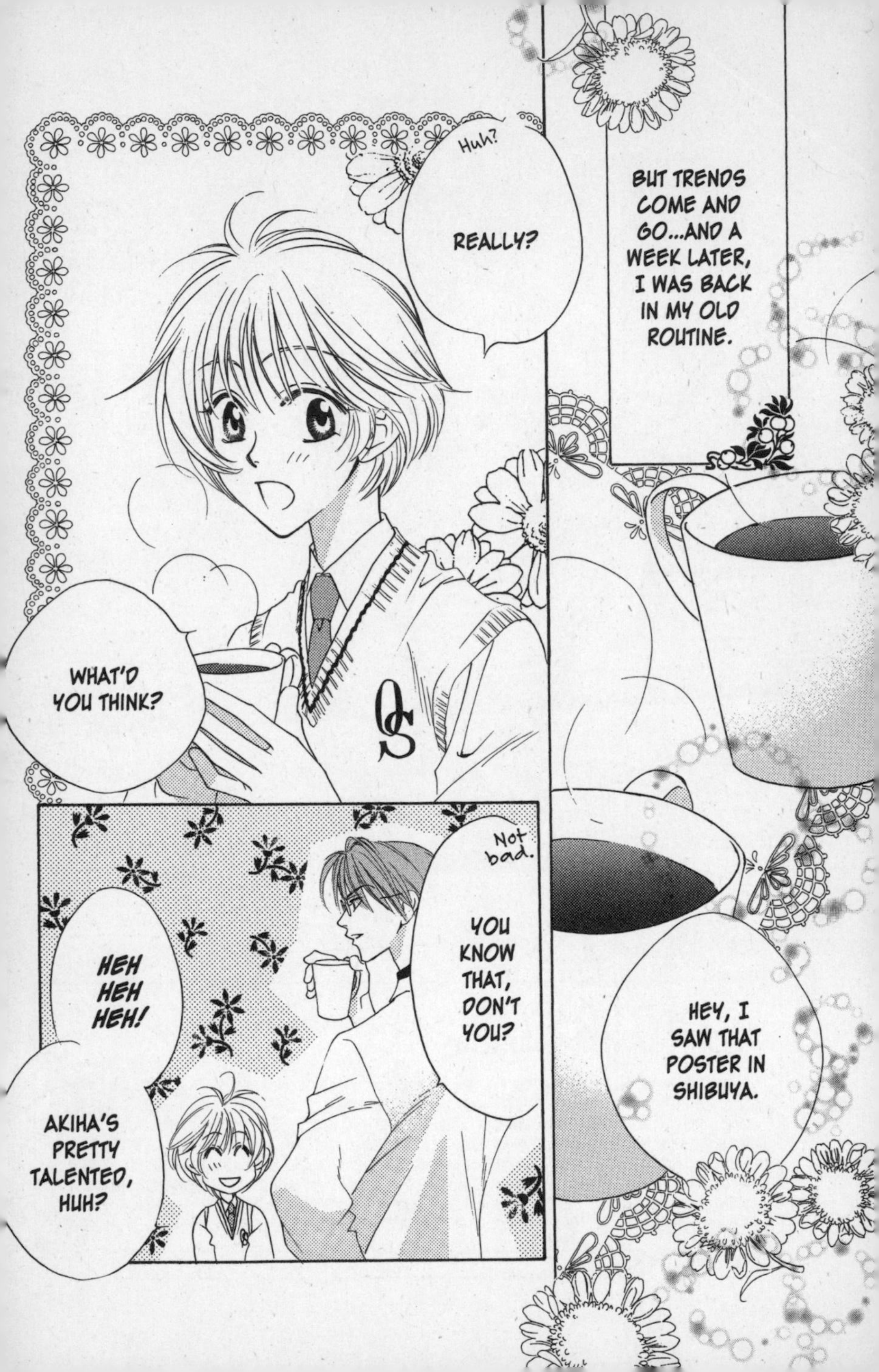
BUT TRENDS COME AND GO...AND A WEEK LATER, I WAS BACK IN MY OLD ROUTINE.
HEY, I SAW THAT POSTER IN SHIBUYA.
Huh?
REALLY?
WHAT'D YOU THINK?
Not bad.
YOU KNOW THAT, DON'T YOU?
HEH HEH HEH!
AKIHA'S PRETTY TALENTED, HUH?

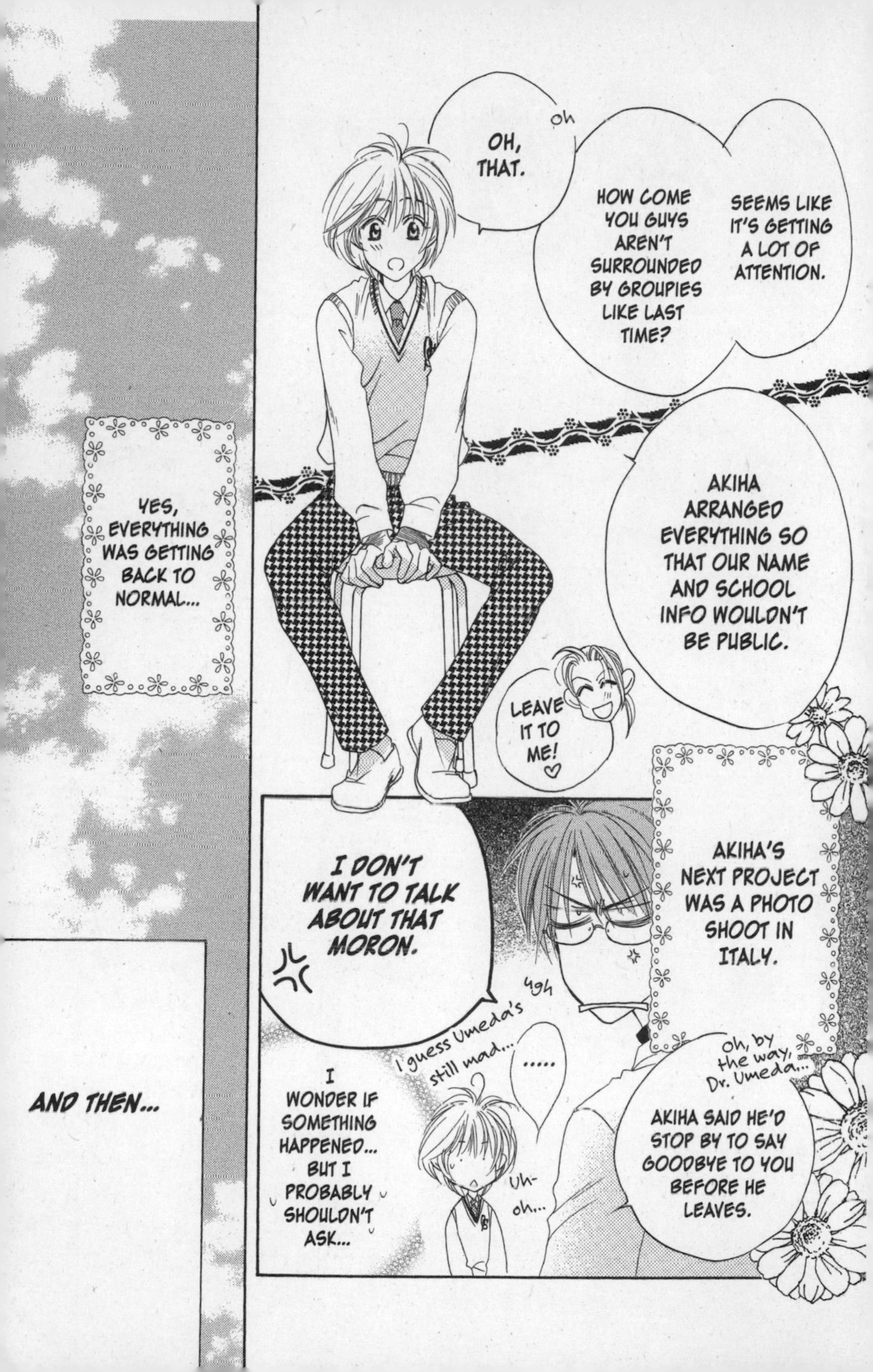
SEEMS LIKE IT'S GETTING A LOT OF ATTENTION.
HOW COME YOU GUYS AREN'T SURROUNDED BY GROUPIES LIKE LAST TIME?
oh
OH, THAT.
AKIHA ARRANGED EVERYTHING SO THAT OUR NAME AND SCHOOL INFO WOULDN'T BE PUBLIC.
LEAVE IT TO ME! ♡
AKIHA'S NEXT PROJECT WAS A PHOTO SHOOT IN ITALY.
I DON'T WANT TO TALK ABOUT THAT MORON.
ugh
Oh, by the way, Dr. Umeda...
AKIHA SAID HE'D STOP BY TO SAY GOODBYE TO YOU BEFORE HE LEAVES.
Uh-oh...
.....
I guess Umeda's still mad...
I WONDER IF SOMETHING HAPPENED... BUT I PROBABLY SHOULDN'T ASK...
YES, EVERYTHING WAS GETTING BACK TO NORMAL...
AND THEN...

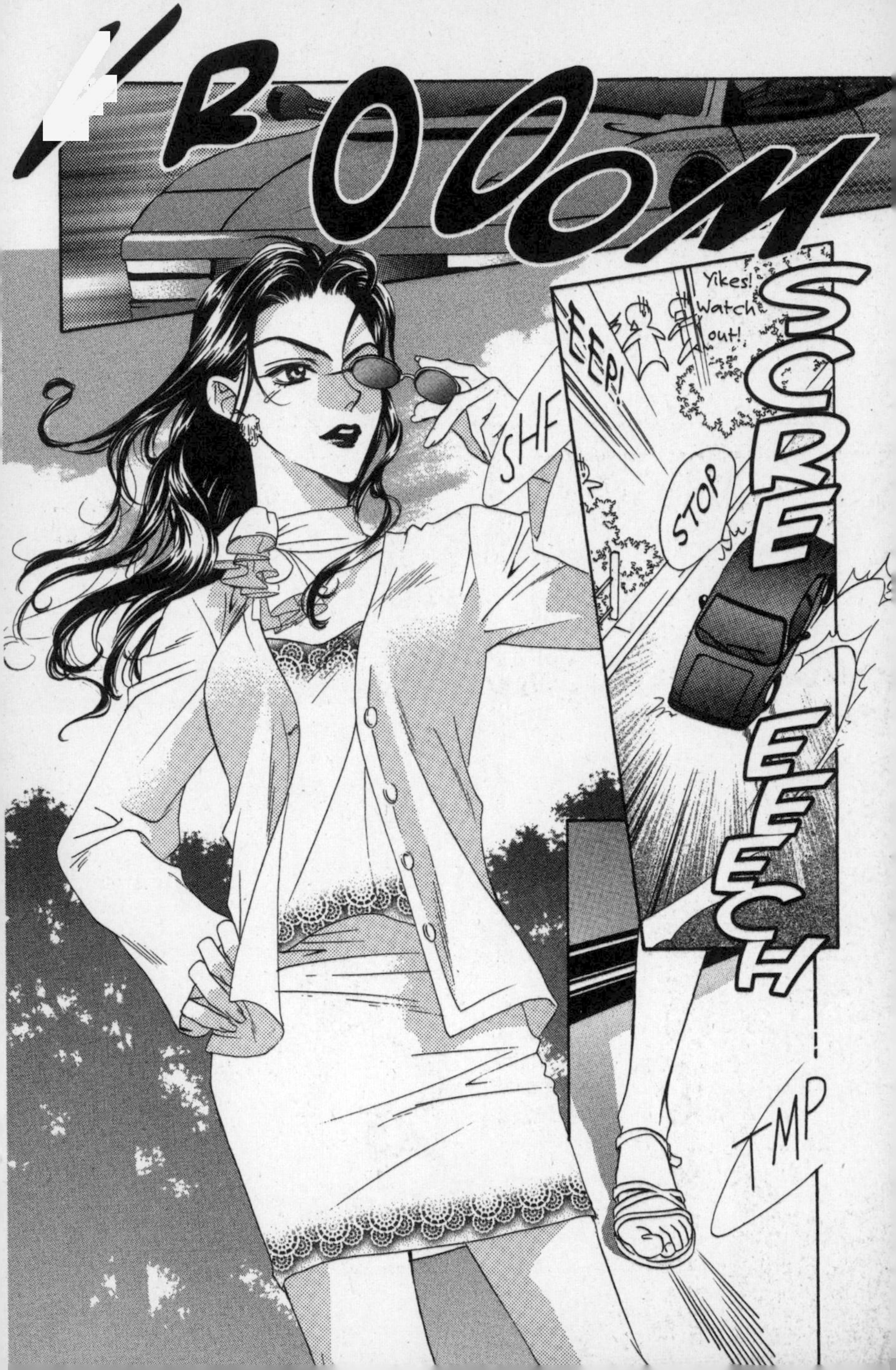
BOOOM
Yikes! Watch out!
EEP!
STOP
SCREEEEECH
SHF
TMP

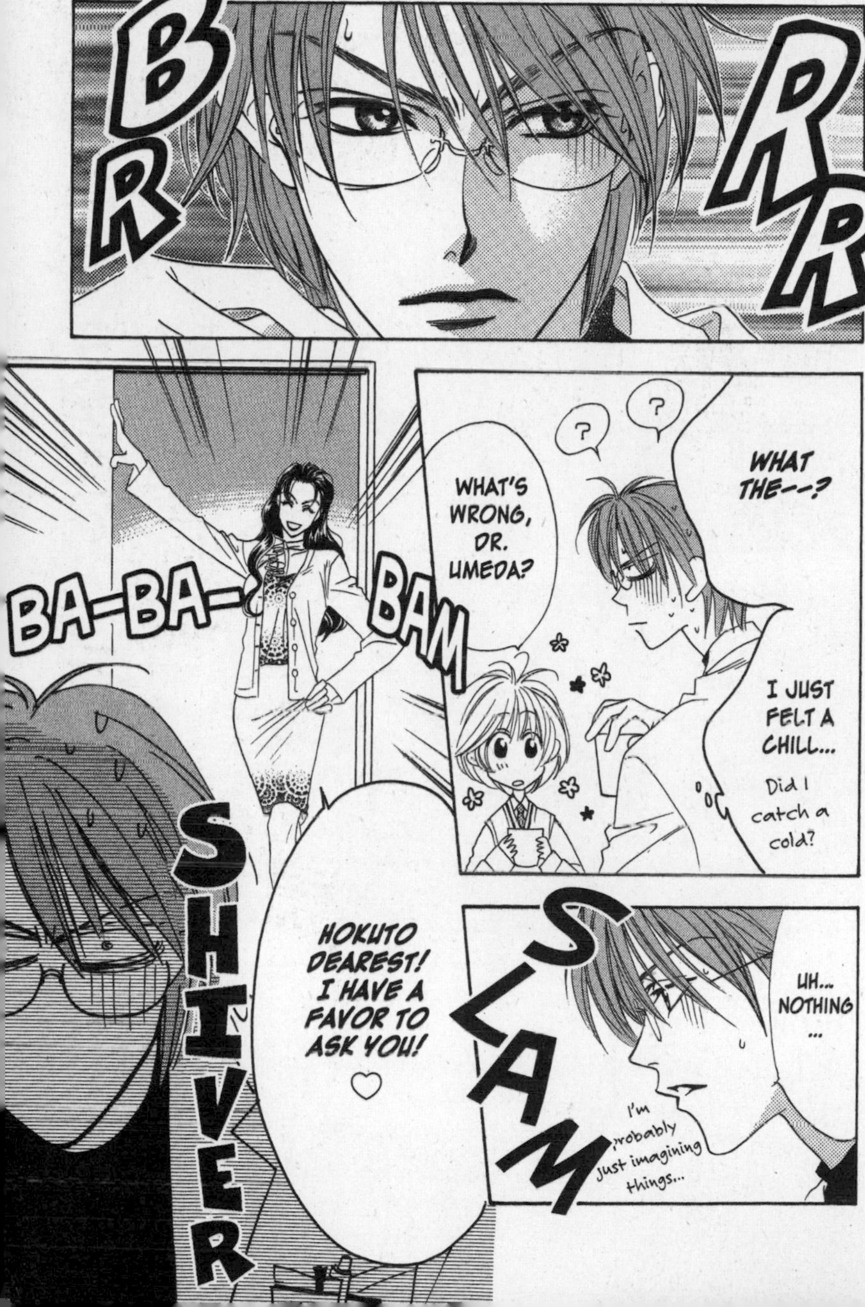
BR
RR
?
?
WHAT THE--?
WHAT'S WRONG, DR. UMEDA?
I JUST FELT A CHILL...
Did I catch a cold?
UH... NOTHING ...
I'm probably just imagining things...
SLAM
BA-BA-BAM
HOKUTO DEAREST! I HAVE A FAVOR TO ASK YOU! ♡
SHIVER

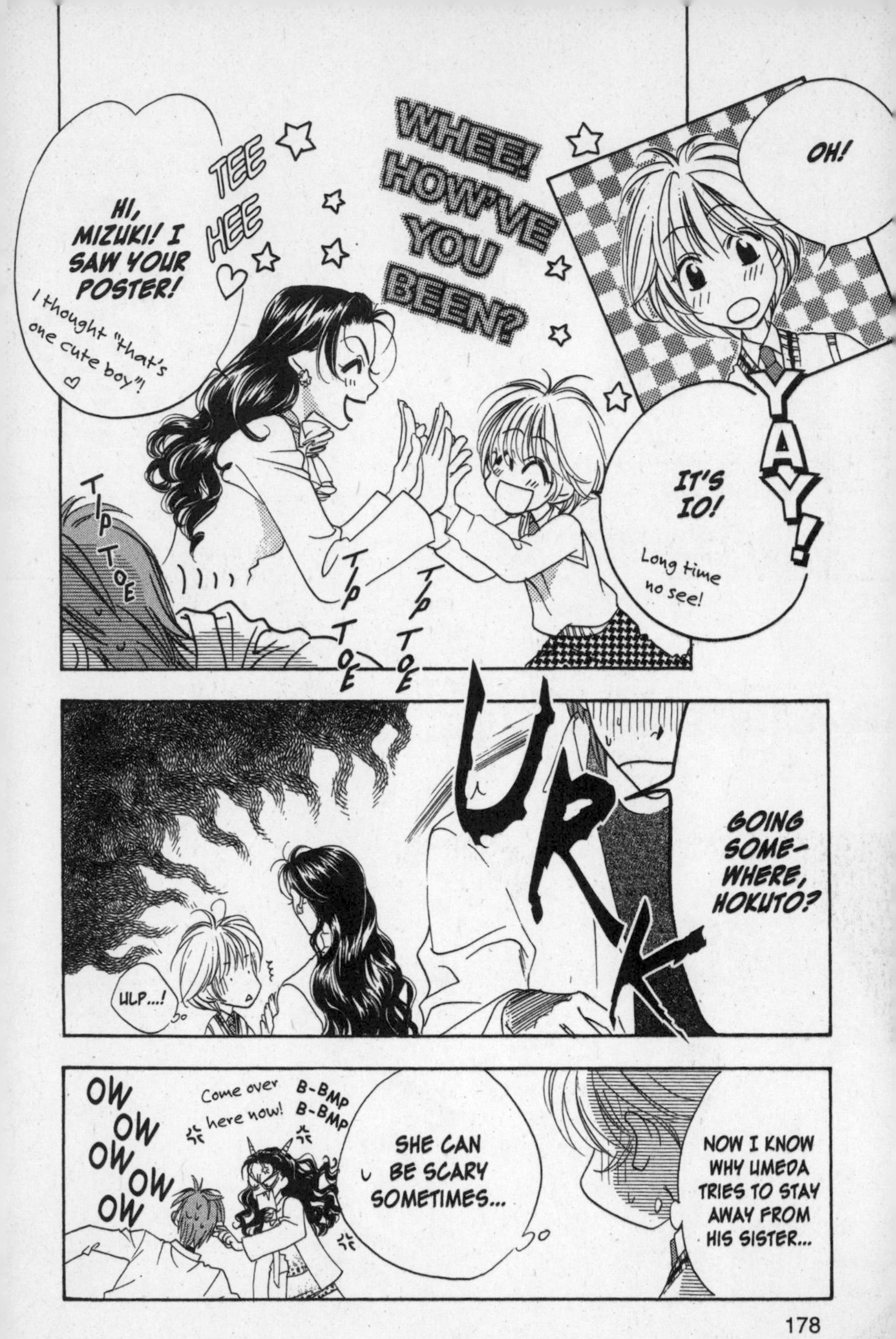
OH!
YAY!
IT'S IO!
Long time no see!
WHEE! HOW'VE YOU BEEN?
TEE HEE
HI, MIZUKI! I SAW YOUR POSTER!
I thought "that's one cute boy"! ♡
TIP TOE
TIP TOE
TIP TOE
GOING SOME-WHERE, HOKUTO?
URK
ULP...!
NOW I KNOW WHY UMEDA TRIES TO STAY AWAY FROM HIS SISTER...
SHE CAN BE SCARY SOMETIMES...
B-BMP B-BMP
Come over here now!
OW OW OW OW OW

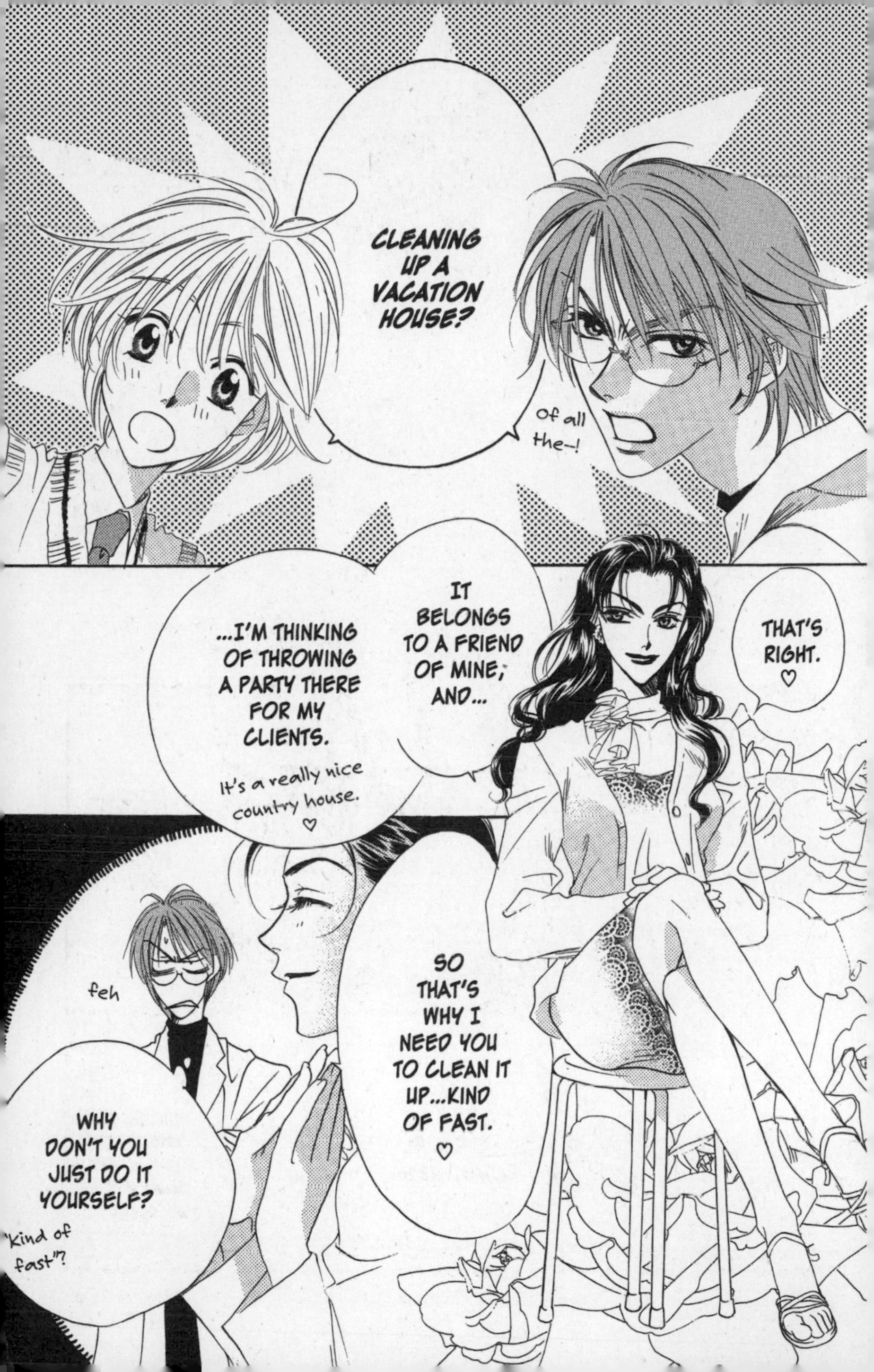
CLEANING UP A VACATION HOUSE?
Of all the–!
THAT'S RIGHT. ♡
IT BELONGS TO A FRIEND OF MINE, AND...
...I'M THINKING OF THROWING A PARTY THERE FOR MY CLIENTS.
It's a really nice country house. ♡
SO THAT'S WHY I NEED YOU TO CLEAN IT UP...KIND OF FAST. ♡
feh
WHY DON'T YOU JUST DO IT YOURSELF?
"Kind of fast"?

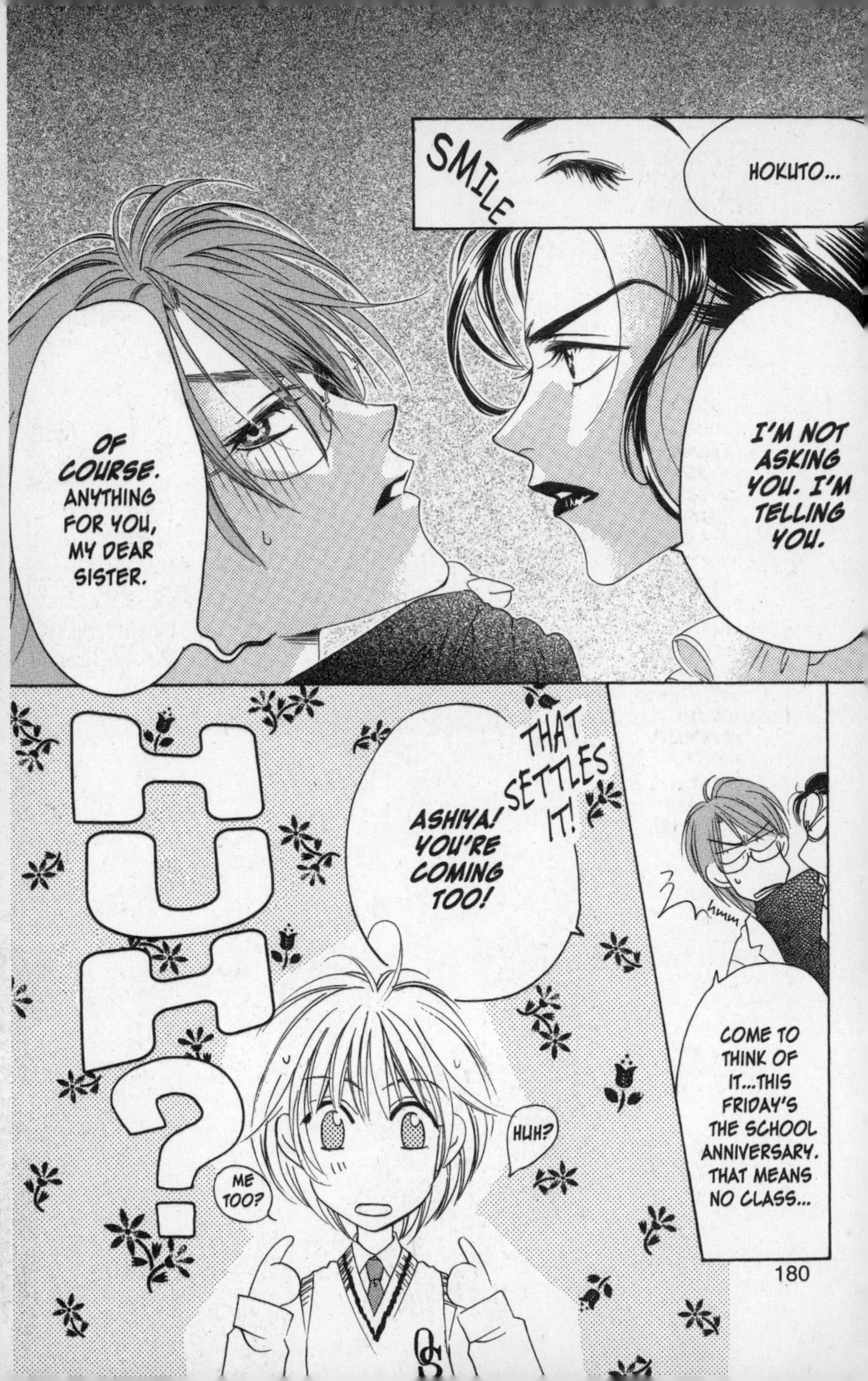
HOKUTO...
SMILE
I'M NOT ASKING YOU. I'M TELLING YOU.
OF COURSE. ANYTHING FOR YOU, MY DEAR SISTER.
hmm
COME TO THINK OF IT...THIS FRIDAY'S THE SCHOOL ANNIVERSARY. THAT MEANS NO CLASS...
THAT SETTLES IT!
ASHIYA! YOU'RE COMING TOO!
HUH?
ME TOO?
HUH?

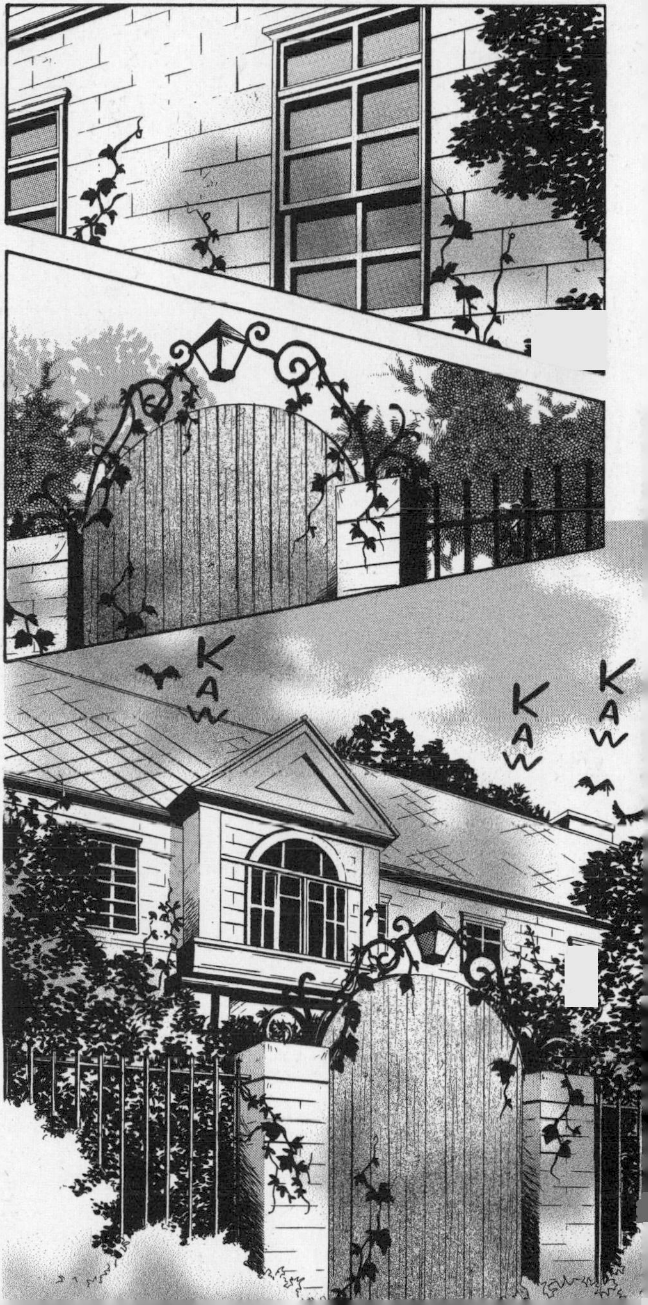
KAW
KAW
KAW

WHISPERED SECRETS

TAIKI KAYASHIMA

BIRTHDAY:
FEBRUARY 22ND
AGE:
16
BLOOD TYPE:
O
SIGN:
PISCES
HEIGHT:
170CM
FAVORITE FOODS:
MISO-FLAVORED FOOD
FAVORITE MUSICIANS:
MASASHI SADA, KITARO, GENIOU-YAMASHIROGUMI, KIJIN
FAVORITE MOVIES:
THE EXORCIST, THE SHINING
FAVORITE SPORTS:
TABLE TENNIS
FAVORITE GENRE:
OCCULT (?)
CHARACTERISTICS:
CAN SEE GHOSTS AND AURAS
IMAGE FLOWER:
GENTIAN

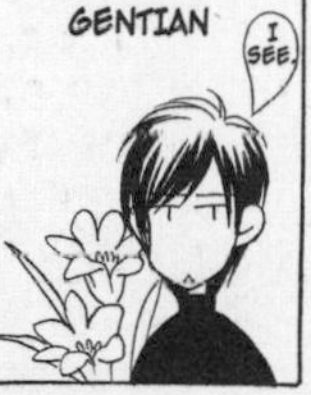
I SEE.

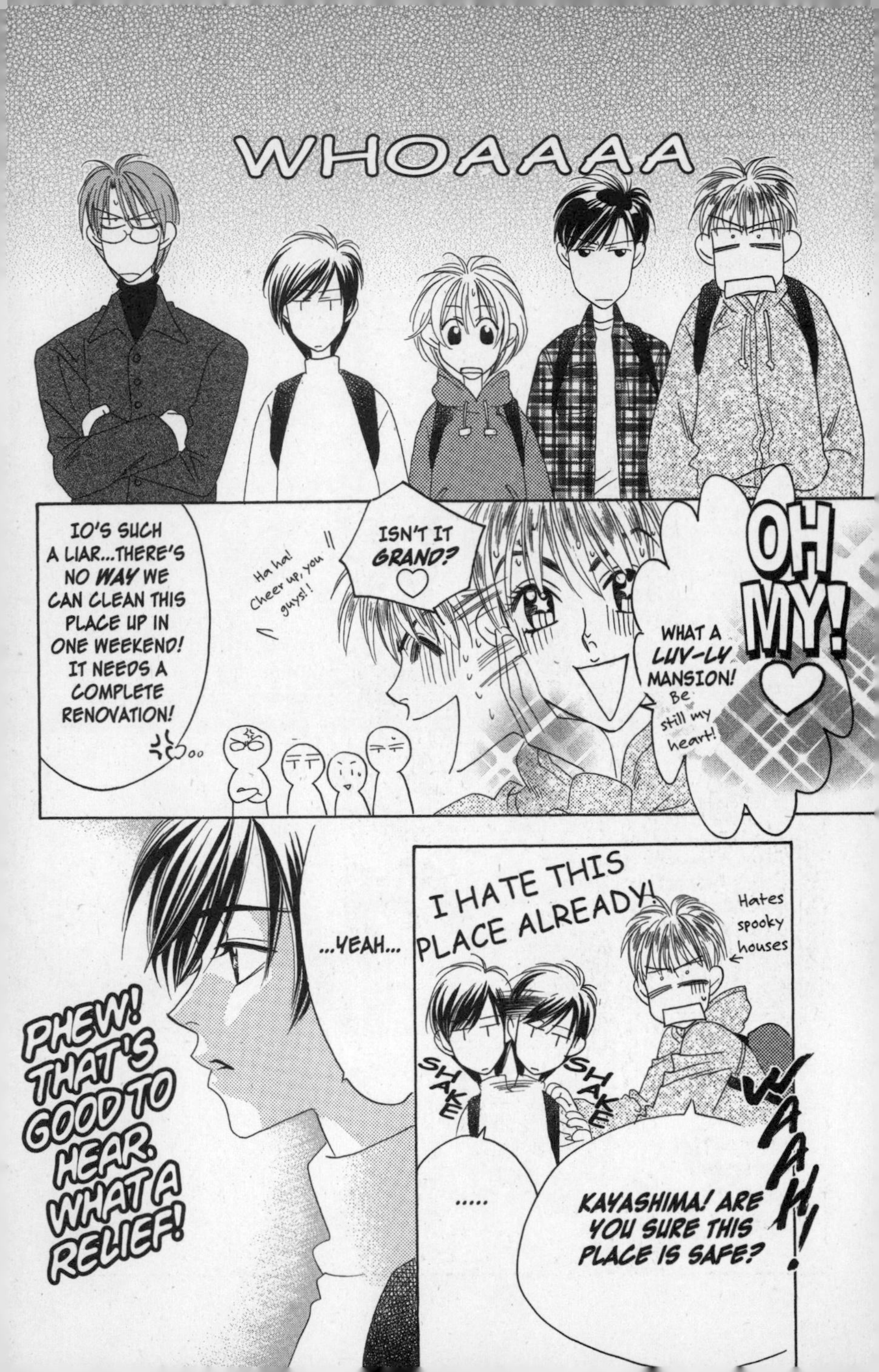
WHOAAAA
OH MY!
WHAT A LUV-LY MANSION! Be still my heart!
ISN'T IT GRAND?
Ha ha! Cheer up, you guys!!
IO'S SUCH A LIAR...THERE'S NO WAY WE CAN CLEAN THIS PLACE UP IN ONE WEEKEND! IT NEEDS A COMPLETE RENOVATION!
Hates spooky houses
I HATE THIS PLACE ALREADY!
WAAAH!
SHAKE
SHAKE
KAYASHIMA! ARE YOU SURE THIS PLACE IS SAFE?
.....
...YEAH...
PHEW! THAT'S GOOD TO HEAR. WHAT A RELIEF!

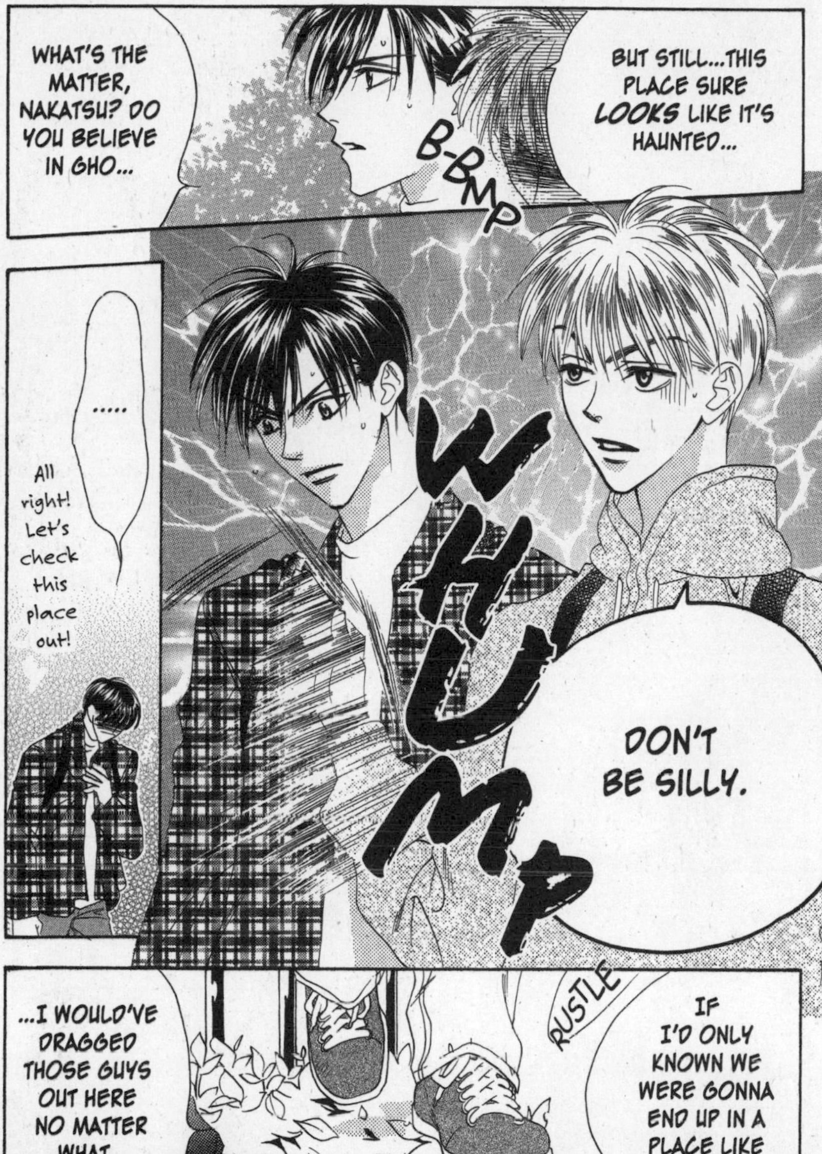
BUT STILL...THIS PLACE SURE LOOKS LIKE IT'S HAUNTED...
B-BMP
WHAT'S THE MATTER, NAKATSU? DO YOU BELIEVE IN GHO...
WHUMP
DON'T BE SILLY.
.....
All right! Let's check this place out!
IF I'D ONLY KNOWN WE WERE GONNA END UP IN A PLACE LIKE THIS...
RUSTLE
...I WOULD'VE DRAGGED THOSE GUYS OUT HERE NO MATTER WHAT.

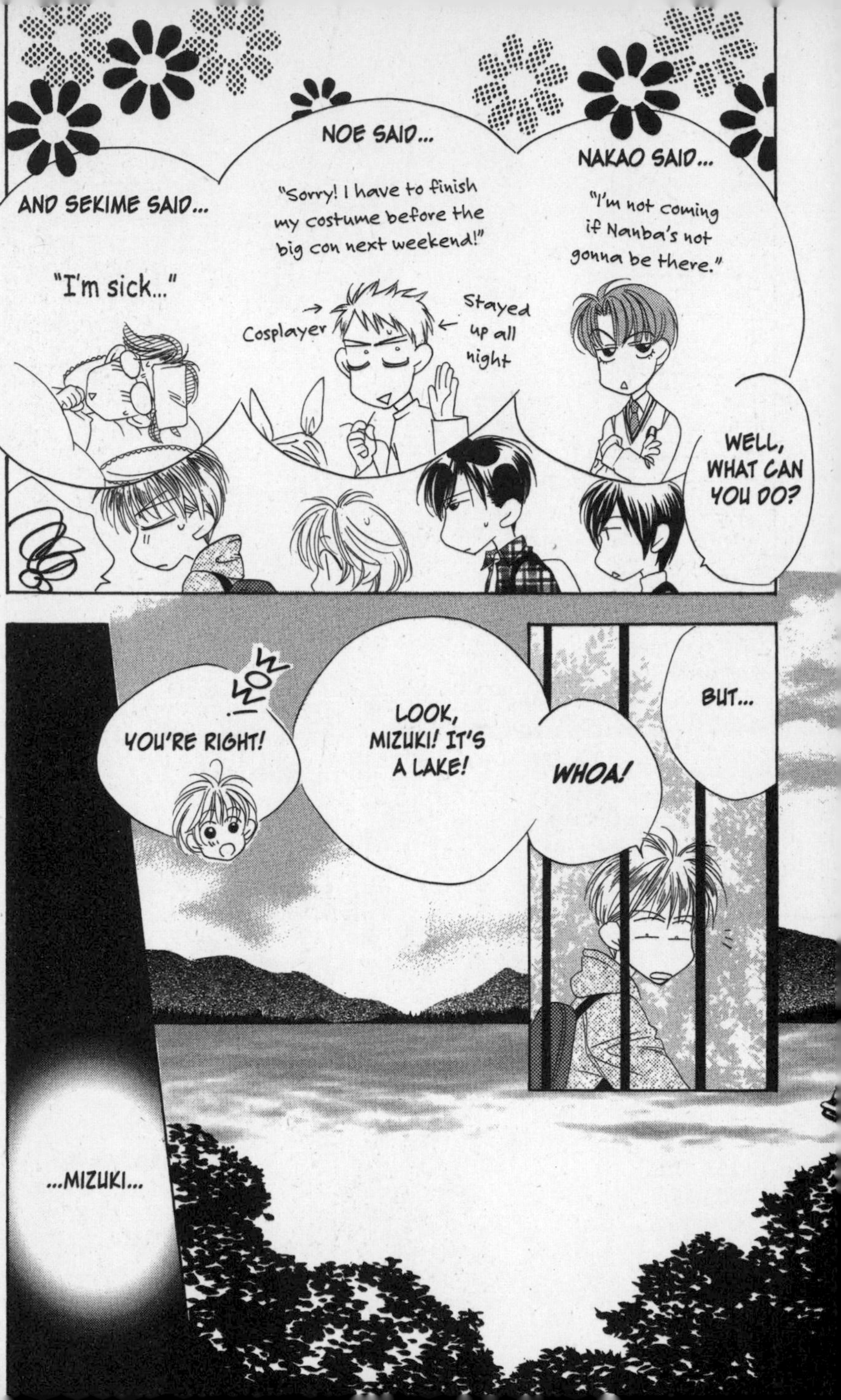
NAKAO SAID...
"I'm not coming if Nanba's not gonna be there."
NOE SAID...
"Sorry! I have to finish my costume before the big con next weekend!"
Stayed up all night
Cosplayer
AND SEKIME SAID...
"I'm sick..."
WELL, WHAT CAN YOU DO?
BUT...
WHOA!
LOOK, MIZUKI! IT'S A LAKE!
WOW!
YOU'RE RIGHT!
...MIZUKI...

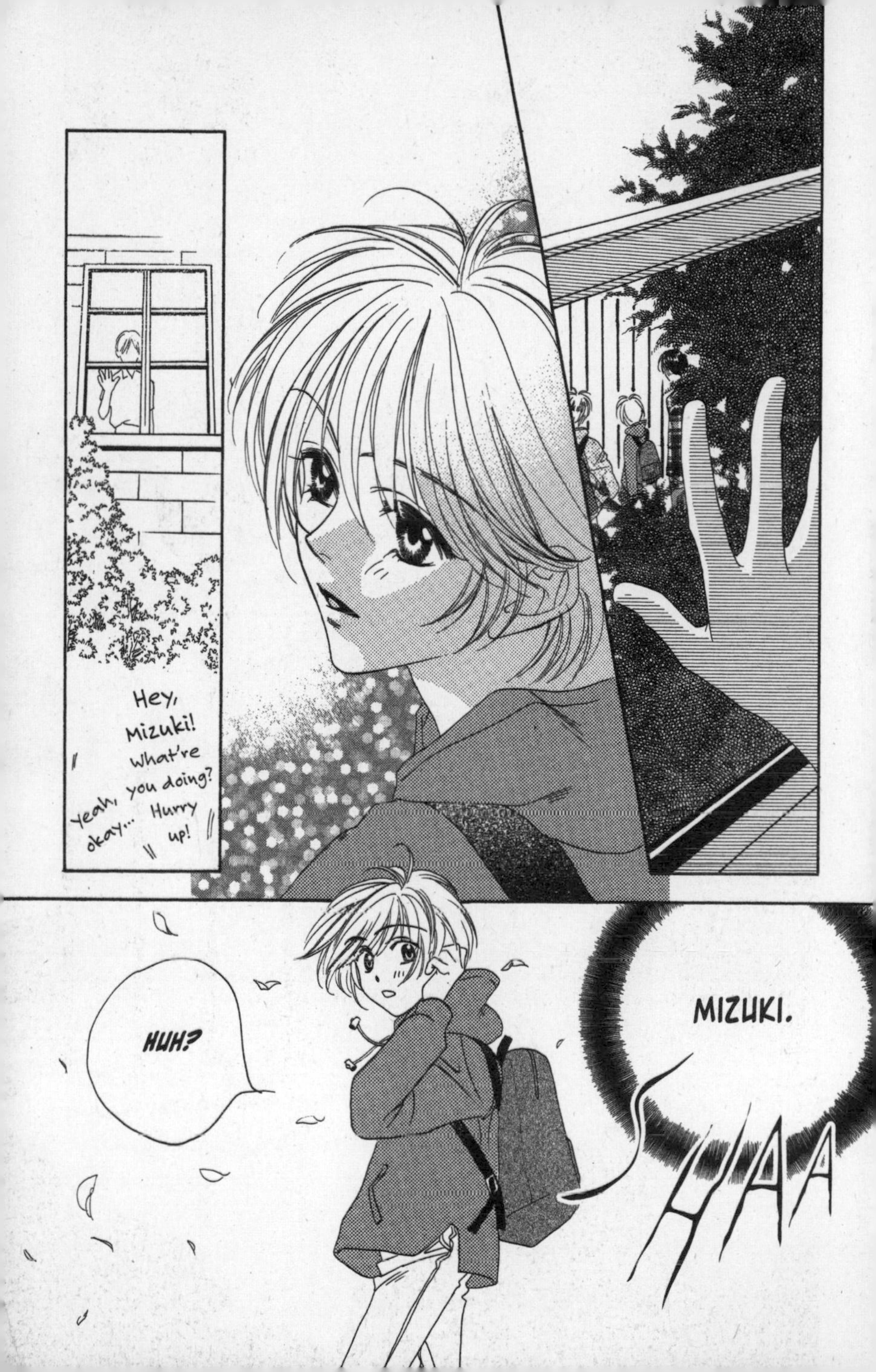
Hey, Mizuki! What're you doing? Hurry up!
Yeah, okay...
MIZUKI.
SHAA
HUH?

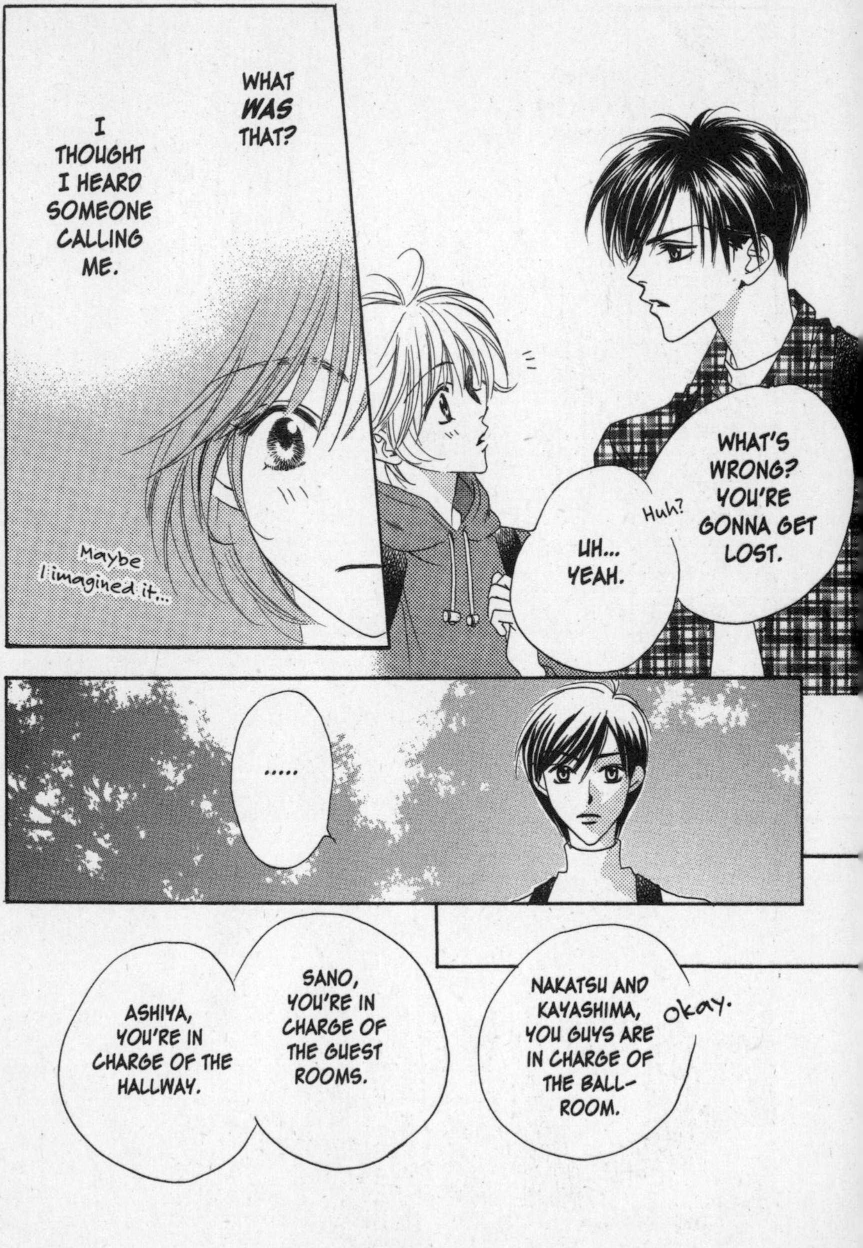
WHAT'S WRONG? YOU'RE GONNA GET LOST.
Huh?
UH... YEAH.
WHAT WAS THAT?
I THOUGHT I HEARD SOMEONE CALLING ME.
Maybe I imagined it...
.....
NAKATSU AND KAYASHIMA, YOU GUYS ARE IN CHARGE OF THE BALL-ROOM.
Okay.
SANO, YOU'RE IN CHARGE OF THE GUEST ROOMS.
ASHIYA, YOU'RE IN CHARGE OF THE HALLWAY.

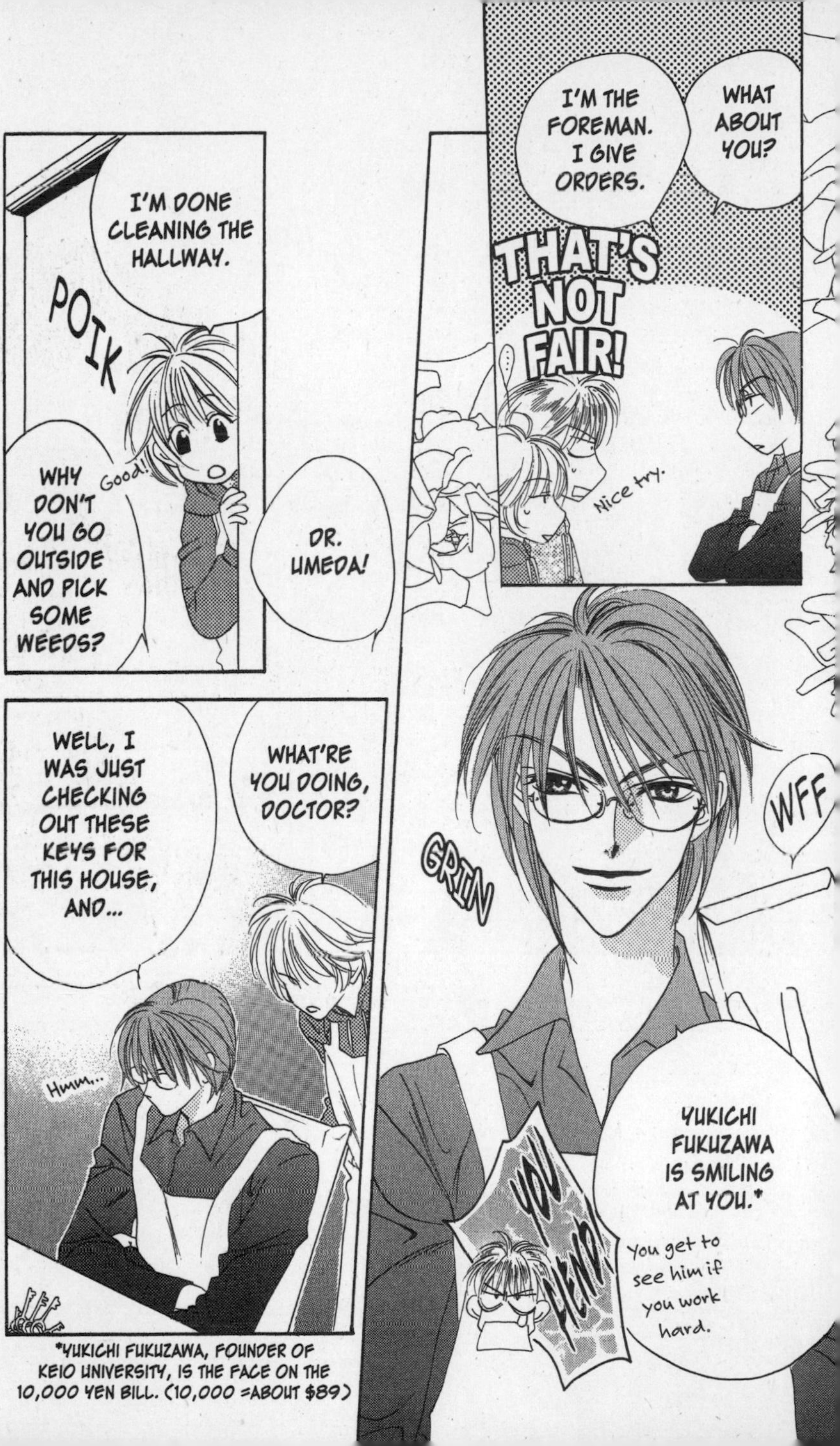
WHAT ABOUT YOU?
I'M THE FOREMAN. I GIVE ORDERS.
THAT'S NOT FAIR!
Nice try.
WFF
GRIN
YUKICHI FUKUZAWA IS SMILING AT YOU.*
You get to see him if you work hard.
YOU FIEND!
I'M DONE CLEANING THE HALLWAY.
POIK
DR. UMEDA!
Good!
WHY DON'T YOU GO OUTSIDE AND PICK SOME WEEDS?
WHAT'RE YOU DOING, DOCTOR?
WELL, I WAS JUST CHECKING OUT THESE KEYS FOR THIS HOUSE, AND...
Hmm...

*YUKICHI FUKUZAWA, FOUNDER OF KEIO UNIVERSITY, IS THE FACE ON THE 10,000 YEN BILL. (10,000 =ABOUT $89)

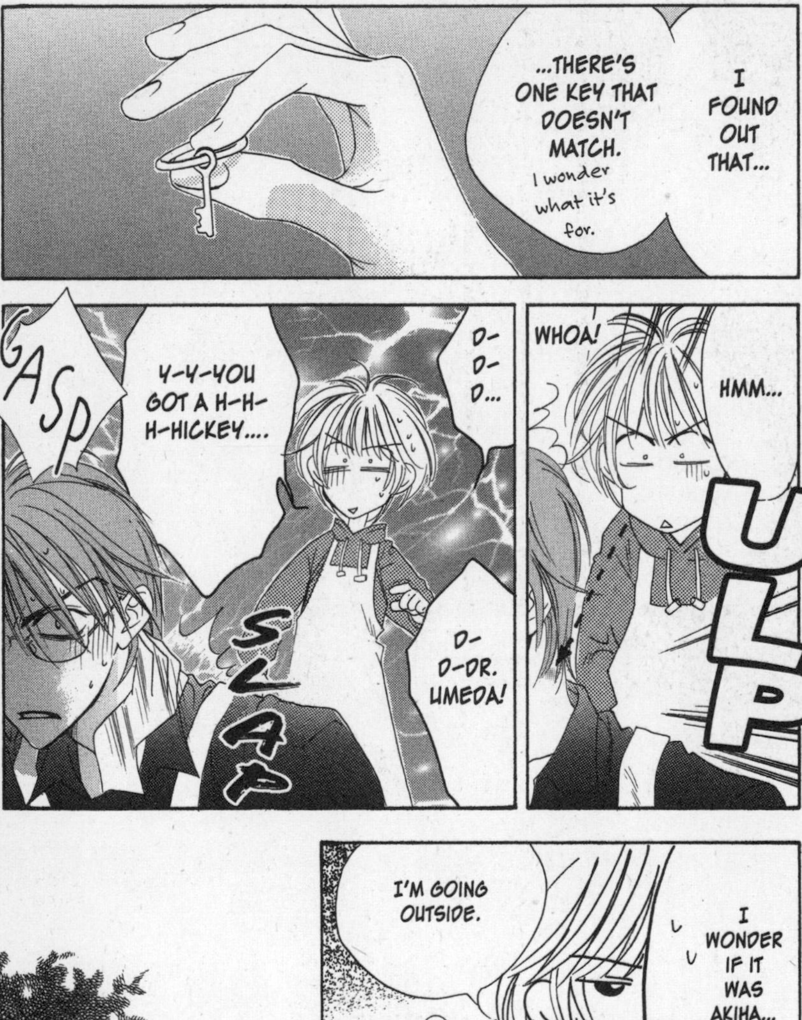
I FOUND OUT THAT...
...THERE'S ONE KEY THAT DOESN'T MATCH.
I wonder what it's for.
HMM...
WHOA!
ULP
D-D-D...
D-D-DR. UMEDA!
Y-Y-YOU GOT A H-H-H-HICKEY....
GASP
SLAP
I WONDER IF IT WAS AKIHA...
I'd better not ask.
I'M GOING OUTSIDE.
...OKAY.

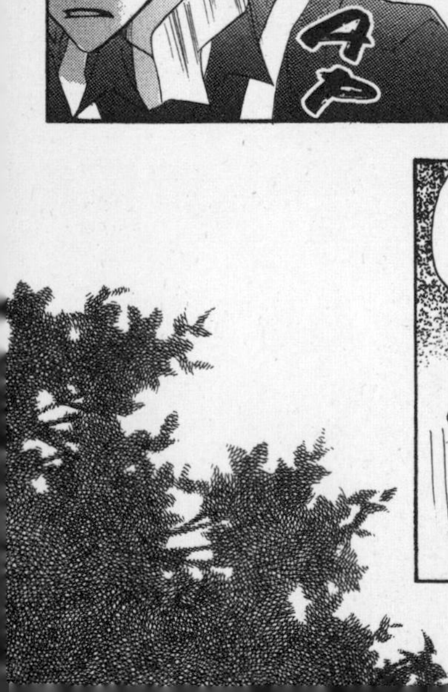

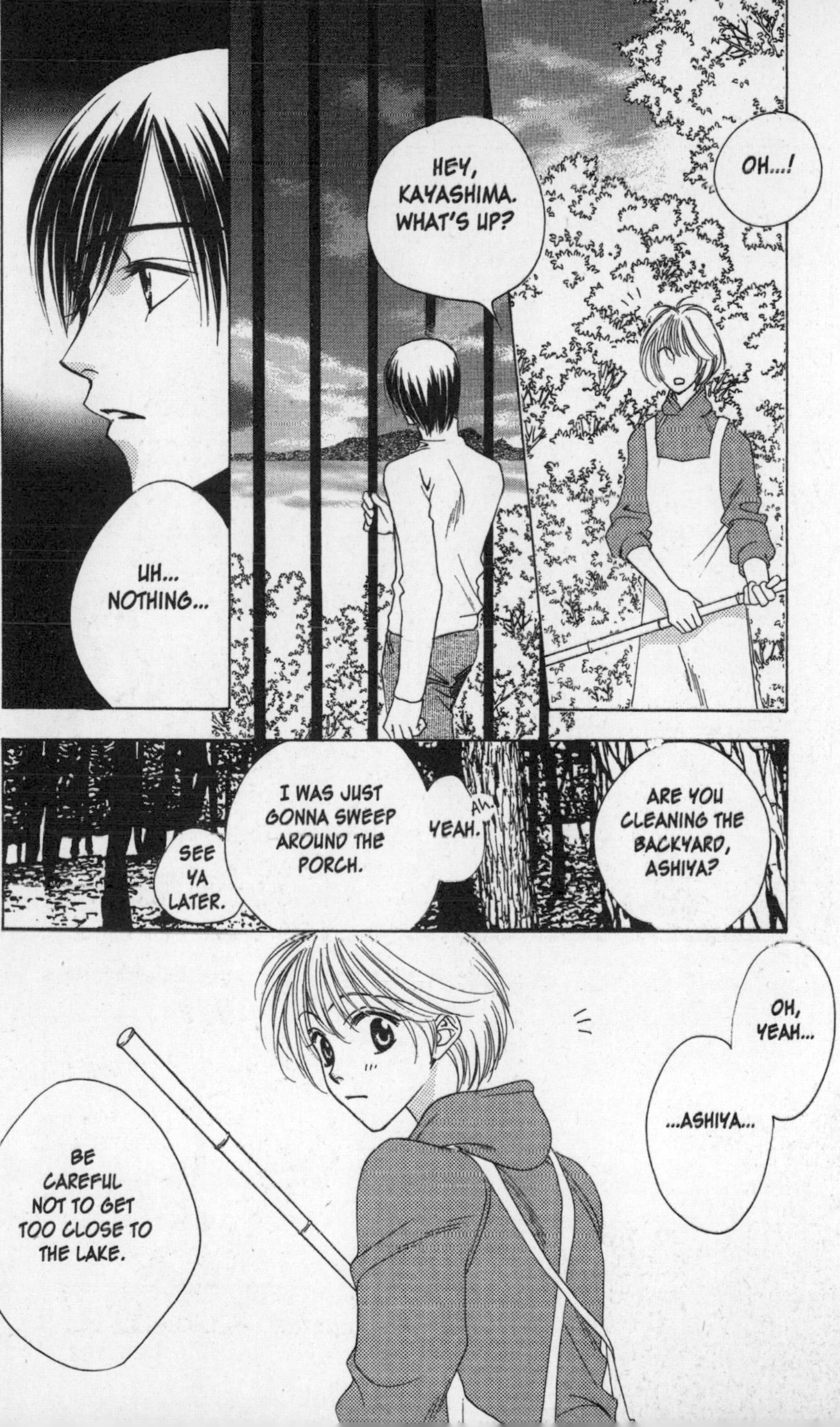
OH...!
HEY, KAYASHIMA. WHAT'S UP?
UH... NOTHING...
ARE YOU CLEANING THE BACKYARD, ASHIYA?
AH.
YEAH.
I WAS JUST GONNA SWEEP AROUND THE PORCH.
SEE YA LATER.
OH, YEAH...
...ASHIYA...
BE CAREFUL NOT TO GET TOO CLOSE TO THE LAKE.

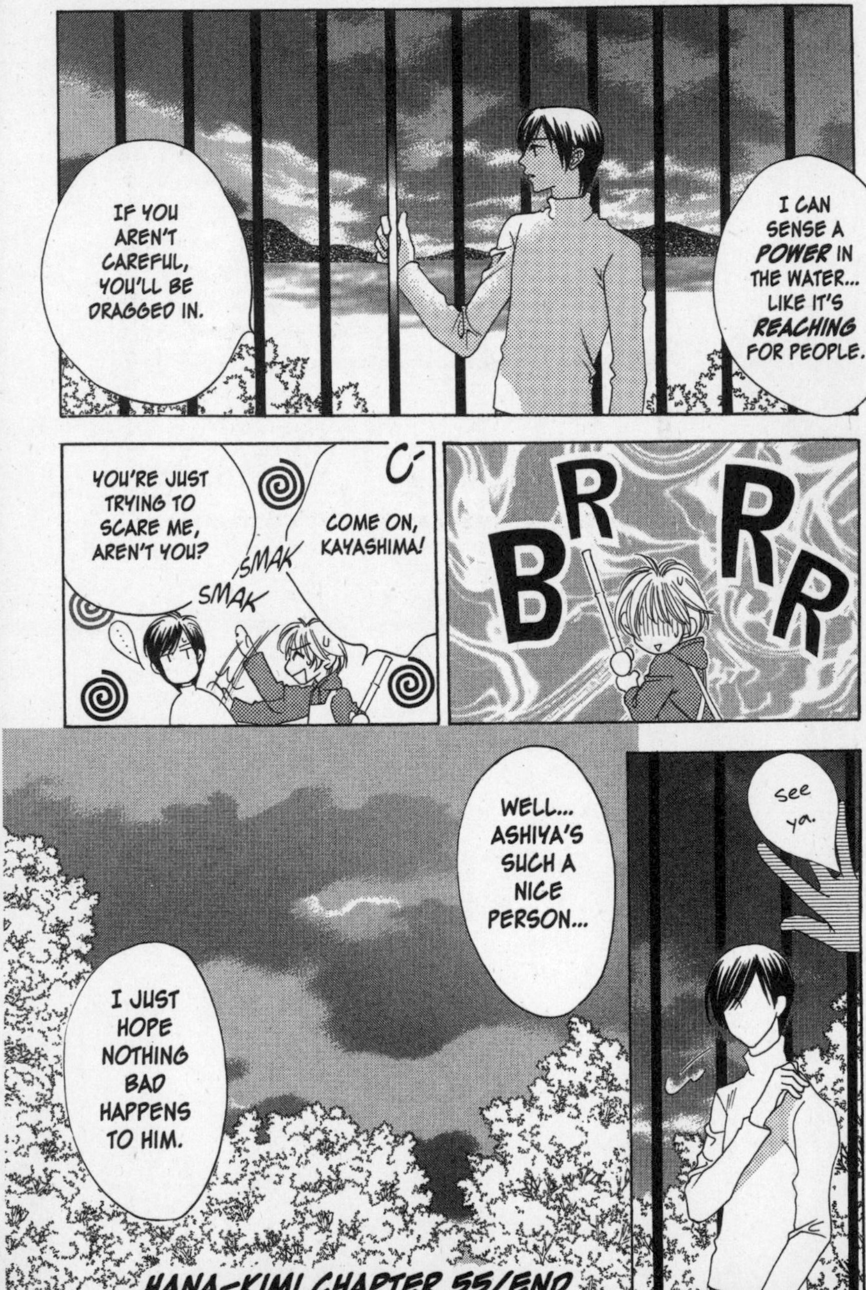
I CAN SENSE A POWER IN THE WATER... LIKE IT'S REACHING FOR PEOPLE.
IF YOU AREN'T CAREFUL, YOU'LL BE DRAGGED IN.
BRRRR
C-
COME ON, KAYASHIMA!
YOU'RE JUST TRYING TO SCARE ME, AREN'T YOU?
SMAK
SMAK
...
See ya.
WELL... ASHIYA'S SUCH A NICE PERSON...
I JUST HOPE NOTHING BAD HAPPENS TO HIM.

HANA-KIMI CHAPTER 55/END

ABOUT THE AUTHOR

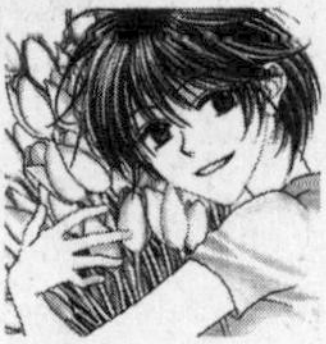

Hisaya Nakajo's manga series **Hanazakari no Kimitachi he** (For You in Full Blossom, casually known as **Hana-Kimi**) has been a hit since it first appeared in 1997 in the shôjo manga magazine **Hana to Yume** (Flowers and Dreams). In Japan, two **Hana-Kimi** art books and several "drama CDs" have been released. Her other manga series include **Missing Piece** (2 volumes) and **Yumemiru Happa** (The Dreaming Leaf, 1 volume).

Hisaya Nakajo's website:
www.wild-vanilla.com

IN THE NEXT VOLUME ...

Is the vacation house really haunted? Are Mizuki and her friends ready for a real paranormal encounter? Then, the ghosts turn holy as the boys of Osaka High School get ready for Christmas...and the annual *co-ed Christmas Dance!* But when Saint Blossom High School turns out to be a few girls short, prom queen Hibari Hanayashiki comes up with a brilliant idea: *pay boys to dress up like girls!* And guess who's her first choice...

バチバチバチッ
なんかすご～く知ってる人みたいだよ
類友や類友っ
ひそっ
ひそ
時間のムダですわね
……まあ!!
ばたりー
かわいいですわ
ぎゃー
ひえええん

AVAILABLE NOW!

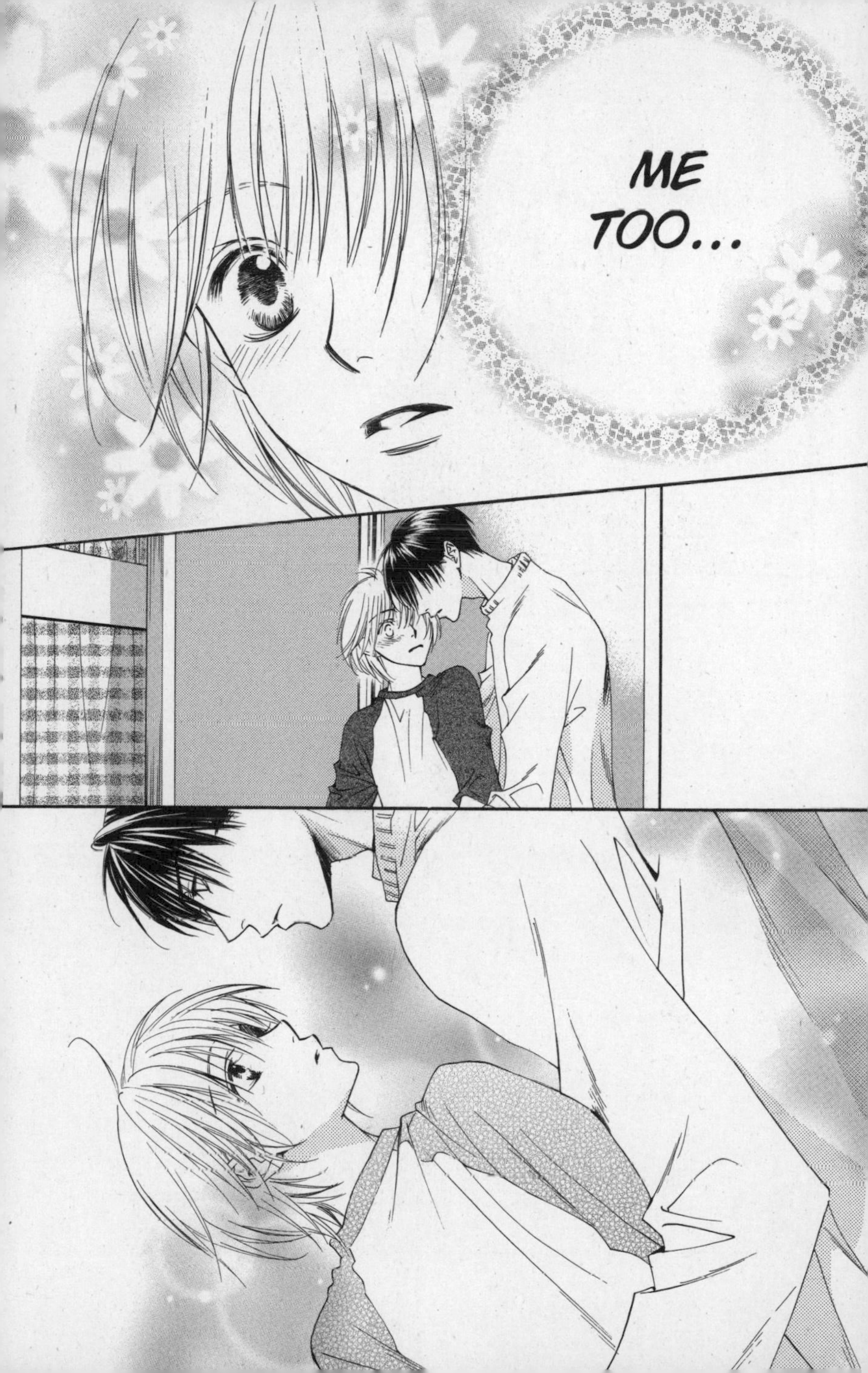
ME TOO...

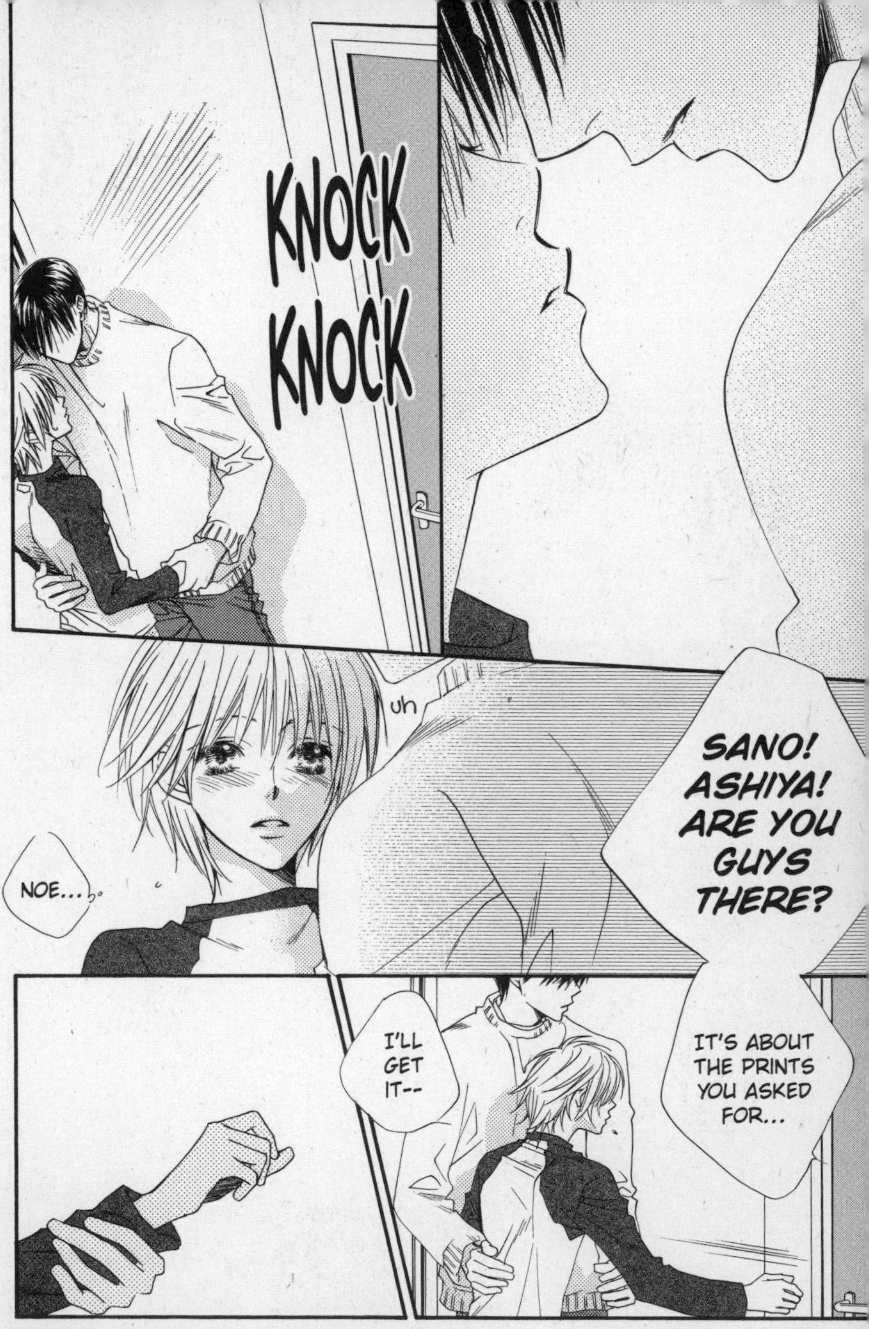
KNOCK KNOCK
SANO! ASHIYA! ARE YOU GUYS THERE?
uh
NOE...
IT'S ABOUT THE PRINTS YOU ASKED FOR...
I'LL GET IT--